1st Workshop on Vector Space Modeling for Natural Language Processing 2015

Held at NAACL HLT 2015

Denver, Colorado, USA
5 June 2015

ISBN: 978-1-5108-0432-6

Printed from e-media with permission by:

Curran Associates, Inc.
57 Morehouse Lane
Red Hook, NY 12571

CURRAN ASSOCIATES INC.
proceedings
.com

Some format issues inherent in the e-media version may also appear in this print version.

Printed by Curran Associates, Inc. (2015)

Association for Computational Linguistics
209 N. Eighth Street
Stroudsburg, Pennsylvania 18360

Phone: 1-570-476-8006
Fax: 1-570-476-0860

acl@aclweb.org

Additional copies of this publication are available from:

Curran Associates, Inc.
57 Morehouse Lane
Red Hook, NY 12571 USA
Phone: 845-758-0400
Fax: 845-758-2634
Email: curran@proceedings.com
Web: www.proceedings.com

NAACL HLT 2015

The 1st Workshop on Vector Space Modeling for Natural Language Processing (in NAACL 2015)

Proceedings of the Workshop

June 5, 2015
Denver, Colorado, USA

Order print-on-demand copies from:

Curran Associates
57 Morehouse Lane
Red Hook, New York 12571
USA
Tel: +1-845-758-0400
Fax: +1-845-758-2633
curran@proceedings.com

Introduction

The idea of statistical analysis of language is an old idea, but modern NLP started with a focus on methods based on pure symbolic analysis of language. Statistical methods were introduced to NLP in its current form in the 1980s/1990s, allowing "soft" reasoning about language, and made NLP more data-driven. Over the last decade another step has been taken in this direction – it was proposed to represent and analyze language in vector spaces. Now-a-days, context, symbolic and high-dimensional representations are often augmented with relatively low-dimensional vector-space representations. Vector space representations have been successfully used in different areas of NLP such as syntax and semantics.

This workshop is an opportunity to explore state of the art in the use of vector spaces in order to computationally analyze natural language. The focus of the workshop is on the use of vector spaces to learn latent representations.

The goal of the workshop is to bring together researchers from areas such as deep learning and representation learning, spectral learning, distributional compositional semantics and others, in order to see their relevance to each other, and learn about the state of the art in these areas.

This is the first time that this workshop is held. There were other similar workshops in the past, such as the Workshop on Continuous Vector Space Models and their Compositionality.

The program this year includes 27 papers that cover different areas under the realm of vector space modeling in NLP, all of which are presented in two poster sessions. There are also 3 invited speakers, Marco Baroni, Chris Manning and Xavier Carreras, with each of their talks covering a different aspect of vector space modeling in NLP.

We would like to thank the Program Committee members who reviewed the papers this year. We would also like to thank the workshop participants. Last, a word of thanks also goes to our two sponsors: Google Deepmind and Textkernel.

Phil Blunsom, Shay Cohen, Paramveer Dhillon and Percy Liang

Co-Organizers

Organizers:

Phil Blunsom (University of Oxford)
Shay Cohen (University of Edinburgh)
Paramveer Dhillon (Massachusetts Institute of Technology)
Percy Liang (Stanford University)

Program Committee:

Waleed Ammar (Carnegie Mellon University)
Apoorv Agarwal (Columbia University)
Borja Balle (McGill University)
William Blacoe (University of Edinburgh)
Jordan Boyd-Graber (University of Colorado)
Xavier Carreras (XRCE)
Tejaswini Deoskar (University of Edinburgh)
Weisi Duan (Carnegie Mellon University)
Edward Grefenstette (University of Oxford)
Manaal Frauqui (Carnegie Mellon University)
Lea Frermann (University of Edinburgh)
Karl Moritz Hermann (University of Oxford)
Thang Minh Luong (Stanford University)
Annie Louis (University of Edinburgh)
Jeff Mitchell (University of Edinburgh)
Ankur Parikh (Carnegie Mellon University)
Rohan Ramanath (Carnegie Mellon University)
Siva Reddy (University of Edinburgh)
Roi Reichart (Technion)
Sebastian Riedel (University College London)
Richard Socher (Stanford University)
Karl Stratos (Columbia University)
Lyle Ungar (University of Pennsylvania)
Eva Maria Vecchi (University of Cambridge)

Invited Speakers:

Marco Baroni (University of Trento)
Xavier Carreras (XRCE)
Chris Manning (Stanford University)

Sponsors:

Google DeepMind
Textkernel (*http://www.textkernel.com*: machine learning for matching people and jobs)

Table of Contents

Conference Program

9:00–9:15 ***Opening Remarks***

9:15–10:15 ***Invited Talk (Chris Manning)***

10:15–12:15 ***Poster session 1***

A Simple Word Embedding Model for Lexical Substitution
Oren Melamud, Omer Levy and Ido Dagan

Unsupervised Text Normalization Using Distributed Representations of Words and Phrases
Vivek Kumar Rangarajan Sridhar

A Multi-classifier Approach to support Coreference Resolution in a Vector Space Model
Ana Zelaia, Olatz Arregi and Basilio Sierra

Neural context embeddings for automatic discovery of word senses
Mikael Kågebäck, Fredrik Johansson, Richard Johansson and Devdatt Dubhashi

Distributional Representations of Words for Short Text Classification
Chenglong Ma, Weiqun Xu, Peijia Li and Yonghong Yan

Relation Extraction: Perspective from Convolutional Neural Networks
Thien Huu Nguyen and Ralph Grishman

Distributional Semantic Concept Models for Entity Relation Discovery
Jay Urbain, Glenn Bushee and George Kowalski

A Deep Architecture for Non-Projective Dependency Parsing
Erick Fonseca and Sandra Aluísio

Short Text Clustering via Convolutional Neural Networks
jiaming xu, peng wang, guanhua tian, bo xu, jun zhao, fangyuan wang and hongwei hao

A Word-Embedding-based Sense Index for Regular Polysemy Representation
Marco Del Tredici and Núria Bel

No Day Set (continued)

Simple Semi-Supervised POS Tagging
Karl Stratos and Michael Collins

Learning Distributed Representations for Multilingual Text Sequences
Hieu Pham, Thang Luong and Christopher Manning

Combining Distributed Vector Representations for Words
Justin Garten, Kenji Sagae, Volkan Ustun and Morteza Dehghani

12:15–13:30 ***Lunch***

13:30–14:30 ***Invited Talk (Xavier Carreras)***

14:30–16:30 ***Poster session 2***

Dependency Link Embeddings: Continuous Representations of Syntactic Substructures
Mohit Bansal

DeepNL: a Deep Learning NLP pipeline
Giuseppe Attardi

A Vector Space Approach for Aspect Based Sentiment Analysis
Abdulaziz Alghunaim, Mitra Mohtarami, Scott Cyphers and Jim Glass

Word Embeddings vs Word Types for Sequence Labeling: the Curious Case of CV Parsing
Melanie Tosik, Carsten Lygteskov Hansen, Gerard Goossen and Mihai Rotaru

Morpho-syntactic Regularities in Continuous Word Representations: A multilingual study.
Garrett Nicolai, Colin Cherry and Grzegorz Kondrak

Towards Combined Matrix and Tensor Factorization for Universal Schema Relation Extraction
Sameer Singh, Tim Rocktäschel and Sebastian Riedel

Neural word embeddings with multiplicative feature interactions for tensor-based compositions
Joo-Kyung Kim, Marie-Catherine de Marneffe and Eric Fosler-Lussier

No Day Set (continued)

Bilingual Word Representations with Monolingual Quality in Mind
Thang Luong, Hieu Pham and Christopher D. Manning

Distributed Word Representations Improve NER for e-Commerce
Mahesh Joshi, Ethan Hart, Mirko Vogel and Jean-David Ruvini

Semantic Information Extraction for Improved Word Embeddings
Jiaqiang Chen and Gerard de Melo

Named Entity Recognition for Arabic Social Media
Ayah Zirikly and Mona Diab

Vector Space Models for Scientific Document Summarization
John Conroy and Sashka Davis

Unsupervised Topic Modeling for Short Texts Using Distributed Representations of Words
Vivek Kumar Rangarajan Sridhar

Estimating User Location in Social Media with Stacked Denoising Auto-encoders
Ji Liu and Diana Inkpen

16:30–17:30 ***Invited Talk (Marco Baroni)***

17:30–17:45 ***Concluding Remarks and Prizes***

17:45–19:00 ***Farewell Reception***

A Simple Word Embedding Model for Lexical Substitution

Oren Melamud **Omer Levy** **Ido Dagan**
Department of Computer Science
Bar-Ilan University
Ramat-Gan, Israel
{melamuo,omerlevy,dagan}@cs.biu.ac.il

Abstract

The lexical substitution task requires identifying meaning-preserving substitutes for a target word instance in a given sentential context. Since its introduction in SemEval-2007, various models addressed this challenge, mostly in an unsupervised setting. In this work we propose a simple model for lexical substitution, which is based on the popular skip-gram word embedding model. The novelty of our approach is in leveraging explicitly the *context embeddings* generated within the skip-gram model, which were so far considered only as an internal component of the learning process. Our model is efficient, very simple to implement, and at the same time achieves state-of-the-art results on lexical substitution tasks in an unsupervised setting.

1 Introduction

Lexical substitution tasks have become very popular for evaluating context-sensitive lexical inference models since the introduction of the original task in SemEval-2007 (McCarthy and Navigli, 2007) and additional later variants (Biemann, 2013; Kremer et al., 2014). In these tasks, systems are required to predict substitutes for a target word instance, which preserve its meaning in a given sentential context. Recent models addressed this challenge mostly in an unsupervised setting. They typically generated a word instance representation, which is biased towards its given context, and then identified substitute words based on their similarity to this biased representation. Various types of models were proposed, from sparse syntax-based vector models (Thater et al., 2011), to probabilistic graphical models (Moon and Erk, 2013) and LDA topic models (Ó Séaghdha and Korhonen, 2014).

Word embeddings are low-dimensional vector representations of word types that recently gained much traction in various semantic tasks. Probably the most popular word embedding model today is *skip-gram*, introduced in Mikolov et al. (2013) and available as part of the *word2vec* toolkit.[1] word2vec learns for every word type two distinct representations, one as a target and another as a context, both embedded in the same space. However, the context representations are considered internal to the model and are discarded after training. The output word embeddings represent context-insensitive target word types.

Few recent models extended word embeddings by learning a distinct representation for each sense of a target word type, as induced by clustering the word's contexts (Huang et al., 2012; Neelakantan et al., 2014). They then identify the relevant sense(s) for a given word instance, in order to measure context-sensitive similarities. Although these models may be considered for lexical substitution, they have so far been applied only to 'softer' word similarity tasks which include topical relations.

In this work we propose a simple approach for *directly* utilizing the skip-gram model for context-sensitive lexical substitution. Instead of discarding the learned context embeddings, we use them in conjunction with the target word embeddings to model target word instances. A suitable substitute for a

[1] https://code.google.com/p/word2vec/

Proceedings of NAACL-HLT 2015, pages 1–7,

target word instance is then identified via its combined similarity to the embeddings of both the target and its given context. [2] Our model is efficient, can be implemented literally in a few lines of code, and at the same time achieves state-of-the-art results on two lexical substitution datasets in an unsupervised setting.

2 Skip-gram Word Embeddings

In this section we provide technical background on skip-gram embeddings, which are used in our model. As mentioned, skip-gram embeds both target words and contexts in the same low-dimensional space. In this space, the vector representations of a target and context are pushed closer together the more frequently they co-occur in a learning corpus. Thus, the Cosine distance between them can be viewed as a first-order *target-to-context* similarity measure, indicative of their syntagmatic compatibility. Indirectly, this also results in assigning similar vector representations to target words that share similar contexts, thereby suggesting the Cosine distance between word embeddings as a second-order *target-to-target* distributional similarity measure.

word2vecf[3] (Levy and Goldberg, 2014a) is an extension of the skip-gram implementation in word2vec, which supports arbitrary types of contexts rather than only word window contexts. Levy and Goldberg (2014a) used word2vecf to produce syntax-based word embeddings, where context elements are the syntactic contexts of the target words. Specifically, for a target word t with modifiers m_1,...,m_k and head h, they considered the context elements (m_1, r_1),...,(m_k, r_k),(h, r_h^{-1}), where r is the type of the ('collapsed') dependency relation between the head and the modifier (e.g. *dobj*, *prep_of*) and r^{-1} denotes an inverse relation. Similarly to traditional syntax-based vector space models (Padó and Lapata, 2007), they show that these embeddings tend to capture functional word similarity (as in *manage* ∼ *supervise*) rather than topical similarity or relatedness (as in *manage* ∼ *manager*). Figure 1 illustrates a syntax-based embedding space using t-SNE (Van der Maaten and Hinton, 2008), which visualizes the similarities in the original higher-dimensional space.

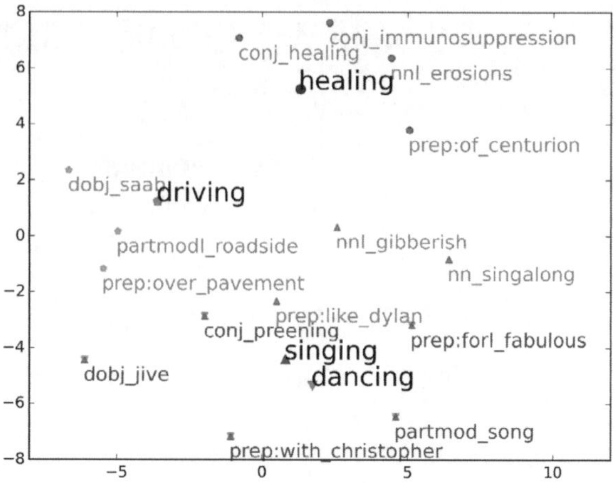

Figure 1: A 2-dimensional visualization of the gerunds *singing*, *dancing*, *driving*, and *healing* with their top syntactic contexts in an embedded space. *singing* and *dancing* share many similar contexts (e.g. *partmod_song* and *dobj_jive*) and therefore end up with very similar vector representations.

3 Lexical Substitution Model

Our model is based on the natural assumption that a good lexical substitute for a target word instance, under a given context, needs to be both (1) semantically similar to the target word and (2) compatible with the given context. Hence, we wish to propose a context-sensitive substitutability measure for potential substitutes, which reflects a combination of the above. We estimate the semantic similarity between a substitute word and the target word using a second-order target-to-target similarity measure, and the compatibility of a substitute word with the given context using a first-order target-to-context similarity measure. Conveniently, as described in Section 2, both target-to-target and target-to-context similarities can be estimated by the vector Cosine distance between the respective skip-gram embeddings, i.e. using both target word embeddings and the 'internal' context embeddings. Specifically, we choose syntax-based skip-gram embeddings (Levy

[2] While in this work we focus on skip-gram embeddings, we note that there are also other potentially relevant word embedding methods that can generate context representations in addition to the 'standard' target word representations. See, for example, GloVe (Pennington et al., 2014) and SVD-based methods (Levy et al., 2015).

[3] https://bitbucket.org/yoavgo/word2vecf

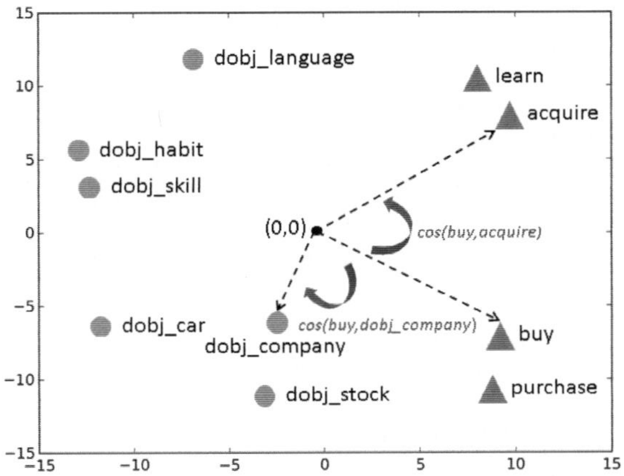

Figure 2: Identifying substitutes for the target word *acquire* under the syntactic context *dobj_company*, visualized in a 2-dimensional embedded space. Even though *learn* is the closest word to *acquire*, the word *buy* is both reasonably close to *acquire* as well as to the context *dobj_company* and is therefore considered a better substitute.

and Goldberg, 2014a) since lexical substitutes need to exhibit strict functional similarity to the target word. Figure 2 illustrates our approach.

We next describe the details of our model. Our model introduces a context-sensitive substitutability measure (or metric) for estimating the suitability of a lexical substitute for a target word in a given sentential context. This measure weighs the semantic similarity score between the substitute and the target word type, together with one or more context compatibility scores, estimating the compatibility of the substitute with each of the target's context elements in the given sentential context.

To keep our method as simple as possible we do not employ any tunable weighting parameters to optimize our proposed measure. Instead, we choose to focus only on evaluating the four measure variants described in Table 1. These measures reflect two basic metric design choices. The first choice is between using an arithmetic mean (as in Add and BalAdd) and a geometrical mean (as in Mult and BalMult) to combine the score elements together. These are two common methods, which were recently investigated in the context of analogy detection tasks (Levy and Goldberg, 2014b). The multiplicative combinations, Mult and BalMult, reflect a stricter

Add	$\frac{cos(s,t)+\sum_{c\in C} cos(s,c)}{\lvert C\rvert+1}$
BalAdd	$\frac{\lvert C\rvert\cdot cos(s,t)+\sum_{c\in C} cos(s,c)}{2\cdot\lvert C\rvert}$
Mult	$\sqrt[\lvert C\rvert+1]{pcos(s,t)\cdot\prod_{c\in C} pcos(s,c)}$
BalMult	$\sqrt[2\cdot\lvert C\rvert]{pcos(s,t)^{\lvert C\rvert}\cdot\prod_{c\in C} pcos(s,c)}$

Table 1: The different substitutability measures considered in our model for a lexical substitute s of the target word t in sentential context C. C is represented by the set of the target word's context elements in the context sentence, where c denotes an individual context element. cos is the vector Cosine function applied to the vector representations of the words or contexts, and $pcos(v,v')=\frac{cos(v,v')+1}{2}$ is used to avoid negative values in Mult and BalMult.

logical 'AND-like' approach requiring high similarities in all elements of the product to get a high score. In particular, they reward substitutes that show substantial similarity to both the target word and each of the context elements. In contrast, the additive combinations, Add and BalAdd, can yield a high score even if one of the elements in the sum is zero.

The second design choice concerns the relative contribution of the context compatibility component with respect to the word similarity component. In Add and Mult, the relative weight of context compatibility with respect to word similarity becomes greater the more there are context elements for the target word in the given context sentence. In contrast, the balanced combinations, BalAdd and BalMult, keep an equal balance between these two factors, under the hypothesis that the overall contribution of the context compatibility should be fixed regardless to the number of context elements.

As a motivating example, Table 2 shows how our model uses a single informative context element to generate context-sensitive lexical substitutions for polysemous target words.

4 Evaluation

In the original lexical substitution task (McCarthy and Navigli, 2007) all of the participating sys-

$t = jaguar$		$t = cool$		$t = employ$	
$c = poss^{-1}\ engine$	$c = poss^{-1}\ paws$	$c = amod^{-1}\ outfit$	$c = amod^{-1}\ weather$	$c = dobj\ technique$	$c = dobj\ specialist$
daimler	cheetah	preppy	wintery	employs	employing
lancia	tiger	old-skool	drizzly	employing	employs
maserati	puma	kick-ass	spring-like	employed	recruit
bmw	leopard	sexy	unseasonably	adopt	employed
rover	jaguars	chilled-out	warm	utilise	appoint
daihatsu	cat	snazzy	balmy	using	redeploy
lamborghini	hyena	funky	hot	utilize	remunerate
volvo	wildcat	super-cool	anticyclonic	re-learn	recruited
gt6	panda	half-decent	cooler	adopting	recruiting

Table 2: The top lexical substitutes for example target words t under different syntactic contexts c, using Mult.

tems predicted substitutes by first using manually-constructed thesauri to generate substitute candidates and then developing candidate ranking models to choose the most appropriate ones. Later works focused mostly on the candidate ranking part, where candidates are provided as part of the datasets. In this section we present the evaluation of our model both on the substitute candidates ranking task, and on the original substitutes prediction task (no candidates provided), using two different lexical substitution datasets.

4.1 Lexical substitutions datasets

The dataset introduced in the lexical substitution task of SemEval-2007 (McCarthy and Navigli, 2007), denoted here LS-SE, is the most widely used for the evaluation of lexical substitution. It consists of 10 sentences extracted from a web corpus for each of 201 target words (nouns, verbs, adjectives and adverbs), or altogether 2,010 word instances in sentential context, split into 300 trial sentences and 1,710 test sentences. The gold standard provided with this dataset is a weighted lemmatized substitute list for each word instance, based on manual annotations.

A more recent large-scale 'all-words' dataset, called 'Concepts in Context', was introduced in Kremer et al. (2014) and denoted here LS-CIC. This dataset provides the same kind of data as LS-SE, but instead of choosing specific target words that tend to be ambiguous as done in LS-SE, the target words here are all the content words in text documents extracted from news and fiction corpora, and are therefore more naturally distributed. LS-CIC is also much larger than LS-SE with over 15K target word instances.

4.2 Compared methods

We used ukWaC (Ferraresi et al., 2008), a two billion word web corpus, as our learning corpus. We parsed both ukWaC and the sentences in the lexical substitution datasets with Stanford's Neural Network Dependency Parser (Chen and Manning, 2014).[4] Following Levy and Goldberg (2014a), we learned syntax-based skip-gram word and context embeddings using word2vecf (with 600 dimensions and 15 negative sampling), converting all tokens to lowercase, discarding words and syntactic contexts that appear less than 100 times in the corpus and 'collapsing' dependencies that include prepositions. This resulted in a vocabulary of about 200K word embeddings and 1M context embeddings. [5] Finally, for every instance in the lexical substitution datasets, we extracted the syntactic contexts of the target word and used each of our measures, Add, BalAdd, Mult and BalMult, to compute the substitute scores. In addition to our measures, we evaluated as a baseline a context-insensitive method, denoted Base, assigning scores according to the Cosine similarity between the target and the substitute word embeddings, ignoring the context. We also compare our results to the state-of-the-art.

4.3 Candidate ranking task

Most works that used the LS-SE dataset after SemEval-2007, as well as the one on LS-CIC, focused on ranking substitute candidates. They obtained the set of substitute candidates for a target type by pooling the annotated gold-standard substi-

[4]http://nlp.stanford.edu/software/nndep.shtml

[5]Our embeddings are available at: www.cs.biu.ac.il/nlp/resources/downloads/lexsub_embeddings/

Method	Resources	LS-SE	LS-CIC
Mult	ukWaC	**53.6**	**48.1**
BalMult		51.5	48.3
Add		**52.9**	**48.3**
BalAdd		50.3	48.0
Base		44.9	46.2
Random	n/a	30.0	33.8
Kremer, 2014†	Gigaword	52.5	47.8
Séaghdha, 2014	Wikipedia,BNC	49.5	n/a
Moon, 2013	ukWaC,BNC,WN Gigaword,WN	47.1 46.7	n/a n/a
Szarvas, 2013	LLC,WN	55.0*	n/a

Table 3: GAP scores for compared methods on the candidate ranking task. Resources used by these methods: ukWaC, Wikipedia, Gigaword (Parker et al., 2011), WN = WordNet (Fellbaum, 2010), BNC = British National Corpus (Aston and Burnard, 1998), and LLC (Richter et al., 2006).
† A re-implementation of the model in Thater, 2011.
* Obtained by a supervised method.

tutes from all of its instances.[6] Furthermore, all of these works discarded multi-word expression substitutes from the gold standards, and omitted instances who thus remained with no gold substitutes.[7] The quality of the rankings with respect to the gold standard was measured using Generalized Average Precision (GAP) (Kishida, 2005). We follow the same evaluation settings for this task, using the substitute scores of our compared methods to rank the candidates.

Our results, compared with the most recent state-of-the-art, are illustrated in Table 3. First, we see that all of our methods yield significant performance gains over the context-insensitive Base baseline. Similarly to the behavior reported in (Kremer et al., 2014), this gain is much more substantial in LS-SE than in LS-CIC, which seems to be due to the target words in LS-SE being more ambiguous by construction. Next, we see that the non-balanced methods, Mult and Add, perform a little better on the LS-SE dataset. This suggests that giving more weight to context compatibility at the expense of word similarity is beneficial when ranking substitute candidates of ambiguous words. This can be justified considering that all the substitute candidates already bear some semantic similarity with the target by way of construction. Finally, the multiplicative combinations seem to perform slightly better than the additive ones on LS-SE.

In comparison to previous works our results are slightly better than state-of-the-art, with the exception of Szarvas et al. (2013). However, we note that Szarvas et al. (2013) is a supervised model, evaluated on the LS-SE gold standard with 10-fold cross validation and therefore is not directly comparable with unsupervised models, such as our own.

4.4 Substitute prediction task

In the original lexical substitution task of SemEval-2007, the organizers evaluated participant systems on their ability to predict the substitutes in the gold standard of the LS-SE test-set in a few subtasks (1) *best* and *best-mode* - evaluate the quality of the best predictions (2) *oot* and *oot-mode* (out of ten) - evaluate the coverage of the gold substitute list by the top ten best predictions.[8] We performed this evaluation on both the LS-SE and LS-CIC datasets, using our measures to predict the most suitable substitutes. We note that this task is a lot more challenging than the candidate ranking task, as it requires to identify the best substitutes out of the entire word vocabulary. To the best of our knowledge, Biemann and Riedl (2013), denoted here BR-2013, is the only prior work that reported such results on the LS-SE dataset, learning only from corpus data like we do. They used a syntax-based distributional thesaurus to generate a list of substitute candidates and then ranked the candidates according to their compatibility with the given context. As their learning corpus, they merged Gigaword (Parker et al., 2011) and LLC (Richter et al., 2006), which is similar in size to ours. Both Biemann and Riedl (2013) and our model do not attempt to identify and therefore always fail to predict the multi-word expression substitutes in the gold standard. There is no previously reported result

[6] A target type is defined as the pair (word lemma, pos), where pos ∈ {noun, verb, adjective, adverb}.

[7] In cases where this procedure was not clearly described in the paper, we verified it with the authors.

[8] For brevity we do not describe the details of these subtasks. We report only *recall* scores as in this task *recall=precision* for all methods that predict substitutes to all of the instances in the dataset as we did.

Method	best	best-mode	oot	oot-mode
LS-SE test-set				
Mult	6.64	10.89	23.16	33.58
BalMult	**8.09**	**13.41**	**27.65**	**39.19**
Add	7.37	12.11	25.52	36.59
BalAdd	**8.14**	**13.41**	**27.42**	**39.11**
Base	7.81	13.41	23.38	33.98
BR-2013	n/a	n/a	27.48	37.19
LS-CIC				
Mult	4.08	8.36	15.07	26.02
BalMult	**5.51**	**11.72**	**19.59**	**33.32**
Add	4.82	9.97	17.11	29.48
BalAdd	**5.62**	**11.89**	**20.03**	**33.75**
Base	5.17	10.93	18.01	30.29

Table 4: *best* and *oot* subtasks scores for all compared methods on the substitute prediction task.

for this task on LS-CIC.

The results are shown in Table 4. In contrast to the candidate ranking task, we see that in the prediction task the balanced methods perform significantly better than the non-balanced ones. This suggests that in the absence of a substitute candidate 'oracle' it is important for the models to balance both word similarity and context compatibility. The balanced methods, BalAdd and BalMult, perform similarly, and show significant advantage over the context-insensitive Base baseline in the *oot* subtasks. On the *best* sub-tasks they show very little improvement. Finally, our results are on par with the results reported by Biemann and Riedl (2013).

5 Conclusions

In this paper we showed how the skip-gram model can be utilized directly to perform context-sensitive lexical substitution. This is achieved by exploiting its internally-learned context embeddings in conjunction with the 'standard' target word embeddings, to weigh context compatibility together with word similarity. Despite its simplicity, our model achieves state-of-the-art results on lexical substitution tasks using two different datasets.

Word embeddings in general, and skip-gram embeddings in particular, have recently become very popular in many NLP tasks since they achieve state-of-the-art performance, and at the same time are easy to use and efficient both in learning and inference time. Our work shows how these attractive properties can be easily carried over when addressing context-sensitive lexical substitution.

In future work, we hypothesize that our simple model may be further optimized. One reason to believe so is that although our balanced weighting methods showed robust performance across all the tasks in our evaluations, we did see that other strategies, which put more weight on context compatibility, achieve the best results in a substitute candidate ranking setting. This suggests that applications may benefit from adapting our model to the task at hand. For example, a possible direction is using a tunable weighting parameter for interpolating between the components of our substitutability measure.

Finally, while focusing on skip-gram embeddings in this work, it would be interesting to explore how well our approach generalizes to other types of embeddings that can represent both target words and contexts (Pennington et al., 2014; Levy et al., 2015).

Acknowledgments

This work was partially supported by the Israel Science Foundation grant 880/12 and the German Research Foundation through the German-Israeli Project Cooperation (DIP, grant DA 1600/1-1).

References

Guy Aston and Lou Burnard. 1998. *The BNC handbook: exploring the British National Corpus with SARA*. Capstone.

Chris Biemann and Martin Riedl. 2013. Text: Now in 2D! A framework for lexical expansion with contextual similarity. *Journal of Language Modelling*, 1(1):55–95.

Chris Biemann. 2013. Creating a system for lexical substitutions from scratch using crowdsourcing. *Language Resources and Evaluation*, 47(1):97–122.

Danqi Chen and Christopher D Manning. 2014. A fast and accurate dependency parser using neural networks. In *Proceedings of EMNLP*.

Christiane Fellbaum. 2010. *WordNet*. Springer.

Adriano Ferraresi, Eros Zanchetta, Marco Baroni, and Silvia Bernardini. 2008. Introducing and evaluating ukwac, a very large web-derived corpus of English. In *Proceedings of the 4th Web as Corpus Workshop (WAC-4)*.

Eric H. Huang, Richard Socher, Christopher D. Manning, and Andrew Y. Ng. 2012. Improving word representations via global context and multiple word prototypes. In *Proceedings of ACL*.

Kazuaki Kishida. 2005. *Property of average precision and its generalization: An examination of evaluation indicator for information retrieval experiments*. National Institute of Informatics Tokyo, Japan.

Gerhard Kremer, Katrin Erk, Sebastian Padó, and Stefan Thater. 2014. What substitutes tell us-analysis of an all-words lexical substitution corpus. In *Proceedings of EACL*.

Omer Levy and Yoav Goldberg. 2014a. Dependency-based word embeddings. In *Proceedings of ACL*.

Omer Levy and Yoav Goldberg. 2014b. Linguistic regularities in sparse and explicit word representations. In *Proceedings of CoNLL-2014*.

Omer Levy, Yoav Goldberg, and Ido Dagan. 2015. Improving distributional similarity with lessons learned from word embeddings. *Transactions of the Association for Computational Linguistics*, 3.

Diana McCarthy and Roberto Navigli. 2007. Semeval-2007 task 10: English lexical substitution task. In *Proceedings of SemEval*.

Tomas Mikolov, Kai Chen, Greg Corrado, and Jeffrey Dean. 2013. Efficient estimation of word representations in vector space. *arXiv preprint arXiv:1301.3781*.

Taesun Moon and Katrin Erk. 2013. An inference-based model of word meaning in context as a paraphrase distribution. *ACM Trans. Intell. Syst. Technol.*, 4(3):42:1–42:28, July.

Arvind Neelakantan, Jeevan Shankar, Alexandre Passos, and Andrew McCallum. 2014. Efficient non-parametric estimation of multiple embeddings per word in vector space. In *Proceedings of EMNLP*.

Diarmuid Ó Séaghdha and Anna Korhonen. 2014. Probabilistic distributional semantics with latent variable models. *Computational Linguistics*, 40(3):587–631.

Sebastian Padó and Mirella Lapata. 2007. Dependency-based construction of semantic space models. *Computational Linguistics*, 33(2):161–199.

Robert Parker, David Graff, Junbo Kong, Ke Chen, and Kazuaki Maeda. 2011. English gigaword fifth edition, june. *Linguistic Data Consortium, LDC2011T07*.

Jeffrey Pennington, Richard Socher, and Christopher Manning. 2014. Glove: Global vectors for word representation. In *Proceedings of the EMNLP*.

Matthias Richter, Uwe Quasthoff, Erla Hallsteinsdóttir, and Chris Biemann. 2006. Exploiting the Leipzig corpora collection. *Proceesings of the IS-LTC*.

György Szarvas, Róbert Busa-Fekete, and Eyke Hüllermeier. 2013. Learning to rank lexical substitutions. In *Proceedings of EMNLP*.

Stefan Thater, Hagen Fürstenau, and Manfred Pinkal. 2011. Word meaning in context: A simple and effective vector model. In *Proceedings of IJCNLP*.

Laurens Van der Maaten and Geoffrey Hinton. 2008. Visualizing data using t-sne. *Journal of Machine Learning Research*, 9:2579–2605.

Unsupervised Text Normalization Using Distributed Representations of Words and Phrases

Vivek Kumar Rangarajan Sridhar*
AT&T Labs - Research
1 AT&T Way, Bedminster, NJ 07920

Abstract

Text normalization techniques that use rule-based normalization or string similarity based on static dictionaries are typically unable to capture domain-specific abbreviations (*custy, cx* → *customer*) and shorthands (*5ever, 7ever* → *forever*) used in informal texts. In this work, we exploit the property that noisy and canonical forms of a particular word share similar context in a large noisy text collection (millions or billions of social media feeds from Twitter, Facebook, etc.). We learn distributed representations of words to capture the notion of contextual similarity and subsequently learn normalization lexicons from these representations in a completely unsupervised manner. We experiment with linear and non-linear distributed representations obtained from log-linear models and neural networks, respectively. We apply our framework for normalizing customer care notes and Twitter. We also extend our approach to learn phrase normalization lexicons (*g2g* → *got to go*) by training distributed representations over compound words. Our approach outperforms Microsoft Word, Aspell and a manually compiled urban dictionary from the Web and achieves state-of-the-art results on a publicly available Twitter dataset.

1 Introduction

Text normalization is a prerequisite for a variety of tasks involving speech and language. Most natural language processing (NLP) tasks require a tight and compact vocabulary to reduce the model complexity in terms of feature size. As a consequence, applications such as syntactic tagging and parsing, semantic tagging, named entity extraction, information extraction, machine translation, language models for speech recognition, etc., are trained on clean data that is normalized and restricted to some user defined vocabulary. Conventionally, most NLP researchers perform such normalization through rule-based mapping that can get unwieldily and cumbersome for extremely noisy texts as in SMS, chat or social media.

Unnormalized text, as witnessed in social media forums such as Facebook, Twitter and message boards, or short messaging service (SMS), have a variety of issues with spelling that include repeating letters, eliminating vowels, using phonetic spellings, substituting letters (typically syllables) with numbers, using shorthands and user created abbreviations for phrases. The remarkable property of such texts is that new variants of canonical words and phrases evolve constantly (e.g., *jghome* → *just got home*). Hence, it is important to design a framework that can learn the mapping between unnormalized and canonical forms of such words and phrases in an unsupervised and extensible manner.

Conventional edit distance (Levenshtein, 1966) based approaches are not accurate for predicting spelling correction for large number of edits in abbreviations and shorthands found in informal texts. In this work, we exploit the property that noisy and canonical forms of a particular word share similar context in a large noisy text collection (millions or billions of social media feeds from Twitter, Facebook, etc.). We represent the words in a vector space using distributed representations to capture the notion contextual similarity and subsequently learn normalization lexicons from these representations. The distributed representations are induced either through neural networks (non-linear embeddings) or log-linear models (linear embeddings). The proposed approach uses the property of contextual similarity between canonical and noisy versions of a particular word to cluster them in $\mathbb{R}^D$, where D is the dimension of the distributed representation. We also extend our framework to learn one-to-many mappings (e.g., *ily* → *i love you*, *nbd* → *no big deal*

*The author is currently with Apple, Inc., and can be contacted at vrangarajansridh@apple.com.

Proceedings of NAACL-HLT 2015, pages 8–16,
Denver, Colorado, May 31 – June 5, 2015. ©2015 Association for Computational Linguistics

by learning distributed representations over words and phrases.

We demonstrate the fidelity of our approach on customer care domain and Twitter. We also compare our approach with Microsoft Word, Aspell, custom dictionaries compiled from the Web as well as state-of-the-art techniques for unsupervised normalization.

2 Related Work

Text normalization has been traditionally performed in a task specific manner through string edit operations. While a large proportion of NLP researchers still perform this exercise manually by writing regular expression patterns, several automatic procedures have been proposed. A simple way to perform this string edit operation is by using a noisy channel model (Brill and Moore, 2000). However, this requires supervised training data in the form of the canonical and erroneous strings. Since words are spoken using phonetics, it is instructive to look at the problem from the point of pronunciation changes. For example, (Toutanova and Moore, 2002) extended the noisy channel framework to include word pronunciation information. The **aspell** tool for spelling correction also works on a phonetic algorithm for string normalization (Philips, 1990).

(Cook and Stevenson, 2009) introduced an unsupervised noisy channel model that considered several word formation processes in a generative model. Another popular way to normalize or even punctuate text is by using phrase-based machine translation. (Aw et al., 2009) used a character level phrase-based machine translation approach to translate SMS text into clean English text. However, such an approach still requires supervised training data. Furthermore, noisy channel models typically do not use wider context in resolving the normalization problem. Clearly, many of the unnormalized forms appear in the same context as the canonical form and exploiting such information is critical.

Social media text normalization using contextual graph random walks was recently proposed in (Hassan and Menezes, 2013). They use a lexicon based approach where the normalization lexicon is obtained in an unsupervised manner by performing random walks on contextual similarity graphs (bipartite) constructed from n-gram sequences. A similar approach using distributional similarity was also proposed in (Han et al., 2012a) where a pairwise similarity deems two words with identical context to be normalization equivalences. Due to the pairwise computation, it does not result in a globally optimized equivalence. Our framework is most similar to (Hassan and Menezes, 2013) as we also use the notion of distributional similarity between strings at a corpus level to identify normalization equivalences in an unsupervised manner. In contrast, we use distributed representation of words to capture contextual similarity and learn unsupervised lexicons using both lexical and vector space feature functions. The proposed approach is relatively simple, scalable and easily reproducible.

3 Distributed Representation of Words

Conventional NLP applications typically use one-hot encoding where each word in the vocabulary is represented by a bit vector. Such a representation exacerbates the data sparsity problem and does not exploit any semantic or syntactic relationship that may be present amongst subset of words. Distributed representation of words (also called word embeddings or continuous space representation of words) has become a popular way for capturing distributional similarity (lexical, semantic or even syntactic) between words. The basic idea is to represent each word $w_i \in V$ with a real-valued vector of some fixed dimension D, i.e., $w_i \in \mathbb{R}^D \;\; \forall \;\; i = 1, \cdots, V$. The idea of representing words in vector space was originally proposed in (Rumelhart et al., 1986; Elman, 1991). However, improved training techniques and tools in the recent past have made it possible to obtain such representations for large vocabularies.

Distributed representations can be induced for a given vocabulary V in several ways. While they are typically induced in the context of a deep neural network framework for a given task (Bengio et al., 2003; Collobert and Weston, 2008; Bengio et al., 2009; Turian et al., 2010; Mikolov et al., 2010), recent work in (Mikolov et al., 2013) has also shown that they can also be induced by using simple log-linear models. Since in many practical NLP applications, the distributed representations are learnt along with the task, the word vectors will have some notion of task dependent distributional similarity. It is this exact notion of contextual and distributional similarity that we exploit in this work to learn normalization lexicons in an un-

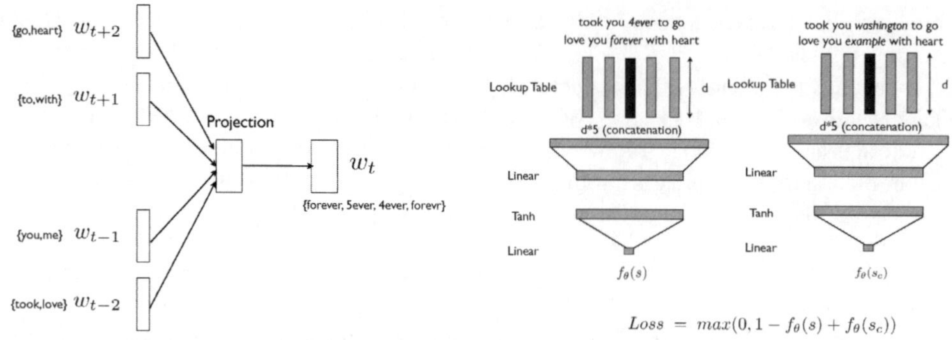

(a) Continuous Bag-of-Words Architecture

(b) Neural Network Architecture

Figure 1: Illustration of obtaining distributed representations for text normalization using two different approaches

supervised manner.

Figure 1 shows two different architectures for inducing distributed representations. On the left side, the architecture for the continuous bag-of-words model (Mikolov et al., 2013) is shown while the neural network learning architecture for inducing distributed representations in language models (Collobert and Weston, 2008) is shown on the right. Both these frameworks essentially perform a similar function in that the word representations are created based on contextual similarity. Figure 1 also shows an example of the contextual similarity that can be exploited such that canonical and noisy versions of a particular word have similar vector representation (in terms of some similarity metric). It is shown that the words $\{$*forever, 4ever, 5ever, forevr*$\}$ share similar context. It is also interesting to note that the word *5ever* that is used to mean *longer than 4ever* can be identified to mean *forever* that edit distance matching is typically not able to capture.

	Language	
	en	
Corpus	Vocabulary	#Sentences
Customer care	7846840	870491324
Twitter	8371078	178770137

Table 1: Statistics of the data used to learn distributed representations

4 Data

We use two sources of data in our work. One is internal anonymized customer care notes and the other is Twitter. The customer care data refers to notes made by agents at mobility call centers when customers make a call. Each call typically results in one record and the notes typically consist of a brief summary of the call from the representative side. The data we use does not contain any metadata beyond the text description. We used all the data between Dec 2012 and Jan 2014. The text data is extremely noisy as the agents are making these notes either during their interaction or immediately afterward. Hence, the data contains several spelling errors and abbreviations that need to be corrected before performing any large scale data analytics.

We also acquired a 10% random sample of Twitter firehose data across all languages. As a first step, we filtered the tweets by language code. Since the language code is a property set in the user profile, the language code does not guarantee that all tweets are in the same language. We used a simple frequency threshold for language identification based on language specific word lists. Subsequently, we performed some basic clean-up such as replacing usernames, hashtags, web addresses and numerals with generic symbols such as *_user_*, *_hashtags_*, *_url_* and *_number_*. Finally, we removed all punctuations from the strings and lowercased the text. In this work, we perform our experiments on English.

5 Training Distributed Representations

We used two approaches (see Figure 1) for learning both linear and non-linear distributed representations of words. For the non-linear neural network approach, we used an architecture identical to that in (Collobert and Weston, 2008), i.e., the network consisted of a lookup table, hidden layer with 100 nodes and a linear layer with one output. However, we used a right and left context of 5 (or 7) words and corrupted the centre word instead of the last word to learn the distributed representations. Given a text window $s = \{w\}_1^{wlen}$, $wlen$[1] is the window length, and a set of parameters associated with the network θ, the network outputs a score $f_\theta(x)$. The approach then minimizes the ranking criterion with respect to θ such that:

$$\theta \mapsto \sum_{s \in \mathcal{X}} \sum_{w \in \mathcal{V}} max\{0, 1 - f_\theta(s) + f_\theta(s_c)\} \quad (1)$$

where $\mathcal{X}$ is the set of all windows of length $wlen$ in the training data, $\mathcal{V}$ is the vocabulary and s_c denotes the corrupted version of s with the middle word replaced by a random word w in $\mathcal{V}$. We used a frequency threshold of 10 occurrences for the centre word, i.e., all words below this frequency was not considered in training. We performed stochastic gradient minimization over 1000 epochs on each dataset and used the Torch toolkit (Collobert et al., 2011) to train the representation.

We also used a log-linear model for inducing the distributed representations using the continuous-bag-of-words architecture proposed in (Mikolov et al., 2013). The continuous-bag-of-words model is similar to the neural network language model (Bengio et al., 2003) with the non-linear layer replaced by a sum pooling layer, i.e., the model uses a bag of surrounding words to predict the centre word. Since the implementation of this architecture was readily available through the word2vec tool[2], we used it for inducing the representations. We used hierarchical sampling for reducing the vocabulary during training and used a minimum count of 10 occurrences for each word.

The framework presented in this paper can also work with word vectors obtained using other techniques such as latent semantic indexing, convolutional neural networks, recurrent neural networks, etc.

6 Learning Normalization Lexicons

Once we obtain the set of word embeddings $w_i \mapsto \mathbf{d}_i, \forall i \in V; \mathbf{d}_i \in \mathbb{R}^D$, our framework requires a list of canonical words as input. For English, we used a wordlist from Project Gutenberg (`http://www.gutenberg.org/ebooks/3201`) consisting of 113809 words. Given a canonical word **s1**, we find the K-nearest neighbors in the vector space and objectively measure the similarity between **s1** and the neighbors, i.e., from each pair of strings **s1** and **s2** with corresponding vectors **u** and **v**, we obtain lexical and vector space features described below.

6.1 Similarity Cost

The cosine distance between two D-dimensional vectors **u** and **v** is defined as,

$$cosine\ \ similarity = \frac{\sum_{i=1}^{D} u_i \times v_i}{\sqrt{\sum_{i=1}^{D}(u_i)^2 \times \sum_{i=1}^{D}(v_i)^2}} \quad (2)$$

The lexical similarity cost is computed similar to that presented in (Hassan and Menezes, 2013).

$$lexical\ \ similarity(\mathbf{s1}, \mathbf{s2}) = \frac{LCSR(\mathbf{s1}, \mathbf{s2})}{ED(\mathbf{s1}, \mathbf{s2})} \quad (3)$$

$$LCSR(\mathbf{s1}, \mathbf{s2}) = \frac{LCS(\mathbf{s1}, \mathbf{s2})}{Max\ Length(\mathbf{s1}, \mathbf{s2})} \quad (4)$$

where LCSR refers to the Longest Common Subsequence Ratio (Melamed, 1995), LCS refers to Longest Common Subsequence and ED refers to the edit distance between the two strings. For English, the edit distance computation was modified to find the distance between the consonant skeleton of the two strings **s1** and **s2**, i.e., all the vowels were removed. Repetition in the strings was reduced to a single letter and numbers in the words were substituted by their equivalent letters. The general algorithm for learning a normalization lexicon through our approach is presented in Algorithm 1. While it is possible to learn optimal weights for several feature functions through minimum error rate training (Och, 2003), we use uniform weights in the absence of a significant held-out set for optimization.

6.2 Representation of Lexicons using FSTs

We compile the lexicon $\mathcal{L}$ obtained using Algorithm 1 into a finite-state transducer with the arc score equal to the negative logarithm of the similarity cost (for finding the path with least cost).

[1] $wlen$ in our work is an odd number, e.g., $wlen = 11$ implies a left and right context of 5 words

[2] https://code.google.com/p/word2vec/

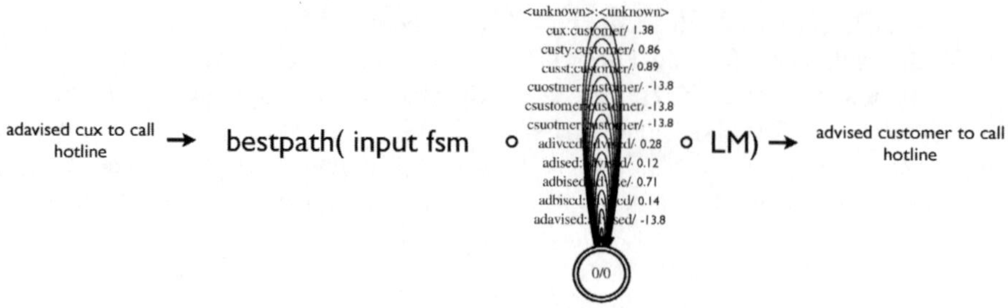

Figure 2: Illustration of the normalization technique using finite state transducers. The unknown words in the input are preserved in the output.

Algorithm 1 Unsupervised Lexicon Learning

input $\{\mathbf{d}_i\}_{i=1}^{|V|}$: distributed representation of words for vocabulary $|V|$
input K: number of nearest neighbors
input $COST$: lexical similarity metric
input W: list of canonical words
for each $w \in W$ **do**
  for each $i \in |V|$ **do**
    if $w_i \mapsto \mathbf{d}_i \notin W$ **then**
      Compute cosine distance between $\mathbf{d}_i$ and $\mathbf{d}(w)$
      Store top K neighbors in map $L(w)$
for each $w \in W$ **do**
  for each $o \in L(w)$ **do**
    Compute $COST(w,o)$
    Push $w \mapsto \{o, COST(w,o)\}$ into D
Invert the map D to obtain lexicon $\mathcal{L}$

The normalization lexicon is converted into a single state finite-state transducer (FST) with the input and output labels being the noisy and canonical word, respectively. In all our experiments, we used the number of nearest neighbors $K = 25$.

Given a sentence that needs to be normalized, we form a linear FSM s from the text string and compose it with the FST lexicon $\mathbf{N}$. The resulting FSM is then composed with a language model (LM) $\mathbf{L}$, if available, and the best path is found to obtain s_{norm}. We used a trigram language model that was trained on a variety of texts (English Gigaword, Web, Opensubtitles, etc.). We used Kneser-Ney discounting and the LM was not optimized in any way.

$$s_{norm} = bestpath(s \circ \mathbf{N} \circ \mathbf{L}) \quad (5)$$

Figure 2 illustrates this procedure. The unknown words in the input are preserved in the output (the language model is trained with an open vocabulary).

6.3 Evaluation

First, we evaluated our approach on customer care data. A set of 300 sentences from the customer care data was randomly selected and the reference sentences were created manually by a professional transcriber. A total of 2387 tokens were normalized by the transcribers. The distributed representation was trained on the remaining customer care data through neural network learning approach (Collobert and Weston, 2008) over a window of 11 words with a vector dimension of 100. We compare our approach with Microsoft Word and Aspell, where the best option was manually chosen (oracle) from the suggestion list. If no option was appropriate, the word was left in it's original form. We measure the fidelity of normalization using precision and recall. The results are presented in Table 2.

Tokens	Model	Precision (%)	Recall (%)	F1 (%)
All	Microsoft Word (Oracle)	53.2	55.0	54.0
	Aspell (Oracle)	33.0	41.2	36.7
	Our approach without LM	59.8	58.2	59.0
	Our approach with LM	64.2	70.4	67.1
Edit distance > 2	Microsoft Word (Oracle)	62.3	49.7	55.3
	Aspell (Oracle)	41.9	36.4	38.9
	Our approach without LM	44.4	58.2	50.4
	Our approach with LM	50.61	75.1	60.5

Table 2: Sentence level normalization on customer care notes

Our approach achieves good performance on the customer care notes. We achieve precision and recall of 64.2% and 70.4%. The performance using our approach outperforms the oracle accuracy using Microsoft Word and Aspell. It is important

Category	Model	Precision (%)	Recall (%)	F1 (%)
Word	Microsoft Word (Oracle)	72.7	30.8	43.3
	Aspell (Oracle)	83.0	35.4	49.6
	Web dictionary with LM	79.8	24.2	37.1
	Neural Network ($wlen$:11+D:100) lexicon without LM	53.4	74.7	62.3
	Neural Network ($wlen$:11+D:100) lexicon with LM	54.4	77.1	63.8
	Neural Network ($wlen$:11+D:200) lexicon with LM	50.5	75.1	60.4
	Neural Network ($wlen$:15+D:100) lexicon with LM	54.2	73.5	62.4
	Neural Network ($wlen$:15+D:200) lexicon with LM	48.5	75.4	59.0
	Log-Linear Model ($wlen$:11+D:100) lexicon with LM	54.5	77.2	63.9
	Log-Linear Model ($wlen$:11+D:200) lexicon with LM	51.2	75.9	61.1
	Log-Linear Model ($wlen$:15+D:100) lexicon with LM	54.6	76.1	63.5
	Log-Linear Model ($wlen$:15+D:200) lexicon with LM	47.1	75.1	57.9

Table 3: Sentence level word normalization on English Twitter data

to note that while our approach is customized to the domain, the baseline comparisons are not. The performance for noisy words that differ in edit distance by more than 2 from the canonical word is also shown in Table 2. Our framework achieves significantly better performance for abbreviations that typically have edit distance > 2. Since our approach combines the strength of distributional and lexical similarity as opposed to most approaches that rely only on string similarity, we are also able to correctly normalize domain specific abbreviations, e.g., *custy* → *customer*, *cx* → *customer*, *lqd* → *liquid*, *bal* → *balance*, *exp* → *expectations*, etc. The use of a language model significantly improves the normalization accuracy.

We also performed sentence (tweet) level normalization on Twitter data. We manually annotated (expanded abbreviations, shorthands and spelling errors) 1000 tweets and performed normalization using our approach. The annotation was performed serially by two professional transcribers. We compare our approach with Microsoft Word, Aspell and a dictionary compiled from several websites. We use a log-linear model (continuous-bag-of-words) as well as a neural network (see Section 5) to automatically learn normalization lexicons. For each model, we experimented with window length ($wlen$) of 11 and 15 while the dimension of distributed representation was either 100 or 200. The results in Table 3 indicate that using Algorithm 1 we achieve impressive performance with both models in comparison with the other schemes. The log-linear model works just as well as the non-linear model and is much quicker to train. One should note that the results from Microsoft Word and Aspell overestimate the fidelity of normalization since the task was performed manually, i.e., we picked the best option from the suggestion list. In case of no correct suggestion, we left the original form as is. Hence, the results are skewed towards achieving high precision. In contrast, our approach is completely unsupervised in design and evaluation. We also compared our approach with a Twitter and SMS dictionary compiled from several websites. The dictionary contained entries for 3864 words and 3536 phrases. The dictionary was compiled into a FST and the procedure in Section 6.2 was used for evaluation. Since, the dictionary entries do not have an associated score, the FST lexicon **N** is unweighted. Our results clearly indicate that for construction of the normalization lexicon all we need is a reliable distributed representation trained on large amount of noisy text. The non-linearity with the neural network does not help significantly for this task.

Approach	Precision (%)	Recall (%)	F1 (%)
(Han et al., 2012b)	70.0	17.9	26.3
(Hassan and Menezes, 2013)	85.3	56.4	69.9
Our approach	64.8	76.3	70.1

Table 4: Sentence level normalization on Twitter test set from (Han et al., 2012b)

We also tested our approach on a publicly available Twitter test set (Han et al., 2012b) comprising of 548 sentences to compare our framework with other state-of-the-art approaches. The training data and approach for each of these schemes is different and we did not optimize our model in any way on the test domain or data. The normalization was performed at the sentence level and we used the language model described in Section 6.2. The results in Table 4 demonstrates that our framework performs favorably in comparison with other techniques.

Category	Model	Precision (%)	Recall (%)	F1 (%)
Phrase	Microsoft Word (Oracle)	99.2	18.7	31.5
	Aspell (Oracle)	75.0	0.4	0.8
	Web dictionary with LM	34.0	19.0	24.4
	Neural Network ($wlen$:11+D:100) without LM	91.4	60.7	73.0
	Neural Network ($wlen$:11+D:100) with LM	92.4	71.3	80.5
	Neural Network ($wlen$:11+D:200) lexicon with LM	92.5	71.8	80.8
	Neural Network ($wlen$:15+D:100) lexicon with LM	92.4	71.4	80.6
	Neural Network ($wlen$:15+D:200) lexicon with LM	92.5	71.8	80.8
	Log-Linear Model ($wlen$:11+D:100) lexicon with LM	92.6	72.0	81.0
	Log-Linear Model ($wlen$:11+D:200) lexicon with LM	92.3	71.1	80.3
	Log-Linear Model ($wlen$:15+D:100) lexicon with LM	92.6	71.5	80.6
	Log-Linear Model ($wlen$:15+D:200) lexicon with LM	92.0	70.9	80.0

Table 5: Sentence level phrase normalization on English Twitter data

7 Learning Phrase Normalizations

A major drawback of inducing normalization lexicons using most approaches described in Section 2 is that they are restricted to learning one-to-one word mappings. However, social media text is strewn with abbreviations that span multiple words, e.g., *ily2* refers to *i love you too*. With our framework, one can obtain 1-to-many (or vice versa) mappings if the training data is modified to contain compound words, i.e., *i love you too* is replaced with *i_love_you_too* and treated as a single token. The biggest obstacle is to get a reliable list of such phrases since they keep changing and growing. Unsupervised phrase induction using likelihood ratio test, point-wise mutual information, etc., may be used for such a task but they typically do not capture phrases formed from high frequency function words.

We used a dataset of speech-based SMS message transcriptions for compiling a list of common phrases. The SMS messages were collected through a smartphone application and a majority of them were collected while the users used the application in their cars. We had access to a total of 41.3 million English messages. The speech transcripts were mostly automatic and only a subset of around 400K utterances were manually transcribed. To avoid the use of erroneous transcripts, we sorted the messages by frequency and picked phrases between length 2 and 4 that resulted in 27356 English phrases. The training data was then phrasified (words were compounded) with the above phrase lists and the experiments to learn distributed representations was repeated. We performed this experiment only on Twitter data.

Once the representations were learned, we computed the K-nearest neighbors using the cosine

Tokens	Canonical phrase
tyvm, tysm, ty, thxs	thank you very much
idk, idfk, irdk, idkk	i don't know
ihy, ihu,	i hate you
ily, ilym, ilyy, ilu	i love you
lmk, hum	let me know
omw, omww, otw	on my way
jgh, jghome	just got home
g2g, gottago	got to go
2b, 2ba	to be
2u, 2us	to you
4u, 4you	for you
cme, callme	call me

Table 6: Phrase normalizations learned through our framework

similarity metric for each phrase. The lexical similarity cost was computed differently for the phrases. The first character of each word in the phrase was picked to form a new string (e.g., *i_love_you_too* would be converted into *ilyt*) and a similar technique was used on the nearest neighbors; singleton numbers were expanded into strings (e.g., *ily2* would be converted into *ilyt*). The lexical similarity metric in Equation (3) was then used to compute the distance between the two strings. The normalization table was subsequently inverted and compiled into a FST. Table 6 shows some of the phrase normalizations learnt by our framework. The phrase normalization results for English are presented in Table 5. Our framework learns phrase normalizations quite well. We achieve precision and recall of 92.6% and 72.0%, respectively. Even the mistakes committed are not very different from the ground truth, e.g., *idk* → *i_do_not_know* while the reference is *i_don't_know*, *wtf* → *what_the_hell* instead of *what_the_f**** and *omfg* → *oh_my_god* in place of *oh_my_f****_god*. Our framework does not capture expansions of geographic locations present in the reference data such as *nz* → *new_zealand*, *la* → *los_angeles* and some highly context dependent expansions such as *dw* → *doctor_who*, *dm* → *direct_message*, etc., since the compiled phrase list did not contain these entries.

8 Discussion

The normalization lexicons learned in this work are completely unsupervised. The quality and coverage of the lexicon is dependent on the size and distribution of words in the training data. Our approach assumes that the data contains both the noisy and canonical form of a word. In practice, we have observed that for large text collections, such as millions of tweets, words appear in both canonical and noisy forms. One can also augment noisy corpora with clean text to improve the distributional similarity of the two forms. Choosing the optimal size of noisy data set and appropriate augmentation is beyond the scope of this work.

The main parameters in our model are $wlen$, D and K. The choice of K is dependent on the size of the training data, i.e., a larger K can potentially yield more noisy to canonical mappings. For our datasets, the choice of $K = \{25, 50, 100\}$ did not result in any significant difference in performance. Hence, we used $K = 25$ to increase the speed of Algorithm 1. We also performed several experiments to understand the choice of dimension D. In general, the choice of D is dependent on the vocabulary size of the training data. For vocabulary size between 100K-500K, we found that vector dimension of $D = 50$ is sufficient and for vocabulary size greater than $1M$, $D = 100$ works well empirically. For $wlen$, a context of 5 words to the left and right, i.e., $wlen = 11$ works well and adding more context does not necessarily improve performance. We conjecture that this is due to the length of an average customer care note (12 words) and tweet (15 words). For datasets with longer sentences, larger values of $wlen$ may be beneficial.

The performance reported using Microsoft Word and Aspell was obtained by manually selecting the best suggestion. We resorted to this approach since both schemes do not provide an option to automatically normalize a document. In choosing the best suggestion option, we focused on precision, i.e., picked the best suggestion or left the original form as is. If we had forcefully picked an option from the suggestion list for all corrections, the recall would have been higher at the cost of lower precision. The results using the Web dictionary and our unsupervised framework performs a blind evaluation.

In contrast with conventional string similarity based normalization schemes, our approach is good at modeling abbreviations. Abbreviations are generally hard to normalize with Levenshtein distance based approaches but the combination of distributional and lexical similarity is very helpful in learning the mapping between abbreviated and canonical forms. In most off-the-shelf systems, e.g., Microsoft Word, a standard dictionary is used and any corrections for domain specific spellings are typically performed manually. Since our scheme can be trained with raw data, we are able to address the domain specific idiosyncrasies.

The word and phrase normalizations learned in this work use a particular type of lexical similarity metric. While it captures abbreviations well for English, our framework is open to the use of any linguistically motivated lexical similarity metric. Such metrics can be designed by language experts and linguistic knowledge can potentially be incorporated into the unsupervised scheme, thus, lending a way to embed linguistic rules into a statistical framework.

9 Conclusion

We presented an unsupervised framework for normalizing domain-specific and informal noisy texts using distributed representation of words. Our approach exploits the property that noisy and canonical forms of a particular word share similar context in a large noisy text collection (millions or billions of social media feeds from Twitter, Facebook, etc.). Subsequently, we use a combination of distributional and lexical similarity between canonical and noisy form of words to automatically construct a normalization lexicon. The distributed representations were learned using both log-linear and non-linear models and we used a finite-state transducer framework for representing the lexicons and performing normalization. Our experiments on customer care data and Twitter indicate that our approach can capture spelling errors of different types and achieves good performance in comparison with several baselines and state-of-the-art approaches. Finally, we used our framework to learn phrase normalizations by learning distributed representations over compound words.

References

A. Aw, M. Zhang, J. Xiao, and J. Su. 2009. A phrase-based statistical model for SMS text normalization. In *Proceedings of COLING*, pages 33–40.

Y. Bengio, R. Ducharme, P. Vincent, and C. Jauvin. 2003. A neural probabilistic language model. *Journal of Machine Learning Research*, 3:1137–1155.

Y. Bengio, J. Louradour, R. Collobert, and J. Weston. 2009. Curriculum learning. In *Proceedings of ICML*.

E. Brill and R. C. Moore. 2000. An improved error model for noisy channel spelling correction. In *Proceedings of ACL*, pages 286–293.

R. Collobert and J. Weston. 2008. A unified architecture for natural language processing: deep neural networks with multitask learning. In *Proceedings of ICML*.

R. Collobert, K. Kavukcuoglu, and C. Farabet. 2011. Torch7: A matlab-like environment for machine learning. In *BigLearn, NIPS Workshop*.

P. Cook and S. Stevenson. 2009. An unsupervised model for text message normalization. In *Proceedings of Workshop on Computational Approaches to Linguistic Creativity*, pages 71–78.

J. L. Elman. 1991. Distributed representations, simple recurrent networks, and grammatical structure. *Machine Learning*, 7(2-3):195–225.

B. Han, P. Cook, and Baldwin. 2012a. Automatically constructing a normalization dictionary for microblogs. In *Proceedings of EMNLP*, pages 421–432.

B. Han, P. Cook, and T. Baldwin. 2012b. Automatically constructing a normalisation dictionary for microblogs. In *EMNLP-CoNLL 2012*, pages 421–432.

H. Hassan and A. Menezes. 2013. Social text normalization using contextual graph random walks. In *Proceedings of ACL*, pages 1577–1586.

V. I. Levenshtein. 1966. Binary codes capable of correcting deletions, insertions, and reversals. *Soviet Physics Doklady (in English)*, 10(8):707710, February.

D. Melamed. 1995. Automatic evaluation and uniform filter cascades for inducing n-best translation lexicons. In *Proceedings of the 3rd ACL Workshop on Very Large Corpora (WVLC)*.

T. Mikolov, S. Kopecký, L. Burget, J. Černocký, and S. Khudanpur. 2010. Recurrent neural network based language model. In *Proceedings of Interspeech*.

T. Mikolov, K. Chen, G. Corrado, and J. Dean. 2013. Efficient estimation of word representations in vector space. In *Proceedings of Workshop at ICLR*.

F. J. Och. 2003. Minimum error rate training in statistical machine translation. In *Proceedings of ACL*.

L. Philips. 1990. Hanging on the metaphone. *Computer Language*, 7(12):39–43.

D. E. Rumelhart, G. E. Hinton, and R. J. Williams. 1986. Parallel distributed processing: Explorations in the microstructure of cognition, vol. 1. chapter Learning Internal Representations by Error Propagation, pages 318–362.

K. Toutanova and R. C. Moore. 2002. Pronunciation modeling for improved spelling correction. In *Proceedings of ACL*, pages 141–151.

J. Turian, L. Ratinov, and Y. Bengio. 2010. Word representations: a simple and general method for semi-supervised learning. In *Proceedings of ACL*.

A Multi-classifier Approach to support Coreference Resolution in a Vector Space Model

Ana Zelaia
UPV/EHU
Manuel Lardizabal, 1
Donostia, 20018
Basque Country, Spain
ana.zelaia@ehu.eus

Olatz Arregi
UPV/EHU
Manuel Lardizabal, 1
Donostia, 20018
Basque Country, Spain
olatz.arregi@ehu.eus

Basilio Sierra
UPV/EHU
Manuel Lardizabal, 1
Donostia, 20018
Basque Country, Spain
b.sierra@ehu.eus

Abstract

In this paper a different machine learning approach is presented to deal with the coreference resolution task. This approach consists of a multi-classifier system that classifies mention-pairs in a reduced dimensional vector space. The vector representation for mention-pairs is generated using a rich set of linguistic features. The SVD technique is used to generate the reduced dimensional vector space.

The approach is applied to the OntoNotes v4.0 Release Corpus for the column-format files used in CONLL-2011 coreference resolution shared task. The results obtained show that the reduced dimensional representation obtained by SVD is very adequate to appropriately classify mention-pair vectors. Moreover, we can state that the multi-classifier plays an important role in improving the results.

1 Introduction

Coreference resolution deals with the problem of finding all expressions that refer to the same entity in a text (Mitkov, 2002). It is an important subtask in Natural Language Processing that require natural language understanding, and hence, it is considered to be difficult.

A coreference resolution system has to automatically identify the mentions of entities in text and link the corefering mentions (the ones that refer to the same entity) to form coreference chains. Systems are expected to perform both, mention detection and coreference resolution.

Preliminary researches proposed heuristic approaches to the task, but thanks to the annotated coreference corpora made available in the last years and the progress achieved in statistical NLP methods, machine learning approaches to the coreference resolution task are being proposed. (Ng, 2010) presents an interesting survey of the progress in coreference resolution.

In this paper we present a different machine learning approach to deal with the coreference resolution task. Given a corpus with annotated mentions, the multi-classifier system we present classifies mention-pairs in a reduced dimensional vector space. We use the typical mention-pair model, where each pair of mentions is represented by a rich set of linguistic features; positive instances correspond to mention-pairs that corefer. Coreference resolution is tackled as a binary classification problem (Soon et al., 2001) in this paper; the subsequent linking of mentions into coreference chains is not considered. In fact, the aim of our experiment is to measure to what extent working with feature vectors in a reduced dimensional vector space and applying a multi-classifier system helps to determine the coreference of mention-pairs. To the best of our knowledge, there are no approaches to the coreference resolution task which make use of multi-classifier systems to classify mention-pairs in a reduced dimensional vector space.

This paper gives a brief description of our approach to deal with the problem of identifying whether two mentions corefer and shows the results obtained. Section 2 presents related work. In Section 3 our approach is presented. Section 4 presents the case study, where details about the dataset used in the experiments and the preprocessing applied are

Proceedings of NAACL-HLT 2015, pages 17–24,
Denver, Colorado, May 31 – June 5, 2015.

given. In Section 5 the experimental setup is briefly introduced. The experimental results are presented and discussed in Section 6, and finally, Section 7 contains some conclusions and comments on future work.

2 Related Work

Much attention has been paid to the problem of coreference resolution in the past two decades. Conferences specifically focusing coreference resolution have been organized since 1995. The sixth and seventh Message Understanding Conferences (MUC-6, 1995; MUC-7, 1998) included a specific task on coreference resolution. The Automatic Context Extraction (ACE) Program focused on identifying certain types of relations between a predefined set of entities (Doddington et al., 2004) while the Anaphora Resolution Exercise (ARE) involved anaphora resolution and NP coreference resolution (Orăsan et al., 2008).

More recently, SemEval-2010 Task 1 was dedicated to coreference resolution in multiple languages. One year later, in the CoNLL-2011 shared task (Pradhan et al., 2011), participants had to model unrestricted coreference in the English-language OntoNotes corpora and CoNLL-2012 Shared Task (Pradhan et al., 2012) involved predicting coreference in three languages: English, Chinese and Arabic.

Recent work on coreference resolution has been largely dominated by machine learning approaches. In the SemEval-2010 task on Coreference Resolution in Multiple Languages (Recasens et al., 2010), most of the systems were based on these techniques (Broscheit et al., 2010; Uryupina, 2010; Kobdani et al., 2010). The same occurs at CoNLL-2011, where (Chang et al., 2011; Björkelund et al., 2011; dos Santos et al., 2011) were based on machine learning techniques. The advantage of these approaches is that there are many open-source platforms for machine learning and machine learning based coreference systems such as BART (Versley et al., 2008), the Illinois Coreference Package (Bengtson et al., 2008) or the Stanford CoreNLP (Manning et al., 2014), among others.

Nevertheless, rule-based systems have also been applied successfully (Lappin et al., 1994; Mitkov, 1998; Lee et al., 2013). The authors of this last system propose a coreference resolution system that is an incremental extension of the multi-pass sieve system proposed by (Raghunathan et al., 2010). This system is shifting from the supervised learning setting to an unsupervised setting, and obtained the best result in the CoNLL-2011 Shared Task.

Some very interesting uses of vector space models for the coreference resolution task can be found in the literature. (Nilsson et al., 2009) investigate the effect of using vector space models as an approximation of the kind of lexico-semantic and commonsense knowledge needed for coreference resolution for Swedish texts. They also work with reduced dimensional vector spaces and obtain encouraging results. In an attempt to increase the performance of a coreference resolution engine, (Bryl et al., 2010) make use of structured semantic knowledge available in the web. One of the strategies they adopt is to apply the SVD to Wikipedia articles and classify mentions in a reduced dimensional vector space.

3 Proposed Approach

The approach we present consists of a multi-classifier system which classifies mention-pairs in a reduced dimensional vector space. This multi-classifier is composed of several k-NN classifiers. A set of linguistic features is used to generate the vector representations for the mention-pairs. The training dataset is used to create a reduced dimensional vector space using the SVD technique. Mention-pairs in the training, development and test sets are represented using the same linguistic features and projected onto the reduced dimensional space.

The classification process is performed in the reduced dimensional space. To create the multi-classifier, we apply random subsampling and obtain training datasets $TD_1, \ldots, TD_i$ for the reduced dimensional space. Given a testing case q, the k-NN classifier makes a label prediction c^i based on each one of the training datasets TD_i, and predictions $c^1, \ldots c^i$ are combined to obtain the final prediction c_j using a Bayesian voting scheme. It is a binary classification system where the final prediction c_j may be positive (mentions tested corefer) or negative (mentions do not corefer). Figure 1 shows an illustration of the fundamental steps of the experi-

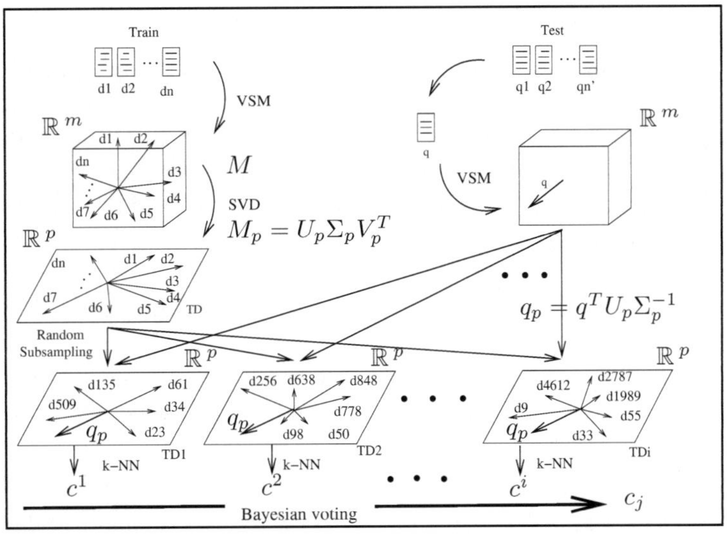

Figure 1: Fundamental steps of the proposed approach. $\mathbb{R}^m$ is the original vector space, $\mathbb{R}^p$ is the reduced dimensional space where vectors are projected. The multi-classifier is composed of several k-NN classifiers. c_j is the final classification label for testing case q.

ment.

In the rest of this section, details about the SVD dimensionality reduction technique, the k-NN classification algorithm, the combination of classifiers and the evaluation measures used are briefly reviewed.

3.1 The SVD Dimensionality Reduction

The classical Vector Space Model (VSM) has been successfully employed to represent documents in text categorization and Information Retrieval tasks. Latent Semantic Indexing (LSI) [1] (Deerwester et al., 1990) is a variant of the VSM in which documents are represented in a lower dimensional vector space created from a training dataset. To create such a lower dimensional vector space, LSI generates a term-document matrix M and computes its SVD matrix decomposition, $M = U\Sigma V^T$. As a result, r singular values are obtained, and terms and documents are mapped to the r-dimensional vector space. By reducing the r to p, a reduced dimensional space is created, the p-dimensional space onto which vectors are projected. This reduced dimensional space is used for classification purposes, and the cosine similarity is usually used to measure the similarity between vectors (Berry et al., 1995).

[1] http://lsi.research.telcordia.com,http://www.cs.utk.edu/~lsi

It has been proved that computing the similarity of vectors in the reduced dimensional space gives better results than working in the original space. In fact, LSI is said to be able to capture the latent relationships among words in documents thanks to the word co-occurrence analysis performed by the SVD technique, and therefore, cluster semantically terms and documents. This powerful technique is being used to better capture the semantics of texts in applications such as Information Retrieval (Berry et al., 2005). LSI is referred to as Latent Semantic Analysis (LSA) when it is used as a model of the acquisition, induction and representation of language and the focus is on the analysis of texts (Dumais, 2004).

For the sake of the coreference resolution task, each document corresponds to a mention-pair, and words in each document are the linguistic feature values for the associated mention-pair. Section 4.2 gives details about the linguistic features used to represent each mention-pair. Matrix M is constructed for the selected feature values (terms) and all mention-pairs considered (documents). The SVD decomposition is computed and the p-dimensional reduced space is created. We use U as the reduced dimensional representation, and compute the coordinates to project mention-pair vectors onto the reduced space and compare them.

3.2 The k-NN classification algorithm

k-NN is a distance based classification approach. According to this approach, given an arbitrary testing case, the k-NN classifier ranks its nearest neighbors among the training cases, and uses the class of the k top-ranking neighbors to do the prediction for the testing case being analyzed (Dasarathy, 1991).

In our experiments, parameter k is set to 3. Given a testing mention-pair vector, the 3-NN classifier is used to find the three nearest neighbor mention-pair vectors in the reduced dimensional vector space. The cosine is used to measure vector similarity and find the nearests.

We also consider the k-NN classifier provided with the Weka package (Hall et al., 2009; Aha et al., 1991). We use it to obtain a honest comparison for the results.

3.3 Multi-classifier systems

The combination of multiple classifiers has been intensively studied with the aim of improving the accuracy of individual components (Ho et al., 1994). A widely used technique to implement this approach is *bagging* (Breiman, 1996), where a set of training datasets TD_i is generated by selecting n training cases drawn randomly with replacement from the original training dataset TD of n cases. When a set of $n_1 < n$ training cases is chosen from the original training collection, the bagging is said to be applied by random subsampling. In fact, this is the approach used in our work and the n_1 parameter is set to be 60% of the total number of training cases n. The proportion of positive and negative cases in the training dataset TD is preserved in the different TD_i datasets generated.

According to the random subsampling, given a testing case q, the classifier makes a label prediction c^i based on each one of the training datasets TD_i. Label predictions c^i may be either positive or negative. One way to combine the predictions is by Bayesian voting (Dietterich, 1998), where a confidence value $\mathrm{cv}^i_{c_j}$ is calculated for each training dataset TD_i and label to be predicted. These confidence values are calculated based on the training collection. Confidence values are summed by label; the label c_j that gets the highest value is finally proposed as a prediction for the testing case q.

3.4 Evaluation measures

The approach presented in this paper is a binary classification system where the final prediction c_j may be positive (mentions tested corefer) or negative (mentions do not corefer). There are many metrics that can be used to measure the performance of a classifier. In binary classification problems precision and recall are very widely used. Precision (Prec) is the number of correct positive results divided by the number of all positive results, and recall (Rec) is the number of correct positive results divided by the number of positive results that should have been returned.

In general, there is a trade-off between precision and recall. Thus, a classifier is usually evaluated by means of a measure which combines them. The F_1-score can be interpreted as a weighted average of precision and recall; it reaches its best value at 1 and worst score at 0.

$$F_1 = \frac{2 \cdot \mathrm{Prec} \cdot \mathrm{Rec}}{\mathrm{Prec} + \mathrm{Rec}}$$

Accuracy is also used as a statistical measure of performance in binary classification tasks. Accuracy is the proportion of true results (both true positives and true negatives) among the total number of cases tested.

4 Case study

This section briefly reviews the dataset used in the experiments and the preprocessing applied.

4.1 Dataset

The OntoNotes v4.0 Release Corpus is used in the experiments[2]. It provides a large-scale multi-genre corpus with multiple layers of annotation (syntactic, semantic and discourse information) which also include coreference tags. A nice description of the coreference annotation in OntoNotes can be found in (Pradhan et al., 2007a) and (Pradhan et al., 2007b).

Although OntoNotes is a multi-lingual resource for English, Chinese and Arabic, for the scope of this paper, we just look at the English portion. We

[2]Downloaded from Linguistic Data Consortium (LDC) Catalog No.: LDC2011T03, https://catalog.ldc.upenn.edu/LDC2011T03. For more information, see OntoNotesRelease4.0.pdf and coreference/english-coref.pdf files in LDC directory

use English texts for five different genres or types of sources: broadcast conversations (BC), broadcast news (BN), magazine articles (MZ), newswires (NW) and web data (WB).

The English language portion of the OntoNotes v4.0 Release Corpus was used in the CONLL-2011 coreference resolution Shared task[3]. The task was to automatically identify mentions of entities and events in text and to link the corefering mentions together to form mention chains (Pradhan et al., 2011; Pradhan et al., 2012). Since OntoNotes coreference data spans multiple genre, the task organizers created a test set spanning all the genres. The training, development and test files were downloaded from the CONLL-2011 website, and the *_conll files were generated from each corresponding *_skel files using the scripts made available by the organizers.

The *_conll files contain information in a tabular structure where the last column contains coreference chain information. Two types of *_conll files may be generated, depending on how the annotation was generated; *gold_conll files were hand-annotated and adjudicated quality, whereas annotations in *auto_conll files were produced using a combination of automatic tools. *gold_conll files are used in the experiments presented in this paper.

4.2 Preprocessing

In order to obtain the vector representation for each pair of mentions, we used the features defined by (Sapena et al., 2011). The 127 binary features they define are related to distance, position, lexical information, morphological information, syntactic dependencies and semantic features. The authors developed a coreference resolution system called RelaxCor[4] and participated in the CoNLL-2011 shared task obtaining very good results. It is an open source software available for anyone who wishes to use it.

RelaxCor is a constraint-based hypergraph partitioning approach to coreference resolution, solved by relaxation labeling. It generates feature vectors for all mention-pairs in the *_conll files as part of the system and uses them to solve the task. We decided to use the perl scripts distributed by the authors and generate the positive and negative feature vectors for all *_conll files. These feature vectors consist of binary values for the 127 binary features and a label: a positive label (+) indicates that the feature vector corresponds to a corefering mention-pair, whereas a negative label (-) indicates that the two mentions do not corefer.

Note that each mention in a file is combined with all the rest of mentions in the same file to form mention-pairs and consequently, a very large amount of negative examples is generated, specially for large files. We decided to reduce the amount of negative examples, in a similar manner as (Sapena et al., 2011) and therefore, negative examples with more than five feature values different from any positive example in each file were eliminated. In order to obtain the training, development and test corpora for the 5 genres, we brought together the examples generated from files of the same split and genre. We removed contradictions (negative examples with identical feature values as a positive example) and examples that appeared more than once in the same corpus. We noticed that the size of the corpora was too large for some of the genres; the broadcast conversations (BC) genre training corpus for instance had more than 4 million examples. We decided to reduce all corpora to a reasonable size to compute the SVD.

	BC	BN	MZ	NW	WB
Train (+)	20206	44515	25103	31034	24501
Train (-)	26623	55921	23568	50687	26948
Dev (+)	4056	5920	3873	4776	3531
Dev (-)	5831	8609	4864	7615	5732
Test (+)	29363	10771	3918	15857	17146
Test (-)	16591	12480	3209	15759	5505

Table 1: Size of corpora used in the experiments.

Table 1. gives detailed information about the number of positive and negative mention-pairs in the training, development and test corpora used in the experiments. A matrix is constructed for each of the training corpus. Feature values that appear at least once in the corpus are selected as terms. Even though theoretically we could have a maximum number of 254 different terms in each training corpus (127 $\times$ 2, because the 127 features are binary), the real value is between 227 and 230. The

[3]http://conll.cemantix.org/2011/introduction.html

[4]http://nlp.lsi.upc.edu/relaxcor/

sizes of the matrices created are given by the number of terms and documents (sum of (+) and (-) examples in the training corpus) and can be seen in Table 2.

	BC	BN	MZ	NW	WB
Terms	227	230	227	229	230
Docs	46829	100436	48671	81721	51449

Table 2: Size of term-document matrices M.

5 Experimental Setup

To optimize the behaviour of the multi-classifier system, the number of TD_i training datasets is adjusted in a parameter tuning phase. This optimization process is performed in an independent way for each of the genres because the five genres correspond to texts coming from different sources and may have very different characteristics (Uryupina et al., 2012). Therefore, we treat them as five different classification problems.

The five development corpora are used to adjust parameter i (the amount of TD_i training datasets). We experimented with the following values for i: 5, 10, 20, 30, 40, 50, 60, 70, 80. Table 3 shows the optimal values obtained for each genre. This means that testing cases for the BC genre, for instance, are classified by a multi-classifier formed by 60 k-NN classifiers, after having generated 60 TD_i training datasets from the original TD.

	BC	BN	MZ	NW	WB
Optimal i	60	30	50	20	40
Singular Values	83	86	85	86	87

Table 3: Optimal values for the number of TD_i datasets. Number of singular values computed by SVD

Two different dimensional representations are experimented for mention-pair vectors. On the one hand, we consider mention-pair vectors represented in the original 127 dimensions. On the other hand, the SVD-computed dimensional vector representation is being experimented. Table 3 shows the number of singular values (dimensions) computed by SVD for each of the genres.

6 Experimental Results

Three experiments were carried out in the test phase using the optimal values for parameter i and the two different representations for mention-pair vectors. Table 4 shows the results obtained for each of the experiments: accuracy values in a first row (Acc.) and F_1-scores in a second (F_1).

In a first experiment (Exp.1), the Weka 3-NN classifier is applied to classify testing cases represented in the original 127 dimensional space. The same 3-NN classifier is applied in a second experiment (Exp.2), but training and testing cases are represented using the dimensions computed by SVD (see Singular Values in Table 3). In a last experiment (Exp.3), our approach is applied and a multi-classifier system classifies testing vectors in the same SVD-dimensional vector space as in the previous experiment. The multi-classifier is generated according to the optimal values for parameter i in each genre.

Exp.	BC	BN	MZ	NW	WB	Mean
1 Acc.	**0.719**	0.704	**0.706**	0.707	0.669	0.701
F_1	**0.762**	0.686	**0.731**	0.679	0.744	0.720
2 Acc.	0.672	0.725	0.662	0.725	**0.783**	0.713
F_1	0.742	0.71	0.717	0.715	**0.85**	**0.747**
3 Acc.	0.669	**0.755**	0.661	**0.742**	0.776	**0.721**
F_1	0.739	**0.728**	0.707	**0.716**	0.841	0.746

Table 4: Accuracy and F_1-score for the test corpora. Exp.1: 3-NN and 127 dimensions. Exp.2: 3-NN and SVD dimensions. Exp.3: multi-classifier and SVD dimensions. Last column: mean values

The results shown in bold in the first part of Table 4 are the best for each genre. Note that the two performance measures computed (accuracy and F_1-score) are very correlated in the five cases. Taking into account that the proportion of positive and negative examples varies from genre to genre, this correlation gives consistency to the interpretation of the results obtained.

The best results for BC and MZ genres are obtained in the first experiment, applying the 3-NN classifier to the 127 dimensional vectors (Exp.1, F_1-scores: 0.762 and 0.731, respectively). For the rest of the genres, the best results are obtained for the SVD-dimensional vectors. An F_1-score of 0.85 is obtained for the WB genre in the second experiment (Exp.2). The approach proposed in this paper (Exp.3) achieves the best results for two out of the five genre, with an F_1-score of 0.728 for BN and 0.716 for NW.

The last column in Table 4 shows the mean accuracy and F_1-scores obtained in each experiment, taking into account the five genres as a whole (the best are shown in bold). The best mean F_1-score is obtained in Experiment 2, where vectors are classified in the SVD-dimensional vector space. In fact, this result is very closely followed by the one obtained in Experiment 3 with our approach, (mean F_1-scores: 0.747 and 0.746, respectively). The best mean accuracy is obtained when our approach is applied (mean accuracy: 0.721). This good results seem to suggest that the dimensions computed by the SVD technique are very appropriate to represent mention-pairs and classify them. Moreover, the use of the multi-classifier system gets to achieve even better results, outperforming the ones obtained by the other classification systems.

7 Conclusions and Future Work

In this paper a different machine learning approach to deal with the coreference resolution task is presented: a multi-classifier system that classifies mention-pairs in a reduced dimensional vector space created by applying the SVD technique. The results obtained for the OntoNotes corpus are very good, outperforming the ones obtained by other classification systems for some genres. Moreover, when mean results per experiment are considered, the SVD generated dimensional representation always achieves the best results, which seems to suggest that it is a very robust and suitable representation for coreference mention-pairs.

As future work, we plan to experiment with some other kind of multi-classifer systems and basic classifiers such as SVM. It is important to note that the approach may be applied to corpora in other languages as well.

Acknowledgments

We gratefully acknowledge Emili Sapena, who helped us solve some file format problems. This work was supported by the University of the Basque Country, UPV/EHU, ikerketaren arloko errektoreordetza / Vicerrectorado de Investigaci6n.

References

David W. Aha, Dennis Kibler, and Marc K. Albert. 1991. *Machine Learning*, volume 6(1).

Eric Bengtson and Dan Roth. 2008. *Understanding the value of features for coreference resolution.* Proceedings of the EMNLP '08: 294–303.

Michael W. Berry, Susan T. Dumais, and Gavin W. O'Brien. 1995. *Using Linear Algebra for Intelligent Information Retrieval*, volume 37(4):573–595. SIAM.

Michael W. Berry and Murray Browne. 2005. *Understanding Search Engines: Mathematical Modeling and Text Retrieval.* SIAM.

Anders Bjrkelund and Pierre Nugues. 2011. *Exploring lexicalized features for coreference resolution.* Proceedings of the CONLL'11 Shared Task, 45–50.

Leo Breiman. 1996. *Bagging Predictors.* Machine Learning, volume 24(2):123–140.

Samuel Broscheit, Massimo Poesio, Simone Paolo Ponzetto, Kepa Joseba Rodriguez, Lorenza Romano, Olga Uryupina, Yannick Versley, and Roberto Zanoli. 2010. *BART: A multilingual anaphora resolution system.* Proceedings of the SemEval-2010, pages 104–107.

Volha Bryl, Claudio Giuliano, Luciano Serafini, and Kateryna Tymoshenko. 2010. *Using Background Knowledge to Support Coreference Resolution.* IOS Press, volume 215:759–764.

Kai-Wei Chang, Rajhans Samdani, Alla Rozovskaya, Nick Rizzolo, Mark Sammons, and Dan Roth. 2011. *Inference protocols for coreference resolution.* Proceedings of the CoNLL'11 Shared Task, 40–44.

Belur V. Dasarathy. 1991. *Nearest Neighbor (NN) Norms: NN Pattern Recognition Classification Techniques.* IEEE Computer Society Press.

Scott Deerwester, Susan T. Dumais, George W. Furnas, Thomas K. Landauer, and Richard Harshman. 1990. *Indexing by Latent Semantic Analysis.* Journal of the American Society for Information Science, 41(6):391–407.

Thomas G. Dietterich. 1998. *Machine Learning Research: Four Current Directions.* The AI Magazine, volume 18(4):97–136.

George Doddington, Alexis Mitchell, Mark Przybocki, Lance Ramshaw, Stephanie Strassel, and Ralph Weischedel. 2004. *The Automatic Content Extraction (ACE) Program-Tasks, Data, and Evaluation.* Proceedings of the LREC-2004, 837–840.

Susan T. Dumais. 2004. *Latent Semantic Analysis*. ARIST (Annual Review of Information Science Technology), volume 38:189–230.

Mark Hall, Eibe Franke, Geoffrey Holmes, Bernhard Pfahringer, Peter Reutemann, and Ian H. Witten. 2009. *The WEKA Data Mining Software: An Update*. SIGKDD Explorations, volume 11(1):10–18.

Tin K. Ho, Jonathan J. Hull, and Sargur N. Srihari. 1994. *Decision Combination in Multiple Classifier Systems*. IEEE Transactions on Pattern Analysis and Machine Intelligence, volume 16(1):66–75.

Hamidreza Kobdani and Hinrich Schütze. 2010. *Sucre: A modular system for coreference resolution*. Proceedings of the SemEval-2010, pp. 92–95.

Heeyoung Lee, Angel Chang, Yves Peirsman, Nathanael Chambers, Mihai Surdeanu, and Dan Jurafsky. 2013. *Deterministic coreference resolution based on entity-centric, precision-ranked rules*. Computational Linguistics, 39(4):885–916.

Shalom Lappin and Herbert J. Leass. 1994. *An algorithm for pronominal anaphora resolution*. Computational linguistics, 20(4):535–561.

Christopher D. Manning, Mihai Surdeanu, John Bauer, Jenny Finkel, Steven J. Bethard, and David McClosky. 2014. *The Stanford CoreNLP Natural Language Processing Toolkit*. Proceedings of 52nd Annual Meeting of the Association for Computational Linguistics: System Demonstrations, 55–60.

Ruslan Mitkov. 1998. *Robust pronoun resolution with limited knowledge*. Proceedings of the COLING'98, volume 2: 869–875.

Ruslan Mitkov. 2002. *Anaphora Resolution*. Pearson Education.

MUC-6. 1995. *Coreference task definition*. Proceedings of the MUC, 335–344.

MUC-7. 1998. *Coreference task definition*. Proceedings of the MUC.

Vincent Ng. 2010. *Supervised Noun Phrase Coreference Research: The First Fifteen Years*. Proceedings of the ACL'10, 1396–1411.

Kristina Nilsson and Hans Hjelm. 2009. *Using Semantic Features Derived from Word-Space Models for Swedish Coreference Resolution*. Proceedings of the NoDaLiDa'09, volume 4:134–141.

Constantin Orăsan, Dan Cristea, Ruslan Mitkov, and António Branco. 2008. *Anaphora Resolution Exercise: an Overview*. Proceedings of the LREC'08.

Sameer Pradhan, Eduard Hovy, Mitchell Marcus, Martha Palmer, Lance Ramshaw, and Ralph Weischedel 2007a. *Ontonotes: a Unified Relational Semantic Representation*. International Journal of Semantic Computing, volume 1(4):405–419.

Sameer Pradhan, Lance Ramshaw, Ralph Weischedel, Jessica MacBride, and Linnea Micciulla. 2007b. *Unrestricted Coreference: Identifying Entities and Events in OntoNotes*. Proceedings of the ICSC, pp. 446–453.

Sameer Pradhan, Martha Palmer, Lance Ramshaw, Ralph Weischedel, Mitchell Marcus, and Nianwen Xue. 2011. *CoNLL-2011 Shared Task: Modeling Unrestricted Coreference in OntoNotes*. Proceedings of the CONLL'11 Shared Task, 1–27.

Sameer Pradhan, Alessandro Moschitti, Nianwen Xue, Olga Uryupina, and Yuchen Zhang. 2012. *CoNLL-2012 Shared Task: Modeling Multilingual Unrestricted Coreference in OntoNotes*. Proceedings of the CONLL'12 Shared Task, 1–40. Association for Computational Linguistics.

Karthik Raghunathan, Heeyoung Lee, Sudarshan Rangarajan, Nathanael Chambers, Mihai Surdeanu, Dan Jurafsky, and Christopher Manning. 2010. *A multi-pass sieve for coreference resolution*. Proceedings of the EMNLP'10, pp. 492–501.

Marta Recasens, Lluís Márquez, Emili Sapena, M. Antónia Martí, Mariona Taulé, Véronique Hoste, Massimo Poesio, and Yannick Versley. 2010. *SemEval-2010 Task 1: Coreference Resolution in Multiple Language*. Proceedings of the SemEval-2010, pp. 1–8.

C. N. dos Santos and D. L. Carvalho. 2011. *Rule and tree ensembles for unrestricted coreference resolution*. Proceedings of the CONLL'11 Shared Task, pp. 51–55.

Emili Sapena, Lluís Padró, and Jordi Turmo. 2011. *RelaxCor Participation in CoNLL Shared Task on Coreference Resolution*. Proceedings of the CONLL'11 Shared Task, pp. 35–39.

Wee M. Soon, Hwee Ng, and Daniel C. Y. Lim. 2001. *A Machine Learning Approach to Coreference Resolution of Noun Phrases*. Association for Computational Linguistics, volume 27(4): 521–544.

Olga Uryupina. 2010. *Corry: A system for coreference resolution*. Proceedings of the SemEval-2010, 100–103.

Olga Uryupina, and Massimo Poesio. 2012. *Domain-specific vs. Uniform Modeling for Coreference Resolution*. Proceedings of the LREC-2012: 187–191.

Yannick Versley, Simone Paolo Ponzetto, Massimo Poesio, Vladimir Eidelman, Alan Jern, Jason Smith, Xiaofeng Yang, and Alessandro Moschitti. 2008. *Bart: a modular toolkit for coreference resolution*. Proceedings of the HLT-Demonstrations'08, pp. 9–12.

Neural context embeddings for automatic discovery of word senses

Mikael Kågebäck, Fredrik Johansson, Richard Johansson[†], Devdatt Dubhashi
Computer Science & Engineering, Chalmers University of Technology
SE-412 96, Göteborg, Sweden
[†]Språkbanken, University of Gothenburg
Box 200, Göteborg, Sweden
{kageback,frejohk,dubhashi}@chalmers.se
richard.johansson@svenska.gu.se

Abstract

Word sense induction (WSI) is the problem of automatically building an inventory of senses for a set of target words using only a text corpus. We introduce a new method for embedding word instances and their context, for use in WSI. The method, *Instance-context embedding* (ICE), leverages neural word embeddings, and the correlation statistics they capture, to compute high quality embeddings of word contexts. In WSI, these context embeddings are clustered to find the word senses present in the text. ICE is based on a novel method for combining word embeddings using continuous Skip-gram, based on both semantic and a temporal aspects of context words. ICE is evaluated both in a new system, and in an extension to a previous system for WSI. In both cases, we surpass previous state-of-the-art, on the WSI task of SemEval-2013, which highlights the generality of ICE. Our proposed system achieves a 33% relative improvement.

1 Introduction

Ambiguity is pervasive in natural language and this is particularly true of word meaning: a word string may refer to several different concepts or senses. *Word sense induction* (WSI) is the problem of using a text corpus to automatically determine 1) the inventory of senses, and 2) which sense a particular occurrence of a word belongs to. This stands in contrast to the related task of *word sense disambiguation* (WSD), which is concerned with linking an occurrence of a word to an external sense inventory, e.g. WordNet. The result of a WSI system is a set of local sense labels, consistent within the system but not linked to a universal set of labels. A wide range of applications have been proposed where WSI could be useful, ranging from basic linguistic and lexicographical research (Nasiruddin et al., 2014), machine reading (Etzioni et al., 2006) and information retrieval (Véronis, 2004). WSI is of particular interest in situations where standard lexical resources are unreliable or inapplicable, such as when tracking changes of word meaning over time (Mitra et al., 2014).

According to the distributional hypothesis (Harris, 1954), word meaning is reflected in the set of contexts in which a word occurs. This intuition makes it natural to operationalize the meaning of a word – and of its contexts – using a vector-space representation, where geometric proximity corresponds to similarity of meaning. A common approach used in several successful WSI systems is to apply this geometric intuition and represent each context of a polysemous word as a vector, look for coherent clusters in the set of context vectors, and let these define the senses of the word. This approach was pioneered by Schütze (1998) using second order co-occurrences to construct the context representation. It is clear that in order to be useful in a WSI system, a geometric representation of context meaning must be designed in a way that makes clusters distinct.

Recently, neural embeddings, such as the popular Skip-gram model (Mikolov et al., 2013a), have proven efficient and accurate in the task of embedding words in vector spaces. As of yet, however, neural embeddings have not been considered for representing contexts in WSI. The systems that seem

Proceedings of NAACL-HLT 2015, pages 25–32,
Denver, Colorado, May 31 – June 5, 2015.

most relevant in this context are those that train *multi-prototype* embeddings: more than one embedding per word (Huang et al., 2012). In particular, Neelakantan et al. (2014) described a modified Skip-gram algorithm that clusters instances on the fly, effectively training several vectors per word. However, whether this or any other similar approach is useful if considered as a WSI system is still an open question, since they have never been evaluated in that setting.

We make the following contributions: (1) We define the *Instance-context embedding* (ICE), a novel way for representing word instances and their context. ICE combines vectors representing context words using a novel weighting schema consisting of a semantic component, and a temporal component, see Section 3. (2) We propose two methods for using our embeddings in word sense induction, see Section 4. The first adopts a batch clustering scheme, where senses are induced after the word embeddings are computed. The number of senses is automatically chosen, based on data. The second extends an existing method for simultaneous embedding and clustering of words (Neelakantan et al., 2014). We show that our extension substantially improves the model. (3) We evaluate both proposed methods in the WSI task. We show that the two components of our proposed weighting schema both contribute to an increased overall performance. Further, we compare our method to state-of-the-art methods on Task 13 of SemEval-2013, achieving a 33% relative improvement see, Section 6.

2 Context clustering

Context clustering is an approach to WSI in which each instance of a word is represented by its context, embedded in a geometric space. These *context embeddings* are then clustered to form centroids representing the different senses of the target word. The context clustering approach was pioneered by Schütze (1998) who used second order co-occurrences to construct the context embedding. In this setting, the output of a WSI system is a set $\mathcal{S}_w = \{\mathbf{s}_{w,1}, \ldots, \mathbf{s}_{w,k}\}$ of k locally defined senses of a word w, with corresponding sense embeddings $\mathbf{s}_{w,j}$. We refer to $\mathcal{S}_w$ as the *induced sense inventory* of w. The WSI problem is often paired with the related task of *word sense disambiguation* (WSD), concerned with linking a previously unseen occurrence of a word to an existing sense inventory. Given an instance w_i, of a possibly polysemous word, let its context be represented by an embedding, $\mathbf{c}_i$. The sense of w_i is determined by finding the nearest neighbor to $\mathbf{c}_i$, in the sense inventory $\mathcal{S}_{w_i}$,

$$sense(w_i) = \operatorname*{arg\,min}_{j\,:\,\mathbf{s}_j \in \mathcal{S}_{w_i}} d(\mathbf{c}_i, \mathbf{s}_j) \,, \qquad (1)$$

where $d(\cdot,\cdot)$ is some distance function. In this work, d is the cosine distance $d(\mathbf{x}, \mathbf{y}) = 1 - \mathbf{x}^T\mathbf{y}/(\|\mathbf{x}\|\|\mathbf{y}\|)$. We proceed to review *distributed word embeddings*, used in this work to create context embeddings.

2.1 Distributed word embeddings

A word embedding is a continuous vector representation that captures semantic and syntactic information about a word. Such representations are often based on the *distributional hypothesis* of Harris (1954), stating that the meaning of a word is largely determined by the contexts in which it appears. For word embeddings, this is realized by assigning similar embeddings to words that appear in similar contexts. These representations can be used to unveil multiple dimensions of similarity between words, such as number, topic and gender (Mikolov et al., 2013b). Word embeddings computed using neural networks were introduced by Bengio et al. (2003) and are often called *neural word embeddings*.

Continuous Skip-gram is an algorithm for computing word embeddings that was introduced by Mikolov et al. (2013a). This model has received a lot of attention recently, being one of the models used in the software package *word2vec* (Mikolov, 2013). The model is trained to predict the context surrounding a given *target* word. Each word w is represented by two vectors, one for when the word is the target, denoted $\mathbf{u}_w$, and one for when it is in the context of another word, denoted $\mathbf{v}_w$.

We follow the interpretation of the negative sampling method for Skip-gram in Levy and Goldberg (2014). Let D denote the observed data, as a set of pairs of target and context words. Then, the probability of observing the pair (w_c, w_i) of a context word c and target word i in the data is,

$$p((w_c, w_i) \in D) = \frac{1}{1 + e^{-\mathbf{v}_c^T \mathbf{u}_i}}, \quad (2)$$

where $\mathbf{u}_i$ is the vector representation of the target word w_i and $\mathbf{v}_c$ is the vector representation of the context word w_c. The vectors $\mathbf{u}_i$ and $\mathbf{v}_c$ are referred to as *word embeddings* and *context-word embeddings* respectively. Training of the Skip-gram model with negative sampling corresponds to finding embeddings that maximize $p((w_c, w_i) \in D)$ for observed context pairs and $p((w_c, w_i) \notin D)$ for random (negative) context pairs. This is usually achieved using stochastic gradient descent.

2.2 Clustering word instances

Clustering of vector-valued observations is a well-studied subject. Perhaps the most widely used algorithm for this purpose, k-means clustering, embodies many of the intuitions and difficulties of the problem. In our setting, the vectors to cluster represent instances of a single word and k corresponds to the number of senses of the word. Clearly, k is highly dependent on the word, and is not easily set by hand. Although many algorithms have been proposed to solve the problem for a given k, choosing k itself remains a problem in its own right. The frequently used Gap statistic (Tibshirani et al., 2000) gives a method for solving this problem. Unfortunately, it can be prohibitively slow for use in repeated clustering of large numbers of points, as the method relies on Monte Carlo simulations. Pham et al. (2005) proposed an alternative method in which a function defined by the cluster distortion for different values of k, is used to evaluate cluster quality.

In the setting described above, the embeddings are assumed to be computed before clustering into senses. In contrast, Multi-sense Skip-gram (MSSG) (Neelakantan et al., 2014) attempts to learn several embeddings of a word, one for each of its different senses, by extending the Skip-gram method of Mikolov et al. (2013a). This involves a simultaneous embedding and clustering of word instances. A drawback is that their method limits the training of multi-sense embeddings to the M most common words, forcing a complete re-training of the model should a new word of interest appear.

3 Instance-context embeddings

We propose a new method for creating context embeddings for WSI. The embeddings are based on word embeddings and context-word embeddings computed using the Skip-gram model as described in Section 2.1. Our method differs from previous approaches in that it assigns different weights to the context words based on their influence on the meaning of the target word.

More precisely, the context embedding ($\mathbf{c}$) for word instance i is computed as the weighed average of the context-word embeddings representing surrounding words

$$\mathbf{c}_i = \frac{1}{Z} \sum_{\substack{-T \le c \le T \\ c \ne 0}} \psi_{i,c} \mathbf{v}_c \,. \quad (3)$$

Here, $\psi_{i,c}$ is the weight for context word c, $\mathbf{v}_c$ is the context-word embedding for the same word and T is the number of words, to the left and right, which are considered part of the context of target word i. Z is a normalizing factor to put $\mathbf{c}_i$ on the unit sphere.

Perhaps the simplest weighting schema is the uniform, or *non-informative* schema, $\psi_{i,c}^{\text{uniform}} = \frac{1}{2T} \forall i, c$. Context embeddings using uniform weights were used in the Multi-Sense Skip-Gram (MSSG) model by Neelakantan et al. (2014) for computing sense embeddings. However, in the context of WSI it is not hard to imagine a situation where an informed weighted sum would perform better. For example, in the phrase "the rock band" the word "band" is clearly more indicative for the sense of "rock" than the word "the", and should therefore have a larger impact on the instance representation. To address this caveat we propose context embeddings based on a novel weighting schema, *Instance-context embeddings* (ICE), that leverages co-occurrence statistics naturally captured by the Skip-gram model.

3.1 Semantic context weights

The first component of ICE is based on the assumption that context words that strongly correlate with the target word is more important for the meaning of the target word. In the example phrase from Section 3, the word "band" is clearly a strong indicator for the presence of the word "rock", while the word "the" occurs everywhere in English text and will therefore not have a strong correlation with "rock".

To leverage this idea, we use the Skip-gram output probability, see (2), to weight context words by

$$\psi_{i,c}^{\text{semantic}} = \frac{1}{1 + e^{-\mathbf{v}_c^T \mathbf{u}_i}}, \tag{4}$$

where $\mathbf{v}_c$ is the context-word embedding for the word c, and $\mathbf{u}_i$ is the word embedding of target word i. Using ψ^{semantic} in (3) has the effect of assigning bigger importance to context words that have a semantic relation to the target word. Context words that are not useful in characterizing the sense of the target are weighted less. This is in stark contrast to the uniform weighting schema.

Levy and Goldberg (2014) discovered an interesting connection between the Skip-gram model and Pointwise Mutual Information (PMI) (Church and Hanks, 1990). Consider the optimizers of the Skip-gram objective, word and context-word embeddings, $\mathbf{u}_i$, $\mathbf{v}_c$, trained using k negative samples. Levy and Goldberg showed that for sufficiently large dimensionality, these vectors satisfy the following relation, ${\mathbf{u}_i}^T\mathbf{v}_c = PMI(w_i, w_c) - \log k$. Let $\sigma(\cdot)$ be the logistic function. For vectors satisfying the conditions stated above, we have $\psi_{i,c}^{\text{semantic}} = \sigma(PMI(w_i, w_c) - \log k)$, establishing a connection between the semantic weights applied to Skip-gram embeddings, and PMI, a function frequently used for measuring word similarity (Pantel and Lin, 2002).

3.2 Temporal context weights

Window functions are used to extract local information from a sequence. In the context of NLP this translates to extracting a phrase of a given length from a larger text. The most common window function used in WSI is the rectangular window function, where T words are extracted from each side of the target word. However, this approach is not optimal. In part, because it ignores the distance between the target word and the context word, but also because the sharp border makes the approach more noisy with respect to the chosen T.

To address these issues we instead apply a triangular window function to the context. This is inspired by the Skip-gram model, where this is achieved by uniformly sampling the context width $\in \{1 \ldots T\}$. In our model we weight the context words according to target word distance as

$$\psi_{i,c}^{\text{temporal}} = \frac{1}{T} \max(0, T - |i - c|) \, . \tag{5}$$

3.3 Instance-context embeddings (ICE)

Finally, by combining the results of Section 3.1 and 3.2 we arrive at the definition of our proposed weighting schema

$$\psi_{i,c}^{\text{ice}} = \psi_{i,c}^{\text{semantic}} \psi_{i,c}^{\text{temporal}} \, . \tag{6}$$

4 Word sense induction using ICE

We devise two methods for performing word sense induction using ICE. The first is based on the k-means clustering algorithm. Here, word and context-word embeddings are computed using Skip-gram. Then, context embeddings are computed for all instances of a word, according to (3), and clustered using k-means, with Pham's heuristic for choosing k (Pham et al., 2005), to form centroids representing word senses. As clustering is performed in batch, after embedding, we refer to this method as ICE-kmeans.

The second method is an extension of the MSSG model (Neelakantan et al., 2014), in which we during training of the model embed word instances using ICE. This improves the disambiguation performed at every iteration of MSSG. As this method performs the clustering in an *online* fashion, we refer to this method as ICE-online. For this, we have modified the code provided by Jeevan Shankar[1].

5 Evaluation

We evaluate our methods for word sense induction on shared task 13 of SemEval-2013, *Word Sense Induction for Graded and Non-Graded Senses* (Jurgens and Klapaftis, 2013). Henceforth, we let "SemEval-2013" refer to this specific task. We also investigate the influence of our weighting schema on both methods. Further, we study qualitative properties of the word instance embeddings produced by our method.

[1]https://bitbucket.org/jeevan_shankar/multi-sense-skipgram/

5.1 SemEval-2013, Task 13

The SemEval-2013 (test) data contains 4664 instances, each inflections of one of 50 lemmas (Jurgens and Klapaftis, 2013). The competition included both single-sense instances and instances with a graded mixture of senses. Because the manual annotations were deemed too poor, only 10% of instances were labeled with multiple senses (Jurgens and Klapaftis, 2013), which led the organizers to publish results both for all instances, and for single-sense instances only. For this reason, we consider only single-sense instances. Each instance is represented by a phrase, annotated with part-of-speech (POS) tags, comprising the word for which to determine the sense, and its context.

The rules of SemEval-2013 allowed the use of a specific corpus, ukWaC, for training of the submitted models. We have cleaned this corpus, removing formatting and making it lowercase. We extract common n-grams from the corpus and include them as entities in our vocabulary, e.g. Kuala Lumpur $\rightarrow$ Kuala_Lumpur. Frequency thresholds were set to 10 times for $n = 1$, 20 times for $n = 2$, and 50 times for $n \in \{3, 4\}$. Longer phrases are not considered. Following SemEval-2013, we evaluate systems for *unsupervised* WSI using two different scores, Fuzzy B-Cubed (FBC) and Fuzzy Normalized Mutual Information (FNMI) (Jurgens and Klapaftis, 2013). FBC compares two *fuzzy* covers, clusterings of the data with partial memberships, on a per-item basis. The score is sensitive to cluster size skew. FNMI is a generalization of normalized mutual information for fuzzy covers. It measures the dependence between two clusterings independently of cluster sizes. As as a final, combined score, we compute the harmonic mean (HM) of FBC and FNMI. To allow direct comparison with published results, we use the fuzzy measures even though we only consider single-sense instances.

We compare our results to two baselines from SemEval-2013. "One sense" predicts that all instances have the same sense. "One per instance" predicts that every instance has its own sense.

5.2 Experimental setup

For ICE-kmeans, we train a 300 dimensional Skip-gram model on the ukWaC corpus using standard parameter settings. I.e. context width set to 20 (10 before and 10 after), and 10 negative samples. We let the model iterate over the training data 9 times to improve the embeddings. For sense induction, we sample 1800 instances of very target word at random, from the ukWaC corpus. Using more instances did not improve the results in our experiments, however, for larger datasets this might not be valid. To remain general, we opted not to use the POS tags available in ukWaC, even though using them might have improved the result. Also, due to the noisy nature of the corpus, we exclude contexts where more than 30% of the words contain non-alphabetic characters. We cluster the selected instances using k-means clustering with the heuristic of Pham et al. (2005) for choosing k. For both ICE-kmeans and ICE-online, when computing the ICE vectors, the context width for was set to 20 when using the full schema, see (6), and 10 otherwise, as the full schema is less sensitive to irrelevant context words. For the MSSG part of ICE-online, we use the parameters reported in Neelakantan et al. (2014).

5.3 Current state-of-the-art

We compare the perfomance of our system to that of state-of-the-art systems for WSI.

First, we compare to the systems with the current best results on SemEval 2013 task 13 for single-sense word instances, AI-KU and unimelb. AI-KU (Baskaya et al., 2013) uses an approach based on substitute word vectors, inferred using a statistical language model. AI-KU achieved the highest FNMI score of the systems submitted to SemEval-2013. unimelb (Lau et al., 2013), who achieved the highest FBC score at SemEval-2013, is a system based on the topic model Latent Dirichlet Allocation and its non-parametric equivalent, Hierarchical Dirichlet Processes. Word instances are clustered based on the topic distributions inferred by the model.

The related problem of training neural embeddings of polysemous words was addressed by Huang et al. (2012) and subsequently by Neelakantan et al. (2014) with the model Multi-sense Skip-gram (MSSG), see Section 2.2. As a second experiment we extend MSSG for WSI. MSSG has not previously been used for WSI, however it produces one word embedding for each word sense, and performs a simple disambiguation procedure during training.

MSSG is thus a natural candidate for comparison. We use the standard variant of MSSG, as it achieved the best overall results in the original paper Neelakantan et al. (2014). MSSG disambiguates instances by assigning them to the sense with embedding closest to the average context-word vector of the instance, i.e. using uniform weighting. We use the parameters reported in Neelakantan et al. (2014), with the number of senses per word set to 3. MSSG takes a parameter M specifying the number of words for which multiple sense vectors are computed. Like in Neelakantan et al. (2014), we set this parameter to $M = 30000$. We note that only 43 out of 50 lemmas in SemEval-2013 were in the M most common words assigned multiple vectors by the MSSG methods. For the remaining 7 words, a single sense was predicted. Making sure all relevant words are included is not trivial in practice, without knowledge of the test set, as the training time of the model depends greatly upon M.

6 Results

We report the results of all experiments below.

6.1 Qualitative evaluation of instance vectors

Consider the word "paper". WordNet (Miller, 1995) lists seven senses of "paper" as a noun: 1) a medium for written communication, 2) an essay (especially one written as an assignment), 3) a scholarly article describing the results of observations or stating hypotheses, 4) a daily or weekly publication on folded sheets; contains news and articles and advertisements, 5) a business firm that publishes newspapers, 6) a material made of cellulose pulp derived mainly from wood or rags or certain grasses, 7) the physical object that is the product of a newspaper publisher. Assigning an instance to one of these senses can be challenging even for a human reader.

The word "paper" is one of the 50 lemmas in the SemEval-2013 evaluation data with corresponding instances that cover six of the senses listed in WordNet. In Figure 1, we show context embeddings for these instances, plotted using the dimensionality reduction tool t-SNE (Van der Maaten and Hinton, 2008). Figure 1a represents context embeddings computed using a uniform average, and Figure 1b plots the instance context embeddings computed with using ICE, as described in Section 3. The colors and markers correspond to gold-standard WordNet annotations provided by SemEval. The size of a marker in Figure 1b is proportional to the average ICE weight of words in the context of an instance and is indicative of the confidence in the instance vector. A low average ICE weight indicates that the context is not predictive of the target word.

For the senses, "material", "scholarly article", "newspaper" and "essay", the instances in Figure 1b are noticeably more clustered than in Figure 1a. This shows that the senses of these words are better represented using ICE weighting for context embeddings than a uniform schema.

6.2 Semeval WSI results

The results of the WSI evaluation on shared task 13 of SemEval-2013 are presented in Table 1. Here, our system ICE-kmeans, and our MSSG extension ICE-online, use the ICE weighting schema, see (6). MSSG is the system presented in Neelakantan et al. (2014) without modifications. AI-KU and unimelb represent the best systems submitted to SemEval-2013, and AI-KU the current state-of-the-art in WSI.

First, we note that ICE-kmeans achieves the overall best results with respect to both scores, corresponding to a relative improvement of 31.1% in FNMI and 15.9% in FBC. Further we note that the previous best FBC and FNMI belong to different methods. This is important since, as with precision and recall, achieving a high score in one of these measures can be achieved using a trivial baseline, see the first two methods in Table 1. Hence, a better benchmark, analogue to the F_1-score, is the harmonic mean (HM) of the two complementary scores. Considering this our results are even more impressive with a 33% relative improvement.

6.3 Semantic and temporal component of ICE

We evaluate the impact of using context embeddings based on the different weighting schemas defined in Section 3, over embeddings based on uniform weights. The results are presented, as harmonic mean and relative improvement over previous state-of-the-art AI-KU, in Table 2.

First, we note that both variants of our full system (ICE) offers a substantial relative improvement over AI-KU. We note that the results are always

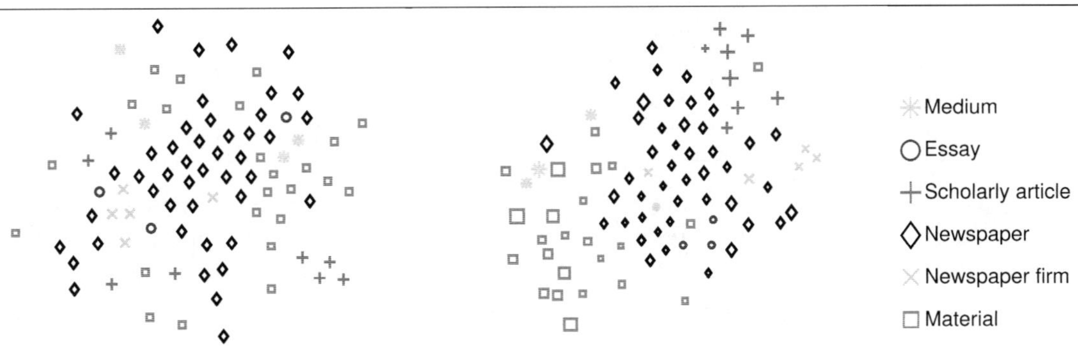

(a) Uniform context embeddings (b) Instance-context embeddings (ICE)

Figure 1: Context embeddings for instances of the noun "paper" in the SemEval-2013 test data, plotted using t-SNE. The legend refers to WordNet gold standard embeddings.

Method	**FBC(%)**	**FNMI(%)**	**HM**
One sense	57.0	0	0
One per instance	0	4.8	0
Unimelb	44.1	3.9	7.2
AI-KU	35.1	4.5	8.0
MSSG	45.9	3.7	6.8
ICE-online	48.7	5.5	9.9
ICE-kmeans	**51.1**	**5.9**	**10.6**

Table 1: Results for single-sense instances on the WSI task of SemEval-2013. HM is the harmonic mean of FBC and FNMI.

better when using semantic weights, Eq (5), over uniform, and always *best* when using the full ICE schema, Eq (6). These results clearly indicate that both the semantic and temporal weight components contribute to a better system. We note that the k-means systemis consistently better than the online version. This conforms to expectations as the online system has access to less information at every cluster assignment. The two top left results (in gray) correspond to the original MSSG system.

7 Conclusion

We have presented Instance-context embedding (ICE), a method for embedding word instances and their context for use in word sense induction (WSI). At the heart of the system are instance representations based on neural embeddings of context words, combined using a novel weighting schema.

We have shown that ICE is sucessful in representating instances of polysemous words, not just in our own WSI system, but in an extension of an existing model as well. In an evaluation on the WSI task of SemEval-2013, our system beat previous state-of-the-art methods, achieving a 33% relative improvement. Further, we have established the benefits of using ICE over a uniform weighting schema, by showing empirically that each of its components contribute to a more accurate system.

Acknowledgments

The authors would like to acknowledge the project *Towards a knowledge-based culturomics* supported by a framework grant from the Swedish Research Council (2012–2016; dnr 2012-5738), and the project *Data-driven secure business intelligence* grant IIS11-0089 from the Swedish Foundation for Strategic Research (SSF). The third author was supported by Swedish Research Council grant 2013–4944, *Distributional methods to represent the meaning of frames and constructions*.

References

Osman Baskaya, Enis Sert, Volkan Cirik, and Deniz Yuret. 2013. Ai-ku: Using substitute vectors and co-occurrence modeling for word sense induction and disambiguation. *Atlanta, Georgia, USA*, page 300.

Method	Uniform HM	Uniform Impr.(%)	ICE (Sem. only) HM	ICE (Sem. only) Impr.(%)	ICE HM	ICE Impr.(%)
ICE-online	6.8†	-14†	7.9	-1.1	9.9	24
ICE-kmeans	7.6	-5.2	9.6	20	**10.6**	**33**

Table 2: Impact of the two different components of ICE on SemEval-2013 task 13 (single-sense). Imprv. is the relative improvement over the state-of-the-art system AI-KU (with an HM of 8.0). †Gray numbers correspond to the original MSSG system. The weighting schemas are: **Uniform**, Section 3, **ICE (Semantic only)**, Eq (4), and **ICE**, Eq (6).

Yoshua Bengio, Réjean Ducharme, Pascal Vincent, and Christian Jauvin. 2003. A neural probabilistic language model. *Journal of Machine Learning Research*, 3:1137–1155.

Kenneth Ward Church and Patrick Hanks. 1990. Word association norms, mutual information, and lexicography. *Comput. Linguist.*, 16(1):22–29, March.

Oren Etzioni, Michele Banko, and Michael J Cafarella. 2006. Machine reading, proceedings of the 21st national conference on artificial intelligence.

Zellig Harris. 1954. Distributional structure. *Word*, 10(23):146–162.

Eric Huang, Richard Socher, Christopher Manning, and Andrew Ng. 2012. Improving word representations via global context and multiple word prototypes. In *Proceedings of the 50th Annual Meeting of the Association for Computational Linguistics (Volume 1: Long Papers)*, pages 873–882, Jeju Island, Korea, July. Association for Computational Linguistics.

David Jurgens and Ioannis Klapaftis. 2013. Semeval-2013 task 13: Word sense induction for graded and non-graded senses. In *Second Joint Conference on Lexical and Computational Semantics (* SEM)*, volume 2, pages 290–299.

Jey Han Lau, Paul Cook, and Timothy Baldwin. 2013. unimelb: Topic modelling-based word sense induction. In *Second Joint Conference on Lexical and Computational Semantics (* SEM)*, volume 2, pages 307–311.

Omer Levy and Yoav Goldberg. 2014. Neural word embedding as implicit matrix factorization. In Z. Ghahramani, M. Welling, C. Cortes, N.D. Lawrence, and K.Q. Weinberger, editors, *Advances in Neural Information Processing Systems 27*, pages 2177–2185. Curran Associates, Inc.

Tomas Mikolov, Kai Chen, Greg Corrado, and Jeffrey Dean. 2013a. Efficient estimation of word representations in vector space. In *Workshop at ICLR*.

Tomas Mikolov, Wen-tau Yih, and Geoffrey Zweig. 2013b. Linguistic regularities in continuous space word representations. In *Proceedings of NAACL-HLT*, pages 746–751.

Tomas Mikolov. 2013. word2vec. `https://code.google.com/p/word2vec/`.

George A Miller. 1995. Wordnet: a lexical database for english. *Communications of the ACM*, 38(11):39–41.

Sunny Mitra, Ritwik Mitra, Martin Riedl, Chris Biemann, Animesh Mukherjee, and Pawan Goyal. 2014. That's sick dude!: Automatic identification of word sense change across different timescales. In *Proceedings of the 52nd Annual Meeting of the Association for Computational Linguistics (Volume 1: Long Papers)*, pages 1020–1029, Baltimore, Maryland, June. Association for Computational Linguistics.

Mohammad Nasiruddin, Didier Schwab, Andon Tchechmedjiev, Gilles Sérasset, Hervé Blanchon, et al. 2014. Induction de sens pour enrichir des ressources lexicales. In *Actes des 21ème conférence sur le Traitement Automatique des Langues Naturelles (TALN 2014)*.

Arvind Neelakantan, Jeevan Shankar, Alexandre Passos, and Andrew McCallum. 2014. Efficient non-parametric estimation of multiple embeddings per word in vector space. In *Proceedings of EMNLP*.

Patrick Pantel and Dekang Lin. 2002. Discovering word senses from text. In *Proceedings of the eighth ACM SIGKDD international conference on Knowledge discovery and data mining*, pages 613–619. ACM.

Duc Truong Pham, Stefan S Dimov, and CD Nguyen. 2005. Selection of k in k-means clustering. *Proceedings of the Institution of Mechanical Engineers, Part C: Journal of Mechanical Engineering Science*, 219(1):103–119.

Hinrich Schütze. 1998. Automatic word sense discrimination. *Computational linguistics*, 24(1):97–123.

Robert Tibshirani, Guenther Walther, and Trevor Hastie. 2000. Estimating the number of clusters in a dataset via the gap statistic. 63:411–423.

Laurens Van der Maaten and Geoffrey Hinton. 2008. Visualizing data using t-sne. *Journal of Machine Learning Research*, 9(2579-2605):85.

Jean Véronis. 2004. Hyperlex: lexical cartography for information retrieval. *Computer Speech & Language*, 18(3):223–252.

Distributional Representations of Words for Short Text Classification

Chenglong Ma, Weiqun Xu, Peijia Li, Yonghong Yan
The Key Laboratory of Speech Acoustics and Content Understanding
Institute of Acoustics, Chinese Academy of Sciences
No. 21 North 4th Ring West Road, Haidian District, 100190 Beijing, China
{machenglong,xuweiqun,lipeijia,yanyonghong}@hccl.ioa.ac.cn

Abstract

Traditional supervised learning approaches to common NLP tasks depend heavily on manual annotation, which is labor intensive and time consuming, and often suffer from data sparseness. In this paper we show how to mitigate the problems in short text classification (STC) through word embeddings – distributional representations of words learned from large unlabeled data. The word embeddings are trained from the entire English Wikipedia text. We assume that a short text document is a specific sample of one distribution in a Bayesian framework. A Gaussian process approach is used to model the distribution of words. The task of classification becomes a simple problem of selecting the most probable Gaussian distribution. This approach is compared with those based on the classical maximum entropy (MaxEnt) model and the Latent Dirichlet Allocation (LDA) approach. Our approach achieved better performance and also showed advantages in dealing with unseen words.

1 Introduction

With the boom of e-commerce and social media, short texts, such as instant messages, microblogs and product reviews, become more available in diverse forms than before. These short forms of documents have become convenient presentations of information. It is becoming more and more important to understand those short text documents and to efficiently detect what users are interested in. Unlike long documents such as news articles and blogs, it is hard to measure similarities among these short texts since they do not share much in common (Phan et al., 2008). This poses a great challenge to short text classification (STC).

The task of short text classification can be described as follows: given a short text *S*, the aim is to identify its target theme *T*. Several supervised learning approaches have been proposed for short text classification. They have been shown to be effective and yielded good performance. These approaches are effective because they leverage a large body of linguistic knowledge and related corpora. However, the supervised learning approaches depend heavily on manual annotation, which is labor intensive and time consuming, and often suffer from data sparseness.

To tackle the above problems, we exploit word embeddings. A word embedding $W{:}words \rightarrow R^n$ is a distributed representation for a word which is usually learned from a large corpus. Many researches have found that the learned word vectors capture linguistic regularities and collapse similar words into groups (Mikolov et al., 2013b).

In this paper, we apply an information theoretic approach which assumes that the short text is generated from a predefined parametric model, and estimate its optimal parameters from training data. We use Gaussian models to describe the distribution of words embeddings since it can describe any continuous distribution in common practice. Then, we classify new short texts using the Bayesian rule to get the posterior probability (Baker and McCallum, 1998).

The paper is organized as follows. Some related work is presented in Section 2. The word embedding

Proceedings of NAACL-HLT 2015, pages 33–38,
Denver, Colorado, May 31 – June 5, 2015.

based approach to short text classification is presented in Section 3. The dataset and evaluation metrics are described in Section 4. Experimental results on short text classification are given in Section 5. Some conclusions are drawn in Section 6.

2 Related Work

Learning to identify the theme of a short text document has been extensively studied during the past decade. Because the text length is short, data sparseness is an outstanding issue. Several approaches have been explored to overcome the data sparseness in order to get better performance.

Some try to calculate the similarity between short texts. E.g., (Zelikovitz and Hirsh, 2000) utilizes a corpus of unlabeled longer documents to compute the similarity between the test sample and the training one. To avoid collecting the specific longer documents, Web search engines (e.g. Google) are used to measure the similarity score (Bollegala et al., 2007; Yih and Meek, 2007) . But the efficiency of those approaches is a severe problem because they repeatedly queried search engines.

Some try to select more useful contextual information to expand and enrich the original text, e.g. using large unlabeled corpora, such as Wikipedia (Banerjee et al., 2007) and WordNet (Hu et al., 2009). A disadvantage of these approaches is that their adaptability would be an issue for certain languages because some of those external resources may be unavailable. Another approach is to integrate the context data with a set of hidden topics discovered from related corpora. E.g., (Phan et al., 2008; Chen et al., 2011) manually built a large and rich universal dataset, and derived a set of hidden topics through topic models such as Latent Dirichlet Allocation (LDA) (Blei et al., 2003) from these corpora. This approach has achieved satisfactory results, but it requires manual collection of the corpora. These researches have shown good improvement, but they rely too much on external resources which are difficult to get in some cases.

With the recent revival of interest in deep neural networks, many researchers have concentrated on learning a real-valued vector representation in a continuous space, where similar words are likely to have similar vectors. This is called word embedding (Turian et al., 2010). In fact, the learned word vectors capture linguistic regularities in a very simple way. In the embedding space, the vector offsets can measure specific relationship, such as the offset between *vec ("King")* and *vec ("Man")* is very close to that between *vec ("Woman")* and *vec ("Queen")* (Mikolov et al., 2013b).

3 Methodology

This section describes the proposed Gaussian classification approaches that use the learned word embeddings to model a classifier for the task of short text classification.

3.1 Word Representation

To get word representation, each input word token is transformed into a vector by looking up word embeddings learned from language model (Zeng et al., 2014). Distributed representations of words in word embedding space are shown to explicitly encode many syntactic and semantic regularities. Word embeddings have been used to help to achieve better performance in several NLP tasks (Collobert et al., 2011). There are some free tools for training word embeddings (Turian et al., 2010). We directly utilize *Word2Vec* tool provided by Mikolov et al. (Mikolov et al., 2013a) to train word embeddings on the Wikipedia corpus.

3.2 Our Approach

As mentioned in Section 3.1, all of the words are represented as word vectors. Word embeddings can be taken as an observation from an unsupervised generative model. We assume that a short text d_j is generated by theme t_k (parameterized by λ_k) according to the domain prior $p(t_k|\lambda_k)$. Similar to language modeling, we assume that a word embedding w_j^i for the i-th word in short text d_j depends only on the preceding words. Under this assumption, the probability of a document given theme t_k is,

$$p(d_j|t_k;\lambda_k) = \prod_{i=1}^{|d_j|} p(w_j^i|t_k;\lambda_k;w_j^m, m < i) \quad (1)$$

Next we assume that each word in a document is independent of its context, which is the same as that for uni-gram language model. Then we rewrite equation 1 as

$$p(d_j|t_k;\lambda_k) = \prod_{i=1}^{|d_j|} p(w_j^i|t_k;\lambda_k) \quad (2)$$

Gaussian model is used to describe the distribution. We use the training data to estimate the parameters $\lambda_k = \{\mu_k, \Sigma_k\}$, where μ_k and Σ_k denote the mean vector and covariance matrix. We also assume that the covariance matrix of Gaussian is diagonal. λ_k can be estimated through Maximum Likelihood (ML) estimation as $\hat{\lambda}_k$:

$$\hat{\mu}_k = \frac{1}{|w_k|}\sum_{i=1}^{|w_k|} w_k^i \quad (3)$$

$$\hat{\Sigma}_k = \frac{1}{|w_k|}\sum_{i=1}^{|w_k|}(w_k^i - \hat{\mu}_k)(w_k^i - \hat{\mu}_k)^T \quad (4)$$

where $|w_k|$ is the total number of words in theme t_k on the training set, w_k^i is the i-th word.

Given estimates of the model parameters, new test data can be classified using the Bayesian theorem. A new short test text can be assigned the most likely theme as follows,

$$p(t_k|d_j;\hat{\lambda}_k) = \frac{p(t_k|\hat{\lambda}_k)\prod_{i=1}^{|d_j|} p(w_j^i|t_k;\hat{\lambda}_k)}{p(d_j|\hat{\lambda}_k)} \quad (5)$$

A uniform prior is used to choose the most probable theme which minimizes cross entropy on the test document. In equation 5, we drop the denominator (which is the same constant across all domains), and take the log of the entire expression. This results in

$$\sum_{i=1}^{|d_j|} \log(p(w_j^i|t_k;\hat{\lambda}_k)) \quad (6)$$

4 Dataset and Evaluation Metrics

To evaluate the performance of the above approach, we use the Web snippet dataset used in (Phan et al., 2008; Chen et al., 2011; Sun, 2012). The dataset contains 10,060 training and 2,280 test snippets of 8 domains, as shown in Table 1. The snippets of search results are (Phan et al., 2008), who collected various phrases belonging to different domains to query the web search engine (Google) and selected the top 20 or 30 snippets from the search results. Different phrases for the training and test data were used to make sure that test data were difficult to classify (Phan et al., 2008). The dataset has an average of 18 words in each snippet. Column 2 of Table 2 shows that the test data include about 4,378 words (about 43.62%) which do not appear in the training data. Column 3 shows the sizes of unseen words after Porter stemming (Sparck Jones, 1997). This table shows that there are more than 40% unseen words in the test data.

Domain	Training data	Test data
business	1,200	300
computer	1,200	300
cul.-arts-ent.	1,880	330
engineering	220	150
health	880	300
politics-soc.	1,200	300
sports	1,120	300
edu.-sci.	2,360	300
Total	10,060	2,280

Table 1: Statistics of the Web Snippets data

	Original	After stemming
Training Vocabulary	26,265	21,596
Test Vocabulary	10,037	8,200
Unseen Words	4,378	3,677
Difference (%)	43.62	44.84

Table 2: The number of unseen words

We downloaded the English Wikipedia dump of October 8, 2014, [1] which was used for training word embeddings. After removing all the non-roman characters and MediaWiki markups, we had 14,941,377 articles. The hyper-parameters used in *Word2Vec* are the same as that in (Mikolov et al., 2013a). To compare our results with the previous studies, we adopt accuracy as the performance metric, which is the proportion of the true results in the test output.

[1] Available at http://download.wikipedia.com/enwiki/.

Method	Feature	Classifier	Acc (%)
1	words (TF*IDF)	MaxEnt	65.75
2	words (TF*IDF) +topics	MaxEnt	82.18
Proposed	words (word embeddings, 400 dimensions)	Our Method	85.48

Table 3: Short Text Classification Performance

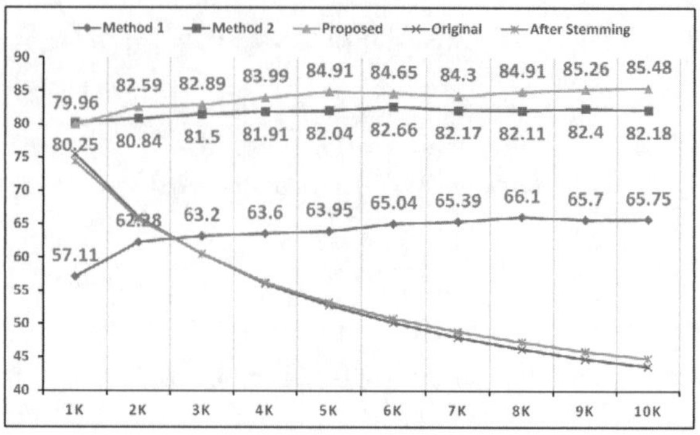

Figure 1: Evaluation with Different Sizes of Training Data.

5 Experiments

We conducted three sets of experiments. In the first set of experiments, we compare the performance of our approach with the previous studies. The second is to test the capability of our approach in dealing with the unseen words using different size of training data. The third is to investigate the effect of the word representation dimension on STC.

5.1 Comparison with Previous Work

For comparison, we select two approaches from (Phan et al., 2008) and the results are given in Table 3. The first method took the short text document as a bag of words (Salton, 1989) and used classical TF/IDF to represent the contribution of each term to its theme. In the second method, topic models are estimated from related corpus using LDA, then topics of the short text are inferred from those models. Thus, the features in method 2 contain topic distributions and bag-of-word vectors. The two approaches employ MaxEnt classifiers.

Table 3 illustrates the results for the three approaches. The best result is obtained from our proposed method with an absolute gain of 3.3 percent. It is clear that using word embeddings which were trained from universal dataset mitigated the problem of unseen words. Unlike the simple representations based on word frequencies (with some simplifications) (Clinchant and Perronnin, 2013) used in the previous studies, an important advantage is that our approach makes better use of the semantics from all the words in the short text document.

5.2 Dealing with Unseen Words

To validate the importance and influence of the size of training data in our approach, we increase the size of training data from 1,000 to 10,000 and measure the performance on the same test set. Since less training data will lead to more unseen words in the test phase, this experiment shows the capability in coping with unseen words, as shown the lines of Original and After Stemming in Figure 1. We directly cited the results of (Phan et al., 2008) because we could not crawl the related corpora which contained 3.5GB Wikipedia documents to re-implement their work.

The results of this experiment are shown in Figure 1. It can be seen that our approach based on the Gaussian process with word embeddings achieved good performance using relatively small data and reduced the cost of collecting and annotating training data.

5.3 The Effect of Word Representation Dimensions on STC

In our method, there is a free parameter in building word embeddings, i.e., the dimension of word representations. We empirically show the effect on the test data.

Figure 2 presents the short text classification performance obtained with different dimensions of word embeddings. In this section, we used all the training data as our experimental data. The best performance is about 85.83% when the size of word embedding space is 550 dimensions. The system achieves 7.23% absolute improvement when the di-

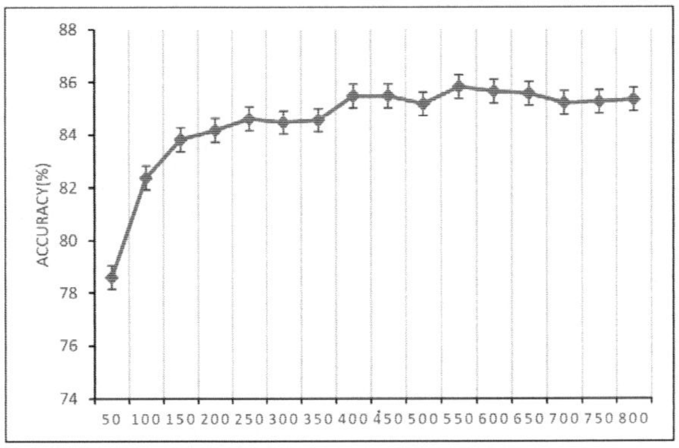

Figure 2: The effect of word embedding dimensions on STC performance.

mension of word embeddings increases from 50 to 550.

6 Conclusion

In this paper, we proposed to use Gaussian process with continuous word embeddings for short text classification. The experimental results show that our approach is effective and that the word embeddings capture syntactic and semantic relationships between words can make good contributions to handle unseen data. For future work, we would like to investigate how continuous word embeddings will work on other genres of short texts like microblogs or on conventional (long) texts, in topic and sentiment classification.

Acknowledgments

This work is partially supported by the National Natural Science Foundation of China (Nos. 11161140319, 91120001, 61271426), the Strategic Priority Research Program of the Chinese Academy of Sciences (Grant Nos. XDA06030100, XDA06030500), the National 863 Program (No. 2012AA012503) and the CAS Priority Deployment Project (No. KGZD-EW-103-2).

References

L Douglas Baker and Andrew Kachites McCallum. 1998. Distributional clustering of words for text classification. In *Proceedings of the 21st annual international ACM SIGIR conference on Research and development in information retrieval*, pages 96–103. ACM.

Somnath Banerjee, Krishnan Ramanathan, and Ajay Gupta. 2007. Clustering short texts using wikipedia. In *Proceedings of the 30th annual international ACM SIGIR conference on Research and development in information retrieval*, pages 787–788. ACM.

David M Blei, Andrew Y Ng, and Michael I Jordan. 2003. Latent dirichlet allocation. *the Journal of machine Learning research*, 3:993–1022.

Danushka Bollegala, Yutaka Matsuo, and Mitsuru Ishizuka. 2007. Measuring semantic similarity between words using web search engines. In *Proceedings of the 16th International Conference on World Wide Web*, WWW '07, pages 757–766, New York, NY, USA. ACM.

Mengen Chen, Xiaoming Jin, and Dou Shen. 2011. Short text classification improved by learning multi-granularity topics. In *Proc. of IJCAI 2011*, pages 1776–1781.

Stephane Clinchant and Florent Perronnin. 2013. Aggregating continuous word embeddings for information retrieval. In *Proceedings of the Workshop on Continuous Vector Space Models and their Compositionality*, pages 100–109, Sofia, Bulgaria, August. Association for Computational Linguistics.

Ronan Collobert, Jason Weston, Lon Bottou, Michael Karlen, Koray Kavukcuoglu, and Pavel Kuksa. 2011. Natural language processing (almost) from scratch. *The Journal of Machine Learning Research*, 12:2493–2537.

Xia Hu, Nan Sun, Chao Zhang, and Tat-Seng Chua. 2009. Exploiting internal and external semantics for the clustering of short texts using world knowledge. In *Proceedings of the 18th ACM conference on Information and knowledge management*, pages 919–928. ACM.

Tomas Mikolov, Ilya Sutskever, Kai Chen, Greg S Corrado, and Jeff Dean. 2013a. Distributed representations of words and phrases and their compositionality. In *Advances in Neural Information Processing Systems*, pages 3111–3119.

Tomas Mikolov, Wen-tau Yih, and Geoffrey Zweig. 2013b. Linguistic regularities in continuous space word representations. In *Proceedings of NAACL-HLT*, pages 746–751.

Xuan-Hieu Phan, Le-Minh Nguyen, and Susumu Horiguchi. 2008. Learning to classify short and sparse text & web with hidden topics from large-scale data collections. In *Proceedings of the 17th international conference on World Wide Web*, pages 91–100. ACM.

Gerard Salton. 1989. *Automatic Text Processing: The Transformation, Analysis, and Retrieval of Information by Computer*. Addison-Wesley.

Karen Sparck Jones, editor. 1997. *Readings in information retrieval*. Morgan Kaufmann.

Aixin Sun. 2012. Short text classification using very few words. In *Proceedings of the 35th international ACM SIGIR conference on Research and development in information retrieval*, pages 1145–1146. ACM.

Joseph Turian, Lev Ratinov, and Yoshua Bengio. 2010. Word representations: a simple and general method for semi-supervised learning. In *Proceedings of the 48th annual meeting of the association for computational linguistics*, pages 384–394. Association for Computational Linguistics.

Wen-Tau Yih and Christopher Meek. 2007. Improving similarity measures for short segments of text. In *Proceedings of the 22Nd National Conference on Artificial Intelligence - Volume 2*, AAAI'07. AAAI Press.

Sarah Zelikovitz and Haym Hirsh. 2000. Improving short text classification using unlabeled background knowledge to assess document similarity. In *Proceedings of the Seventeenth International Conference on Machine Learning*, volume 2000, pages 1183–1190.

Daojian Zeng, Kang Liu, Siwei Lai, Guangyou Zhou, and Jun Zhao. 2014. Relation classification via convolutional deep neural network. In *Proceedings of COLING*, pages 2335–2344.

Relation Extraction: Perspective from Convolutional Neural Networks

Thien Huu Nguyen
Computer Science Department
New York University
New York, NY 10003 USA
thien@cs.nyu.edu

Ralph Grishman
Computer Science Department
New York University
New York, NY 10003 USA
grishman@cs.nyu.edu

Abstract

Up to now, relation extraction systems have made extensive use of features generated by linguistic analysis modules. Errors in these features lead to errors of relation detection and classification. In this work, we depart from these traditional approaches with complicated feature engineering by introducing a convolutional neural network for relation extraction that automatically learns features from sentences and minimizes the dependence on external toolkits and resources. Our model takes advantages of multiple window sizes for filters and pre-trained word embeddings as an initializer on a non-static architecture to improve the performance. We emphasize the relation extraction problem with an unbalanced corpus. The experimental results show that our system significantly outperforms not only the best baseline systems for relation extraction but also the state-of-the-art systems for relation classification.

1 Introduction

Learning to extract semantic relations between entity pairs from text plays a vital role in information extraction, knowledge base population and question answering, to name a few. The *relation extraction* (RE) task can be divided into two steps: detecting if a relation utterance corresponding to some entity mention pair of interest in the same sentence represents some relation and classifying the detected relation mentions into some predefined classes. If we only need to categorize the given relation mentions that are known to express some expected relation (perfect detection), we are left with the *relation classification* (RC) task. One variation of relation classification is that one might have non-relation examples in the dataset but the number of those is comparable to the number of the other examples. The non-relation examples, therefore, can be treated as a usual relation class. Relation extraction, on the other hand, often comes with a tremendously unbalanced dataset where the number of the non-relation examples far exceeds the others, making relation extraction more challenging but more practical than relation classification. Our present work focuses on the relation extraction task with an unbalanced corpus.

In the last decade, the relation extraction literature has been dominated by two methods, distinguished by the nature of the relation representation: the feature-based method (Kambhatla, 2004; Boschee et al., 2005; Zhou et al., 2005; Grishman et al., 2005; Jiang and Zhai, 2007; Chan and Roth, 2010; Sun et al., 2011; Nguyen and Grishman, 2014) and the kernel-based method (Zelenko et al., 2003; Culotta and Sorensen, 2004; Bunescu and Mooney, 2005a; Bunescu and Mooney, 2005b; Zhang et al., 2006; Zhou et al., 2007; Qian et al., 2008; Nguyen et al., 2009; Sun and Han, 2014). The common characteristic of these methods is the leverage of a large body of linguistic analysis and knowledge resources to transform relation mentions into some rich representation to be used by some statistical classifier such as Support Vector Machines (SVM) or Maximum Entropy (MaxEnt). The linguistic analysis pipeline which is *hand-designed* itself includes tokenization, part of speech tagging, chunking, name tagging as well as parsing, often performed by existing natural language processing (NLP) modules.

Proceedings of NAACL-HLT 2015, pages 39–48,
Denver, Colorado, May 31 – June 5, 2015. ©2015 Association for Computational Linguistics

While these methods allow the RE systems to inherit the knowledge discovered by the NLP community for the pre-processing tasks, they might be subject to the error propagation introduced by the imperfect quality of the supervised NLP toolkits. For instance, all the tasks mentioned in the pipeline above are known to suffer from a performance loss when they are applied to out-of-domain data (Blitzer et al., 2006; Daumé III, 2007; McClosky et al., 2010), causing the collapse of the RE systems based on them. In this paper, we target an independent RE system that both avoids complicated feature engineering and minimizes the reliance on the supervised NLP modules for features, potentially alleviating the error propagation and advancing our performance in this area.

To be concrete, our relation extraction system is provided only with raw sentences marked with the positions of the two entities of interest[1]. The only elements we can derive from this structure are the words, the n-grams and their positions in the sentences, suggesting a paradigm in which relation mentions are represented by features that depend on these elements. Eventually, word embeddings that are capable of capturing latent semantic and syntactic properties of words (Bengio et al., 2001; Mnih and Hinton, 2007; Collobert and Weston, 2008; Mnih and Hinton, 2009; Turian et al., 2010; Mikolov et al., 2013) and convolutional neural networks (CNNs) that are able to recognize specific classes of n-gram and induce more abstract representations (Kalchbrenner et al., 2014) are a natural combination one should apply to obtain more effective representations for RE in this setting.

Convolutional neural networks (dating back to the 1980s) are a type of feed-forward artificial neural networks whose layers are formed by a convolution operation followed by a pooling operation (LeCun et al., 1988; Kalchbrenner et al., 2014). Recently, with the emerging interests of the community in deep learning, CNNs have been revived and effectively applied in various NLP tasks, including semantic parsing (Yih et al., 2014), search query retrieval (Shen et al., 2014), sentence modeling and classification (Kalchbrenner et al., 2014; Kim, 2014), name tagging and semantic role labeling (Collobert et al., 2011). For relation classification and extraction, there are two very recent works on CNNs for relation classification (Liu et al., 2013)[2] and (Zeng et al., 2014); however, to the best of our knowledge, there has been no work on employing CNNs for relation extraction so far. This paper is the first attempt to fill in that gap and serves as a baseline for future research in this area.

Our convolutional neural network is built upon that of Kalchbrenner et al. (2014) and Kim (2014) which are originally proposed for sentence classification and modeling. We adapt the network for relation extraction by introducing the position embeddings to encode the relative distances of the words in the sentence to the two entities of interest. Compared to the models in Liu et al. (2013) and Zeng et al. (2014) for relation classification that apply a single window size, our model for relation extraction incorporates various window sizes for convolutional filters, allowing the network to capture wider ranges of n-grams to be helpful for relation extraction. In addition, rather than initializing the word embeddings randomly as do Liu et al. (2013) and fixing the randomly generated position embeddings during training as do Zeng et al. (2014), we use pre-trained word embeddings for initialization and optimize both word embeddings and position embeddings as model parameters. More importantly, rather than using exterior features (either from human annotation or other pre-processing modules) to enrich the representation as do Liu et al. (2013) and Zeng et al. (2014), our model (adapted for RC where entity heads are given) avoids usage of manual linguistic resources and supervised NLP toolkits constructed externally, utilizing word embeddings that can be trained automatically in an unsupervised framework as the only external resource for the whole system.

We explore different model architectures systematically and demonstrate that the best model performance is achieved when multiple window sizes are implemented and the word embeddings, once initialized by some "universal" embeddings, are allowed to vary during the optimization process to reach an

[1]For evaluation purpose, we assume the positions of the two entities of interest in the sentence like most previous studies in this area (listed above). These are the only external features we need to achieve an end-to-end relation extractor.

[2]The title of the paper (Liu et al., 2013) on relation extraction is misleading since the authors actually do relation classification, according to the experimental description.

effective state for relation extraction. We evaluate our models on both relation classification and relation extraction tasks. For relation classification, experiments show that our model (without any external features and resources) outperforms the state-of-the-art models whether the external features are included in these models or not. For relation extraction, our model is significantly better than the baseline models that use the words and the embeddings themselves as the features. In the following, we discuss related work in Section 2 and present our model in Section 3. We detail an extensive evaluation in Section 4 and finally conclude in Section 5.

2 Related Work

As our present work focuses on the supervised framework for relation extraction, we concentrate on the supervised systems in this section. Besides the supervised systems (either feature-based or kernel-based) mentioned above, some recent systems have employed the *distant supervision* (DS) approach for relation extraction. This approach is essentially similar to the traditional systems in representing relation mentions but attempts to generate training data automatically by leveraging large knowledge bases of facts and corpus (Mintz et al., 2009; Riedel et al., 2010; Hoffmann et al., 2011; Surdeanu et al., 2012).

Regarding neural networks, their first application to NLP is language modeling which has been useful to learn distributed representations (embeddings) for words (Bengio et al., 2001; Mnih and Hinton, 2007; Collobert and Weston, 2008; Mnih and Hinton, 2009; Turian et al., 2010; Mikolov et al., 2013). These word embeddings have opened a new direction for many other NLP tasks grounded on neural networks. Some of them are mentioned above. Other than that, a class of recursive neural networks (RNNs) and neural tensor networks are proposed for paraphrase detection (Socher et al., 2011), parsing (Socher et al., 2013a), sentiment analysis (Socher et al., 2013b), knowledge base completion (Socher et al., 2013c), question answering (Mohit et al., 2014) etc. Among these RNN systems, the study that is most related to our relation extraction problem is Socher et al. (2012) that learns compositional vector representations for phrases and sentences through syntactic parse trees and applies these representations for relation classification. However, this method inherently requires syntactic parse trees in contrast to our target of avoiding use of any external features and resources for RC.

3 Convolutional Neural Network for Relation Extraction

Our convolutional neural network for relation extraction consists of four main layers: (i) the look-up tables to encode words in sentences by real-valued vectors, (ii) the convolutional layer to recognize n-grams, (iii) the pooling layer to determine the most relevant features and (iv) a logistic regression layer (a fully connected neural network with a softmax at the end) to perform classification (Collobert et al., 2011; Kim, 2014; Kalchbrenner et al., 2014). Figure 1 gives an overview of the network.

3.1 Word Representation

The input to the CNN for relation extraction consists of sentences marked with the two entity mentions of interest. As CNNs can only work with fixed length inputs, we compute the maximal separation between entity mentions linked by a relation and choose an input width greater than this distance. We insure that every input (relation mention) has this length by trimming longer sentences and padding shorter sentences with a special token.

Let n be the length of the relation mentions and $x = [x_1, x_2, \ldots, x_n]$ be some relation mention where x_i is the i-th word in the mention. Also, let x_{i_1} and x_{i_2} be the two heads of the two entity mentions of interest . Before entering the network, each word x_i is first transformed into a vector e_i by looking up the word embedding table $\mathbf{W}$ that can be initialized either by a random process or by some pretrained word embeddings. Besides, in order to embed the positions of the two entity heads as well as the other words in the relation mention into the representation, for each word x_i, its relative distances to the two entity heads $i - i_1$ and $i - i_2$ are also mapped into real-value vectors d_{i_1} and d_{i_2} respectively using a position embedding table $\mathbf{D}$ (initialized randomly) (Collobert et al., 2011; Liu et al., 2013; Zeng et al., 2014). Note that the relative distances only range from $-n+1$ to $n-1$ so the position embedding matrix $\mathbf{D}$ has size $(2n-1) \times m_d$ (m_d is a hyperparameter indicating the dimensionality of the position embedding vectors). Finally, the word embeddings

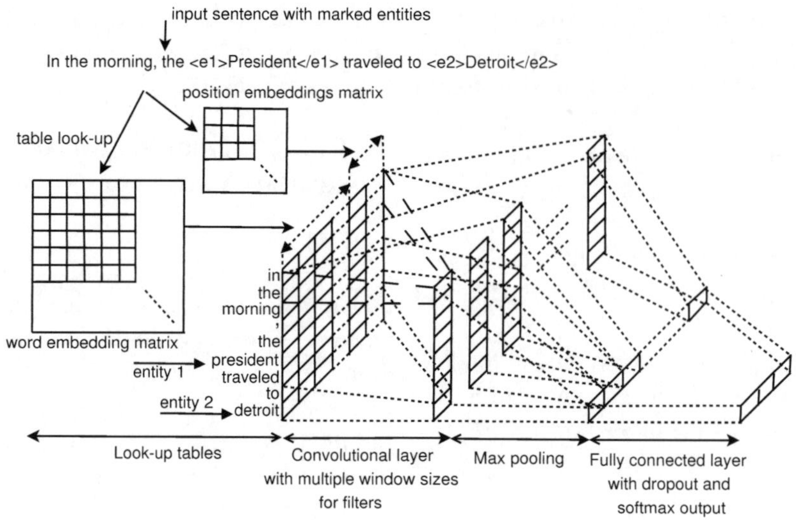

Figure 1: Convolutional Neural Network for Relation Extraction.

e_i and the position embeddings d_1 and d_2 are concatenated into a single vector $\mathbf{x}_i = [e_i, d_{i_1}, d_{i_2}]^\top$ to represent the word x_i. As a result, the original sentence x can now be viewed as a matrix $\mathbf{x}$ of size $(m_e + 2m_d) \times n$ where m_e is the dimensionality of the word embedding vectors.

$$\mathbf{x} = [\mathbf{x}_1, \mathbf{x}_2, \ldots, \mathbf{x}_n]$$

3.2 Convolution

In the next step, the matrix $\mathbf{x}$ representing the input relation mention is fed into the convolutional layer to extract higher level features. Given a widow size w, a filter is seen as a weight matrix $\mathbf{f} = [\mathbf{f}_1, \mathbf{f}_2, \ldots, \mathbf{f}_w]$ ($\mathbf{f}_i$ is a column vector of size $m_e + 2m_d$). The core of this layer is obtained from the application of the convolutional operator on the two matrices $\mathbf{x}$ and $\mathbf{f}$ to produce a score sequence $\mathbf{s} = [s_1, s_2, \ldots, s_{n-w+1}]$:

$$s_i = g(\sum_{j=0}^{w-1} \mathbf{f}_{j+1}^\top \mathbf{x}_{j+i}^\top + b)$$

where b is a bias term and g is some non-linear function. This process can then be replicated for various filters with different window sizes to increase the n-gram coverage of the model.

For relation extraction, we call the n-grams accompanied with relative positions of its words the augmented n-grams. It is instructive to think about the filter $\mathbf{f}$ as representing some hidden class of the augmented n-grams and the scores s_i as measuring the possibility the augmented n-gram at position i belongs to the corresponding hidden class (although these scores are not probabilities at all). The trained weights of the filter f would then amount to a feature detector that learns to recognize the hidden class of the augmented n-grams (Kalchbrenner et al., 2014).

3.3 Pooling

The rationale of the pooling layer is to further abstract the features generated from the convolutional layer by aggregating the scores for each filter to introduce the invariance to the absolute positions but preserve the relative positions of the n-grams between themselves and the entity heads at the same time. The popular aggregating function is $\max$ as it bears responsibility for identifying the most important or relevant features from the score sequence. Concretely, for each filter $\mathbf{f}$, its score sequence $\mathbf{s}$ is passed through the $\max$ function to produce a single number: $p_\mathbf{f} = \max\{\mathbf{s}\} = \max\{s_1, s_2, \ldots s_{n-w+1}\}$ which can be interpreted as estimating the possibility some augmented n-gram of the hidden class of $\mathbf{f}$ appears in the context.

3.4 Regularization and Classification

In the final step, the pooling scores for every filter are concatenated into a single feature vector $\mathbf{z} = [p_1, p_2, \ldots, p_m]$ to represent the relation mention. Here, m is the number of filters in the model and p_i is the pooling score of the i-th filter. Before actually applying this feature vector, following (Kim, 2014; Hinton et al., 2012), we execute a dropout for regularization by randomly setting to zero a proportion ρ of the elements of the feature vector[3] $\mathbf{z}$ to produce the vector $\mathbf{z}_d$. The dropout vector $\mathbf{z}_d$ is then fed into a fully connected layer of standard neural networks followed by a softmax layer in the end to perform classification. The fully connected layer induces a weight matrix $\mathbf{C}$ as model parameters. At test time, the unseen relation mentions are scored using the feature vectors that are not dropped out. We also rescale the weights whose l_2-norms exceed a hyperparameter as Kim (2014).

Overall, the parameters for the presented CNN are: the word embedding matrix $\mathbf{W}$, the position embedding matrix $\mathbf{D}$, the m filter matrices, the weight matrix $\mathbf{C}$ for the fully connected layer. The gradients are computed using back-propagation while training is done via stochastic gradient descent with shuffled mini-batches and the AdaDelta update rule (Zeiler, 2012; Kim, 2014).

4 Experiments

4.1 Hyperparameters and Resources

For all the experiments below, we use: tanh for the non-linear function, 150 filters for each window size in the model and position embedding vectors with dimensionality of $m_d = 50$[4]. Regarding the other parameters, we use the same values as do Kim (2014), i.e, the dropout rate $\rho = 0.5$, the mini-batch size of 50, the hyperparameter for the l_2 of 3.

Finally, we utilize the pre-trained word embeddings `word2vec` from Mikolov et al. (2013) which have dimensionality of $m_e = 300$ and are trained on 100 billion words of Google News using the continuous bag-of-words architecture. These embeddings are publicly available here[5]. Vectors for the words not included in the pre-trained embeddings are initialized randomly. Besides the word embeddings `word2vec`, the model does not use any other NLP toolkits or resources.

4.2 Datasets

We evaluate our models on two datasets: the SemEval-2010 Task 8 dataset (Hendrickx et al., 2010) for relation classification and the ACE 2005 dataset for relation extraction.

ACE 2005 (87,512)		**SemEval 2010 (10,717)**	
Relation	%	Relation	%
ORG-AFF	2.8	Cause-Effect	12.4
PER-SOC	1.2	Component-Whole	11.7
ART	1.0	Entity-Destination	10.6
PART-WHOLE	1.4	Entity-Origin	9.1
GEN-AFF	1.1	Product-Producer	8.8
PHYS	2.1	Member-Collection	8.6
Other	**90.4**	Message-Topic	8.4
		Content-Container	6.8
		Instrument-Agency	6.2
		Other	**17.4**

Table 1: ACE 2005 and SemEval 2010 Relation Class Distributions

The SemEval dataset can be downloaded here[6] and contains 10,717 annotated examples, including 8,000 examples for training and 2,717 examples for testing. Each example is a sentence annotated for a pair of entities of interest and the corresponding relation class for this entity pair. There are 9 ordered relationships (with two directions) and an undirected *Other* class, resulting in 19 classes. A pair is counted as correct if the order of the entities in the relationship is correct. For the ACE 2005 dataset, documents are annotated for 6 major relation classes and 7 entity types. In order to generate the non-relation examples or the examples for the *Other* class, we collect every pair of entity mentions within a single sentence and not included in the annotated relation set. To reduce the noise, we truncate the generated dataset by removing all the examples whose distances between the two entity heads are greater than 15. This results in a considerably unbalanced dataset of 8,365 positive examples of the 6 annotated relation classes and 79,147 negative examples of the class *Other*. The distributions of the relation classes on the two datasets are shown in Table 1. As we can see, the ACE dataset is much more biased toward the *Other* class than the SemEval dataset and thus more appropriate for relation extraction experiments.

4.3 Evaluation of Model Architectures

We investigate the effectiveness of different window sizes of filters by running the proposed CNN

[3] Following the Bernoulli distribution

[4] These values produce the best performance during our experimental process.

[5] https://code.google.com/p/word2vec/

[6] http://docs.google.com/View?id=dfvxd49s 36c28v9pmw

		nonstatic.rand			static.word2vec			nonstatic.word2vec		
#	window sizes	P	R	F	P	R	F	P	R	F
1	2	69.56	41.64	52.04	74.66	41.03	52.90	72.74	49.49	58.87
2	3	68.47	42.73	52.57	74.19	42.16	53.73	72.50	50.75	59.66
3	4	68.17	43.39	52.94	73.60	41.90	53.35	72.56	49.81	58.97
4	5	66.83	43.46	52.55	73.52	42.60	53.89	71.70	51.08	59.57
5	4-5	66.18	46.12	54.25	72.69	45.23	55.71	71.88	52.36	60.50
6	3-4-5	67.54	45.73	54.43	71.99	46.85	56.73	71.21	53.24	60.86
7	2-3-4-5	66.42	47.20	55.12	72.60	46.77	56.85	71.25	53.91	**61.32**

Table 2: System Performance on various window size combinations and architectures

model on window sizes of 2, 3, 4 and 5. To understand the behavior of the model on multiple window sizes, we further test it on the following window size combinations: (4,5), (3,4,5) and (2,3,4,5). In each of these window size configurations, we evaluate the system on three different scenarios: (i) the word embeddings and the position embeddings are randomly initialized and optimized during the training process (denoted by *nonstatic.rand*), (ii) the word embeddings are initialized by the pre-trained word embeddings; the position embeddings are initialized randomly and the two embeddings are kept unchanged during the training (denoted by *static.word2vec*), (iii) the two embeddings are initialized as in case (ii) but they are optimized as model parameters when the model is trained (denoted by *nonstatic.word2vec*). These experiments are carried out for relation extraction on the ACE 2005 dataset via 5-fold cross validation. Table 2 presents the system performance on Precision (P), Recall (R) and F1 score (F).

The key observations from the table are[7]:

(i) From rows 1, 2, 3, 4, we see that evaluating window sizes individually is quite intricate. It is unclear which window size is the best size for CNNs on relation extraction. For instance, on the *nonstatic.rand* mode, the window size 4 seems to outperform the others while on the other modes, the window sizes 3 and 5 turn out to be better. Besides, the performance gaps between the window sizes are small, making it hard to draw a conclusive judgement. In any case, the window size 2 seems to be the worst, suggesting that the 2-grams might be less informative than the others on representing relation mentions for CNNs on this dataset.

[7]The statements at points (ii) and (iii) are significant at confidence levels $\geq 95\%$.

(ii) While the results on evaluating single window sizes are hard to analyze, the results for multiple window sizes are quite clear and conclusive. Moving from single window sizes of 2, 3, 4 or 5 (rows 1, 2, 3 and 4 respectively) to the configuration with two window sizes 4 and 5 (row 5) gives us consistent improvements on all the model architectures. The performance is then consistently enhanced when more window sizes are included, resulting in the best performance when all the window sizes 2, 3, 4 and 5 are employed. This demonstrates the advantages of the models with multiple window sizes over the single window size models in Liu et al. (2013) and Zeng et al. (2014).

(iii) Regarding different model architectures, the picture is even clearer. No matter which window size configuration is applied, we constantly see the *nonstatic.word2vec* architecture performs most effectively, followed by the *static.word2vect* setting which is in turn followed by the *nonstatic.rand* model. This suggests the undeniable benefits of initializing the word embeddings by some "universal" pre-trained values and updating the embeddings to reflex RE specific embeddings when training the models (Collobert et al., 2011; Kim, 2014). For the next experiments, we always use all the window sizes 2, 3, 4 and 5 with the *nonstatic.word2vec* architecture.

4.4 Relation Extraction Experiment

We compare our system with the traditional feature-based relation extraction systems when these system are only allowed to use the same information and resources as our systems, i.e, the words in the relation mentions, the positions of the two entity heads and the word embeddings. Given the sentences and the positions of the two entity heads, the features that the state-of-the-art feature-based systems extract include: the heads of the two entity mentions; the words in the context before mention 1; after mention 2 and between two mentions; the bigrams, the word sequences between two entities, the order of two mentions, the number of words between two mentions (Zhou et al., 2005; Jiang and Zhai, 2007; Sun et al., 2011). The feature-based system using this feature set is called *Words*. Armed with the word embeddings, one can further introduce these embeddings into the head words or the words in the context as additional features (Nguyen and Grishman, 2014). We call the system *Words* augmented with the embeddings for the two heads *Words-HM-Wed* and *Words* augmented with the embeddings for words in the contexts *Words-WC-Wed*. We apply the MaxEnt framework with L2 regularization in the Mallet toolkit[8] to train these feature-based models (as (Jiang and Zhai, 2007; Sun et al., 2011; Nguyen and Grishman, 2014)). Table 3 shows the performance of the three baseline systems and our proposed CNN via 5-fold cross validation on the ACE 2005 dataset.

System	P	R	F
Words	54.95	43.73	48.69
Words-WC-Wed	50.10	44.47	47.11
Words-HM-Wed	57.01	55.74	56.36
Our CNN	71.25	53.91	**61.32**

Table 3: Performance of Relation Extraction Systems

The first observation is that adding the word embeddings to the words in the context hurt the performance of the feature-based systems while augmenting the heads of the entities with word embeddings significantly improves the feature-based systems. This is consistent with the results reported by Nguyen and Grishman (2014) and demonstrates that the ability to wisely pick the words for embeddings and avoid embeddings on specific locations is crucial to the feature-based systems. More importantly, our proposed CNN significantly outperforms all the baseline models at the confidence levels $\geq 95\%$, an improvement of 4.96% over the best feature-based system *Words-HM-Wed* (Nguyen and Grishman, 2014). This result indicates that CNNs are a better way to employ word embeddings for relation extraction.

[8]http://mallet.cs.umass.edu/

Remember that although the traditional systems can achieve a performance greater than 72% on the ACE dataset (Qian et al., 2008; Sun et al., 2011), they come at the expense of elaborate feature engineering as well as much more expensive feature extraction. In particular, the feature extractors of these feature-based systems require: (i) the perfect entity and mention type information hand-labeled laboriously by human annotators; (ii) the extensive usage of the existing supervised NLP toolkits and resources (constituent and dependency parsers, dictionaries, gazetteers etc) which might be unavailable for various domains in reality. The absence of the perfect (hand-annotated) entity and mention type information (i.e point (i) above) greatly impairs these feature-based systems' performance. For instance, both Plank and Moschitti (2013) and Nguyen and Grishman (2014) report a performance less than 60% on the ACE 2005 dataset when the perfect entity type and mention type features are not employed although the other features with extensive feature engineering (i.e point (ii) above) are still included. As a result, in a more realistic setting where hand-annotated features are prohibitive, the proposed CNN requires much less feature engineering and resources but still performs better than the traditional feature-based systems.

4.5 Relation Classification Experiment

In order to further verify the effectiveness of the system, we test the system on the relation classification task with the SemEval 2010 dataset and compare the results with the state-of-the-art systems in this area. Table 4 describes the performance of various traditional systems that are based on classifiers such as MaxEnt and SVM with series of supervised and manual features[9](Hendrickx et al., 2010) as well as the more recent systems based on convolutional neural networks (Zeng et al., 2014) (O-CNN), recursive neural networks (RNN), matrix-vector recursive neural networks (MVRNN) (Socher et al., 2012) or log-quadratic factor-based compositional embedding model (FCM) (Yu et al., 2014)[10].

As we can see, among the systems *not using any*

[9]i.e the features extracted from supervised pre-processing NLP modules and manual resources

[10]These are the macro-averaged F1-scores, computed by the officially provided scorer.

Classifier	Feature Sets	F
SVM	POS, WordNet, morphological features, thesauri, Google n-grams	77.6
MaxEnt	POS, WordNet, morphological features, noun compound system, thesauri, Google n-grams	77.6
SVM	POS, WordNet, prefixes and other morphological features, dependency parse, Levin classes, PropBank, FrameNet, NomLex-Plus, Google n-grams, paraphrases, TextRunner	82.2
RNN	-	74.8
RNN	POS, name tagging, WordNet	77.6
MVRNN	-	79.1
MVRNN	POS, name tagging, WordNet	82.4
O-CNN	-	78.9
O-CNN	WordNet	82.7
FCM	-	80.6
FCM	dependency parse, name tagging	83.0
Our CNN	-	**82.8**

Table 4: Performance of Relation Classification Systems

supervised and manual features (i.e, POS, WordNet, name tagging, dependency parse, patterns etc), our system significantly outperforms the state-of-the-art system FCM (80.6%) (Yu et al., 2014) with an improvement of 2.2%. More interestingly, even without supervised and manual features, our system can still work comparably to the other systems utilizing these features as the vital components. For instance, the supervised features (dependency parse and name tagging) are crucial to FCM (Yu et al., 2014) to significantly improve its performance. We attribute our performance advantage over the closely-related system O-CNN (Zeng et al., 2014) to the multiple window sizes, the optimization of the position embeddings during training and possibly the superiority of the embeddings *word2vec* we use.

4.6 Impact of Unbalanced Dataset

Shifting from relation classification to relation extraction with an unbalanced corpus, we witness a large performance gap as described above. In this section, we study the impact of the unbalanced corpus on the performance of relation extractors for both convolutional neural networks and traditional feature-based approaches (*Words* and *Words-HM-Wed*). In particular, we vary the ratio of positive (true relations) and negative (the class *Other*) examples in the ACE 2005 dataset and see how the system performance responds to this variation. Figure 2 shows the curves. This is a 5-fold cross validation experiment and all the comparisons are significant at confidence levels $\geq 95\%$.

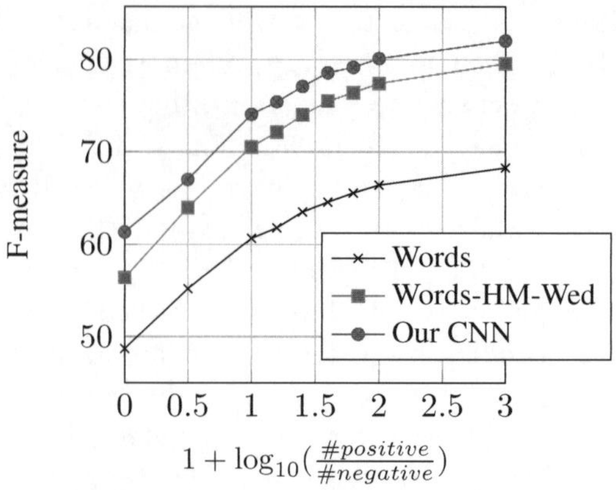

Figure 2: F measures vs positive/negative ratios

From the figure, we see that all the models improve constantly with the increase of the ratio of the positive and negative examples. The performance peaks with an improvement of about 20% for all models when the number of examples of the class *Other* is small relative to the others. In other words, the systems attain their best performance when relation extraction is reduced to the relation classification problem, suggesting that relation extraction is much more challenging than relation classification. Finally, for all the ratio values, we consistently see that the convolutional neural network is superior to the others, once again confirming its advantages.

5 Conclusion

We present a CNN for relation extraction that emphasizes an unbalanced corpus and minimizes usage of external supervised NLP toolkits for features. The network uses multiple window sizes for filters, position embeddings for encoding relative distances and pre-trained word embeddings for initialization in a non-static architecture. The experimental results demonstrate the effectiveness of the proposed CNN on both RC and RE. Our future work includes: (i) to enrich the representation of CNNs with more features for RE, (ii) to study the applications of CNNs on other related tasks, and (iii) to examine other neural network models for RE.

References

Yoshua Bengio, Réjean Ducharme, and Pascal Vincent. 2001. *A Neural Probabilistic Language Model.* In Advances in Neural Information Processing Systems 13 (NIPS'00), pages 932938, MIT Press, 2001.

John Blitzer, Ryan McDonald, and Fernando Pereira. 2006. *Domain Adaptation with Structural Correspondence Learning.* In Proceedings of the 2006 Conference on Empirical Methods in Natural Language Processing, Sydney, Australia.

Elizabeth Boschee, Ralph Weischedel, and Alex Zamanian. 2005. *Automatic Information Extraction.* In Proceedings of the International Conference on Intelligence Analysis.

Razvan C. Bunescu and Raymond J. Mooney. 2005a. *A Shortest Path Dependency Kenrel for Relation Extraction.* In Proceedings of HLT/EMNLP.

Razvan C. Bunescu and Raymond J. Mooney. 2005b. *Subsequence Kernels for Relation Extraction.* In Proceedings of NIPS.

Yee S. Chan and Dan Roth. 2010. *Exploiting Background Knowledge for Relation Extraction.* In Proceedings of the 23rd International Conference on Computational Linguistics (Coling 2010), pages 152-160, Beijing, China, August.

Ronan Collobert and Jason Weston. 2008. *A Unied Architecture for Natural Language Processing: Deep Neural Networks with Multitask Learning.* In International Conference on Machine Learning, ICML, 2008.

Ronan Collobert, Jason Weston, Léon Bottou, Michael Karlen, Koray Kavukcuoglu and Pavel Kuksa. 2011. *Natural Language Processing (Almost) from Scratch.* Journal of Machine Learning Research 12:24932537.

Aron Culotta and Jeffrey Sorensen. 2004. *Dependency Tree Kernels for Relation Extraction.* In Proceedings of ACL 2004.

Hal Daumé III. 2007. *Frustratingly Easy Domain Adaptation.* In Proceedings of the ACL, pages 256-263, Prague, Czech Republic, June 2007.

Ralph Grishman, David Westbrook and Adam Meyers. 2005. *NYUs English ACE 2005 System Description.* ACE 2005 Evaluation Workshop.

Jing Jiang and ChengXiang Zhai. 2007. *A Systematic Exploration of the Feature Space for Relation Extraction.* In Proceedings of the Human Language Technology Conference of the North American Chapter of the Association for Computational Linguistics (NAACL-HLT'07), pages 113-120, 2007.

Iris Hendrickx, Su Nam Kim, Zornitsa Kozareva, Preslav Nakov, Diarmuid Ó Séaghdha, Sebastian Padó, Marco Pennacchiotti, Lorenza Romano, Stan Szpakowicz 2010. *SemEval-2010 Task 8: Multi-Way Classification of Semantic Relations Between Pairs of Nominals.* In Proceedings of the 5th International Workshop on Semantic Evaluation, SemEval 2010.

Geoffrey E. Hinton, Nitish Srivastava, Alex Krizhevsky, Ilya Sutskever, and Ruslan Salakhutdinov. 2012. *Improving Neural Networks by Preventing Co-Adaptation of Feature Detectors.* CoRR, abs/1207.0580.

Raphael Hoffmann, Congle Zhang, Xiao Ling, Luke Zettlemoyer, and Daniel Weld. 2011. *Knowledge-based Weak Supervision for Information Extraction of Overlapping Relations.* In Proceedings of ACL 2011.

Nal Kalchbrenner, Edward Grefenstette and Phil Blunsom. 2014. *A Convolutional Neural Network for Modelling Sentences.* In Proceedings of ACL 2014.

Nanda Kambhatla. 2004. *Combining Lexical, Syntactic, and Semantic Features with Maximum Entropy Models for Information Extraction.* In Proceedings of ACL 2004.

Yoon Kim. 2014. *Convolutional Neural Networks for Sentence Classification.* In Proceedings of EMNLP 2014.

Yann LeCun, Léon Bottou, Yoshua Bengio and Patrick Haffner. 1988. *Gradient-based learning applied to document recognition.* In Proceedings of the IEEE, 86(11):22782324, November, 1988.

ChunYang Liu, WenBo Sun, WenHan Chao, and WanXiang Che. 2013. *Convolution Neural Network for Relation Extraction.* In Proceedings of 9th International Conference on Advanced Data Mining and Applications, Part II (ADMA 2013), Hangzhou, China, December, 2013.

David McClosky, Eugene Charniak, and Mark Johnson. 2010. *Automatic Domain Adaptation for Parsing.* In Proceedings of Human Language Technology Conference of the North American Chapter of the Association for Computational Linguistics, pages 28-36, Los Angeles, California, June 2010.

Tomas Mikolov, Ilya Sutskever, Kai Chen, Greg Corrado, and Jeffrey Dean. 2013. *Distributed Representations of Words and Phrases and their Compositionality.* In Proceedings of NIPS, 2013.

Mike Mintz, Steven Bills, Rion Snow, and Daniel Jurafsky. 2009. *Distant Supervision for Relation Extraction without Labeled Data.* In Proceedings of ACL, 2009.

Andriy Mnih and Geoffrey Hinton. 2007. *Three new Graphical Models for Statistical Language Modelling.* In Proceedings of ICML'07, pages 641-648, Corvallis, OR, 2007.

Andriy Mnih and Geoffrey Hinton. 2009. *A Scalable Hierarchical Distributed Language Model.* In NIPS, page 1081-1088.

Mohit Iyyer, Jordan Boyd-Graber, Leonardo Claudino, Richard Socher and Hal Daumé III. 2014. *A Neural*

Network for Factoid Question Answering over Paragraphs. In Proceedings of EMNLP 2014.

Thien Huu Nguyen and Ralph Grishman. 2014. *Employing Word Representations and Regularization for Domain Adaptation of Relation Extraction.* In Proceedings of ACL 2014, pages 68-74, Baltimore, Maryland, USA.

Truc-Vien T. Nguyen, Alessandro Moschitti, and Giuseppe Riccardi. 2009. *Convolution Kernels on Constituent, Dependency and Sequential Structures for Relation Extraction.* In Proceedings of EMNLP 09, pages 1378-1387, Stroudsburg, PA, USA.

Barbara Plank and Alessandro Moschitti. 2013. *Embedding Semantic Similarity in Tree Kernels for Domain Adaptation of Relation Extraction.* In Proceedings of the ACL 2013, pages 1498-1507, Sofia, Bulgaria.

Longhua Qian, Guodong Zhou, Qiaoming Zhu and Peide Qian. 2008. *Exploiting Constituent Dependencies for Tree Kernel-based Semantic Relation Extraction.* In Proceedings of COLING, pages 697-704, Manchester.

Sebastian Riedel, Limin Yao, and Andrew McCallum. 2010. *Modeling Relations and their Mentions without Labeled Text.* In Proceedings of ECML PKDD, 2010.

Yelong Shen, Xiaodong He, Jianfeng Gao, Li Deng and Grégoire Mesnil. 2014. *Learning Semantic Representations Using Convolutional Neural Networks for Web Search.* In Proceedings of WWW 2014.

Richard Socher, Eric H. Huang, Jeffrey Pennington, Andrew Y. Ng, and Christopher D. Manning. 2011. *Dynamic Pooling and Unfolding Recursive Autoencoders for Paraphrase Detection.* In Proceedings of NIPS 2011.

Richard Socher, Brody Huval, Christopher D. Manning and Andrew Y. Ng. 2012. *Semantic Compositionality through Recursive Matrix-Vector Spaces.* In Proceedings of EMNLP 2012.

Richard Socher, John Bauer, Christopher D. Manning and Andrew Y. Ng. 2013. *Parsing with Compositional Vector Grammars.* In Proceedings of ACL 2013.

Richard Socher, Alex Perelygin, Jean Wu, Jason Chuang, Chris Manning, Andrew Ng and Chris Potts. 2013. *Recursive Deep Models for Semantic Compositionality Over a Sentiment Treebank.* In Proceedings of EMNLP 2013.

Richard Socher, Danqi Chen, Christopher D. Manning, Andrew Y. Ng. 2013. *Reasoning With Neural Tensor Networks for Knowledge Base Completion.* In Proceedings of NIPS 2013.

Ang Sun, Ralph Grishman, and Satoshi Sekine. 2011. *Semi-supervised Relation Extraction with Large-scale Word Clustering.* In Proceedings of ACL-HLT, pages 521-529, Portland, Oregon, USA.

Le Sun and Xianpei Han 2014. *A Feature-Enriched Tree Kernel for Relation Extraction.* In Proceedings of ACL 2014, pages 61-67, Baltimore, Maryland, USA.

Mihai Surdeanu, Julie Tibshirani, Ramesh Nallapati and Christopher D. Manning 2012. *Multi-instance Multi-label Learning for Relation Extraction.* In Proceedings of EMNLP-CoNLL 2012.

Joseph Turian, Lev Ratinov, and Yoshua Bengio. 2010. *Word representations: A simple and general method for semi-supervised learning.* In Proceedings of the 48th Annual Meeting of the Association for Computational Linguistics (ACL'10), pages 384-394, Uppsala, Sweden, July, 2010.

Wen-tau Yih, Xiaodong He, and Christopher Meek. 2014. *Semantic Parsing for Single-Relation Question Answering.* In Proceddings of ACL 2014.

Mo Yu, Matthew R. Gormley, and Mark Dredze. 2014. *Factor-based Compositional Embedding Models.* In the NIPS Learning Semantics Workshop 2014.

Matthew D. Zeiler. 2012. *ADADELTA: An Adaptive Learning Rate Method.* CoRR, abs/1212.5701.

Dmitry Zelenko, Chinatsu Aone, and Anthony Richardella. 2003. *Kernel Methods for Relation Extraction.* Journal of Machine Learning Research, 3:10831106.

Daojian Zeng, Kang Liu, Siwei Lai, Guangyou Zhou and Jun Zhao. 2014. *Relation Classification via Convolutional Deep Neural Network.* In Proceedings of COLING 2014.

Min Zhang, Jie Zhang, Jian Su, and GuoDong Zhou. 2006. *A Composite Kernel to Extract Relations between Entities with both Flat and Structured Features.* In Proceedings of COLING-ACL-06, pages 825-832, Sydney.

Guodong Zhou, Jian Su, Jie Zhang, and Min Zhang. 2005. *Exploring various Knowledge in Relation Extraction.* In Proceedings of ACL'05, pages 427-434, Ann Arbor, USA, 2005.

Guodong Zhou, Min Zhang, DongHong Ji, and QiaoMing Zhu. 2007. *Tree Kernel-based Relation Extraction with Context-sensitive Structured Parse Tree Information.* In Proceedings of EMNLP-CoNLL-07, pages 728-736, Prague.

Distributional Semantic Concept Models for Entity Relation Discovery

Jay Urbain
Milwaukee School of Engineering
CTSI, MCW
1025 N. Broadway Ave.
Milwaukee, WI, USA
urbain@msoe.edu

Glenn Bushee
Clinical Translational Science Institute
Medical College of WI
8701 Watertown Plank
Milwaukee, WI, USA
gbushee@mcw.edu

Paul Knudson
Clinical Translational Science Institute
Medical College of WI
8701 Watertown Plank
Milwaukee, WI, USA
knudson@mcw.edu

George Kowalski
Clinical Translational Science Institute
Medical College of WI
8701 Watertown Plank
Milwaukee, WI, USA
gkowalski@mcw.edu

Brad Taylor
Clinical Translational Science Institute
Medical College of WI
8701 Watertown Plank
Milwaukee, WI, USA
btaylor@mcw.edu

Abstract

We present an ad hoc concept modeling approach using distributional semantic models to identify fine-grained entities and their relations in an online search setting. Concepts are generated from user-defined seed terms, distributional evidence, and a relational model over concept distributions. A dimensional indexing model is used for efficient aggregation of distributional, syntactic, and relational evidence. The proposed semi-supervised model allows concepts to be defined and related at varying levels of granularity and scope. Qualitative evaluations on medical records, intelligence documents, and open domain web data demonstrate the efficacy of our approach.

1 Introduction

Knowledge discovery could be facilitated with the ability to define concepts ad hoc, and from these concepts identify semantically related named entities and entity relations. In an online search setting, identification of specific named entities may not be available, or may not have the granularity to support specific information needs. Attempting to provide models for all possible entity and relation types is computationally intractable, so there is a need for a more flexible, fine-grained, user-driven approach.

These needs are in contrast to named entities identified by models defined in advance from labeled training data, knowledge bases, or embedded in a set of rules. Entities identified from these models may be too general, e.g., person *versus* terrorist, or disease *versus* diabetes; or domain specific, e.g., protein type in a dietary *versus* a molecular biology sense. This can be an impediment to search and discovery since many discoveries are serendipitous in nature and are found by identifying linkages between more specialized concepts within and across domains. Using a flexible dimensional index for efficient aggregation of distributional statistics and a distributional relational model over concept distributions, we propose a new, more flexible approach for creating fine-grained, user-driven concept models for identification of semantically related entity relations.

First, we present an information-seeking scenario to motivate our approach. This is followed by a presentation of our proposed distributional semantic concept model and qualitative results.

1.1 Ad hoc information seeking scenario

Interactive knowledge discovery can be modeled using a dual representation of concepts and relations (Bollegala, et al., 2010). Concepts can be defined by the relations they participate in, and by their lexical and semantic similarity. Relations can be defined by their participating concepts, and by semantically similar relations. In the following scenario, we are interested in identifying relations between *Alzheimer's disease (AD)* and other diseases. We've heard of studies linking *Type 2 Diabetes Mellitus (T2DM)* with *AD*, so we start with the query "*Diabetes related to Alzheimers*." The system extracts candidate *entity* instances and *relations* from the query (Table 1).

Proceedings of NAACL-HLT 2015, pages 49–55,
Denver, Colorado, May 31 – June 5, 2015. ©2015 Association for Computational Linguistics

Query: ***Diabetes related to Alzheimers***
Concepts:
Diabetes - *id: /en/diabetes_mellitus, type: /medicine/disease*
Alzheimers - *id: /en/alzheimers_disease, type: /medicine/disease*
Relations - (concept1, relation 1, 2,..., concept2):
diabetes; related to; alzheimers -> disease; related to; disease

Table 1. Parsed query with semantically related entities.

A structured representation of the query is generated that integrates syntactic and lexical evidence with distributional semantic concept models of each candidate entity. Sentences semantically *relevant* to the query are retrieved and rank ordered. A sample search result for "Diabetes related to Alzheimer's" with extracted concepts and relations are shown in Table 2(a). Table 2(b) shows a entity-relation-entity graph of the query and a retrieved sentence.

a) Retrieved Sentence with concepts & relational dependencies	**Diabetes is a risk factor for vascular dementia.** *Dependency relations: (concept1; relation 1, 2,...;concept2)* diabetes; ; risk_factor risk_factor; *for*; vascular_dementia diabetes; *risk_factor_for*; vascular_dementia
b) Concept-relation graph: Query + Sentence	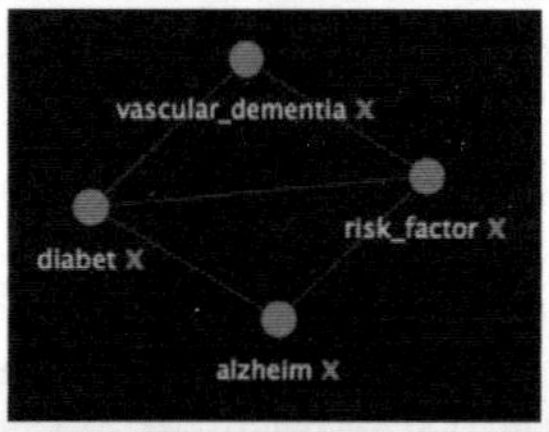
c) Semantic similarity graph: query: *(vascular dementia; risk factor; *).*	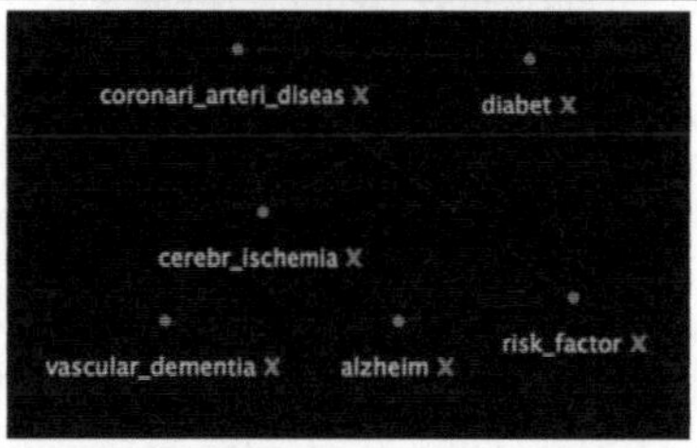

Table 2. (a) Concept-relation search result for query: *Diabetes related to Alzheimer's*. (b) Graph of query and sentence result. (c) Concept-relation graph search results for query: (*vascular dementia; risk factor;* *).

The search result and query provide a relational lattice linking diabetes, vascular dementia, and Alzheimer's with risk factors. From analyzing the results of the query, the user may be interested in identifying other concepts related to risk factors and vascular dementia. For example, the user may expand the scope of the search space by querying for any concept related as a risk factor to vascular dementia.

A dimensional index is used for efficiently aggregating distributional statistics and relating evidence of concepts and relations within the search index with information from the query. Table 2(c) shows the results using a force-directed graph. The user can now identify new concepts participating in some form of risk factor relation. From these results, other relations for one or more concepts or any combination of concept relation could be explored. Table 4 lists the ranked retrieval process.

1. The user presents a natural language query.
2. The NLP engine parses the query, extracts candidate entities, dependency relations, syntax, and textual context.
3. A structured query is generated from the evidence extracted by the NLP engine.
4. A distributional semantic model is generated for each entity within the query from the dimensional index.
5. Word and phrase search within the context of individual sentences and documents.
6. Query model (4) applied to the top ranking sentences from (step 5).
7. User can provide relevance feedback to the system.

Iterate over search results.

Table 4. Ranked retrieval process (top) and architecture (bottom).

2 Dimensional Indexing

A dimensional indexing model (Kimball, 1996; Gray, et al. 1997) is used for efficient search and aggregation of distributional statistics. The model represents a Vector Space Model (VSM) of distributional statistics for defining concepts, and a data warehousing style (dimensional data model) inverted index of words, phrases, named entities, relations, and sentences. The grain of the index is the individual word with attributes for position, part-of-speech, and phrase. Semantic concepts are defined over word distributions from the index. An *entity-relation-entity* index is also created during indexing to link candidate entity instances (noun phrases) with their shortest path dependency relation within sentences. The same NLP is used for query processing, and sentence parsing during indexing.

Importantly, the dimensional index facilitates efficient OLAP style SQL queries for aggregating distributional statistics, and for executing relational queries over concepts. The index also supports aggregation over word, phrase, entity, relation, sentence, or document. A variation on this indexing approach has been scaled to several hundred Gigabytes for chemical patent retrieval (Urbain, et al. 2009). Indexes can be created from local collections and integrated with indexes created from online web search results.

3 Distributional Semantic Model

Distributional semantics quantifies and categorizes semantic similarities between linguistic terms based on their distributional properties in large samples of text. The central assumption is that the context surrounding a given word provides important information about its meaning (Church et al., 1989, 1991; Firth, 1968; Harris, 1954; Turney and Pantel, 2010). VSMs provide a mechanism for representing term, concept, relation, or sentence meaning by using distributional statistics. The semantic properties of words are captured in a multi-dimensional space by vectors that are constructed from large bodies of text by observing the distributional patterns of co-occurrence with their neighboring words. These vectors can then be used as measures of text similarity between words, phrases, abstract concepts, entities, relations, or snips of arbitrary text.

We base our distributional measures of semantic similarity using pointwise mutual information (PMI). PMI measures the pointwise mutual information between two objects as the log ratio of the joint probability of two objects co-occurring relative to the probability of those objects occurring independently. PMI using information retrieval (PMI-IR) was suggested by Turney (2001) as an unsupervised measure for the evaluation of the semantic similarity of words (Eq. 1). Turney defined words as words co-occurring if they co-occurred within a 10-word window.

$$PMI(w1,w2) = log_2\left(\frac{p(w1,w2)}{p(w1)p(w2)}\right) \quad (1)$$

Multiple evaluations have demonstrated the effectiveness of PMI on semantic similarity benchmarks (Mihalecea, 2006; Eneko, 2012). We are also attracted to its simplicity and efficiency for generating distributional concept models online within our dimensional data model. Tables 6 and 7 show the PMI of words for the concepts Diabetes and CHF (Congestive Heart Failure). The distribution of semantically similar words (shown in lexically stemmed form) for each disease can be used to infer the underlying concepts Diabetes and CHF respectively.

Concept	Stem term	PMI
diabet	mellitu	4.12
diabet	depend	3.52
diabet	type	2.67
diabet	retinopathi	2.14
diabet	insulin	2.13
diabet	nephropathi	2.02
diabet	noninsulin	1.84
diabet	hyperlipidemia	1.76
diabet	esrd	1.54
diabet	adult	1.52
diabet	glaucoma	1.42
diabet	hypercholesterolemia	1.10

Table 6. PMI of words for Diabetes.

Concept	**Stem term**	**PMI**
chf	exacerb	2.34
chf	ef	1.5
chf	drainag	1.4
chf	leukocytosi	0.71
chf	lvh	0.47
chf	treat	0.34
chf	secondari	0.33
chf	etiolog	0.31
chf	cad	0.29
chf	diuresi	0.27
chf	evid	0.25
chf	pleural	0.21

Table 7. PMI of words for CHF.

Mihalecea, et al. (2006) extended semantic similarity measurements to two arbitrary text segments. Given a measurement for the semantic similarity of two unordered (bag of words) text segments and a measurement for term specificity, the semantic similarity of two text segments *C1* and *C2* can be defined using a model that combines the semantic similarities of each text segment in turn with respect to the other text segment. We extended the original bag-of-words text-to-text measurement to include phrases (candidate entities and their relation dependencies). Using PMI as the underlying measure of semantic similarity, we developed the following 2nd order PMI-based model for measuring the semantic similarity between concepts C1, C2. (Eq. 2).

$$SemSim(C_1, C_2) = \frac{1}{2}\left(\frac{\sum_{w\in(W_1\cap W_2)}\left(PMI(C_1,w) * idf(w) + \left(PMI(C_2,w) * idf(w)\right)\right)}{\sum_{w\in(W_1\cap W_2)}\left(idf(w)\right)}\right) \quad (2)$$

Concept1	Concept2	Co-term	$PMI(C_1, w) * idf(w)$	$PMI(C_2, w) * idf(w)$	Average
afghanistan	pakistan	india	6.00	6.66	6.33
afghanistan	pakistan	iran	6.10	6.04	6.07
afghanistan	pakistan	china	6.15	5.94	6.05
afghanistan	pakistan	franc	6.03	5.94	5.99
afghanistan	pakistan	russia	5.63	6.04	5.83
afghanistan	pakistan	tajikistan	5.48	6.10	5.79
afghanistan	pakistan	arabia	4.93	5.88	5.41
afghanistan	pakistan	soviet	5.42	5.09	5.25
afghanistan	pakistan	britain	5.63	4.48	5.06

Table 7. Semantic similarity (*SemSim*) between concepts Afghanistan and Pakistan

$$RelDepSim(R_1, R_2) = \propto \sum_{w\in(R_1\cap R_2)}\left(NIRDF(w)\right) + (1-\propto)\sum_{i=1}^{2} SemSim(e_{r1i}, e_{r2i}) \quad (3)$$

$$LexSim(S_1, S_2) = \propto_1 \sum_{e\in(E_1\cap E_2)}(1) + \propto_2 BM25(S_1, S_2) + \propto_3 BM25(D_1, D_2) \quad (4)$$

Where $\propto_1 > \propto_2 > \propto_3$.

$$AggSim(CR_1, CR_2) = \propto_1 SemSim(C_1, C_2) + \propto_2 RelDepSim(R_1, R_2) + \propto_3 LexSim(S_1, S_2) + \propto_4 PRSim(S_1, S_2) \quad (5)$$

Where $\propto_1 > \propto_2 > \propto_3 > \propto_4$.

Concept instances used in Eq. 2 may be any text segment. PMI is calculated over the inner product (relational join) of all mutually co-occurring words between *C1* and *C2* is weighted by their respective semantic similarity (*SemSim*) and their normalized inverse document frequency (*NIDF*). This measurement is completely unsupervised and can be used to compare any ordered or non-ordered text segment across any domain. To demonstrate the open domain capability of the semantic similarity measurement, we list the top co-occurring *PMI*IDF* measurements for *Afghanistan* and *Pakistan* in a post 9/11 intelligence document collection Table 7.

For reference we provide information retrieval measurements for relational dependency similarity (Eq.3), lexical similarity (Eq. 4) using Robertson's *BM25* (2000), and an aggregate similarity measurement integrating semantic, relational dependency, and lexical similarity (Eq. 5).

3.1 Learning Semantic Concepts

Figure 1 illustrates the following process for defining semantic concepts.

1) Users provide seed terms to bootstrap learning of a semantic concept. In this case, the user defines the semantic concept *CAD*, and seed terms *CAD* and *coronary artery disease. Note: Seed terms may be any combination of individual words or phrases.*

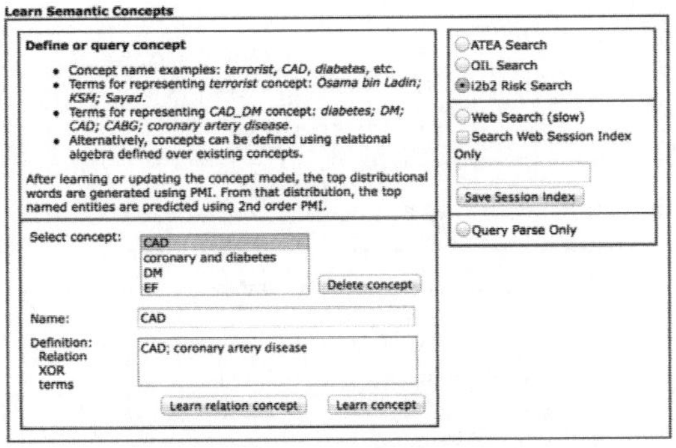

Figure 1. Learning semantic concepts

2) Concept terms can come from different conceptual areas to meet specific information retrieval needs. For example, terms from *finance* and *terrorism*, or terms identifying medical co-morbidities such as *coronary artery disease* and *diabetes*. Additional terms can also be added for increased specificity.

A vector-space model of a concept's distribution is generated from 2nd order probabilistic likelihood of co-occurring terms (PMI) (Figure 2):

Termid	Term	Idf	N	Pmi	NPmi
2349	cabg	0.331	2	3.757	1
90	fhx	0.629	1	3.171	0.844
1249	anterosept	0.608	1	2.317	0.617
13612	pnc	0.803	1	2.16	0.575
1675	imi	0.608	1	2.102	0.559
112	known	0.189	2	2.084	0.555
2211	leukemia	0.589	1	1.956	0.521
3410	pvd	0.363	1	1.837	0.489
1635	chf	0.286	1	1.785	0.475
115	coronari	0.159	2	1.76	0.468
93	cad	0.151	1	1.749	0.466
6869	psychosi	0.712	1	1.716	0.457
3646	gastriti	0.53	1	1.646	0.438
2350	septemb	0.43	1	1.525	0.406
276	mi	0.207	2	1.476	0.393
133	arteri	0.142	1	1.453	0.387
139	stent	0.232	2	1.448	0.385
105	hyperlipidemia	0.155	2	1.424	0.379
889	ptca	0.46	1	1.344	0.358
100	hx	0.207	1	1.28	0.341

Figure 2. Distributional concept model for CAD

Qualitative review of concept terms demonstrates the accuracy of this approach. To properly evaluate the sematic model, we should be able to take the model and predict relevant named entities.

3) From the concept model CAD, we can predict the likelihood of semantic relatedness of candidate entities (Figure 3). *Note: Candidate entities are noun phrases identified during indexing or query processing.*

Entityid	Term	Idf	SC
86	cad	0.267	1
320	histori	0.163	0.439
204	coronari_arteri_diseas	0.597	0.406
39	htn	0.157	0.363
166	dm	0.182	0.329
321	cabg	0.455	0.328
454	hypertens	0.339	0.261
666	diabet	0.267	0.241
2311	risk	0.666	0.23
40	pt	0.101	0.204
288	chf	0.316	0.2
1614	ag	0.629	0.199
1885	pvd	0.57	0.196
2031	septemb	0.545	0.18

Figure 3. Named entitities predicted for concept *CAD*

4) From the semantic concept model, CAD, we can predict the likelihood of generating sentences by using this model for sentence information retrieval (Figure 4).

100 **Sentence Search Results** *order by aggregate*

N	ID	2nd Order PMI	Text
1	215-215-8528	0.122	Ehlers) CABG x 4 (LIMA - LAD/ Sequential graft: SVG1 connects Aorta to D1 then OM1/ SVG2 - LVB2 Incidental anomalous circumflex off the right coronary artery Pre-op EF 50-55% with infero-posterior hypokineses (?post-op) Bicuspid aortic valve (not replaced with CABG according to notes) Mild AS, Mild AI only on pre-CABG echo 2097 Hypertension Dyslipidemia Diabetes Type II Perioperative hyperglycemia post CABG Exsmoker Quit 2097, >50 pack years Peripheral arterial disease Occluded distal aorta (diagnosed after cardiac catheterization attempt in 2097) Small infrarenal abdominal aortic aneurysm 3.6cm Paroxysmal atrial fibrillation (x2 years at least) On coumadin for stroke prevention and amiodarone from maintenance of NSR Currently in NSR BPH Chronic back pain Renal insufficiency (Creatinine 4.1) non-oliguric - ?cause Cr normal November 2097 Gradually increased over November from 1.1-1.6,
2	161-161-6298	0.112	PMH: DM x 20 years, peripheral neuropathy HTN CAD Anteroseptal MI in 03/91, PTCA and stent EF 32% (last echo 2092) Hemorrhoids (normal colo 2095) Iritis, corneal dystrophy Osteoporosis Diverticulosis (?) Meds: Glipizide 2.5 QD Asa 325 QD Lisinopril 5mg QD Lopressor 50 mg BID Lipitor 10 mg QD Amitryptilline 25 mg QHS Prednisone gtt Caltrate + D (CALCIUM Carbonate 1500 Mg (600 Mg Elem Ca)/ Vit D 200 Iu) 1 TAB PO BID All: Acetaminophen--rash SH: Tob: 43 year pack hx, quit 2060 EtOH: denies Illicits: denies FH: Mother: pernicious anemia Father: died in accident at young age Brother: leukemia ROS: As in HPI. - General: no weight loss/gain, no fatigue, no fevers, no chills, no change in appetite - Respiratory: no cough, no SOB, no DOE, no hemoptysis, no wheezing - HEENT: no neck stiffness, no hoarseness, no hearing loss - Cardiac: chest pain/pressure as above, no palpitations, no orthopnea, no PND - Gastrointestinal: no nausea, no vomiting, no diarrhea, no constipation, no bleeding - Neurologic: diminished sensation in LLE bilaterally - Lymph nodes: no enlarged lymph nodes - Musculoskeletal: No back pain, no neck pain, no leg pain, no arm pain - Urologic: No hematuria, no dysuria, no polyuria, no nocturia - Hematologic: No bruising, no bleeding - Exposures: No sick contacts, no recent travel Exam: VS: 97.7 74 18 98% supine 108/54 standing 127/70 HEENT: NC/AT, PERRL, nonicteric.
3	123-123-4822	0.111	PMH: Duchenne's muscular dystrophy, COPD (2.5L home O2), IDDM, recurrent UTIs w/ previous Candida tropicalis fungemia (followed by Dr. Phoebe Abreu), B ureteral obstruction s/p ureteral stent placement, CAD s/p CABG, PVD, SZ disorder, hyperkalemia secondary to hyperaldosteronemia (type III RTA), CRI (baseline 1.5) PSH: CABG; cystoscopy, B RPG, B ureteral stent placement 11/93; cystoscopy, B ureteral stent change 2/94 MED: vancomycin, ceftriaxone, fluconazole, lactulose, senna, kayexalate, tramadol, sarna, nystatin, paxil, lipitor, lantus, humalog ISS, keppra, labetalol, meclizine, prilosec ALL: PCN PE: AVSS NAD; alert, responsive, and interactive S/NT/ND Phallus uncircumcised w/ easily retractible foreskin; meatus WNL Testes descended bilaterally and nontender Foley to gravity draining clear urine with sediment LABS: Chem7 (12/24) – 137/6.0/108/16/83/2.7/79

Table 4. Sentence retrieved from the semantic concept model, CAD

3.2 Distributional relational model

A distributional relational model can be defined over semantic concept distributions. For example, we may be interested in searching the intersection of concepts *Terrorist* and *Yemen*. So we could define a relational *natural join* operation (⋈) over *Terrorist* and *Yemen* concept distributions to identify semantically related terms at the intersection of *Terrorist* and *Yemen*. From this result set we could predict the most semantically related entities, relations, or sentences

We may also be interested in major cities in *Afghanistan* and *Pakistan*, i.e., what are the most prominent semantically similar attributes of major cities in Afghanistan Pakistan? In this case, we could formulate a query using relational addition ('+') or UNION. Alternatively, we could use relational subtraction ('-'). For example, what is specific to COPD (Chronic Obstructive Pulmonary Disorder) that is not shared by CAD (Coronary Artery Disease)?

Defining relational operators for addition and subtraction over distributions requires some thought. Given matching terms in separate distributions, how are distributions coalesced? Our approach for defining distributional operators are summarized below:

- *Natural join* (⋈) – set intersection. Only maintain matching terms in each distribution.
- *Boolean addition*: set UNION. Set semantic similarity coefficient (SSC) to the arithmetic mean of matching terms.
- *Boolean subtraction*: set SUBTRACTION. Remove terms from second operand distribution from first distribution.
- *Distributional addition*: set UNION. Set semantic similarity coefficient (SSC) to sum of matching terms, maximum 1.
- *Distributional subtraction: set SUBTRACTION.* Subtract SSC of matching terms in second operand distribution from first operand distribution, minimum 0.

Relational query operations are defined as a first-order relational algebra and can be of arbitrary complexity. Query expressions are recursively parsed into a postfix expression:

Expression (Given):
((Karachi+Islamabad+Lahore)-Pakistan)+Afghanistan
Parse (Output):
[ADD, Afghanistan, SUBTRACT, Pakistan, ADD, Lahore, ADD, Islamabad, Karachi]

The postfix expression is tranlated to a series of SQL statements, which are executed against concept distribution tables. The result set of the query defines a new concept that can in turn be used as any other distributional concept to predict entities, relations, or sentences.

4 Conclusion

We have presented an ad hoc concept modeling approach using distributional semantic models to identify and relate fine-grained entities in an online search setting. We have also presented, a novel distributional relational model for relating semantically similar concepts. The distributional concept and relational models provide a framework for future research. For example, quantitatively determining the most effective concept distribution models and distributional relational operators. What are the best architectures for scaling ad hoc distributional semantics?

Acknowledgments

This publication and project was supported by the National Center for Advancing Translational Sciences, National Institutes of Health, through Grant Number 8UL1TR000055. Its contents are solely the responsibility of the authors and do not necessarily represent the official views of the NIH.

This material is based on past research sponsored by the Air Force Research Laboratory and Air Force Office of Science and Research Visiting Faculty Research and Summer Faculty Fellowship Programs (2010-2011) agreement number (13.20.02.B4488), and current research being sponsored by the Air Force Research Laboratory under agreement number (FA8750-12-1-0031). The U.S. Government is authorized to reproduce and distribute reprints for Governmental purposes notwithstanding any copyright notation thereon.

References

Bollegala, D.T., Yutaka M., and Mitsuru I. (2010. Relational duality: Unsupervised extraction of semantic relations between entities on the web. Proceedings of the 19th international conference on World wide web. ACM.

Church, K.W., Hanks, P. 1989. Word Association Norms, Mutual Information and Lexicography. Proceedings of the 27th Annual Conference of the Association of Computational Linguistics, 76-83.

Church, K., Gale, W., Hanks, P., Hindle, D. 1991. Using Statistics in Lexical Analysis. In: Uri Zernik (ed.), Lexical Acquisition: Exploiting On-Line Resources to Build a Lexicon. New Jersey: Lawrence Erlbaum 115-164.

Copi, I. 1998. Introduction to Logic (1998). Prentice Hall College Div,

Eneko, A., et al. 2012. Semeval-2012 task 6: A pilot on semantic textual similarity. Proceedings of the First Joint Conference on Lexical and Computational Semantics-Volume 1: Proceedings of the main conference and the shared task, and Volume 2: Proceedings of the Sixth International Workshop on Semantic Evaluation. Association for Computational Linguistics.

Finkel, J., Grenager, T., and Manning, C. 2005. Incorporating Non-local Information into Information Extraction Systems by Gibbs Sampling. Proceedings of the 43nd Annual Meeting of the Association for Computational Linguistics (ACL 2005), pp. 363-370.

Firth, J.R. A synopsis of linguistic theory 1930-1955. In Studies in Linguistic Analysis, 1968. Oxford: Philological Society. (1957). Reprinted in F.R. Palmer (ed.), Selected Papers of J.R. Firth 1952-1959, London: Longman.

Kimball, R. 1996. Data Warehouse Toolkit: Practical Techniques for Building Dimensional Data Warehouses. Ralph, John Wiley.

Gray, J., et al. 1997. Data Cube: A Relational Aggregation Operator Generalizing Group-By, Cross-Tab, and Sub-Totals. Data Mining and Knowledge Discovery, Vol. 1, Issue 1.

Harris, Z. Distributional structure. 1954. Word 10 (23): 146–162.

Mihalcea, R., Corley, C., and Strapparava, C. 2006. Corpus-based and knowledge-based measures of text semantic similarity. AAAI Press. 775-780.

S. Robertson and S. Walker. Okapi/Keenbow at TREC-8,"NIST Special Publication 500-246, 2000.

Sahlgren, M. The Distributional Hypothesis. 2008. Rivista di Linguistica 20 (1): 33–53.

Turney, P. 2001. Mining the Web for Synonyms: PMI-IR versus LSA on TOEFL.

Turney, P., and Pantel, P. 2010. From frequency to meaning: Vector space models of semantics. Journal of artificial intelligence research 37.1 141-188.

Urbain, J., Frieder, O., and Goharian. N. 2009. assage relevance models for genomics search, BMC Bioinformatica, 10 (Suppl 3): S3.

Urbain, J., and Frieder. O. 2010, Exploring contextual models in chemical patent search. Advances in Multidisciplinary Retrieval. Springer Berlin Heidelberg. 60-69.

A Deep Architecture for Non-Projective Dependency Parsing

Erick R. Fonseca
University of São Paulo
Avenida Trabalhador São-carlense, 400
São Carlos, Brazil
erickrf@icmc.usp.br

Sandra M. Aluísio
University of São Paulo
Avenida Trabalhador São-carlense, 400
São Carlos, Brazil
sandra@icmc.usp.br

Abstract

Graph-based dependency parsing algorithms commonly employ features up to third order in an attempt to capture richer syntactic relations. However, each level and each feature combination must be defined manually. Besides that, input features are usually represented as huge, sparse binary vectors, offering limited generalization. In this work, we present a deep architecture for dependency parsing based on a convolutional neural network. It can examine the whole sentence structure before scoring each head/modifier candidate pair, and uses dense embeddings as input. Our model is still under ongoing work, achieving 91.6% unlabeled attachment score in the Penn Treebank.

1 Introduction

Graph-based dependency parsing works by assigning scores to each possible dependency arc between two words (plus the root), and then creating a dependency tree by selecting the arcs which yield the highest score sum (McDonald et al., 2005). The Chu-Liu-Edmonds algorithm is commonly used to extract the maximum spanning tree (MST) of the resulting graph in polynomial time, and inherently allows for non-projective trees.

Most such parsing algorithms obtain the score for an arc from word i to j as the dot product of a weight vector and a vector of binary features, $s(i, j) = \mathbf{w} \cdot \mathbf{f}(i, j)$. Their training procedure is thus essentially optimizing the weight vector.

The features, however, often follow redundant patterns: the same classifier may use as separate features: (i) head word and its POS tag, (ii) head word, and (iii) head word POS tag. This is justified first by data sparseness, since a given word may not have been seen many times in the training set (or not with a given POS tag), and the last two features serve as a fallback. Second, most approaches are based on linear classifiers, which cannot learn complex interactions between features.

Given that the scoring function deals with an arc at a time, graph-based parsers are usually restricted to features of local pairs. This is problematic when determining the head of a given word depends on its modifiers. For example, consider the two sentences in Figure 1, where the preposition *with* may be attached to a verb or a noun, depending on its complement. Including neighboring words as features in the arc scoring function may alleviate the problem, but doesn't account for long range dependencies. A more efficient solution is second or high order features, which include child or sibling arcs in the scoring function (McDonald and Pereira, 2006). Some authors explored higher order features, including, for example, grandparents and grand-siblings (Koo and Collins, 2010) or non-adjacent siblings (Carreras, 2007).

However, each new level (i.e., each higher order) must be defined through manually designed features. Furthermore, finding the exact non-projective MST in such cases is computationally intractable, making it necessary to resort to approximate solutions[1].

Another disadvantage of such systems is that fea-

[1]The projective MST, however, can be obtained in $O(n^{m+1})$ time for a model of m-th order. A common practice is to find the projective MST and then swap some edges.

Proceedings of NAACL-HLT 2015, pages 56–61,
Denver, Colorado, May 31 – June 5, 2015.

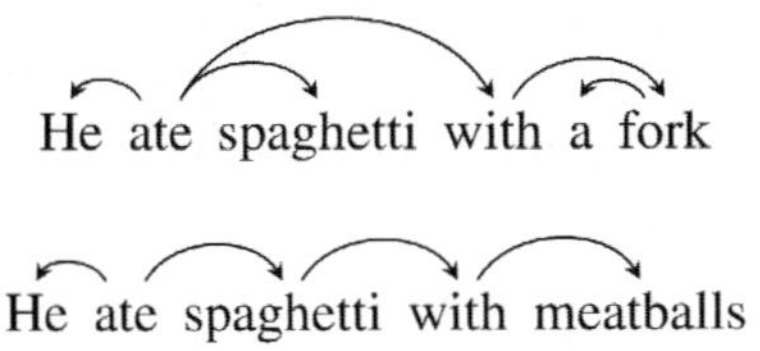

Figure 1: Example of dependency trees with different head words for *with*, depending on its complement.

tures are usually binary. Thus, each word in the system vocabulary is represented as a separate, independent feature. By contrast, a growing trend in the NLP community is to use word embeddings, which are low dimensional, dense vectors representing words (Turian et al., 2010; Collobert, 2011; Mikolov et al., 2013). Word embeddings have the advantage to deliver similar representations to words that tend to occur in the same contexts (and usually have a related meaning), and lower out-of-vocabulary impact.

In this work, we address the limitations described above with a graph-based parser architecture inspired in the SENNA system (Collobert, 2011). It takes word embeddings and POS tags as input, and uses a convolutional neural network that allows it to examine the whole sentence before giving a score for each head-dependent pair. The complexity of the scoring procedure is $O(n^3)$.

The remaining of this paper is organized as follows. Section 2 presents relevant related work with dependency parsing, word embeddings and neural architectures. Section 3 describes our model. Section 4 shows our experimental setup and results found for English, German and Dutch, and Section 5 presents our conclusions.

2 Related Work

Graph based parsers were combined with transition based ones in studies aimed at exploiting global features, which fit better with the latter (Martins et al., 2008; Nivre and McDonald, 2008). Beam search has also been used instead of exact inference in order to allow more complex features and keep the problem computationally tractable (Zhang and Clark, 2008). In contrast, our method works by examining the whole sentence in a straightforward manner before assigning a score to an arc.

There has also been studies on generating word embeddings based on syntactic relations of each word instead of its neighbors in a fixed size window (Padó and Lapata, 2007). Recently, Bansal et al. (2014) and Levy and Goldberg (2014) used similar variants of the skip-gram model (Mikolov et al., 2013) to this end: both studies parsed huge corpora with a dependency parser and then used dependency relations as context for the skip-gram algorithm.

The skip-gram model induces word representations such as to maximize the capabilities of predicting neighboring words w' given a word w. By considering *neighbors* the words with a dependency edge between them, instead of merely occurring near each other, the embeddings are able to capture more syntactic knowledge.

Some other studies employed neural architectures and word embeddings to address parsing. Socher et al. (2013), for example, recurrently combined word vectors into phrase vectors in constituency-based parse trees. Chen and Manning (2014) used an MLP network with one hidden layer to perform transition-based dependency parsing. Their network decides, for each state configuration, which action to take next.

More related to this work, Collobert (2011) used a convolutional network to address constituent parsing. Words are tagged in multiple levels, according to the constituents they are part of. A key component of the network is the convolution layer, which is capable of turning the representation of a sentence of variable size into a fixed size vector.

A very similar architecture had been previously used by Collobert et al. (2011) to perform semantic role labeling. For this task, the network had to classify each token with respect to each predicate in the sentence. We draw on this idea, making our dependency parser, implemented as a convolutional neural network, score each word with respect with a candidate head.

3 Deep Architecture

A way to avoid the need of defining each higher level of features manually is a deep architecture that examines the whole sentence before making each local decision.

Our parser first identifies unlabeled dependency arcs between words and then labels them. In the first stage, it computes a score $s(h, m, x)$ for assigning a given head h to a modifier word m within a sentence x. After having computed scores for all (h, m) combinations, we perform the Chu-Liu-Edmond's algorithm to find the maximum spanning tree.

Then, in the second stage, for each pair (h, m) previously detected, we must label the arc connecting the words. We assign a score $s(l, h, m, x)$ for each possible label l, and the label l' with the highest score is selected by the parser.

3.1 Word Representations

Each word t is represented as a concatenation of four embedding vectors: one representing the word itself, one for its POS tag, one for the relative distance between t and h and one for the relative distance between t and m. As such, the final representation varies according to each pair (h, m) being processed.

The four vectors mentioned above have independent dimensions d^{word}, d^{POS}, d^{hdist} and d^{mdist}. The vectors are drawn from matrices M_{word}, M_{POS}, M_{hdist} and M_{mdist}. As usual in research with vector space models, we take advantage of previously trained embeddings to initialize M_{word}. The other three matrices are initialized randomly; all four are adjusted during training.

The relative distance between two words t_1 and t_2 is determined as the difference in their positions in the sentence, clipped to a maximum absolute value:

$$dist(t_1, t_2) = \min(\alpha, \max(-\alpha, i - j)) \quad (1)$$

Where i and j are the numerical positions of t_1 and t_2 in x, and α is a threshold value. A positive distance means that t_1 comes first in the sentence, and a negative distance means otherwise. The matrices M_{hdist} and M_{mdist} need $2\alpha + 3$ entries: each positive and negative distance, plus a vector for distances greater than the threshold (also positive and negative) and zero. Zero distance means that t_1 and t_2 are the same.

3.2 Edge Detection

For the edge detection stage, the neural network performs as follows. All possible (h, m) pairs are considered, and all words in the sentence are examined for each decision. A convolution layer turns a variable sized input (i.e., the sentence) into a fixed size intermediate vector.

For each (h, m) candidate pair, the convolution layer applies a default weight matrix multiplication over the vectors representing all words and stores the results:

$$[C]_i = W_1 \cdot \mathrm{wr}(i, h, m), 1 \leq i \leq |x| \quad (2)$$

Where W_1 is a weight matrix, $\mathrm{wr}(i, h, m)$ is the representation (concatenation of the four vectors) for the i-th word in the sentence, considering a pair (h, m), C is a matrix containing the convolution results over the whole sentence and $[C]_i$ denotes its i-th row.

After all words in the sentence have been examined, each convolution neuron outputs the maximum value it found[2] and a bias is added to the resulting vector. The whole operation is described in Equations 3 and 4.

$$[c_{max}]_j = \max_{1 \leq i \leq |x|} [C]_{ij}, 1 \leq j \leq |c_{max}| \quad (3)$$

$$c_{out} = c_{max} + b_1 \quad (4)$$

Where c_{max} is the fixed size vector obtained after the convolution and c_{out} has the values forwarded to the next layer. Their dimension is equal to the number of convolution neurons. $[c_{max}]_j$ indicates the j-th element in the vector, and $[C]_{ij}$ indicates the element at cell (i, j) of the matrix. b_1 is a bias vector.

The second hidden layer performs another matrix multiplication and adds another bias vector. We apply a non-linear function over the resulting values: for speed, we use a hard version of the hyperbolic tangent, which just clips values greater than 1 or

[2] In fact, the actual implementation is slightly different in order to avoid repeated calculations: we store a lookup table with pre-computed values in the convolution layer considering only distance vectors, and when scoring a sentence, we create another lookup table with the results *without* considering distance vectors. Then, for each (h, m), we just have to sum the appropriate entries.

smaller than -1. Equation 5 describes the hidden layer operation.

$$h = f(W_2 \cdot c_{out} + b_2) \quad (5)$$

h represents the resulting vector in the layer, $f(\cdot)$ is our non-linear function, W_2 is a weight matrix and b_2 is a bias vector. The output layer in our network has a single neuron which outputs the score $s(h, m, x)$, obtained by a dot product between h and a weight vector w:

$$s(h, m, x) = w \cdot h \quad (6)$$

The representation of the root dependency has been discussed and shown to be a non-trivial decision (Ballesteros and Nivre, 2013). We found that a simple and elegant way to treat a dependency to the dummy root node is to model it as $s(t, t, x)$; that is, the score of a spurious dependency from a word to itself. When $s(t, t, x)$ is higher than $s(u, t, x)$ for all other words u in the sentence, word t can be viewed as not having any other word as a likely head.

During training, we perform stochastic gradient descent, sampling one sentence at a time. After the network has produced all head scores for a modifier, we apply a softmax to the output to obtain a probability distribution:

$$p(h|m, x) = \frac{e^{s(h,m,x)}}{\sum_{j \in x} e^{s(j,m,x)}} \quad (7)$$

The error gradient in the output layer is calculated in a way to increase the score for the correct pair (h^*, m) at the expense of all others:

$$\delta_{h,m} = \begin{cases} 1 - p(h|m, x), & \text{if } h = h^* \\ -p(h|m, x), & \text{otherwise} \end{cases} \quad (8)$$

The error is backpropagated until all feature matrices. The details of calculating the gradients at each layer can be found in Collobert et al. (2011).

3.3 Determining Labels

In order to label each dependency arc, we use a similar architecture. Instead of calculating the distance from each word t to every possible pair (h, m), we only need to consider the pairs that have an actual dependency, which lowers complexity to $O(n^2)$.

Also, the output layer has one neuron for each possible label, requiring a weight matrix instead of a weight vector. Thus, instead of Equation 6, we have Equation 9 for determining the network output.

$$y = W_3 \cdot h + b_3 \quad (9)$$

W_3 and b_3 are, respectively, a weight matrix and a bias vector. We pick the label with the highest score in the output vector y as the parser answer. During training, we apply a softmax on it in order to determine probabilities for each label. Error gradients are found with the same rationale than edge detection, the only difference being that we maximize the log probability of the correct label instead of the correct head.

4 Experiments

We performed experiments with English, German and Dutch data. For English, we used the default Penn Treebank data set, converted to constituency trees to CoNLL dependencies (Johansson and Nugues, 2007) using the LTH conversion tool[3] We trained on sections 2-21, validated on 22, and tested on section 23. We trained and validated models using gold POS tags; for testing, we used a neural network based tagger trained on the default WSJ POS tagging data set (sections 0-18).

For German and Dutch, we used the CoNLL 2006 datasets. We chose these two languages because they have the highest rate of non-projective edges among all languages in CoNLL 2006, and one of our method's strengths is precisely finding non-projective edges as easily as it would find projective ones. As common practice, we used gold POS tags in training, validating and testing on these languages.

We report results obtained with the English word embedding matrix M_{word} initialized with data from SKIP$_{\text{DEP}}$ and Levy and Goldberg (2014)[4] (L&G for short). For German and Dutch, we used word embeddings provided by the Polyglot project[5] (Al-Rfou et al., 2013), generated by a neural language model.

[3] `http://nlp.cs.lth.se/software/treebank_converter/`

[4] It is important to note that neither of them included the WSJ corpus in the data used to generate the embeddings.

[5] Available at `http://bit.ly/embeddings`

Parameter	Value
M_{word} embeddings size (en)[6]	100
M_{word} embeddings size (de/nl)	64
M_{POS} embeddings size	10
M_{mdist} embeddings size	5
M_{hdist} embeddings size	5
Distance threshold α [7]	10
Iterations	15
Learning rate at epoch i	$\frac{0.01}{i}$
Convolution layer size (U)	100
Convolution layer size (L)	200
Second hidden layer size (U)	500
Second hidden layer size (L)	200

Table 1: Parameter values used in experiments. (U) indicates the unlabeled stage, and (L) the labeled one. When neither is present, the same configuration was used in both.

The other matrices were initialized randomly. Since they have a relatively low number of entries, we can expect good embeddings to be obtained during supervised training. Table 1 summarizes the adjustable parameters in our model and their values.

Results are shown in Table 2. SKIP_{DEP} embeddings yielded slightly better accuracy than L&G, but still considerably low when compared to state-of-the-art parsers, which achieve 93.3%, 87.4% and 92.7% UAS on the WSJ, Dutch and German data, respectively (Zhang et al., 2014). On the other hand, the first-order parsers from Zhang et al. (2014) have 91.94%, 84.79% and 90.54% UAS.

Thus, despite our theoretical motivation, our parser's performance is on par with that of first-order models. This suggests that the simpler, local features commonly used by such models are just as effective as examining the whole sentence before issuing each local decision.

Training time is another drawback, with each epoch in edge detection for the WSJ taking around 4 hours (running on an Intel Xeon E7 2.4 GHz). However, as this was preliminary work on evaluating the architecture, we didn't focus on speeding up execution (e.g., using pruning). On the other hand, memory consumption is low: training uses around 1.5 GB of RAM and running a model needs around 320 MB.

[6] L&G embeddings originally had 300 dimensions. We applied Principal Component Analysis in order to reduce them to 100.

[7] The maximum distance is counted separately to the right and to the left. In other words, there are 10 different vectors encoding distance *before* a head/modifier, and 10 encoding distance *after*. Additionally, there is a vector for distance 0 and two for 11 or more, totaling 23 vectors.

	Dev		**Test**	
Vectors	UAS	LAS	UAS	LAS
SKIP_{DEP}	91.9%	89.0%	91.6%	88.9%
L&G	91.6%	88.6%	91.4%	88.7%
Dutch	—	—	83.4%	78.4%
German	—	—	90.1%	87.7%

Table 2: Accuracy values

5 Conclusions

We have presented a graph-based dependency parser built upon a deep architecture as an alternative to explicitly engineered high order features. However, contrary to some advancements recently obtained by such models, ours fell short of state-of-the-art accuracy.

We believe that a more elaborate version of our architecture could achieve competitive performance, while still avoiding the problems related to the input representation pointed out in the introduction. Our code and trained models are available at `https://github.com/erickrf/nlpnet`.

References

[Al-Rfou et al.2013] Rami Al-Rfou, Bryan Perozzi, and Steven Skiena. 2013. Polyglot: Distributed Word Representations for Multilingual NLP. In *Proceedings of the Seventeenth Conference on Computational Natural Language Learning*, pages 183–192, Sofia, Bulgaria, August. Association for Computational Linguistics.

[Ballesteros and Nivre2013] Miguel Ballesteros and Joakim Nivre. 2013. Going to the Roots of Dependency Parsing. *Computational Linguistics*, 39(1):5–13.

[Bansal et al.2014] Mohit Bansal, Kevin Gimpel, and Karen Livescu. 2014. Tailoring Continuous Word Representations for Dependency Parsing. In *Proceedings of the 52nd Annual Meeting of the Association for Computational Linguistics (Short Papers)*, pages 809–815.

[Carreras2007] Xavier Carreras. 2007. Experiments with a Higher-Order Projective Dependency Parser. In

Proceedings of the CoNLL Shared Task Session of EMNLP-CoNLL 2007, pages 957–961.

[Chen and Manning2014] Danqi Chen and Christopher D. Manning. 2014. A Fast and Accurate Dependency Parser using Neural Networks. In *Proceedings of the 2014 Conference on Empirical Methods in Natural Language Processing (EMNLP)*, pages 740–750.

[Collobert et al.2011] Ronan Collobert, Jason Weston, Léon Bottou, Michael Karlen, Koray Kavukcuoglu, and Pavel Kuksa. 2011. Natural Language Processing (Almost) from Scratch. *Journal of Machine Learning Research*, 12:2493–2537.

[Collobert2011] Ronan Collobert. 2011. Deep Learning for Efficient Discriminative Parsing. In *Proceedings of the 14th International Con- ference on Artificial Intelligence and Statistics (AISTATS)*.

[Johansson and Nugues2007] Richard Johansson and Pierre Nugues. 2007. Extended constituent-to-dependency conversion for english. In *NODALIDA 2007 Proceedings*.

[Koo and Collins2010] Terry Koo and Michael Collins. 2010. Efficient Third-Order Dependency Parsers. In *Proceedings of the 48th Annual Meeting of the Association for Computational Linguistics*, pages 1–11.

[Levy and Goldberg2014] Omer Levy and Yoav Goldberg. 2014. Dependency-Based Word Embeddings. In *Proceedings of the 52nd Annual Meeting of the Association for Computational Linguistics (Short Papers)*, pages 302–308.

[Martins et al.2008] André F. T. Martins, Dipanjan Das, Noah A. Smith, and Eric P. Xing. 2008. Stacking Dependency Parsers. In *Proceedings of the 2008 Conference on Empirical Methods in Natural Language Processing*, pages 157–166.

[McDonald and Pereira2006] Ryan McDonald and Fernando Pereira. 2006. Online Learning of Approximate Dependency Parsing Algorithms. In *Proceedings of the 11th Conference of the European Chapter of the Association for Computational Linguistics*, pages 81–88.

[McDonald et al.2005] Ryan McDonald, Fernando Pereira, Kiril Ribarov, and Jan Hajič. 2005. Non-projective Dependency Parsing using Spanning Tree Algorithms. In *Proceedings of Human Language Technology Conference and Conference on Empirical Methods in Natural Language Processing*, pages 523–530.

[Mikolov et al.2013] Tomas Mikolov, Kai Chen, Greg Corrado, and Jeffrey Dean. 2013. Efficient estimation of word representations in vector space. In *Proceedings of the ICLR*.

[Nivre and McDonald2008] Joakim Nivre and Ryan McDonald. 2008. Integrating Graph-Based and Transition-Based Dependency Parsers. In *Proceedings of ACL-08: HLT*, pages 950–958.

[Padó and Lapata2007] Sebastian Padó and Mirella Lapata. 2007. Dependency-Based Construction of Semantic Space Models. *Computational Linguistics*, 33(2):161–199.

[Socher et al.2013] Richard Socher, John Bauer, Christopher D Manning, and Andrew Y Ng. 2013. Parsing with Compositional Vector Grammars. In *Proceedings of the 51st Annual Meeting of the Association for Computational Linguistics*, pages 455–465.

[Turian et al.2010] Joseph Turian, Lev Ratinov, and Yoshua Bengio. 2010. Word representations : A simple and general method for semi-supervised learning. In *Proceedings of the 48th Annual Meeting of the Association for Computational Linguistics*, pages 384–394.

[Zhang and Clark2008] Yue Zhang and Stephen Clark. 2008. A Tale of Two Parsers : investigating and combining graph-based and transition-based dependency parsing using beam-search. In *Proceedings of the 2008 Conference on Empirical Methods in Natural Language Processing*, pages 562–571.

[Zhang et al.2014] Yuan Zhang, Tao Lei, Regina Barzilay, and Tommi Jaakkola. 2014. Greed is Good if Randomized : New Inference for Dependency Parsing. In *Proceedings of the 2014 Conference on Empirical Methods in Natural Language Processing (EMNLP)*, pages 1013–1024.

Short Text Clustering via Convolutional Neural Networks

Jiaming Xu, Peng Wang, Guanhua Tian, Bo Xu, Jun Zhao,
Fangyuan Wang, Hongwei Hao
Institute of Automation, Chinese Academy of Sciences. 100190, Beijing, P.R. China
{jiaming.xu, peng.wang, boxu, guanhua.tian}@ia.ac.cn,
jzhao@nlpr.ia.ac.cn, {fangyuan.wang, hongwei.hao}@ia.ac.cn

Abstract

Short text clustering has become an increasing important task with the popularity of social media, and it is a challenging problem due to its sparseness of text representation. In this paper, we propose a Short Text Clustering via Convolutional neural networks (abbr. to STCC), which is more beneficial for clustering by considering one constraint on learned features through a self-taught learning framework without using any external tags/labels. First, we embed the original keyword features into compact binary codes with a locality-preserving constraint. Then, word embeddings are explored and fed into convolutional neural networks to learn deep feature representations, with the output units fitting the pre-trained binary code in the training process. After obtaining the learned representations, we use K-means to cluster them. Our extensive experimental study on two public short text datasets shows that the deep feature representation learned by our approach can achieve a significantly better performance than some other existing features, such as term frequency-inverse document frequency, Laplacian eigenvectors and average embedding, for clustering.

1 Introduction

Different from the normal text clustering, short text clustering has the problem of sparsity (Aggarwal and Zhai, 2012). Most words only occur once in each short text, as a result, the term frequency-inverse document frequency (TF-IDF) measure cannot work well in the short text setting. In order to address this problem, some researchers work on expanding and enriching the context of data from Wikipedia (Banerjee et al., 2007) or an ontology (Fodeh et al., 2011). However, these methods involve solid natural language processing (NLP) knowledge and still use high-dimensional representation which may result in a waste of both memory and computation time. Another way to overcome these issues is to explore some sophisticated models to cluster short texts. For example, Yin and Wang (2014) proposed a Dirichlet multinomial mixture model-based approach for short text clustering and Cai et al. (2005) clustered texts using Locality Preserving Indexing (LPI) algorithm. Yet how to design an effective model is an open question, and most of these methods directly trained based on bag-of-words (BoW) are shallow structures which cannot preserve the accurate semantic similarities.

With the recent revival of interest in Deep Neural Network (DNN), many researchers have concentrated on using Deep Learning to learn features. Hinton and Salakhutdinov (2006) use deep auto encoder (DAE) to learn text representation from raw text representation. Recently, with the help of word embedding, neural networks demonstrate their great performance in terms of constructing text representation, such as Recursive Neural Network (RecNN) (Socher et al., 2011; Socher et al., 2013) and Recurrent Neural Network (RNN) (Mikolov et al., 2011). However, RecNN exhibits high time complexity to construct the textual tree, and RNN, using the layer computed at the last word to represent the text, is a biased model (Lai et al., 2015). More recently, Convolution Neural Network (CNN), applying convolutional filters to capture local features, has achieved a better performance in many NLP applications, such as sentence modeling (Blunsom et al., 2014), relation classification (Zeng et al., 2014), and other traditional NLP tasks (Collobert et al., 2011). Most of the previous works focus CNN on solving supervised NLP tasks, while in this paper we aim to explore the power of CNN on one unsupervised NLP task, short text clustering.

To address the above challenges, we systematically introduce a short text clustering method via con-

Proceedings of NAACL-HLT 2015, pages 62–69,
Denver, Colorado, May 31 – June 5, 2015. ©2015 Association for Computational Linguistics

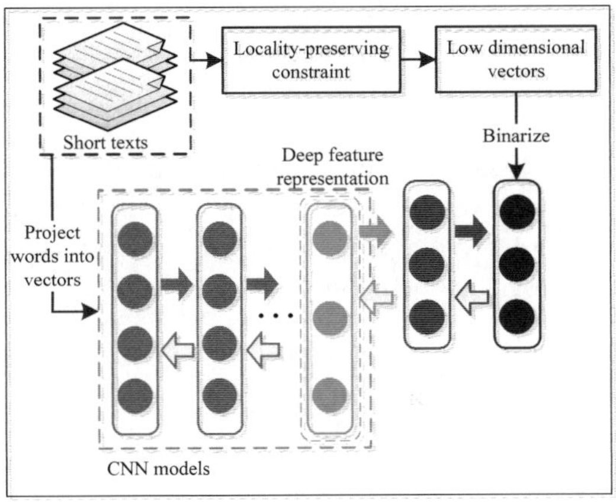

Figure 1: Architecture of the proposed short text clustering via convolutional neural networks

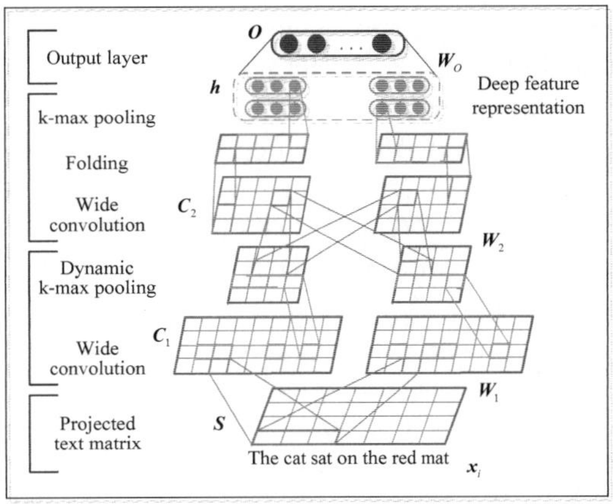

Figure 2: Dynamic convolutional neural network used for extracting deep feature representation

volutional neural networks. An overall architecture of the proposed method is illustrated in Figure 1. Given a short text collection $\mathbf{X}$, the goal of this work is to cluster these texts into clusters $\mathbb{C}$ based on the deep feature representation $\mathbf{h}$ learned from CNN models. In order to train the CNN models, we, inspired by (Zhang et al., 2010), utilize a self-taught learning framework in our work. In particular, we first embed the original features into compact binary code $\mathbf{B}$ with a locality-preserving constraint. Then word vectors $\mathbf{S}$ projected from word embeddings are fed into a CNN model to learn the feature representation $\mathbf{h}$ and the output units are used to fit the pre-trained binary code $\mathbf{B}$. After obtaining the learned features, traditional K-means algorithm is employed to cluster texts into clusters $\mathbb{C}$. The main contributions of this paper are summarized as follows:

1). To the best of our knowledge, this is the first attempt to explore the feasibility and effectiveness of combining CNN and traditional semantic constraint, with the help of word embedding to solve one unsupervised learning task, short text clustering.

2). We learn deep feature representations with locality-preserving constraint through a self-taught learning framework, and our approach do not use any external tags/labels or complicated NLP pre-processing.

3). We conduct experiments on two short text datasets. The experimental results demonstrate that the proposed method achieves excellent performance in terms of both accuracy and normalized mutual information.

The remainder of this paper is organized as follows: In Section 2, we first describe the proposed approach STCC and implementation details. Experimental results and analyses are presented in Section 3. In Section 4, we briefly survey several related works. Finally, conclusions are given in the last Section.

2 Methodology

2.1 Convolutional Neural Networks

In this section, we will briefly review one popular deep convolutional neural network, Dynamic Convolutional Neural Network (DCNN) (Blunsom et al., 2014), which is the foundation of our proposed method.

Taking a neural network with two convolutional layers in Figure 2 as an example, the network transforms raw input text to a powerful representation. Particularly, let $\mathbf{X} = \{\mathbf{x}_i : \mathbf{x}_i \in \mathbb{R}^{d \times 1}\}_{i=1,2,\dots,n}$ denote the set of input n texts, where d is the dimensionality of the original keyword features. Each raw text vector $\mathbf{x}_i$ is projected into a matrix representation $\mathbf{S} \in \mathbb{R}^{d_w \times s}$ by looking up a word embedding $\mathbf{E}$, where d_w is the dimension of word embedding features and s is the length of one text. We also let $\tilde{\mathbf{W}} = \{\mathbf{W}_i\}_{i=1,2}$ and $\mathbf{W}_O$ denote the weights of the neural networks. The network defines a transformation $f(\cdot) : \mathbb{R}^{d \times 1} \rightarrow \mathbb{R}^{r \times 1}$ $(d \gg r)$ which transforms an raw input text $\mathbf{x}$ to a r-dimensional deep representation $\mathbf{h}$. There are three basic operations described as follows:

– **Wide one-dimensional convolution** This operation is applied to an individual row of the sentence matrix $\mathbf{S} \in \mathbb{R}^{d_w \times s}$, and yields a set of sequences $\mathbf{C}_i \in \mathbb{R}^{s+m-1}$ where m is the width of convolutional filter.

– **Folding** In this operation, every two rows in a feature map component-wise are simply summed. For a map of d_w rows, folding returns a map of $d_w/2$ rows, thus halving the size of the representation.

– **Dymantic k-max pooling** Given a fixed pooling parameter k_{top} for the topmost convolutional layer, the parameter k of k-max pooling in the l-th convolutional layer can be computed as follows:

$$k_l = \max(k_{top}, \left\lceil \frac{L-l}{L} s \right\rceil), \quad (1)$$

where L is the total number of convolutional layers in the network.

2.2 Locality-preserving Constraint

Here, we first pre-train binary code $\mathbf{B}$ based on the keyword features with a locality-preserving constraint, and choose Laplacian affinity loss, also used in some previous works (Weiss et al., 2009; Zhang et al., 2010). The optimization can be written as:

$$\begin{aligned} &\min_{\mathbf{B}} \sum_{i,j=1}^{n} S_{ij} \left\| \mathbf{b}_i - \mathbf{b}_j \right\|_F^2 \\ &s.t.\ \mathbf{B} \in \{-1,1\}^{n \times q},\ \mathbf{B}^T \mathbf{1} = \mathbf{0},\ \mathbf{B}^T\mathbf{B} = \mathbf{I}, \end{aligned} \quad (2)$$

where S_{ij} is the pairwise similarity between texts $\mathbf{x}_i$ and $\mathbf{x}_j$, and $\|\cdot\|_F$ is the Frobenius norm. The problem is relaxed by discarding $\mathbf{B} \in \{-1,1\}^{n \times q}$, and the q-dimensional real-valued vectors $\tilde{\mathbf{B}}$ can be learned from Laplacian Eigenmap. Then, we get the binary code $\mathbf{B}$ via the media vector $median(\tilde{\mathbf{B}})$. In particular, we construct the $n \times n$ local similarity matrix $\mathbf{S}$ by using heat kernel as follows:

$$S_{ij} = \begin{cases} \exp(-\frac{\|\mathbf{x}_i - \mathbf{x}_j\|^2}{2\sigma^2}), & if\ x_i \in N_k(\mathbf{x}_j)\ or\ vice\ \text{versa} \\ 0, & otherwise \end{cases} \quad (3)$$

where, σ is a tuning parameter (default is 1) and $\mathbf{N}_k(\mathbf{x})$ represents the set of k-nearest-neighbors of $\mathbf{x}$.

The last layer of CNN is an output layer as follows:

$$\mathbf{O} = \mathbf{W}_O \mathbf{h}, \quad (4)$$

where, $\mathbf{h}$ is the deep feature representation, $\mathbf{O} \in \mathbb{R}^q$ is the output vector and $\mathbf{W}_O \in \mathbb{R}^{q \times r}$ is weight matrix. In order to fit the pre-trained binary code $\mathbf{B}$, we apply q logistic operations to the output vector $\mathbf{O}$ as follows:

$$p_i = \frac{\exp(\mathbf{O}_i)}{1 + \exp(\mathbf{O}_i)}. \quad (5)$$

2.3 Learning

All of the parameters to be trained are defined as θ.

$$\theta = \{\mathbf{E}, \tilde{\mathbf{W}}, \mathbf{W}_O\}. \quad (6)$$

Given the training text collection $\mathbf{X}$, and the pre-trained binary code $\mathbf{B}$, the log likelihood of the parameters can be written down as follows:

$$J(\theta) = \sum_{i=1}^{n} \log p(\mathbf{b}_i | \mathbf{x}_i, \theta). \quad (7)$$

Following the previous work (Blunsom et al., 2014), we train the network with mini-batches by back-propagation and perform the gradient-based optimization using the Adagrad update rule (Duchi et al., 2011). For regularization, we employ dropout with 50% rate to the penultimate layer (Blunsom et al., 2014; Kim, 2014).

2.4 K-means for Clustering

With the given short texts, we first utilize the trained deep neural network to obtain the semantic representations $\mathbf{h}$, and then employ traditional K-means algorithm to perform clustering.

3 Experiments

3.1 Datasets

We test our algorithm on two public text datasets, and the summary statistics of the datasets are described in Table 1.

SearchSnippets[1]. This dataset was selected from the results of web search transaction using predefined phrases of 8 different domains (Phan et al., 2008).

[1] http://jwebpro.sourceforge.net/data-web-snippets.tar.gz.

StackOverflow[2]. We use the challenge data published in Kaggle.com[3]. This dataset consists 3,370,528 samples through July 31st, 2012 to August 14, 2012. In our experiments, we randomly select 20, 000 question titles from 20 different tags.

For these datasets, we do not remove any stop words or symbols in the text.

Dataset	C	Number	L(mean/max)	$\|V\|$
Snippets	8	12340	17.88/38	30642
Stack	20	20000	8.31/34	22956

Table 1: Statistics for the text datasets. C: the number of classes; Num: the dataset size; L(mean/max): the mean and max length of texts and $|V|$: the vocabulary size.

3.2 Pre-trained Word Vectors

We use the publicly available word2vec tool to train word embeddings, and the most parameters are set as same as Mikolov et al. (2013) to train word vectors on Google News setting[4], excepts of vector dimensionality using 48 and minimize count using 5. For SearchSnippets, we train word vectors on Wikipedia dumps[5]. For StackOverflow, we train word vectors on the whole corpus of the StackOverflow dataset described above which includes the question titles and post contents. The coverage of these learned vectors on two datasets are listed in Table 2, and the words not present in the set of pre-trained words are initialized randomly.

Dataset	$\|V\|$	$\|T\|$
SearchSnippets	23826 (77%)	211575 (95%)
StackOverflow	19639 (85%)	162998 (97%)

Table 2: Coverage of word embeddings on two datasets. $|V|$ is the vocabulary size and $|T|$ is the number of tokens.

3.3 Comparisons

We compare the proposed method with some most popular clustering algorithms:

- **K-means** K-means (Wagstaff et al., 2001) on original keyword features which are respectively weighted with term frequency (TF) and term frequency-inverse document frequency (TF-IDF).
- **Spectral Clustering** This baseline (Belkin and Niyogi, 2001) uses Laplacian Eigenmaps (LE) and subsequently employ K-means algorithm. The dimension of subspace is default set to the number of clusters (Ng et al., 2002; Cai et al., 2005), we also iterate the dimensions ranging from 10:10:200 to get the best performance, that is 20 on SearchSnippets and 70 on StackOverflow in our expriments.
- **Average Embedding** K-means on the weighted average of the word embeddings which are respectively weighted with TF and TF-IDF. Huang et al. (2012) also used this strategy as the global context in their task and Lai et al. (2015) used this in text classification.

3.4 Evaluation Metrics

The clustering performance is evaluated by comparing the clustering results of texts with the tags/labels provided by the text corpus. Two metrics, the accuracy (ACC) and the normalized mutual information metric (NMI), are used to measure the clustering performance (Cai et al., 2005; Huang et al., 2014). Given a text $\mathbf{x}_i$, let c_i and y_i be the obtained cluster label and the label provided by the corpus, respectively. Accuracy is defined as:

$$ACC = \frac{\sum_{i=1}^{n} \delta(y_i, map(c_i))}{n}, \quad (8)$$

where, n is the total number of texts, $\delta(x, y)$ is the indicator function that equals one if $x = y$ and equals zero otherwise, and $map(c_i)$ is the permutation mapping function that maps each cluster label c_i to the equivalent label from the text data by Hungarian algorithm (Papadimitriou and Steiglitz, 1998).

Normalized mutual information (Chen et al., 2011) between tag/label set $\mathbf{Y}$ and cluster set $\mathbb{C}$ is a popular metric used for evaluating clustering tasks. It is defined as follows:

$$NMI(\mathbf{Y}, \mathbb{C}) = \frac{MI(\mathbf{Y}, \mathbb{C})}{\sqrt{H(\mathbf{Y})H(\mathbb{C})}}, \quad (9)$$

[2]https://github.com/jacoxu/StackOverflow.

[3]https://www.kaggle.com/c/predict-closed-questions-on-stack-overflow/download/train.zip.

[4]https://groups.google.com/forum/#!topic/word2vec-toolkit/lxbl_MB29Ic.

[5]http://dumps.wikimedia.org/enwiki/latest/enwiki-latest-pages-articles.xml.bz2.

where, $MI(\mathbf{Y}, \mathbb{C})$ is the mutual information between $\mathbf{Y}$ and $\mathbb{C}$, $H(\cdot)$ is entropy and the denominator $\sqrt{H(\mathbf{Y})H(\mathbb{C})}$ is used for normalizing the mutual information to be in the range of [0, 1].

3.5 Hyperparameter Settings

In our experiments, the most of parameters are set uniformly for these datasets. Following previous study (Cai et al., 2005), the parameter k in Eq. 3 is fixed to 15 when constructing the graph Laplacians in our approach, as well as in spectral clustering. For CNN model, we manually choose a same architecture for the two datasets. More specifically, in our experiments, the networks has two convolutional layers similar as the example in Figure 2. The widths of the convolutional filters are both 3. The value of k for the top k-max pooling is 5. The number of feature maps at the first convolutional layer is 12, and 8 feature maps at the second convolutional layer. Both those two convolutional layers are followed by a folding layer. We further set the dimension of word embeddings d_w as 48. Finally, the dimension of the deep feature representation r is fixed to 480. Moreover, we set the learning rate λ as 0.01 and the mini-batch training size as 200. The output size q in Eq. 4 and Eq. 2 is set same as the best dimensions of subspace in the baseline method, spectral clustering, as described in Section 3.3.

For initial centroids have significant impact on clustering results when utilizing the K-means algorithms, we repeat K-means for multiple times with random initial centroids (specifically, 100 times for statistical significance). The final results reported are the average of 5 trials with all clustering methods on two text datasets.

3.6 Quantitative Results

Here, we firstly evaluate the influence of the iteration number in our method. Figure 3 shows the change of ACC and NMI as the iteration number increases on two text datasets. It can be found that the performance rises steadily in the first ten iterations, which demonstrates that our method is effective. In the period of 10$\sim$20 iterations, ACC and NMI become relatively stable on both two texts. In the following experiments, we report the results after 10 iterations.

We report ACC and NMI performance of all the clustering methods in Table 3. The experimental results show that Spectral Clustering and Average Embedding significantly better than K-means on two datasets. It is because K-means directly construct the similarity structure from the original keyword feature space while Average Embedding and Spectral Clustering extract the semantic features using shallow structure models. Compared with the best baselines, the proposed STCC extracting deep learned representation from convolutional neural network achieves large improvement on these datasets by 2.33%/4.86% and 14.23%/10.01% (ACC/NMI) on SearchSnippets and StackOverflow, respectively. Note that TF-IDF weighting gives a more remarkable improvement for K-means, while TF weighting works better than TF-IDF weighting for Average Embedding. Maybe the reason is that pre-trained word embeddings encode some useful information from external corpus and are able to get even better results without TF-IDF weighting.

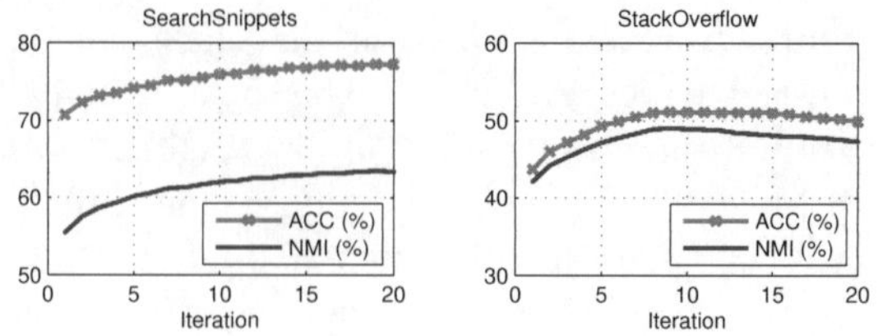

Figure 3: Influence of the iteration number on two text datasets.

In Figure 4 and Figure 5, we further report 2-dimensional embeddings using stochastic neighbor embedding (Van der Maaten and Hinton, 2008)[6] of the feature representations used in the clustering methods. We can see that the 2-dimensional embedding results of deep features representation learned from our STCC show more clear-cut margins among different semantic topics (that is, tags/labels) on two short text datasets.

4 Related Work

In this section, we review the related work from the following two perspectives: short text clustering and deep neural networks.

4.1 Short Text Clustering

There have been several studies that attempted to overcome the sparseness of short representation.

[6]http://lvdmaaten.github.io/tsne/.

	SearchSnippets		StackOverflow	
Method	ACC (%)	NMI (%)	ACC (%)	NMI (%)
K-means (TF)	24.75±2.22	9.03±2.30	13.51±2.18	7.81±2.56
K-means (TF-IDF)	33.77±3.92	21.40±4.35	20.31±3.95	15.64±4.68
Spectral Clustering	63.90±5.36	48.44±2.39	27.55±0.93	21.03±0.37
Spectral Clustering (best)	74.76±5.08	58.30±1.97	37.17±1.62	26.27±0.86
Average Embedding (TF-IDF)	62.05±5.27	46.64±1.87	37.02±1.29	35.58±0.84
Average Embedding (TF)	64.63±4.84	50.59±1.71	37.22±1.57	38.43±1.13
STCC	**77.09±3.99**	**63.16±1.56**	**51.13±2.80**	**49.03±1.46**

Table 3: Comparison of ACC and NMI of clustering methods on two short text datasets. For Spectral Clustering, the dimension of subspace are set to the number of clusters, and Spectral Clustering (best) get the best performance by iterating the dimensions ranging from 10:10:200. More details about the baseline setting are described in Section 3.3

One way is to expand and enrich the context of data. For example, Banerjee et al. (2007) proposed a method of improving the accuracy of short text clustering by enriching their representation with additional features from Wikipedia, and Fodeh et al. (2011) incorporate semantic knowledge from an ontology into text clustering. Another way is to explore some sophisticated models to cluster short text. For example, Yin and Wang (2014) proposed a Dirichlet multinomial mixture model-based approach for short text clustering and Cai et al. (2005) applied the LPI algorithm for text clustering. Moreover, some studies both focus the above two streams. For example, Tang et al. (2012) proposed a novel framework which performs multi-language knowledge integration and feature reduction simultaneously through matrix factorization techniques. However, the former works need solid NLP knowledge while the later works are shallow structures which can not fully capture accurate semantic similarities.

4.2 Deep Neural Networks

With the recent revival of interest in DNN, many researchers have concentrated on using Deep Learning to learn features. Hinton and Salakhutdinov (2006) use DAE to learn text representation. During the fine-tuning procedure, they use backpropagation to find codes that are good at reconstructing the word-count vector.

Recently, researchers propose to use external corpus to learn a distributed representation for each word, called word embedding (Turian et al., 2010), to improve DNN performance on NLP tasks. The skip-gram and continuous bag-of-words models of (Mikolov et al., 2013) propose a simple single-layer architecture based on the inner product between two word vectors, and Jeffrey Pennington et al. (2014) introduce a new model for word representation, called GloVe, which captures the global corpus statistics.

Based on word embedding, neural networks can capture true meaningful syntactic and semantic regularities, such as RecNN (Socher et al., 2011; Socher et al., 2013) and RNN (Mikolov et al., 2011). However, RecNN exhibits high time complexity to construct the textual tree, and RNN, using the layer computed at the last word to represent the text, is a biased model. Recently, CNN, applying convolving filters to local features, has been successfully exploited for many supervised NLP learning tasks as described in Section 1. This paper, to our best knowledge, is the first time to explore the power of CNN and word embedding to solve one unsupervised learning task, short text clustering.

5 Conclusions

In this paper, we proposed a short text clustering based on deep feature representation learned from CNN without using any external tags/labels and complicated NLP pre-processing. As experimental study shows that STCC can achieve significantly better performance than the baseline methods.

Acknowledgments

We thank anonymous reviewers for their comments, and this work is supported by the National Natural

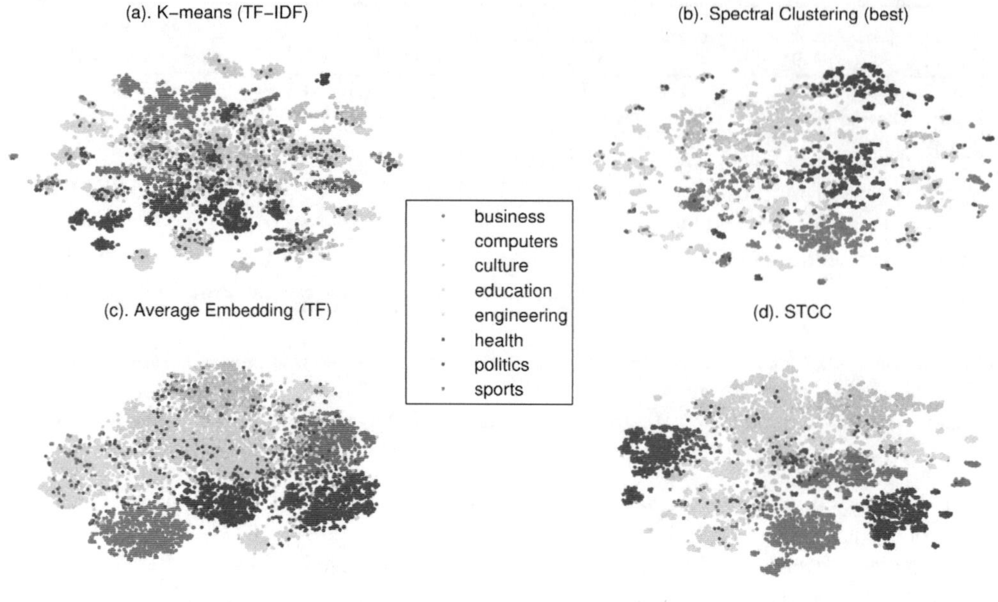

Figure 4: A 2-dimensional embedding of original keyword features weighted with TF-IDF (a), Laplacian eigenvectors (b), average embeddings weighted with TF (c) and deep learned features (d) which are respectively used in K-means (TF-IDF), Spectral Clustering (best), Average Embeddings (TF) and the proposed STCC methods on SearchSnippets. (Best viewed in color)

Science Foundation of China (No. 61203281 and No. 61303172) and Hundred Talents Program of Chinese Academy of Sciences (No. Y3S4011D31).

References

Charu C Aggarwal and ChengXiang Zhai. 2012. A survey of text clustering algorithms. In *Mining Text Data*, pages 77–128. Springer.

Somnath Banerjee, Krishnan Ramanathan, and Ajay Gupta. 2007. Clustering short texts using wikipedia. In *SIGIR*, pages 787–788. ACM.

Mikhail Belkin and Partha Niyogi. 2001. Laplacian eigenmaps and spectral techniques for embedding and clustering. In *NIPS*, volume 14, pages 585–591.

Phil Blunsom, Edward Grefenstette, Nal Kalchbrenner, et al. 2014. A convolutional neural network for modelling sentences. In *ACL*.

Deng Cai, Xiaofei He, and Jiawei Han. 2005. Document clustering using locality preserving indexing. *Knowledge and Data Engineering, IEEE Transactions on*, 17(12):1624–1637.

Wen-Yen Chen, Yangqiu Song, Hongjie Bai, Chih-Jen Lin, and Edward Y Chang. 2011. Parallel spectral clustering in distributed systems. *Pattern Analysis and Machine Intelligence, IEEE Transactions on*, 33(3):568–586.

Ronan Collobert, Jason Weston, Léon Bottou, Michael Karlen, Koray Kavukcuoglu, and Pavel Kuksa. 2011. Natural language processing (almost) from scratch. *JMLR*, 12:2493–2537.

John Duchi, Elad Hazan, and Yoram Singer. 2011. Adaptive subgradient methods for online learning and stochastic optimization. *JMLR*, 12:2121–2159.

Samah Fodeh, Bill Punch, and Pang-Ning Tan. 2011. On ontology-driven document clustering using core semantic features. *Knowledge and information systems*, 28(2):395–421.

Geoffrey E Hinton and Ruslan R Salakhutdinov. 2006. Reducing the dimensionality of data with neural networks. *Science*, 313(5786):504–507.

Eric H Huang, Richard Socher, Christopher D Manning, and Andrew Y Ng. 2012. Improving word representations via global context and multiple word prototypes. In *ACL*, pages 873–882. Association for Computational Linguistics.

Peihao Huang, Yan Huang, Wei Wang, and Liang Wang. 2014. Deep embedding network for clustering. In *Pattern Recognition (ICPR), 2014 22nd International Conference on*, pages 1532–1537. IEEE.

Yoon Kim. 2014. Convolutional neural networks for sentence classification. *arXiv preprint arXiv:1408.5882*.

Siwei Lai, Liheng Xu, Kang Liu, and Jun Zhao. 2015. Recurrent convolutional neural networks for text classification. In *AAAI*.

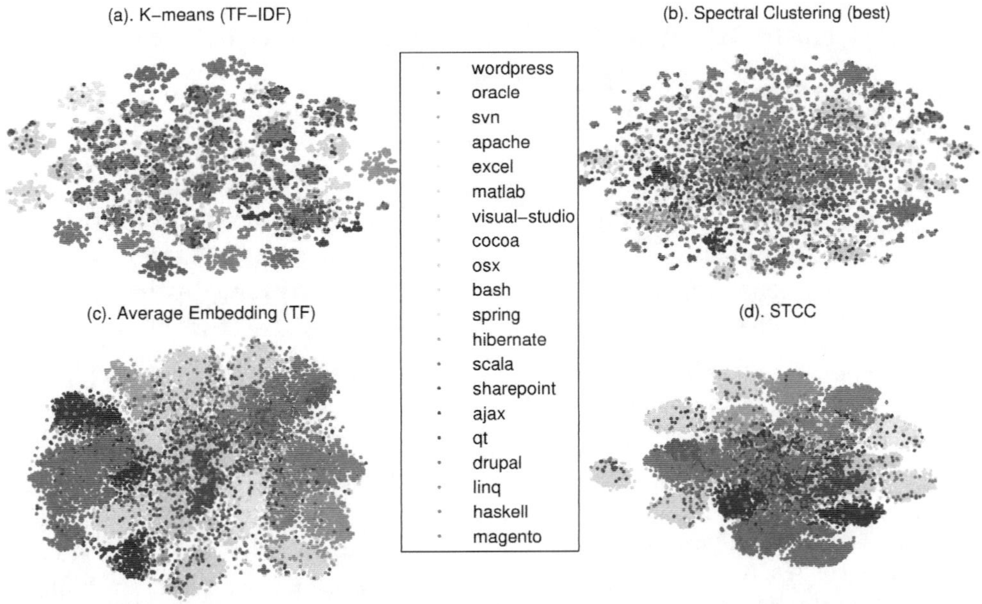

Figure 5: A 2-dimensional embedding of original keyword features weighted with TF-IDF (a), Laplacian eigenvectors (b), average embeddings weighted with TF (c) and deep learned features (d) which are respectively used in K-means (TF-IDF), Spectral Clustering (best), Average Embeddings (TF) and the proposed STCC methods on StackOverflow. (Best viewed in color)

Tomas Mikolov, Stefan Kombrink, Lukas Burget, Jan H Cernocky, and Sanjeev Khudanpur. 2011. Extensions of recurrent neural network language model. In *ICASSP*, pages 5528–5531. IEEE.

Tomas Mikolov, Ilya Sutskever, Kai Chen, Greg S Corrado, and Jeff Dean. 2013. Distributed representations of words and phrases and their compositionality. In *NIPS*, pages 3111–3119.

Andrew Y Ng, Michael I Jordan, Yair Weiss, et al. 2002. On spectral clustering: Analysis and an algorithm. *NIPS*, 2:849–856.

Christos H Papadimitriou and Kenneth Steiglitz. 1998. *Combinatorial optimization: algorithms and complexity*. Courier Corporation.

Jeffrey Pennington, Richard Socher, and Christopher D Manning. 2014. Glove: Global vectors for word representation. *EMNLP*, 12.

Xuan-Hieu Phan, Le-Minh Nguyen, and Susumu Horiguchi. 2008. Learning to classify short and sparse text & web with hidden topics from large-scale data collections. In *WWW*, pages 91–100. ACM.

Richard Socher, Jeffrey Pennington, Eric H Huang, Andrew Y Ng, and Christopher D Manning. 2011. Semi-supervised recursive autoencoders for predicting sentiment distributions. In *EMNLP*, pages 151–161.

Richard Socher, Alex Perelygin, Jean Y Wu, Jason Chuang, Christopher D Manning, Andrew Y Ng, and Christopher Potts. 2013. Recursive deep models for semantic compositionality over a sentiment treebank. In *EMNLP*, volume 1631, page 1642. Citeseer.

Jiliang Tang, Xufei Wang, Huiji Gao, Xia Hu, and Huan Liu. 2012. Enriching short text representation in microblog for clustering. *Frontiers of Computer Science*, 6(1):88–101.

Joseph Turian, Lev Ratinov, and Yoshua Bengio. 2010. Word representations: a simple and general method for semi-supervised learning. In *ACL*, pages 384–394.

Laurens Van der Maaten and Geoffrey Hinton. 2008. Visualizing data using t-sne. *JMLR*, 9(2579-2605):85.

Kiri Wagstaff, Claire Cardie, Seth Rogers, Stefan Schrödl, et al. 2001. Constrained k-means clustering with background knowledge. In *ICML*, volume 1, pages 577–584.

Yair Weiss, Antonio Torralba, and Rob Fergus. 2009. Spectral hashing. In *NIPS*, pages 1753–1760.

Jianhua Yin and Jianyong Wang. 2014. A dirichlet multinomial mixture model-based approach for short text clustering. In *SIGKDD*, pages 233–242. ACM.

Daojian Zeng, Kang Liu, Siwei Lai, Guangyou Zhou, and Jun Zhao. 2014. Relation classification via convolutional deep neural network. In *COLING*, pages 2335–2344.

Dell Zhang, Jun Wang, Deng Cai, and Jinsong Lu. 2010. Self-taught hashing for fast similarity search. In *SIGIR*, pages 18–25. ACM.

A Word-Embedding-based Sense Index for Regular Polysemy Representation

Marco Del Tredici
Universitat Pompeu Fabra
Roc Boronat, 138
Barcelona, Spain
marco.deltredici@upf.edu

Núria Bel
Universitat Pompeu Fabra
Roc Boronat, 138
Barcelona, Spain
nuria.bel@upf.edu

Abstract

We present a method for the detection and representation of polysemous nouns, a phenomenon that has received little attention in NLP. The method is based on the exploitation of the semantic information preserved in Word Embeddings. We first prove that polysemous nouns instantiating a particular sense alternation form a separate class when clustering nouns in a lexicon. Such a class, however, does not include those polysemes in which a sense is strongly predominant. We address this problem and present a sense index that, for a given pair of lexical classes, defines the degree of membership of a noun to each class: polysemy is hence implicitly represented as an intermediate value on the continuum between two classes. We finally show that by exploiting the information provided by the sense index it is possible to accurately detect polysemous nouns in the dataset.

1 Introduction

A major issue in lexical semantics is regular polysemy (also known as *systematic* or *logical* polysemy), the phenomenon whereby words belonging to a semantic class can predictably act as members of another class (Pustejovsky, 1991; Martínez Alonso et al., 2013). For example, the word *chicken* can be considered a member of the class ANIMAL but also of FOOD, thus defining its senses in terms of lexical semantic classes. For some polysemous nouns one sense can be much more frequent than the other, thus causing asymmetry in sense predominance; this is the case of *turkey*, in which the food sense is clearly more frequent than the animal one (Copestake and Briscoe, 1995).

Given its pervasiveness in natural language, regular polysemy has been extensively investigated in lexical semantics (Apresjan, 1974; Nunberg, 1992). However, only few works attempted to computationally model this phenomenon (Copestake, 2013; Boleda et al., 2012b). The vast majority of applications treat regular polysemy like other phenomena of lexical ambiguity, such as homography, not considering the relevant theoretical differences between those phenomena, for example that regular polysemy is predictable, while homography is not (Utt and Padó, 2011). Information on regular polysemy would be valuable for a task like Word Sense Disambiguation, since it would reduce the number of possible options when choosing the right sense of a word. More generally, every lexical resource would benefit from the capability to cope with the shifts of meaning produced by regular polysemy, and this, in turn, would lead to improvements in several NLP applications as such machine translation, textual entailment or text analytics.

In this paper we present a method for polysemy detection and representation based on Word Embeddings (WE) (Mikolov et al., 2013a). WE are low dimensional, dense and real-valued vectors which preserve word syntactic and semantic information in a Vector Space Model (VSM). WE have recently been proved to be efficient in several NLP tasks, such as detection of relational similarity (Mikolov et al., 2013d), word similarity tasks (Mikolov et al., 2013a) and automatic building of bilingual lexica (Mikolov et al., 2013b), in which this word repre-

Proceedings of NAACL-HLT 2015, pages 70–78,
Denver, Colorado, May 31 – June 5, 2015.

sentations outperformed others with state-of-the-art methods (Baroni et al., 2014).

However, at the best of our knowledge, this is the first work in which WE are used to represent and account for regular polysemy. Our work departs from the assumption that lexical classes related by regular polysemy are limited and known and that since the class-related senses of a polysemous nouns can be considered as modulations of meaning of a single lemma (Copestake and Briscoe, 1995), they are to be represented by a single vector. As a first step, we will prove through a clustering task that nouns instantiating a particular sense alternation (e.g. animal/food) group together and separately from non-polysemous nouns, forming a distinct cluster. Such a cluster, however, does not include polysemous nouns with a strong sense asymmetry. Therefore, obtained clustering information is exploited in order to assign each noun a *sense index*, which can be thought as the value associated to a noun on a continuum, whose ends are lexical classes, and where polysemy is implicitly represented as an intermediate value between two classes. Such an index allows to represent sense modulation of disemous nouns (i.e. polysemes with two senses) and to account for the predominance of one the senses, if any, and therefore to accurately detect polysemes.

The main contribution of the work is a novel method for the identification and representation of polysemous nouns, which accounts for the semantic of such nouns and explicitly represents it.

2 Motivation and Related Works

In the field of NLP the information regarding lexical semantic classes has been proved to be crucial for several applications, such as information extraction, machine translation and question answering, and an increasing amount of research has been carried out in order to create models for the automatic classification of nouns (Romeo et al., 2014a; Bel et al., 2013; Schwartz et al., 2014).

Despite the effects of regular polysemy on lexical classification, few work attempted to computationally model the phenomenon. The approaches in the literature for the representation of polysemous words are basically three. Polysemes can be simultaneously represented as members of several classes (e.g. the polysemous word *xy* belongs to both the classes *X* and *Y*); as members of new, independent class which includes only words with the same hybrid distributional behaviour (*xy* belongs to the new class *XY*); on a continuum, thus assigning each word a polysemy index between 0 and 1.

Boleda et al. (2012a) present an in-depth study on adjective categorization with a special focus on polysemy, in which they conclude that multiple attribution is the best way to model polysemy. Boleda et al. (2012b) present a model to determine whether a noun matches a given sense alternation, while Romeo et al. (2013) introduce a supervised model for polysemy detection and conclude that since polysemes demonstrate lexico-syntactic traits of multiple classes, they can be considered as members of such classes. Romeo et al. (2014b) improve the previous approach reaching an accuracy of 60.71% in a polysemous noun classification task.

As pointed out by Boleda et al. (2012a) both the first two approaches are not completely satisfactory: the multi-labelling approach fails to represent the differences between polysemous and monosemous nouns in a class, while the second one does not account for the significant similarities between a polyseme and monosemous nouns belonging to the same classes of its senses. Furthermore, none of the two approaches can provide an adequate representation of the asymmetry of senses in a polysemous word.

The third approach has been explored by Utt and Padó (2011): they introduce a *polysemy index* based on the systematicity of sense variation of polysemous nouns to distinguish between polysemy and homonymy. Building on the same methodology, Frontini et al. (2014) define a threshold based on known basic type alternations, and use such a threshold to calculate the polysemy of new words. Finally, Martínez (2013) proposes an index that ranges from literal to metonymic, and that is used to account for the underspecified sense of polysemes.

Despite the fact that we also propose an index for polysemy representation, there are significant differences with the indexes proposed by the cited works. Martínez (2013) focuses on a particular aspect of polysemy, i.e. underspecification; Utt and Padó (2011) only take into account the distinction between homonimous and polysemous nouns; finally, Frontini et al. (2014) investigate the systematic aspect of the phenomenon, focusing on the detection of new basic sense alternations not considered in literature. Differently, in our work we aim to provide a single representation for each polysemous noun that explicitly accounts for its degree of membership to the basic lexical classes its senses belong to, thus highlighting the differences in distributional behaviour of different polysemes and addressing the problem of sense asymmetry.

3 Polysemy Detection

We present in this section a method for the identification of polysemous nouns. Firstly, a clustering algorithm was employed in order to verify that the semantic information preserved in WE was enough to separate nouns belonging to different lexical classes. Given a gold standard composed of L lexical classes and a set of nouns N=$\{n_1,n_2,...n_i\}$ distributed across these classes, WE representing the nouns in N were clustered in a number L of clusters. As a result of this first task, the clusters were expected to largely correspond to the classes in the gold standard.

Once the reliability of the semantic information in WE was proved, a second clustering task was performed to assess the following hypothesis: since polysemous nouns show distributional patterns that are different from non-polysemous nouns, WE representing polysemes are different from the others, and this difference can be captured by means of a clustering algorithm. This hypothesis was verified by clustering the WE of nouns in N in L+1 clusters: as a result, L clusters of monosemous nouns and one cluster composed of polysemes instantiating a specific alternation were expected. Note that the fact that just one class of polysemous nouns was expected only depended on the fact that all the cases of polysemy in the dataset instantiated a single sense alternation (animal/food).

3.1 Word Embeddings

WE of size 200 were trained using the word2vec toolkit[1] with the CBOW architecture, which has been proved computationally efficient for large datasets (Mikolov et al., 2013b; Baroni et al., 2014). Given the results of some preliminary studies, three relevant choices were made in the training phase. Firstly, WE were trained on a parsed version of the British National Corpus (BNC). The choice is in line with previous research (Levy and Goldberg, 2014) that proved how the embeddings created on input annotated with dependency relations better represent similarity (i.e. the paradigmatic relation existing between words, e.g. *coffee* and *tea*) compared with embedding created on linear contexts, which tend to encode more contextual information, or relatedness (e.g. *coffee* and *cup*).

Second, the size of the window was 1 word either side of the target word: once again, the reason is that smaller context windows have been proved to improve the ability of the model to represent similarity (Kiela and Clark, 2014).

Finally, consistently with the theoretic approach adopted, a single WE was created for each noun; thus, only one vector representation was available for the two senses of a disemous noun.

3.2 Clustering

WE have proved to be a representation that preserves semantic information in a vectorial space. Therefore, since nouns belonging to the same lexical class are close in the semantic space, a clustering algorithm should be capable of discovering the portion of the space where all the members of a class are located and include them in a cluster, thus separating them from nouns of other classes. We used the k-means algorithm, a flat, partitional algorithm that minimizes the distance from objects and their centroid and performs hard clustering.

3.3 Evaluation

For evaluation, we used the dataset proposed by Schwartz et al. (2014), which was built on the CSLB norms dataset created by Devereux et al. (2014), a very rich dataset made up of 638 concepts manually labelled by thirty annotators. Schwarz et al. (2014) applied a filtering mechanism to the original CSLB and obtained a final dataset made up of 346 nouns belonging to four semantic categories: animacy (*ANI*, 146 nouns), edibility (i.e. food items, *EDI*, 115 nouns), tools (*TOO*, 35 nouns) and things that can be worn (*WOR*, 50 nouns). The dataset included 33 disemous nouns which were represented

[1] https://code.google.com/p/word2vec/

cluster	k=4			k=4+1		
	precision	recall	f-score	precision	recall	f-score
0/WOR	0.98	0.92	0.95	1	0.92	0.96
1/EDI	0.83	0.78	0.81	0.87	0.94	0.90
2/ANI	0.85	0.85	0.85	0.89	0.95	0.92
3/TOO	0.77	0.97	0.86	0.81	0.97	0.88
4/ANI_EDI	/	/	/	0.83	0.44	0.65

Table 1: Results of the clustering tasks with *k*=4 and *k*=4+1.

as two lexical items (e.g. for the noun *chicken*, *chicken_ANI* and *chicken_EDI* [2]). The results of the first clustering task (*k*=4) were evaluated against this dataset.

For the second clustering (*k*=4+1), the dataset was slightly modified, and disemous nouns were represented with a new label indicating their polysemy (*chicken_ANI_EDI*).

In table 1 the results of the two clustering tasks are shown. For each cluster and its corresponding class in the dataset (first column) *precision*, *recall* and *f*-score for *k*=4 and *k*=4+1 were computed. The results confirmed that (i) the semantic information kept in WE was enough to include nouns of the same lexical class in the same cluster: this is proved by the high f-scores for *k*=4; (ii) WE preserved enough information to distinguish polysemous nouns instantiating a specific sense alternation from the other nouns in the dataset. As expected, when clustering with *k*=4+1, four out of five clusters were mainly composed of monosemous nouns, thus corresponding to the four classes *ANI*, *EDI*, *WOR* and *TOO* of the dataset, whereas the fifth included polysemes labelled as *ANI_EDI*. The f-score for this cluster was significantly lower than the others, but note that Martínez et al. (2013) report about the difficulties of the task also for human annotators.

The most relevant data are the precision and recall of the cluster *4/ANI_EDI*. We will discuss about the recall in the following section. The high result in precision confirmed that the great majority of the nouns in the cluster were polysemous, and hence that it was possible to find a portion of the semantic space populated only by polysemes.

Finally, the data regarding the f-scores with *k*=4+1 show that considering polysemous nouns as members of a new class led to an improvement of the results for all the other clusters. This confirms that by accounting for regular polysemy it is possible to improve the performance of a system in a task of lexical classification.

3.4 Discussion

From the error analysis, two general errors causes and a specific one for *k*=4 and *k*=4+1 were identified. Firstly, the *association effect*: even if the setting chosen for the creation of the WE was intended to maximize similarity and to minimize relatedness, a noun like *peeler_TOO*, which co-occurs almost exclusively with nouns referring to fruits and vegetables (akin nouns belonging to *EDI*), was included in *1/EDI* instead of *3/TOO*. The same effect has also been found in other works (Hill et al., 2014).

Secondly, the *low frequency effect*: the majority of the misclassified monosemous nouns had less than 50 occurrences in the BNC corpus (e.g. *chipmunk_ANI*, 20 occurrences). Few occurrences of a word seemed to produce less informative WE and this, in turn, less accurate cluster assignment. Note that WE for low frequency words are usually discarded (Mikolov et al., 2013c).

For the first task (*k*=4) the *polysemy effect*: 36 out of 51 errors were due to regular polysemy, an expected result, given that only one embedding for each noun had been used. Thus, for example, since *chicken_ANI* and *chicken_EDI* were represented by the same vector, they were both assigned to *1/EDI*.

Finally, the low recall of the cluster for polysemous nouns in *k*=4+1 was due to the already mentioned sense asymmetry: when one sense is more

[2]The notation '*_CAT*' is used to identify the class in the dataset which a lexical item belongs to, while '*_n/CAT*' identifies the cluster - and the corresponding class - to which a noun is assigned by our method.

taxonomic labelling	production frequency	taxonomic labelling	production frequency
crustacean	6	edible_eaten	20
shellfish	7	seafood	6
tot animal	13	tot food	26
% ANI	33	% EDI	67

Table 2: Taxonomic labelling and production frequency for the noun *prawn*

cluster	% EDI-related human judgements	% ANI-related human judgements
1/EDI	64	36
2/ANI	33	67
4/ANI_EDI	48	52

Table 3: Averaged taxonomic labelling for nouns in *1/EDI*, *2/ANI* and *4/ANI_EDI*

frequent or predominant that the other, the WE is expected to be more similar to those of non ambiguous nouns in a basic class, as it mostly behaves, in distributional terms, like them.

Sense predominance was also observed in the human annotated CSLB dataset. For every concept in the CSLB, information about the taxonomic group the concept belongs to is also provided as well as the relative production frequency, i.e. the number of times the taxonomic group has been associated to the target concept. As an example, for the noun *prawn* the information reported in table 2 is provided. Our assumption was that the difference in taxonomic labelling adequately reflects the difference in sense predominance: hence *prawn*, on average, is associated to the class *EDI* on 67% of times, and to *ANI* in the remaining 33%.

In table 3, we averaged relevant values of production frequency for polysemous nouns in *4/ANI_EDI*, *2/ANI* and *1/EDI*. On average, polysemous nouns that in task *k*=4+1 were included in cluster *1/EDI* were judged to belong to the taxonomic category of food in 64% of cases, and only 36% to the class of animals; polysemous nouns assigned to cluster *2/ANI*, were labelled by humans as animals in 67% of cases (33% food). Finally, polysemous nouns clustered in *4/ANI_EDI* had almost equal average of human labelling for the two senses: 48% food, 52% animal.

Human judgements support our explanation of the low recall of cluster *4/ANI_EDI*: on average, the same polysemous nouns that were incorrectly included in *1/EDI* and *2/ANI* because of their strong sense asymmetry, are mostly considered as food or animal respectively by humans.

On the basis of these data, it is possible to conclude that, as expected, cluster *4/ANI_EDI* included only polysemous nouns, but only those whose senses are *balanced*, i.e. not strongly asymmetric. On the contrary, *unbalanced* polysemous nouns tended to be included in the classes the predominant sense belongs to.

4 Modeling Sense Asymmetry

The clustering introduced above allowed to identify most polysemous nouns for a specific class alternation but failed to handle polysemes with a strong sense asymmetry. In order to overcome this problem, in this section we propose a *sense index* which, given a specific class alternation, makes it possible to identify and represent disemous nouns and their particular sense asymmetries. Such an index allows to detect and accurately represent polysemes, since it locates nouns on a continuum whose ends are the two involved lexical classes: monosemous nouns lay close to one of the ends, while polysemous nouns lay in the middle of the continuum, in a different position depending on the degree of asymmetry of their senses.

The sense index was calculated considering the *k*=4 scenario, that is without taking into account the polysemous class *ANI_EDI*. For each cluster, the centroids *C* were computed. A centroid is an average vector and hence, in our method, it represents the centre of a class; therefore, the closer a noun is to the centroid of a class, higher its degree of membership to such a class is.

Our goal was to identify which nouns were polysemous for a specific class alternation; for this reason the method considered one pair of clusters *X*, *Y* at a time. Given X=$\{x_1, x_2,...x_n\}$ and Y=$\{y_1, y_2,...y_n\}$, and the centroids of the two addressed clusters C_x and C_y, the cosine similarity between each centroid and every noun in the two classes was computed to assess class membership. In what follows, we will refer to this initial value as *absolute cosine class membership* (θAbs).

The highest ($\theta MaxAbs$) and the lowest ($\theta MinAbs$) values of θAbs were then used in order to define a *relative cosine class membership* (θRel). The reason for switching from absolute to relative class membership is the following. WE represent the whole vocabulary of the corpus in a single vector semantic space: since θAbs is computed in this space, it accounts for the distance between the nouns of the dataset and all the other words of the vocabulary. This fact had a major drawback: while accounting for the cosine distance with very distant words in the semantic space, it minimized the distances between class-related nouns. By adopting θRel we overcame this problem, since this measure is aimed to only account for the semantic space in which nouns of two classes and their centroids are included, thus making evident the differences of targeted nouns.

Relative cosine class membership between a centroid and a noun *n* in the dataset can be computed as in (1):

$$\theta Rel = \frac{\theta Abs - \theta MinAbs}{RanMaxMin} \quad (1)$$

where θAbs is the absolute cosine similarity between the target name and the centroid, $\theta MinAbs$ and $\theta MaxAbs$ are the values of cosine similarity between the centroid and the farthest and closest point respectively, and *RanMaxMin* is the range between these two values.

Let's consider the noun *fox* and the centroids C_{ani} and C_{edi}. The θAbs between *fox* and C_{ani} was 0.73, between *fox* and C_{edi} 0.48, while the values of θRel were 0.80 with C_{ani} and 0.30 with C_{edi}. Clearly, relative cosine similarity made more evident the proximity in the semantic space of *fox* to C_{ani}, and stressed the distance between *fox* and C_{edi}.

Finally, the values of θRel between a noun and the two centroids were used to obtain the sense index, whereby the degree of membership of a noun to two classes is defined. Given the two values of relative cosine class membership between a noun and the two centroids θRel_1 and θRel_2 sense index for the first sense was computed as in (2):

$$SenseIndex1 = \frac{\theta Rel_1{}^2}{\theta Rel_1{}^2 + \theta Rel_2{}^2} \quad (2)$$

Since the indexes for the first and the second sense are complementary, the second index was obtained by computing 1-SenseIndex1. For *fox* the final sense index was 0.88 for *ANI* and a corresponding 0.12 *EDI*, a result that indicates a clear membership of the target noun to lexical class of the animals, and therefore that *fox* can be considered a monosemous noun. The differences between monosemous and polysemous are evident for nouns in table 4.

target noun	dataset label	ANI-index	EDI-index
butter	EDI	0.08	0.92
bacon	EDI	0.07	0.93
cheese	EDI	0.08	0.92
eagle	ANI	0.87	0.13
panther	ANI	0.95	0.05
pelican	ANI	0.98	0.02
calf	ANI_EDI	0.51	0.49
shrimp	ANI_EDI	0.40	0.60
chicken	ANI_EDI	0.31	0.69

Table 4: Examples of sense indexes

The indexes in the table allow to distinguish three groups of nouns, a finding which is in line both with those of the clustering method and with the initial hypothesis that polysemous nouns gather together in a specific area of the vectors semantic space. In the first part of the table monosemous nouns labelled as *EDI* in the dataset are listed: their sense index clearly reflects this class attribution, as all the indexes for *EDI* are above 0.90. The same holds true for the nouns in the second part of the table, i.e. those nouns with high *ANI* index. The third part of the table is the most interesting one. Firstly, the polysemy of the nouns in this section can be easily detected by looking at their balanced indexes. Second, the method provided specific information that stresses the differences regarding the distributional behaviour of polysemes: for example, while with the clustering method the only available information was that *calf* and *shrimp* were in the same cluster (*ANI_EDI*), with the present method we know that while the two senses of *calf* are almost perfectly balanced (0.51 *ANI*/0.49 *EDI*), *shrimp* is more similar to the monosemous nouns in *EDI* (0.60) than to those in *ANI* (0.40). Finally, the present method overcame the limitation of the previous one related to sense asymmetry. For example, *chicken* was in the cluster *1/EDI* in *k*=4+1 given its strongly predominant food sense, while its sense index is 0.69 *EDI*/0.31 *ANI*: by comparing this index with that of the monosemous nouns of the first part of the table 4, it becomes clear that *chicken* is not so strictly tied to the food sense, i.e. it is not a monosemous noun, but also that, differently from other polysemous nouns in the third part of the table, its *EDI*-related sense is strongly predominant.

4.1 Evaluation

In order to asses the quality with which our method distinguished between polysemous and monosemous nouns we turned the evaluation of the sense index in a classification task. For this purpose, given a pair of lexical classes, we identified two thresholds 'α' and 'γ' on the continuum between such classes, thus obtaining three separate ranges. For such ranges, we expected the following distribution: monosemous nouns labelled as the first sense in the range [0-α], nouns labelled as the second sense in the range [γ-1] and polysemous nouns instantiating the alternation of the two senses in [α-γ]. The populations of the three ranges were than evaluated against the classes of the dataset annotated with polysemous nouns, from which we removed WE that proved to preserve insufficient information due to low frequency of the noun in the corpus (see 3.4.). We selected two pairs of lexical classes for the evaluation, namely *ANI-EDI*, a typical regular polysemy alternation, and *WOR-EDI*, an impossible alternation according to the literature. While for the former a certain number of polysemes in the middle of the continuum was expected, for the latter the expectation was to find two groups of nouns laying at the ends of the continuum, and nothing in the middle.

Along with Utt and Padó (2011), in order to chose the best threshold for the two pairs of classes we experimented with different values for α and γ and evaluated the resulting populations of the ranges with the Mann-Whitney U-Test, a non parametric test that is used to test whether two populations are significantly different or not. The output of the test is the U-value, which can range from 0 to a number computed considering the values of the two populations in exam. In our case, values of U close to 0 would mean that monosemous and polysemous nouns lay in different ranges, while high values of U indicate that they are approximately evenly distributed on the continuum.

For *ANI-EDI* we identified the best threshold for α=0.23 (U=46 on a maximum value of 5671) and γ=0.59 (U=227, max value 9730), with $p \leq 0.05$ for both the results. As expected, *EDI*-nouns were in the range [0-α], ANI-nouns in the range [γ-1] and polysemes in [α-γ]. The low values of U indicate that, even if there was a partial overlapping of the three populations on the continuum, there were significant differences among them.

For *WOR-EDI* the identification of best values for α and γ was fairly straightforward. Since all the nouns labelled as *WOR* were in the range [0-0.26] and the nouns labelled as *EDI* in the range [0.63-1], the values of the two thresholds were at α=0.26 (U=0, $p \leq 0.05$) and γ=0.63 (U=0, $p \leq 0.05$). In table 5 are shown the results obtained using the polysemy index for the classification of polysemous nouns for the two class pairs *ANI-EDI* and *WOR-EDI*.

	ANI-EDI		
range	precision	recall	f-score
[0-α]/EDI	0.97	0.96	0.96
[α-γ]/ANI_EDI	0.73	0.88	0.81
[γ-1]/ANI	0.97	0.93	0.95
	WOR-EDI		
range	precision	recall	f-score
[0-α]/WOR	1	1	1
[α-γ]/WOR_EDI	/	/	/
[γ-1]/EDI	1	1	1

Table 5: Results of the evaluation of the Sense Index.

4.2 Discussion

For both the class alternations taken into account, the results confirmed our expectation to find monosemous nouns on the ends of the continuum, and disemous nouns (if present) in the middle. This was especially true for *WOR-EDI*, in which nouns were clearly polarized at the ends of the continuum and no polysemous nouns instantiating this alternation were found among them.

Following the comparison of the sense index results for *ANI-EDI* with those of the k=4+1 clustering, some conclusions can be drawn. Firstly, the general improvement in the f-score of *ANI*, *EDI* and *ANI_EDI* proved that the method presented in this section outperformed the clustering algorithm in the task of polysemy detection.

Secondly, the significant improvement in recall for *ANI_EDI* showed that by exploiting the information provided by the sense index it was possible to detect those polysemous nouns with a strongly predominant sense that were misclassified with the previous method, even if there were few exceptions. *Tuna* was found among nouns laying in the *EDI* range, but close to the threshold α (*tuna*'s index is 19, α=23). As for polysemes found in the *ANI* range some explanations can be advanced: *sheep* and *cow* are not usually employed to denote meat as they have a corresponding term specific for this use; *snail* is very seldom meant as food; for *rabbit* we conjecture that there are a number of figurative uses that made it more distant for the group of edible things.

The results show that the sense index has considerably increased *ANI_EDI* recall but, to some extent, at the expenses of the precision, what was already expected after the U-test which showed the existence of some overlap between ranges. Nevertheless, the general increase in f-score terms for the three involved classes shows the benefits of the index approach.

The correspondence of the values of the thresholds α and γ placed on the two continua was almost perfect: 0.23 and 0.59 on *ANI-EDI*, 0.26 and 0.63 on *WOR-EDI*. This means that the separation of the ranges on the continuum was consistent between different senses alternations, thus proving the robustness of the method.

Finally, the considerable distance between the first polysemous noun (*tuna*), laying at point 0.19, and the last one (*octopus*) at point 0.70 on the *ANI-EDI* continuum, reflects the fact that the distributional characteristics of polysemes are more disperse than those of monosemous nouns.

5 Conclusions

We have presented an ongoing work that proposes a method for the detection and representation of polysemous nouns based on the semantic information preserved in WE. We initially showed that polysemous nouns instantiating a particular sense alternation group together in a specific area of the vector semantic space. Subsequently, we proposed a method by which, given a pair of lexical classes, a sense index defining the degree of membership to such classes is assigned to each noun. In this method, polysemy is implicitly represented as a balanced value of the degree of membership. We finally showed that it is possible to identify two thresholds α and γ such that nouns having sense index included in the ranges [0-α] and [γ-1] are monosemous nouns belonging to the first and the second class of the pair respectively, while polysemes are included in the range between α and γ.

Results, although limited in scale, show that the method allows a clear separation between monosemous belonging to a lexical class and polysemous nouns instantiating specific sense alternation, also accounting for those polysemes with a strong asymmetry in sense predominace.

In future work, we plan to double check that the results are independent of the datasets, provided enough data is considered. Furthermore, more experiments with other class alternations are planned as well as particular application of our sense index in actual WSD applications.

6 Acknowledgements

This work was funded with the support of the IULA-UPF PhD fellowship program.

References

Ju D Apresjan. 1974. Regular polysemy. *Linguistics*, 12(142):5–32.

Marco Baroni, Georgiana Dinu, and Germán Kruszewski. 2014. Dont count, predict! a systematic comparison of context-counting vs. context-predicting semantic vectors. In *Proceedings of the 52nd Annual Meeting of the Association for Computational Linguistics*, volume 1, pages 238–247.

Núria Bel, Lauren Romeo, and Muntsa Padró. 2013. Automatic lexical semantic classification of nouns. *arXiv preprint arXiv:1303.1930*.

Gemma Boleda, Sabine Schulte im Walde, and Toni Badia. 2012a. Modeling regular polysemy: A study on the semantic classification of catalan adjectives. *Computational Linguistics*, 38(3):575–616.

Gemma Boleda, Sebastian Padó, and Jason Utt. 2012b. Regular polysemy: A distributional model. In *Proceedings of the First Joint Conference on Lexical and Computational Semantics-Volume 1: Proceedings of the main conference and the shared task, and Volume 2: Proceedings of the Sixth International Workshop on Semantic Evaluation*, pages 151–160. Association for Computational Linguistics.

Ann Copestake and Ted Briscoe. 1995. Semi-productive polysemy and sense extension. *Journal of semantics*, 12(1):15–67.

Ann Copestake. 2013. Can distributional approached improve on goold old-fashioned lexical semantics. In *IWCS Workshop Towards a Formal Distributional Semantics*.

Barry J Devereux, Lorraine K Tyler, Jeroen Geertzen, and Billi Randall. 2014. The centre for speech, language and the brain (cslb) concept property norms. *Behavior research methods*, 46(4):1119–1127.

Francesca Frontini, Valeria Quochi, Sebastian Padó, Jason Utt, and Monica Monachini. 2014. Polysemy index for nouns: an experiment on italian using the parole simple clips lexical database.

Felix Hill, KyungHyun Cho, Sebastien Jean, Coline Devin, and Yoshua Bengio. 2014. Not all neural embeddings are born equal. *arXiv preprint arXiv:1410.0718*.

Douwe Kiela and Stephen Clark. 2014. A systematic study of semantic vector space model parameters. In *Proceedings of the 2nd Workshop on Continuous Vector Space Models and their Compositionality (CVSC) at EACL*, pages 21–30.

Omer Levy and Yoav Goldberg. 2014. Dependency-based word embeddings. In *Proceedings of the 52nd Annual Meeting of the Association for Computational Linguistics*, volume 2, pages 302–308.

Héctor Martínez Alonso, Bolette Sandford Pedersen, and Núria Bel. 2013. Annotation of regular polysemy and underspecification. In *ACL (2)*, pages 725–730.

Héctor Martínez Alonso. 2013. Annotation of regular polysemy: an empirical assessment of the underspecified sense.

Tomas Mikolov, Kai Chen, Greg Corrado, and Jeffrey Dean. 2013a. Efficient estimation of word representations in vector space. *arXiv preprint arXiv:1301.3781*.

Tomas Mikolov, Quoc V Le, and Ilya Sutskever. 2013b. Exploiting similarities among languages for machine translation. *arXiv preprint arXiv:1309.4168*.

Tomas Mikolov, Ilya Sutskever, Kai Chen, Greg S Corrado, and Jeff Dean. 2013c. Distributed representations of words and phrases and their compositionality. In *Advances in Neural Information Processing Systems*, pages 3111–3119.

Tomas Mikolov, Wen-tau Yih, and Geoffrey Zweig. 2013d. Linguistic regularities in continuous space word representations. In *HLT-NAACL*, pages 746–751.

Geoff Nunberg. 1992. Systematic polysemy in lexicology and lexicography.

James Pustejovsky. 1991. The generative lexicon. *Computational linguistics*, 17(4):409–441.

J Pustejovsky. 1995. Tile generative lexicon. *ms. Brandeis University*.

Lauren Romeo, Sara Mendes, and Núria Bel. 2013. Towards the automatic classification of complex-type nominals. In *6th International Conference on Generative Approaches to the Lexicon*, page 21. Citeseer.

Lauren Romeo, Gianluca E Lebani, Núria Bel, and Alessandro Lenci. 2014a. Choosing which to use? a study of distributional models for nominal lexical semantic classification. In *Proceedings of the Ninth International Conference on Language Resources and Evaluation (LREC 2014)*, pages 4366–4373.

Lauren Romeo, Sara Mendes, and Núria Bel. 2014b. A cascade approach for complex-type classification. In *Proceedings of the Ninth International Conference on Language Resources and Evaluation (LREC 2014)*, pages 4451–4458.

Roy Schwartz, Roi Reichart, and Ari Rappoport. 2014. Minimally supervised classification to semantic categories using automatically acquired symmetric patterns. In *Proceedings of COLING 2014 the 25th International Conference on Computational Linguistics*, pages 1612–1623.

Jason Utt and Sebastian Padó. 2011. Ontology-based distinction between polysemy and homonymy. In *Proceedings of the Ninth International Conference on Computational Semantics*, pages 265–274. Association for Computational Linguistics.

Simple Semi-Supervised POS Tagging

Karl Stratos **Michael Collins**

Columbia University, New York, NY 10027, USA
{stratos, mcollins}@cs.columbia.edu

Abstract

We tackle the question: how much supervision is needed to achieve state-of-the-art performance in part-of-speech (POS) tagging, if we leverage lexical representations given by the model of Brown et al. (1992)? It has become a standard practice to use automatically induced "Brown clusters" in place of POS tags. We claim that the underlying sequence model for these clusters is particularly well-suited for capturing POS tags. We empirically demonstrate this claim by drastically reducing supervision in POS tagging with these representations. Using either the bit-string form given by the algorithm of Brown et al. (1992) or the (less well-known) embedding form given by the canonical correlation analysis algorithm of Stratos et al. (2014), we can obtain 93% tagging accuracy with just 400 labeled *words* and achieve state-of-the-art accuracy (> 97%) with less than 1 percent of the original training data.

1 Introduction

While fully supervised POS tagging is largely considered a solved problem today, this is hardly the case for unsupervised POS tagging. Despite much previous work (Smith and Eisner, 2005; Johnson, 2007; Toutanova and Johnson, 2007; Haghighi and Klein, 2006; Berg-Kirkpatrick et al., 2010), results on this task are complicated by varying assumptions and unclear evaluation metrics (Christodoulopoulos et al., 2010). Perhaps most importantly, they are not good enough to be practical. Even with indirect supervision, for example the prototype-driven method of Haghighi and Klein (2006) which assumes a set of word examples for each tag type, the best per-position accuracy remains in the range of mid-70%.

Recent work has taken a middle ground between fully supervised and unsupervised setups by exploiting existing resources, for example by projecting POS tags from a supervised language or using tag dictionaries (Das and Petrov, 2011; Li et al., 2012; Täckström et al., 2013).

In this work, we focus on *minimizing* the amount of labeled data required to obtain a good POS tagger. The key to our approach is the use of lexical representations induced by the clustering model of Brown et al. (1992). We argue that this model is particularly appropriate for representing POS tags given their nearly deterministic nature (Section 2). This sheds light on why the representations derived under this model reveal the underlying POS tag information of words.

We empirically demonstrate the validity of our observation by using these representations to drastically reduce the number of training examples required for good POS tagging performance on English, German, and Spanish newswire datasets. For instance, on the 12-tag English dataset, we obtain tagging accuracy of 93% with just 400 labeled *words*. We obtain tagging accuracy of 97.03% (about a half percent behind fully supervised models) with just 0.74% of the original training data.

Our aim is orthogonal to the discussion in Manning (2011) who investigates what is needed to go beyond the current state-of-the-art POS tagging performance. Our focus is on reaching that performance with as little supervision as possible.

Proceedings of NAACL-HLT 2015, pages 79–87,
Denver, Colorado, May 31 – June 5, 2015.

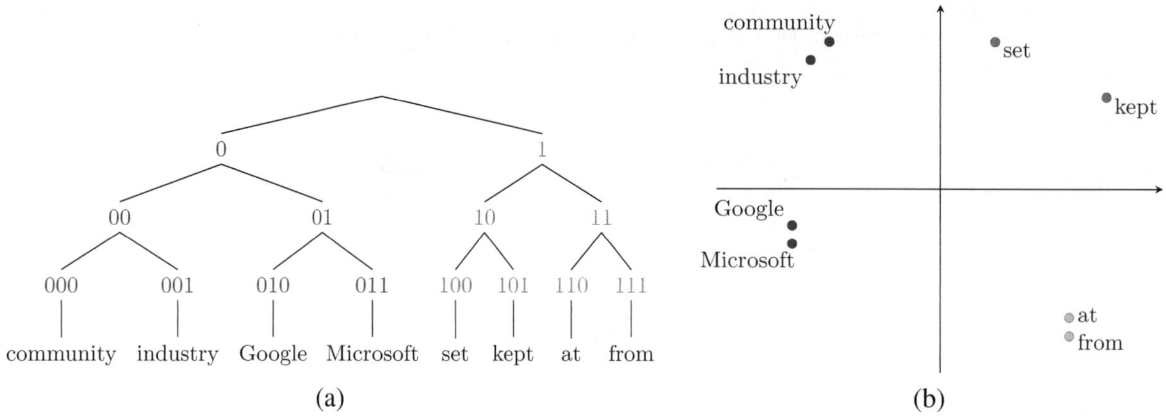

Figure 1: Two representational schemes under the Brown model. (a) Bit-string representations: the path from the root to a word is encoded as a bit-string. (b) CCA vector representations.

2 Motivation

2.1 POS tags are almost deterministic

Certain words are genuinely ambiguous (e.g., `set` can be a verb or a noun): this was the motivation of the use of statistical models in the early days of computational linguistics (Church, 1988). However, it is also true that many words are deterministically mapped to correct POS tags (e.g., `the` is always a determiner). A simple experiment highlights this property. Let $\textbf{count}(w,t)$ be the number of times word w is tagged as t in the training data (likewise, $\textbf{count}(w)$ and $\textbf{count}(t)$ are counts of word w and tag t). Define a deterministic mapping $f : w \mapsto t$ from words to tags as

$$f(w) = \begin{cases} \arg\max_t \textbf{count}(w,t) & \text{if } \textbf{count}(w) > 0 \\ \arg\max_t \textbf{count}(t) & \text{otherwise} \end{cases}$$

In our datasets, this naïve procedure in fact yields reasonable tagging accuracies: 92.22% for coarse tags and 88.50% for fine-grained tags (averaged across three languages).

This observation suggests that the following restricted class of HMMs might be sufficient for modeling the characteristics of POS tags:

- $\pi(t)$ is the prior probability of tag type t.
- $t(t'|t)$ is the probability of transitioning from tag type t to tag type t'.
- $o(w|t)$ is the probability of emitting word type w from tag type t.
- (Restriction) For each word type w, we have $o(w|t) > 0$ only for a *unique* tag type t and $o(w|t') = 0$ for all other tag types $t' \neq t$.

In other words, we assume that tag types partition word types while imposing a first-order sequence structure on tag types.

2.2 Brown et al. (1992) model

This class of restricted HMMs is precisely the model proposed by Brown et al. (1992)—henceforth the Brown model. A popular use of this model is agglomerative word clustering: the result is a hierarchy over word types, such as the one shown in Figure 1(a). In practice, each word type is represented as a bit-string indicating the path from the root. These bit-strings have been used as discrete (binary) features in various natural language tasks such as named-entity recognition (Miller et al., 2004) and dependency parsing (Koo et al., 2008).

Recently, Stratos et al. (2014) showed that a variant of canonical correlation analysis (CCA) (Hotelling, 1936) can be used to provably recover the clusters under the Brown model. Under this method, each word is represented as an m-dimensional vector where m is the number of hidden states in the model: see Figure 1(b) for illustration. This can be used as m real-valued features in discrminative models. Note that real-valued representations can reflect ambiguity (e.g., `set` in the illustration) which can be seen as a benefit over discrete representations.

By the above observation, we conjecture that the hidden states of the Brown model capture POS tags. Then the bit-string and embedding representations essentially "give away" the POS tag associated with a word. In experiments, we show that this is indeed the case and not far removed from the idealized illustration in Figure 1.

3 Method

In this section, we describe our tagging framework MINITAGGER, which is pleasantly simple but surprisingly effective. It uses an off-the-shelf discriminative classifier to map a word's context to a POS tag. Concretely, given a sentence $\boldsymbol{x}$ and a position i in $\boldsymbol{x}$, we extract a feature vector $\phi(\boldsymbol{x}, i) \in \mathbb{R}^d$ and train a multi-class classifier to map $\phi(\boldsymbol{x}, i)$ to a POS tag. To clarify, this is *not* the the HMM model described in the previous section: the HMM model underlies Brown bit-strings and CCA embeddings.

This framework has compelling benefits. First, it allows for learning from partially labeled sentences since each word is an independent sample. Second, training and tagging can be very fast since they do not involve dynamic programming required for structured models. Third, arbitrary features can be easily and effectively incorporated. Finally, there are many well-oiled public implementations of discriminative classifiers such as support-vector machines (SVMs), thus building an efficient and effective MINITAGGER takes only a minimal effort.

3.1 Feature templates

We use a baseline feature function **base** that maps a sentence-position pair $(\boldsymbol{x}, i)$ to a a 0-1 vector $\mathbf{base}(\boldsymbol{x}, i)$ indicating

- Identities of $x_{i-1}, x_{i+1}, x_i, x_{i-2}, x_{i+2}$
- Prefixes and suffixes of x_i up to length 4
- Whether x_i is capitalized, numeric, or non-alphanumeric

Let $\mathbf{bit}(x)$ be a binary vector indicating prefixes of the Brown bit-string corresponding to x.[1] Let $\mathbf{cca}(x) \in \mathbb{R}^m$ be an m-dimensional CCA embedding corresponding to x.

[1]Past work has used various complex schemes on which prefixes to use, e.g., see Koo et al. (2008). For simplicity, we use every prefix in this work.

$\phi(\boldsymbol{x}, i)$	Definition
BASE	$\mathbf{base}(\boldsymbol{x}, i)$
BIT	$\mathbf{base}(\boldsymbol{x}, i) \oplus \mathbf{bit}(x_i) \oplus \mathbf{bit}(x_{i-1}) \oplus \mathbf{bit}(x_{i+1})$
CCA	$\frac{\mathbf{base}(\boldsymbol{x},i)}{\lVert\mathbf{base}(\boldsymbol{x},i)\rVert} \oplus \frac{\mathbf{cca}(x_i)}{\lVert\mathbf{cca}(x_i)\rVert} \oplus \frac{\mathbf{cca}(x_{i-1})}{\lVert\mathbf{cca}(x_{i-1})\rVert} \oplus \frac{\mathbf{cca}(x_{i+1})}{\lVert\mathbf{cca}(x_{i+1})\rVert}$

Table 1: Feature templates for MINITAGGER: $\oplus$ is the vector concatenation operation.

Table 1 shows the feature templates we use to obtain a vector representation of $(\boldsymbol{x}, i)$. $\oplus$ is the vector concatenation operation. BASE is a baseline template which uses only the spelling features of the current word and the identities of neighboring words. BIT is the same as BASE but augmented with Brown bit-strings. CCA is the same as BASE but augmented with CCA embeddings with appropriate normalization.

3.2 Sampling methods

3.2.1 Active learning

We also deploy *active learning* to find the most informative words for labeling in attempt to reduce the amount of training data. While there is a rich literature on this topic (see Settles (2010) for a survey), we focus on a simple form of margin sampling in this work. Every time the model is allowed to have an additional label, it actively selects the word from a pool of unannotated words whose predicted tag is the least confident.

To be precise, let $s(\boldsymbol{x}, i, y)$ be the score of label y for sentence-position pair $(\boldsymbol{x}, i)$. For example, a linear SVM may define $s(\boldsymbol{x}, i, y) = w_y^\top \phi(\boldsymbol{x}, i)$ where w_y is the model parameter and $\phi(\boldsymbol{x}, i)$ is a feature template in Table 1. To obtain M labeled examples, we specify the initial seed size $k \leq M$ and the step size ξ (for simplicity, assume ξ divides $M - k$) and proceed as follows:

1. Select the top k most frequent word types (a random occurrence of each type) for labeling.

2. For $(M - k)/\xi$ times:

    (a) Train a model with the current set of labeled examples.

NOUN		VERB		ADP	ADJ	ADV	NUM
community	Microsoft	kept	is	from	romantic	boldly	1
enterprise	AT&T	made	was	between	mystical	selfishly	2
law	Unocal	invented	were	for	macho	frequently	3
anthem	Chrysler	squandered	are	[on	heroic	cynically	4
invader	Hexcel	lent	had	in	straight-ahead	wisely	6
pastime	Tosco	memorized	becomes	towards	piquant	clumsily	7
heritage	Geico	witnessed	's	betwen	cushy	effectively	8
curriculum	Starwave	enjoyed	has	betweeen	ghoulish	carefully	5

Table 2: Nearest neighbors of some example words along with their associated universal tags (measuring the l_2 distance between CCA word vectors).

(b) Label ξ examples $(\boldsymbol{x}, i)$ with the smallest "confidence" values $s(\boldsymbol{x}, i, y_1) - s(\boldsymbol{x}, i, y_2)$ where

$$y_1 := \arg\max_{y} s(\boldsymbol{x}, i, y)$$

$$y_2 := \arg\max_{y \neq y_1} s(\boldsymbol{x}, i, y)$$

During active learning, the model operates on unannotated data provided that we supply labels for selected examples (we simulate this setting with labeled data). Note that the selection of examples is inherently tied to the choice of features. Indeed, our experiments show that it is crucial to use lexical representations for active learning to work effectively.

Large values of k and ξ can be used to speed up active learning (possibly at the cost of performance loss). Since our focus is on maximizing performance with minimal supervision, we use $k = \xi = 1$. We leave the speed-performance tradeoff of active learning for future work.

3.2.2 Random and frequent-word sampling

In addition to active learning, we consider the following methods for obtaining M labeled words.

- Random sampling: Select M words uniformly at random (without replacement).
- Frequent-word sampling: Select random occurrences of the M most frequent word types.

Note that frequent-word sampling is optimal if there really is a deterministic mapping from word types to tag types. But since the assumption does not hold perfectly, it has severe limitations in practice. We have found that frequent-word sampling outperforms random sampling for small values of M but starts to lag behind as M increases.

4 Experiments

4.1 Setting

We experimented on 3 languages: English, German, and Spanish. For all these languages, we used the train/dev/test datasets of the universal treebank (McDonald et al., 2013)—both the reduced tagset version, which we denote by EN12, GE12, and SP12, and the original tagset version, which we denote by EN45, GE16, and SP24. The number in the dataset name refers to the number of tag types in that dataset: e.g., EN45 is an English dataset with 45 possible tags.

For each language, we derived Brown representations (by which we mean both the bit-string and embedding forms) from a corpus of unlabeled text. For English, we used a corpus of about 772 million words from various sources of (mostly newswire) text. For German and Spanish, we used the n-gram statistics in Google Ngram (Michel et al., 2011). The number of words was about 64 billion for German and 83 billion for Spanish.

We used the implementation of Liang (2005) to derive bit-string word representations for English: for German and Spanish, we used the agglomerative clustering technique of Stratos et al. (2014) since Liang's implementation did not support operating directly on n-grams. We used the CCA algorithm of Stratos et al. (2014) to derive 50-dimensional word embeddings. Table 2 displays nearest neighbors (i.e., words whose associated CCA embeddings are

# labels	Sampling	Features	EN12	GE12	SP12	EN45	GE16	SP24
200	random	BASE	74.52	72.91	77.47	70.00	60.39	67.01
	frequent-word	BASE	79.42	78.36	77.88	74.58	68.83	73.92
	active	BASE	66.67	71.00	69.90	61.05	61.01	64.60
		BIT	88.53	**81.71**	85.18	79.89	71.18	81.39
		CCA	**89.34**	81.30	**87.63**	**81.68**	**76.60**	**86.54**
400	random	BASE	80.18	76.13	79.96	75.26	69.08	76.66
	frequent-word	BASE	85.44	82.69	79.93	82.07	75.68	80.44
	active	BASE	76.06	77.56	80.69	77.24	67.93	79.29
		BIT	**93.00**	87.53	89.94	88.38	77.82	86.53
		CCA	92.29	**88.17**	**91.70**	**88.55**	**80.48**	**89.06**
1000	random	BASE	85.39	81.31	85.92	81.72	73.61	82.53
	frequent-word	BASE	89.94	85.04	88.93	87.53	79.31	85.93
	active	BASE	85.65	86.27	88.16	85.02	78.54	84.91
		BIT	**95.21**	91.18	93.45	**92.81**	83.91	91.73
		CCA	95.03	**92.48**	**94.37**	92.22	**84.40**	**91.97**

Table 3: Dev performance of MINITAGGER when only 200, 400, and 1000 labeled words are used.

the closest in l_2 distance) of some example words. We see that these embeddings are remarkably good at relating the POS tag information to Euclidean distance, confirming our hypothesis in Section 2.

We built a MINITAGGER using the liblinear package of Fan et al. (2008).[2] We primarily compared our model with conditional random fields (CRFs) (Lafferty et al., 2001). We used the implementation of Okazaki (2007).

While we do not rigorously compare runtime performances in this work, we note that the computational advantages of MINITAGGER are very useful in practice. Training/tagging takes only a few seconds with baseline features; with more complex features such as word embeddings, it still takes much less time than what is required by a CRF (which takes hours with baseline features).

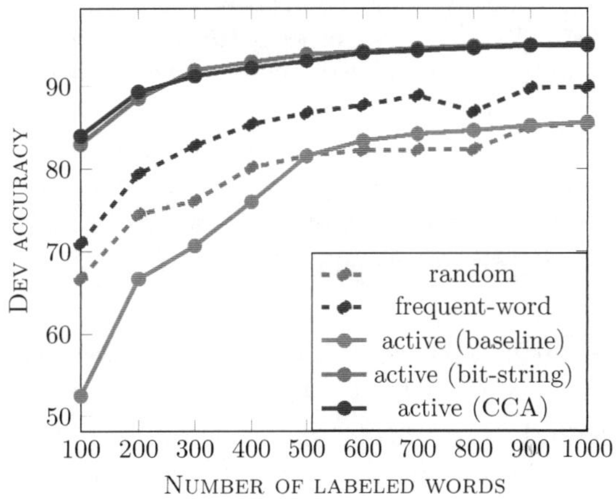

Figure 2: Dev performance of MINITAGGER with varying amounts of supervision (on EN12).

4.2 Effect of Brown representations

4.2.1 With limited supervision

We first look at the effect of using Brown representations when only a limited amount of training data is available: a scenario in which the role of such lexical representations can be prominent. We select a subset of training data (by words) with various sampling schemes described in Section 3.2.

Fixed amount of data. Table 3 shows the performance on the development portion when MINITAGGER is trained on 200, 400, and 1000 labeled words. Active learning together with Brown representations gives dramatic improvement in accuracy when the amount of training data is limited. With 200 randomly sampled labels, the baseline model obtains an average accuracy of 74.97% across EN12, GE12, and SP12. This improves to 86.09% when labels are actively selected with CCA features. A striking result is that we can obtain an accuracy of 93% with only 400 labeled words on the 12-tag English data.

The performance of various sampling methods and features on EN12 is plotted in Figure 2: it is

[2] Our code is available at: `https://github.com/karlstratos/minitagger`.

Dataset	Target acc	BASE	BIT	CCA
EN12	97%	33200	10300	**7000**
GE12	94%	8600	4800	**3000**
SP12	96%	13700	6900	**2700**
EN45	96%	34400	17800	**7700**
GE16	92%	33500	15200	**13200**
SP24	95%	26500	8600	**6000**

(a)

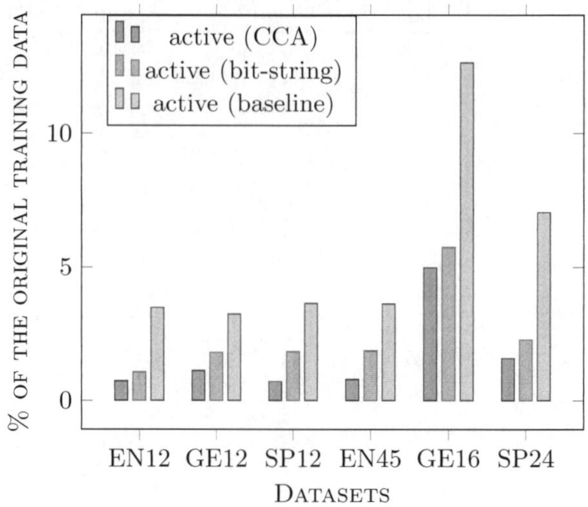

(b)

Table 4: (a) Smallest numbers of actively selected labels required by MINITAGGER to reach the target dev performance: 92–97%. The target performance is defined to be the accuracy of the fully supervised baseline rounded down to a whole number (Table 5). (b) As percentages of the original training data.

clear that active sampling with Brown bit-string or CCA embedding features outperforms others consistently and very significantly.

Fixed target accuracy. Table 4(a) shows the smallest numbers of labeled words required to achieve target performance, where the target performance is defined to be the accuracy of the fully supervised baseline rounded down to a whole number (Table 5). We repeatedly increase the training size by 100 and report the first size that allows MINITAGGER to reach the target accuracy. These numbers are presented as percentages of the size of the original training data in Table 4(b).

We see that active learning with lexical representations provides dramatic reduction in training data while maintaining good performance. In all cases, using CCA embeddings as features for active learning outperforms using Brown bit-strings, although sampling takes much longer with CCA embeddings since there are many more non-zero features. MINITAGGER does almost as well as when fully supervised with less than 1% of the training data on English: $>$ 97% accuracy with 0.74% of the data on the 12-tag version, and $>$ 96% accuracy with 0.81% of the data on the 45-tag version.

4.2.2 With full supervision

We also examine the effect of Brown representations in a fully supervised setting. Table 5 shows the performance of different tagging methods on the development portion when all training data is used. We see that Brown representations are helpful even under full supervision: MINITAGGER, a simple greedy model, outperforms CRF when equipped with Brown representations.

Table 5 also shows the performance of MINITAGGER and CRF on the test portion. For MINITAGGER, we additionally consider a model trained only on the actively selected samples with CCA features in Table 4 which are sufficient to reach state-of-the-art performance on the dev portion. As percentages of the original training data, these samples constitute 0.74% for EN12, 1.13% for GE12, 0.72% for SP12, 0.81% for EN45, 4.98% for GE16, and 1.60% for SP24—1.66% on average. The accuracy of MINITAGGER equipped with Brown representations is again generally higher than that of CRF. Furthermore, MINITAGGER achieves competitive performance using only a fraction of the original training set.

Eval	Model	Features	Data	EN12	GE12	SP12	EN45	GE16	SP24
dev	MINI	BASE	all	97.42	94.91	96.75	96.51	92.44	95.42
		BIT	all	97.56	**95.09**	96.98	96.63	92.67	95.89
		CCA	all	**97.67**	94.94	**97.12**	**96.81**	**92.81**	**95.99**
	CRF	default	all	97.37	94.56	96.59	96.59	91.76	95.61
test	MINI	CCA	all	**97.90**	**94.79**	**95.88**	**97.25**	**92.16**	**94.70**
	MINI	CCA	active	97.20 (0.74)	94.09 (1.13)	94.27 (0.72)	96.43 (0.81)	91.59 (4.98)	93.06 (1.60)
	CRF	default	all	97.54	94.33	94.88	97.03	91.12	93.48

Table 5: Performance of MINITAGGER (MINI in short) and CRF on the dev and test portions. The Data column specifies the amount of training data: "all" means all training data is used, "active" means only the labeled examples actively selected (with the same CCA features) in Table 4 are used: the amount of actively selected examples as a percentage of the original training data is shown in parantheses.

5 Related work

We make a few remarks on related works not already discussed earlier. Our work extends a rich body of previous work on reducing annotation efforts with seed examples, unlabeled data, and training example selection (Yarowsky, 1995; Blum and Mitchell, 1998; Collins and Singer, 1999; Miller et al., 2004; Koo et al., 2008; Kim and Snyder, 2013). In particular, Miller et al. (2004) investigate semi-supervised named-entity recognition based on Brown clusters and active learning. Koo et al. (2008) investigate semi-supervised dependency parsing based on Brown clusters.

The direction that Ringger et al. (2007) pursue is perhaps the most similar to ours. They attempt to reduce supervision required for high POS tagging performance based on active learning. But a critical difference is that they do not use word representations: in contrast, word representations are central to our approach.

Another closely relevant work is the work of Garrette and Baldridge (2013) who aim to learn a good POS tagger from limited resources. Notably, they faithfully simulate tagging resource-poor languages with human annotators. Our contribution is different in several important ways. Most importantly, our results are much more striking in the aspect of minimizing supervision. We obtain $> 90\%$ accuracy with a few hundred labeled words, whereas Garrette and Baldridge (2013) obtain 71-78% with 1,537-2,650 labeled words and tag dictionaries (i.e., the result of two hours of annotation efforts). They also do not make use of word representations which are the highlight of this work.

6 Conclusion

We have argued that that the sequence model of Brown et al. (1992), often used for deriving lexical representations, is particularly appropriate for capturing POS tags. We have demonstrated this claim by drastically reducing the amount of labeled data required for state-of-the-art POS tagging accuracy with word representations derived under the Brown model. Our simple framework MINITAGGER allows one to learn a functioning POS tagger with merely a few hundred labeled tokens, or an accurate POS tagger with less than 1% of the normally considered amount of training data.

We focused on utilizing lexical representations in a greedy framework, which is well-suited for the per-position accuracy metric (which is the standard metric for POS tagging). However, the result may be quite different if other metric is chosen, for instance the per-sentence accuracy metric. Thus improving tagging performance under different metrics using lexical representations may be a fruitful direction.

While they are not considered in this work, lexical representations *not* derived under the Brown model such as the skip-gram model in the WORD2VEC package Mikolov et al. (2013) can certainly be used for the same task. It may be illuminating to compare such different representations.

References

Taylor Berg-Kirkpatrick, Alexandre Bouchard-Côté, John DeNero, and Dan Klein. 2010. Painless unsupervised learning with features. In *Human Language Technologies: The 2010 Annual Conference of the North American Chapter of the Association for Com-*

putational Linguistics, pages 582–590. Association for Computational Linguistics.

Avrim Blum and Tom Mitchell. 1998. Combining labeled and unlabeled data with co-training. In *Proceedings of the eleventh annual conference on Computational learning theory*, pages 92–100. ACM.

Peter F Brown, Peter V Desouza, Robert L Mercer, Vincent J Della Pietra, and Jenifer C Lai. 1992. Class-based n-gram models of natural language. *Computational linguistics*, 18(4):467–479.

Christos Christodoulopoulos, Sharon Goldwater, and Mark Steedman. 2010. Two decades of unsupervised pos induction: How far have we come? In *Proceedings of the 2010 Conference on Empirical Methods in Natural Language Processing*, pages 575–584. Association for Computational Linguistics.

Kenneth Ward Church. 1988. A stochastic parts program and noun phrase parser for unrestricted text. In *Proceedings of the second conference on Applied natural language processing*, pages 136–143. Association for Computational Linguistics.

Michael Collins and Yoram Singer. 1999. Unsupervised models for named entity classification. In *Proceedings of the joint SIGDAT conference on empirical methods in natural language processing and very large corpora*, pages 100–110.

Dipanjan Das and Slav Petrov. 2011. Unsupervised part-of-speech tagging with bilingual graph-based projections. In *Proceedings of the 49th Annual Meeting of the Association for Computational Linguistics: Human Language Technologies-Volume 1*, pages 600–609. Association for Computational Linguistics.

Rong-En Fan, Kai-Wei Chang, Cho-Jui Hsieh, Xiang-Rui Wang, and Chih-Jen Lin. 2008. Liblinear: A library for large linear classification. *The Journal of Machine Learning Research*, 9:1871–1874.

Dan Garrette and Jason Baldridge. 2013. Learning a part-of-speech tagger from two hours of annotation.

Aria Haghighi and Dan Klein. 2006. Prototype-driven learning for sequence models. In *Proceedings of the main conference on Human Language Technology Conference of the North American Chapter of the Association of Computational Linguistics*, pages 320–327. Association for Computational Linguistics.

Harold Hotelling. 1936. Relations between two sets of variates. *Biometrika*, 28(3/4):321–377.

Mark Johnson. 2007. Why doesn't em find good hmm pos-taggers? In *EMNLP-CoNLL*, pages 296–305.

Young-Bum Kim and Benjamin Snyder. 2013. Optimal data set selection: An application to grapheme-to-phoneme conversion. In *HLT-NAACL*, pages 1196–1205.

Terry Koo, Xavier Carreras, and Michael Collins. 2008. Simple semi-supervised dependency parsing.

John Lafferty, Andrew McCallum, and Fernando CN Pereira. 2001. Conditional random fields: Probabilistic models for segmenting and labeling sequence data. In *Proceedings of the 18th International Conference on Machine Learning*, pages 282–289.

Shen Li, Joao V Graça, and Ben Taskar. 2012. Wiki-ly supervised part-of-speech tagging. In *Proceedings of the 2012 Joint Conference on Empirical Methods in Natural Language Processing and Computational Natural Language Learning*, pages 1389–1398. Association for Computational Linguistics.

P. Liang. 2005. Semi-supervised learning for natural language. Master's thesis, Massachusetts Institute of Technology.

Christopher D Manning. 2011. Part-of-speech tagging from 97% to 100%: is it time for some linguistics? In *Computational Linguistics and Intelligent Text Processing*, pages 171–189. Springer.

Ryan T McDonald, Joakim Nivre, Yvonne Quirmbach-Brundage, Yoav Goldberg, Dipanjan Das, Kuzman Ganchev, Keith B Hall, Slav Petrov, Hao Zhang, Oscar Täckström, et al. 2013. Universal dependency annotation for multilingual parsing. In *ACL (2)*, pages 92–97.

Jean-Baptiste Michel, Yuan Kui Shen, Aviva Presser Aiden, Adrian Veres, Matthew K Gray, Joseph P Pickett, Dale Hoiberg, Dan Clancy, Peter Norvig, Jon Orwant, et al. 2011. Quantitative analysis of culture using millions of digitized books. *science*, 331(6014):176–182.

Tomas Mikolov, Ilya Sutskever, Kai Chen, Greg S Corrado, and Jeff Dean. 2013. Distributed representations of words and phrases and their compositionality. In C.J.C. Burges, L. Bottou, M. Welling, Z. Ghahramani, and K.Q. Weinberger, editors, *Advances in Neural Information Processing Systems 26*, pages 3111–3119. Curran Associates, Inc.

Scott Miller, Jethran Guinness, and Alex Zamanian. 2004. Name tagging with word clusters and discriminative training. In *HLT-NAACL*, volume 4, pages 337–342. Citeseer.

Naoaki Okazaki. 2007. Crfsuite: a fast implementation of conditional random fields (crfs).

Eric Ringger, Peter McClanahan, Robbie Haertel, George Busby, Marc Carmen, James Carroll, Kevin Seppi, and Deryle Lonsdale. 2007. Active learning for part-of-speech tagging: Accelerating corpus annotation. In *Proceedings of the Linguistic Annotation Workshop*, pages 101–108. Association for Computational Linguistics.

Burr Settles. 2010. Active learning literature survey. *University of Wisconsin, Madison*, 52:55–66.

Noah A Smith and Jason Eisner. 2005. Contrastive estimation: Training log-linear models on unlabeled data.

In *Proceedings of the 43rd Annual Meeting on Association for Computational Linguistics*, pages 354–362. Association for Computational Linguistics.

Karl Stratos, Do-kyum Kim, Michael Collins, and Daniel Hsu. 2014. A spectral algorithm for learning class-based n-gram models of natural language. In *Proceedings of the thirtieth conference on Uncertainty in Artificial Intelligence*.

Oscar Täckström, Dipanjan Das, Slav Petrov, Ryan McDonald, and Joakim Nivre. 2013. Token and type constraints for cross-lingual part-of-speech tagging. *Transactions of the Association for Computational Linguistics*, 1:1–12.

Kristina Toutanova and Mark Johnson. 2007. A bayesian lda-based model for semi-supervised part-of-speech tagging. In *Advances in Neural Information Processing Systems*, pages 1521–1528.

David Yarowsky. 1995. Unsupervised word sense disambiguation rivaling supervised methods. In *Proceedings of the 33rd annual meeting on Association for Computational Linguistics*, pages 189–196. Association for Computational Linguistics.

Learning Distributed Representations for Multilingual Text Sequences

Hieu Pham **Minh-Thang Luong** **Christopher D. Manning**
Computer Science Department Stanford University, Stanford, CA, 94305
{hyhieu,lmthang,manning}@stanford.edu

Abstract

We propose a novel approach to learning distributed representations of variable-length text sequences in multiple languages simultaneously. Unlike previous work which often derive representations of multi-word sequences as weighted sums of individual word vectors, our model learns distributed representations for phrases and sentences as a whole. Our work is similar in spirit to the recent paragraph vector approach but extends to the bilingual context so as to efficiently encode meaning-equivalent text sequences of multiple languages in the same semantic space. Our learned embeddings achieve state-of-the-art performance in the often used crosslingual document classification task (CLDC) with an accuracy of 92.7 for English to German and 91.5 for German to English. By learning text sequence representations as a whole, our model performs equally well in both classification directions in the CLDC task in which past work did not achieve.

1 Introduction

Distributed representations of words, also known as word embeddings, are critical components of many neural network based NLP systems. Such representations overcome the sparsity of natural languages by representing words with high-dimensional vectors in a continuous space. These vectors encode semantic information of words, leading to success in a wide range of tasks, such as sequence tagging, sentiment analysis, and parsing (Collobert et al., 2011; Maas et al., 2011; Socher et al., 2013a; Chen and Manning, 2014). As a natural extension, being able to learn representations for larger language structures such as phrases or sentences, has also been of interest to the community lately, for instance (Socher et al., 2013b; Le and Mikolov, 2014).

In the multilingual context, most of the recent work in bilingual representation learning such as (Klementiev et al., 2012; Mikolov et al., 2013b; Zou et al., 2013; Hermann and Blunsom, 2014; Kočiský et al., 2014; Gouws et al., 2014) only focus on learning embeddings for words and use simple functions, e.g., idf-weighted sum, to synthesize representations for larger text sequences from their word members. In contrast, our work aims to learn representations for phrases and sentences as a whole so as to represent non-compositional meanings.

In essence, we extend the paragraph vector approach proposed by Le and Mikolov (2014) to the bilingual context to efficiently encode meaning-equivalent multi-word sequences in the same semantic space. Our method only utilizes parallel data and eschews the use of word alignments. When tested on the often used crosslingual document classification (CLDC) tasks, our learned embeddings yield state-of-the-art performance with an accuracy of 92.7 for English to German and 91.5 for German to English. One notable feature of our model is that it performs equally well in both classification directions in the CLDC task in which past work did not achieve as we detail later in the experiment section.

2 Related work

Word representations – Work in learning distributed representations for words can largely be

Proceedings of NAACL-HLT 2015, pages 88–94,
Denver, Colorado, May 31 – June 5, 2015. ©2015 Association for Computational Linguistics

grouped into two categories: (a) pseudo-supervised methods which make use of properties in the unannotated training data as supervised signals and (b) task-specific approaches that utilizes annotated data to learn a prediction task. For the former, word embeddings are often part of neural language models that learn to predict next words given contexts by either minimizing the cross-entropy (Bengio et al., 2003; Morin, 2005; Mnih and Hinton, 2009; Mikolov et al., 2010; Mikolov et al., 2011) or maximizing the ranking margins (Collobert and Weston, 2008; Huang et al., 2012; Luong et al., 2013). Representatives for the latter include (Collobert and Weston, 2008; Maas et al., 2011; Socher et al., 2013a) which finetune embeddings for various tasks such as sequence labelling, sentiment analysis, and constituent parsing.

Larger structure representations – Learning distributed representation for phrases and sentences is harder because one needs to learn both the compositional and non-compositional meanings beyond words. A method that learns distributed representations of sentences, which is closely related to our approach, is the paragraph vector by Le and Mikolov (2014). The method attempts to predict words in N-grams of a sentence, given the same shared sentence vector. Errors are backpropagated to train not only the word vectors but also the sentence vector. This method has an advantage that it only requires training data to be sequences of words unlike other work that require annotated data such as parse trees (Socher et al., 2013b; Socher et al., 2013a).

Multilingual embedding – Previous work to learning multilingual distributed representations, often optimize for a joint objective consisting of several monolingual components, such as neural language models, and a bilingual component to tie representations across languages together. The bilingual objective varies through different approaches and can be formulated as either a multi-task learning objective (Klementiev et al., 2012), a translation probability (Kočiský et al., 2014), or an L_2 distance of various forms between corresponding words (Mikolov et al., 2013b; Zou et al., 2013; Gouws et al., 2014).

The work of Hermann and Blunsom (2014) and Chandar A P et al. (2014) are similar to our work in eliminating the monolingual components and just training a model with bilingual objective to pull distributed representations of parallel sentences together. These approaches, however, only use simple bag-of-word models to compute sentence representations and has a potential disadvantage that it is hard to capture the non-compositional meanings of sentences. Instead, we learn representations for text sequences as a whole, similar to Le and Mikolov (2014), but in the bilingual context.

3 Joint-space bilingual embedding

In this section, we describe our method to learn the distributed representations of sentences from two languages given a parallel corpus. Our learned representations have the property that sequences of words with equivalent meanings across different languages will have their representations clustered together in the shared semantic space. We call this property the clustering constraint.

Our method is based on the following assumptions observed by (Le and Mikolov, 2014): the distributed representation vector of a sequence of words can contribute its knowledge to predict the N-grams in the sequence, and conversely, if a vector can contribute well to the task, then one can think of it as the representation of the sequence. Since the assumption is not made specific to any language, we generalize it to learn the distributed representation of word sequences in multiple languages. However, instead of duplicating the representations to have one vector per sentence per language, we simply force parallel sentences in the languages of consideration to share only one vector. This allows us to avoid a bilingual term in our learning objective function to cluster the corresponding vectors together.

Figure 1 illustrates the architecture of our model. Each word in each language is associated with a D-dimensional vector, whereas each parallel sentence is tied to the same sentence vector of dimension P. These word and sentence vectors are used to predict N-grams in both of the sentences. More precisely, suppose that $s_1, s_2, ..., s_S$ and $t_1, t_2, ..., t_T$ are our two parallel sentences that share the same sentence representation v. For every N-gram $[w_{i-N+1}, w_{i-N+2}, ..., w_i]$, where w can be either s or t, our model computes the N-gram probability as follows

$$p(w_i | w_{i-N+1}, ..., w_{i-1}) = p(w_i | f) \qquad (1)$$

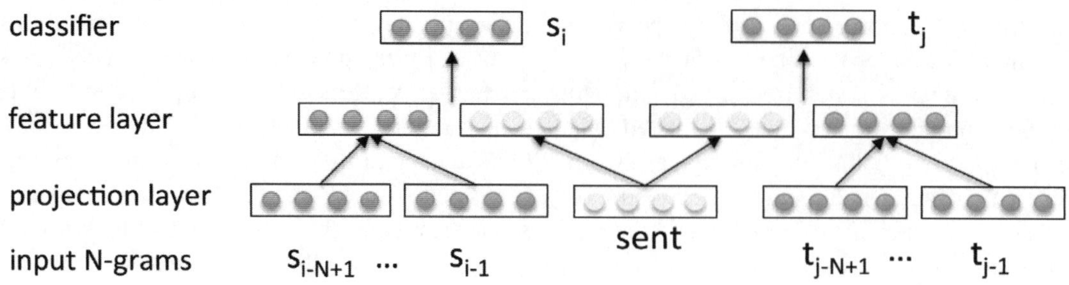

Figure 1: Our architecture to learn bilingual distributed representations of sentences. *sent* is the shared context that contributes to predicting N-grams in both sentences.

where f is a feature vector computed based on the N-gram and the shared sentence vector v.

There are several ways to compute f. As proposed in (Le and Mikolov, 2014), one can either take the average of v and the word embeddings of $w_{i-N+1}, w_{i-N+2}, ..., w_{i-1}$ or concatenate them to form f. In the former "average" approach, one always needs $D = P$, which implies that the contribution of v is less impactful as it needs to compete with the other $(N-1)$ word representations in the average term. In the latter "concatenate" approach, the dimension of f is $P + (N-1) \times D$, which suggests that the model cannot afford to have large word embedding size or longer N-grams. To overcome both problems, we propose to concatenate v with the sum of the word vectors in each of the N-grams. More precisely

$$f = \left[v; \sum_{j=i-N+1}^{i-1} w_j \right] \tag{2}$$

This hybrid approach allows us the freedom to tune D and P for our purpose.

There are also numerous approaches for the classifier that predicts the next word. However, to optimize for efficiency, we narrow our choices to the factorized multiclass classifier, also known as the hierarchical softmax (Morin, 2005). The words in the vocabulary of each language are represented as leaf-nodes of a binary tree. Each node n of the tree has a vector v_p whose dimension is equal to that of the feature vector f. These vectors encode the model's belief whether a f belongs to the left or the right child of n

$$p(\text{go left}|\text{node } n, f) = \sigma\left(f^T \cdot v_n\right) \tag{3}$$

where $\sigma(\cdot)$ is the logistic sigmoid function and v_n is a vector associated to the node n. The probability of seeing a word is then factored into the product of probabilities of the node along the path from the tree's root to the node corresponding to it.

At training time, pairs of parallel sentences are shown to the model for several epochs. The model maintains the shared sentence vectors and updates them, along with the word vectors and hierarchical softmax parameters of both languages, to minimize the cross-entropy prediction error

$$J = -\sum_{(s,t)} \log p(s,t), \tag{4}$$

where the probability of the pair of sentences (s,t) is computed simply based on the Markov assumption

$$\begin{aligned} p(s,t) &= \prod_{i=1}^{S} p(s_i|s_{i-N+1}, ..., s_{i-1}) \\ &\times \prod_{j=1}^{T} p(t_j|t_{j-N+1}, ..., t_{j-1}) \end{aligned} \tag{5}$$

At test time, the model is given one sentence in one of the languages it has been trained on. To compute the representation of that sentence, we randomly initialize a vector and train it in the same setting as above, but to predict only N-grams from one sentence. We update only the sentence vector; other parameters are preserved. We want to emphasize that due to the random initialization, the sentence embeddings computed by our model are not deterministic, in the sense that if the model sees a sentence twice, it is possible that two different embeddings will be learned for the same sentence. This might potentially be a cause of nondeterminism if other models attempt to learn or classify based on these sentence vectors. However, our training objective for each N-gram has the form

$$J_{N\text{-gram}} = -\sum_{n} \log\left(\sigma\left(f^T \cdot v_n\right)\right), \quad (6)$$

Since $\sigma(\cdot)$ is log-concave, our training objective is convex. This guarantees a global minimum sentence embedding vector to which our sentence vectors would converge. Moreover, at train time, the model has been trained to minimize the prediction errors of pairs of sentences that share the same sentence vector, its parameters have adapted to this manner. Hence, at test time, although two sentence vectors are learned independently, one can expect that they converge to close points in the shared semantic space.

4 Experiments

4.1 Training data and procedures

We attempt to learn the distributed representation for arbitrary sequences of words in English and German. We train our model using the `Europarl v7` multilingual corpora (Koehn, 2005), in particular the English-German corpus. The corpus consists of multilingual parliament documents automatically aligned into $1.8M$ equivalent pairs of sentences. We preprocess the corpus by filtering out the tokens that appear less than 5 times and desegment the German compound words. This leads to the final set of $43K$ English words and $95K$ German words.

Parameters of our model are updated using a gradient-based method. While for each pair of sentences, the prediction and N-grams and parameter updates are performed in sequence, our training implementation uses the multithreading approach to train through pairs of sentences in our training corpus in parallel and updates parameters with asynchronous gradient descent. Since our model predicts N-gram probabilities, we tune our hyperparameters, including P, D and the learning rate, based on the model's perplexity on the `newstests` development data provided by the Workshop in Machine Translation[1].

[1]`http://www.statmt.org/wmt15/`

At the beginning of our training procedure, we use `word2vec` (Mikolov et al., 2013a) to guide our hierarchical softmax trees. In particular, first we precompute the distributed representations for all the tokens in all the languages and run the K-Means algorithm to classify our word vectors into C classes based on L_2 distance. Then, we sort each language's vocabulary into contiguous strides of the same class. Finally, we construct our hierarchical softmax tree as the weight-balanced binary tree on each of the sorted vocab. The resulted hierarchical softmax trees thus have the semantic information about the cluster of words held by each of its nodes, similar to the WordNet taxanomy tree (Fellbaum, 1998).

We performed experiments with different settings for the model's architecture, such as the dimension P of sentence vectors, D of word vectors, and N-gram length N, and the learning rate. Our finding is that $P \approx 5D$ generally gives the best performance. Also we used the start learning rate of 0.0001 which decreases as the model is trained for more epochs. We trained all models for 50 epochs. In Section 5, we will discuss the effect of the parameters P and D. Following, we report our best experiment results, with $P = 500$, $D = 100$, $N = 7$ and $C = 500$.

4.2 Document classification on RCV1/RCV2

We test the learned bilingual distributed representations on the English-German Cross-Lingual Document Classification (CLDC, henceforth), proposed by (Klementiev et al., 2012). The corpus consists of documents from Reuter, written in English and German, annotated into 4 categories: Corporate/Industrial, Economics, Government/Social, and Markets. The documents are separated into $1K$ training documents and $5K$ test documents for each language. Each document in the dataset consist of only a few sentences, so the data is similar to the training data that our model has been trained on. The learned models are required to provide the distributed representations of all these documents, which are then passed to a perceptron algorithm to learn from training data and classify test data. The key challenge is that the perceptron algorithm has to learn in English and classify in Germen (`en`$\rightarrow$`de`) or vice versa (`de`$\rightarrow$`en`). To make the learning problem feasible, the document compositional model must satisfy the clustering constraint mentioned in *Section 3*.

As in (Klementiev et al., 2012), the CLDC dataset was proposed to evaluate embeddings of words only, so we follow the author in using the document compositional model where the document vector is computed by taking the sum of all embeddings of the words that appear in the document, weighted by their inverse document frequencies (idf). We refer to this method as `para_sum`. It demonstrates that the English and German word embeddings learned by our model indeed satisfy the clustering constraint. Our model achieves competitive classification result with `para_sum`.

However, our model has not only the word embeddings but also the capability of computing the distributed representation of arbitrary word sequences, so we propose computing the document vectors in this manner. We call this method `para_doc`. We find that `para_doc` gives significantly better results than `para_sum`, especially on the `de→en` direction. In Table 1, we present our classification results on the CLDC task and compare them against strong baselines. Specifically, we first show the results of the original baselines in (Klementiev et al., 2012), then we show the stronger baselines (Chandar A P et al., 2014; Hermann and Blunsom, 2014), which perform considerably better but the gains are uneven between `en→de` and `de→en`. Finally, we show that our method works better than all these baselines. While `para_sum` outperforms the all the baselines but still with a significantly worse result in `de→en`, `para_doc` achieves better results and at once, avoids the asymmetry of all the other approaches.

Model	`en→de`	`de→en`
Majority class	46.8	46.8
Glossed	65.1	68.6
Machine translation	68.1	67.4
I-Matrix	77.6	71.1
Autoencoder	91.8	72.8
Compositional Add+	87.7	77.5
Compositional Bigram+	86.1	79.0
`para_sum`	90.6	78.8
`para_doc`	**92.7**	**91.5**

Table 1: Performances on CLDC English-German. Each model is trained on one language and tested on the other one. The numbers reported are the percentage of correctly predicted test documents. The first four baselines (Klementiev et al., 2012) are less sensitive to languages, so we do not observe large difference between the tasks `en→de` and `de→en`. Other methods that involve weighted sum of word vectors by (Chandar A P et al., 2014) and (Hermann and Blunsom, 2014) perform better on `en→de` than on `de→en`. Our work bridges the gap and simultaneously achieves state-of-the-art performance on both tasks.

5 Discussion

5.1 Symmetry of multilingual model

The key to succeed on the CLDC task is that equivalent documents in English and German should be mapped into similar points in the joint semantic space. This goal, however, is hard to achieve by using the idf weighted sum of word vectors in documents as proposed by (Klementiev et al., 2012). The major reason for this is perhaps due to the linguistic asymmetry between English and German. For example, verbs in German have more conjugations than their English counterparts and there is generally a large number of compound words in German. These phenomena are evidenced by the fact that the German vocab size is about twice of that of English ($95K$ versus $43K$) according to our training data. As a result, many German words appear less often, giving the model less opportunity to optimize for their representations. All these observations explain that it is inferior to simply represent documents as as weighted sum of the embeddings of their words. As highlighted in Table 1, methods that adopt the weighted average approach all suffer from the discrepancy between `en→de` and `de→en` CLDC results. Note that such asymmetry also holds for our learned word vectors when we simply sum them up (the `para_sum` row).

On the other hand, our second approach to compute document vectors does not suffer from this problem. At train time, we have already aimed at learning the same distributed representation for sentences (the clustering constraint on vectors of equivalent words follows only as a consequence). At test time, the same clustering constraint leads the document vectors computed by our model to be more symmetric than the weighted sum of word vectors. This symmetrization explains why our classification results on en→de and de→en using para_doc are about equally strong, and both are better than those of para_sum.

5.2 Effects of embedding dimensions

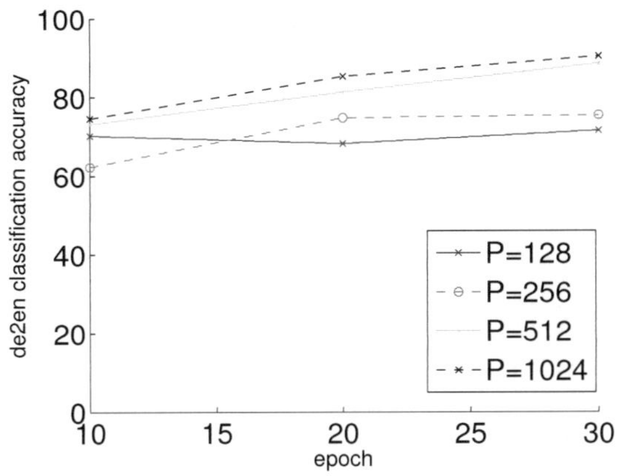

Figure 2: Test results for the de→en CLDC task across training epochs. Larger P gives better result while converging slower at test time.

We train four models on English-German data with with $D = 128$ and $P \in \{128, 256, 512, 1024\}$ and compare their test performances as training progresses. As demonstrated in Figure 2, models with larger P give better classification results (though they require more test iterations to converge to good sentence embeddings).

6 Conclusion

In summary, we have presented our novel approach to computing distributed representations of arbitrary word sequences in different languages from unannotated parallel data. Our method achieves state-of-the-art performance on a bilingual benchmark between English and German. We also gave our intuitions to explain why the model works even though it is nondeterministic while computing sentence vectors at test time. Further intuitions also suggest that it is possible to incorporate new languages into the model without hurting the previously known one. In the future, we plan to investigate the model's capacity to learn embeddings in other languages, such as French.

Acknowledgment

We gratefully acknowledge support from a gift from Bloomberg L.P. and from the Defense Advanced Research Projects Agency (DARPA) Broad Operational Language Translation (BOLT) program under contract HR0011-12-C-0015 through IBM. Any opinions, findings, and conclusions or recommendations expressed in this material are those of the author(s) and do not necessarily reflect the view of DARPA, or the US government. We also thank members of the Stanford NLP Group as well as the annonymous reviewers for their valuable comments and feedbacks.

References

Yoshua Bengio, Rejean Ducharme, Pascal Vincent, and Christian Jauvin. 2003. A neural probabilistic language model. *JMLR*, 3:1137–1155.

Sarath Chandar A P, Stanislas Lauly, Hugo Larochelle, Mitesh Khapra, Balaraman Ravindran, Vikas C Raykar, and Amrita Saha. 2014. An autoencoder approach to learning bilingual word representations. In *NIPS*.

Danqi Chen and Christopher D Manning. 2014. A fast and accurate dependency parser using neural networks. In *EMNLP*.

Ronan Collobert and Jason Weston. 2008. A unified architecture for natural language processing: deep neural networks with multitask learning. In *ICML*.

Ronan Collobert, Jason Weston, Leon Bottou, Michael Karlen, Koray Kavukcuoglu, and Pavel Kuksa. 2011. Natural language processing (almost) from scratch. *JMLR*, 12:2493–2537.

Christiane Fellbaum. 1998. *WordNet: An Electronic Lexical Database*. Bradford Books.

Stephan Gouws, Yoshua Bengio, and Greg Corrado. 2014. Bilbowa: Fast bilingual distributed representations without word alignments. In *NIPS Deep Learning Workshop*.

Karl Moritz Hermann and Phil Blunsom. 2014. Multilingual Models for Compositional Distributional Semantics. In *ACL*.

E. H. Huang, R. Socher, C. D. Manning, and A. Y. Ng. 2012. Improving word representations via global context and multiple word prototypes. In *ACL*.

Alexandre Klementiev, Ivan Titov, and Binod Bhattarai. 2012. Inducing crosslingual distributed representations of words. In *COLING*.

Philipp Koehn. 2005. Europarl: A Parallel Corpus for Statistical Machine Translation. In *MT Summit*.

Tomáš Kočiský, Karl Moritz Hermann, and Phil Blunsom. 2014. Learning Bilingual Word Representations by Marginalizing Alignments. In *ACL*.

Quoc Le and Tomas Mikolov. 2014. Distributed representations of sentences and documents. In *ICML*.

Minh-Thang Luong, Richard Socher, and Christopher D. Manning. 2013. Better word representations with recursive neural networks for morphology. In *CoNLL*.

Andrew L. Maas, Raymond E. Daly, Peter T. Pham, Dan Huang, Andrew Y. Ng, and Christopher Potts. 2011. Learning word vectors for sentiment analysis. In *NAACL-HLT*.

Tomas Mikolov, Martin Karafiát, Lukas Burget, Jan Cernocký, and Sanjeev Khudanpur. 2010. Recurrent neural network based language model. In *Interspeech*.

Tomas Mikolov, Stefan Kombrink, Lukas Burget, Jan Cernocký, and Sanjeev Khudanpur. 2011. Extensions of recurrent neural network language model. In *ICASSP*.

Tomas Mikolov, Kai Chen, Greg Corrado, and Jeffrey Dean. 2013a. Efficient estimation of word representations in vector space. In *ICLR*.

Tomas Mikolov, Quoc V. Le, and Ilya Sutskever. 2013b. Exploiting similarities among languages for machine translation. *CoRR*, abs/1309.4168.

Andriy Mnih and Geoffrey Hinton. 2009. A scalable hierarchical distributed language model. In *NIPS*.

Frederic Morin. 2005. Hierarchical probabilistic neural network language model. In *AISTATS*.

Richard Socher, John Bauer, Christopher D. Manning, and Andrew Y. Ng. 2013a. Parsing With Compositional Vector Grammars. In *ACL*.

Richard Socher, Alex Perelygin, Jean Wu, Jason Chuang, Christopher D. Manning, Andrew Y. Ng, and Christopher Potts. 2013b. Recursive deep models for semantic compositionality over a sentiment treebank. In *EMNLP*.

Will Y. Zou, Richard Socher, Daniel Cer, and Christopher D. Manning. 2013. Bilingual word embeddings for phrase-based machine translation. In *EMNLP*.

Combining Distributed Vector Representations for Words

Justin Garten and **Kenji Sagae** and **Volkan Ustun** and **Morteza Dehghani**
University of Southern California
Los Angeles, CA 90089, USA
{jgarten, mdehghan}@usc.edu, and {sagae, ustun}@ict.usc.edu

Abstract

Recent interest in distributed vector representations for words has resulted in an increased diversity of approaches, each with strengths and weaknesses. We demonstrate how diverse vector representations may be inexpensively composed into hybrid representations, effectively leveraging strengths of individual components, as evidenced by substantial improvements on a standard word analogy task. We further compare these results over different sizes of training sets and find these advantages are more pronounced when training data is limited. Finally, we explore the relative impacts of the differences in the learning methods themselves and the size of the contexts they access.

1 Introduction

Distributed vector representations allow words to be represented in a continuous space. By learning these representations using unsupervised methods over large corpora, these models capture key distributional aspects of word function and meaning. In particular, such representations provide a valuable response to issues of data sparsity by providing simple similarity measures between terms. Whether used indirectly in terms of those similarity measures (e.g. for smoothing in language models) or directly as features to a model for tasks such as parsing (Lei et al., 2014), these representations have proved increasingly valuable to a variety of NLP tasks (Bengio et al., 2013).

Given these benefits, a number of approaches have been explored for generating these representations beginning with early work in connectionist modeling (McClelland et al., 1986) and expanding into applications in text analysis. Recently, in part spurred by the resurgence of neural network methods, vector representations have enjoyed renewed attention, expanding beyond their previous scope with the appearance of a variety of new techniques for their generation and applications for their use.

The various approaches have been shown to have a variety of strengths and weaknesses and it is precisely in the context of this proliferation that our work is focused. Presented with diversity of techniques, other areas of machine learning have found excellent results with the use of ensemble methods (Dietterich, 2000), combining multiple techniques to capture the strengths of each. We examine whether similar gains are available here through the combination of multiple existing techniques for generating semantic vector representations.

Recent work has shown that relationships in these models (such as gender differences or pluralization) are often linear (Mikolov et al., 2013b). Drawing on this, we explore composition through linear combinations of these representational spaces. In particular, we explore combinations of a popular neural network method (Word2Vec) (Mikolov et al., 2013a) with Distributed Vector Representations in Sigma (DVRS) (Ustun et al., 2014), a method based on prior work in holographic representation (Jones and Mewhort, 2007). We demonstrate that various methods of composing these vectors can produce hybrid representations which perform significantly better than either method in isolation. This leap in performance is particularly pronounced when working with smaller datasets, opening up intriguing possibilities for domains which lack large corpora.

Proceedings of NAACL-HLT 2015, pages 95–101,
Denver, Colorado, May 31 – June 5, 2015. ©2015 Association for Computational Linguistics

2 Related Work

Most techniques for generating semantic vector spaces focus on the distributional properties of texts, building representations based on word co-occurrence patterns. Key factors differentiating these methods include the size of the context used in this process, and how the context is used.

Document-level representations consider co-occurrences at the document level, often making use of weighting factors such as *tf-idf*. Techniques such as Latent Semantic Analysis (LSA) (Deerwester et al., 1990) make use of this approach, building a word-document co-occurrence matrix for an entire corpus.

Other methods make use of a sliding window of words in a corpus, considering only words which occur within a certain distance of the target. The skip gram and continuous bag of words methods in Word2Vec are examples of this approach. Rather than a fixed width sampling space, other approaches make use of either sentence level (Levy and Goldberg, 2014a) (critical when using sentence-level parsing information) or paragraph windows, making use of the structure of the text itself to determine the window size.

Yet another class of methods makes use of randomly initialized word values with updates based on the local context. Techniques such as as BEAGLE (Jones and Mewhort, 2007) capture ordering information through the use of circular convolutions while DVRS makes use of piecewise vector multiplications over random projections.

As we make particular use of DVRS and Word2Vec, it is worth looking at the methods used by each in more detail.

2.1 DVRS

DVRS (Ustun et al., 2014) is a method for generating semantic vector representations based on ideas introduced in Jones and Mewhort (2007)'s BEAGLE system. Each word is represented by two vectors. The fixed environmental vector, $e(i)$, is randomly generated by drawing each element of the vector from a uniform distribution on $[-1, 1)$. The lexical vector $l(i)$ captures the word's distributional meaning and is updated over the course of training.

As the corpus is processed, the lexical vector for each encountered word is updated based on its paragraph context $c(k)$ and its sentence order context $o(k)$. The paragraph context is the sum of the environmental vectors in the paragraph, excluding the word being updated.

$$c(k) = \sum_{i=1}^{n} e(i), \text{where } i \neq k$$

The order context is based on the sentence and makes use of sequence vectors, random vectors which correspond the relative positions from the target word (by defaults ± 4). The word order information, $o(k)$, is then calculated as follows (where $*$ is the pointwise product operation):

$$o(k) = \sum_{j=-4}^{4} s(j) * e(k + j),$$

where $j \neq 0$ and $0 < (k + j) \leq n$.

DVRS updates via gradient descent where the gradient is based on the weighted sum of the order and context vectors.

$$l(k) = l(k) + w_c \hat{c(k)} + w_o \hat{o(k)}$$

In this update process, we see a precursor of the compositional techniques described below in that DVRS is already effectively composing two representations (the context and order spaces) into a combined representation.

2.2 Word2Vec

The Word2Vec model learns word representations through a pair of architectures similar to standard feedforward neural net language models. The Continuous Bag-of-Words (CBOW) model effectively averages the vectors of all the words in a given context. The model is trained by predicting the current word based on the projected average of the surrounding context. The continuous Skip-gram model is similar, but instead of predicting the current word based on context, predicts the surrounding words based on the current. Words within a certain distance before and after the current word are predicted with the network optimized for these predictions.

3 Experiment 1: Methods of composing word representations

We extend the underlying concept of DVRS, the notion that multiple vector spaces can be linearly combined to provide more effective distributional representations, by exploring the possibility of combining vector representations from completely separate generation techniques and the impact of different methods of composition. In particular, we explore the composition of Word2Vec and DVRS, effectively combining vectors produced by a neural network approach (particularly the predictive approach provided by the skip-gram model) with the larger context and count-based co-occurrence aggregation of the DVRS model. Across these components, we compare the compositional techniques of direct vector addition with vector concatenation.

We began by exploring alternative methods of combining vector representations. In particular, we looked at the differences between vector addition and concatenation. To get a better sense of the strengths and limits of these methods, we also compared against an oracle method where each of the individual models was tested and, if either was able to provide the correct answer, the oracle provided the answer from that model (exploring a hypothetically ideal simple combination of the two models).

For each of the following methods, we trained vectors against both the first 10^8 bytes of a Wikipedia dump from March 3, 2006 (enwik8) and the first 10^9 bytes of the same dump (enwik9)[1]. The data was initially pre-processed to convert all text to lower case, convert numbers to text, and eliminate links and other references[2].

For Word2Vec, we used the default settings (window size of 10, negative sampling (25), sampling (1e-4), and trained over 15 iterations) to create vectors of 300 and 1024 dimensions using both the skip gram and CBOW models. For DVRS, we created vectors of both 300 and 1024 dimensions, both using the default DVRS combination of order and context vectors and each of these components separately. These numbers were chosen based on previously published results where these values produced the best results for DVRS (1024 dimensions) and Word2Vec (300) respectively.

We tested combining these representational spaces through concatenation and addition. Addition required that the two spaces have the same rank and was accomplished using simple vector addition. The value for each word in the new space was the normalized sum of its two component spaces.

$$x_{new} = x_1 + x_2$$

We compared this against the direct concatenation of the two vectors for a given word. This allowed for the use of vectors with different underlying ranks.

$$x_{new} = x_1 \frown x_2$$

3.1 Results

There are a number of ways of evaluating the quality of vector representations. The space can be evaluated directly, for example by considering target words in terms of their evaluated similarity to their nearest neighbors in the space. Alternately, the space itself can be evaluated in terms of its usefulness as a feature for a known task.

We make use of the set of approximately 20,000 word analogy tests introduced by Mikolov et al (Mikolov et al., 2013a). Covering a mix of semantic and syntactic categories, each problem is based on a simple pattern of the form "A is to A* as B is to B*." Given A, A*, and B, the system is required to predict the correct B*. The test set includes 8,869 semantic test instances (with categories such as national capitals of the form "Athens is to Greece as Helsinki is to [Finland]") and 10,675 syntactic test instances (with categories such as superlatives such as "strong is to strongest as warm is to [warmest]"). We randomly split these tests, reserving 20% of the data for development and optimization and making use of the remaining 80% (15646 questions) for the test results below.

For experiment 1, the results are summarized in Table 1 (representations trained on the enwik8 dataset) and Table 2 (representations trained on the enwik9 dataset). For enwik8, among the individual-model directly-trained vectors, the Word2Vec skip gram model produced the best results with an overall accuracy of 30% on the test set compared to DVRS' best perfromance of 27%. However, while the skip gram model was always the top performer on the syntactic categories, DVRS turned in the best results on the semantic categories.

We then explored several methods of combining these vectors with the results summarized in Table 1. The addition of the 300-dimensional DVRS

[1]Obtained from `http://cs.fit.edu/~mmahoney/compression/textdata.html`.

[2]We used the script provided with the Wikipedia dump by Matt Mahoney.

vectors (overall performance 0.23) with the 300-dimensional skip gram vectors (overall performance 0.30) led to an overall improvement to 0.32. However, concatenating these two vectors improved the overall performance to 39%. Concatenating the best two performing vector sizes for each method (DVRS-1024, SG-300), yielded a slightly below peak overall accuracy of 0.38. Finally, we compared these results to an oracle method where, rather than composing the representations, we had each representation make its prediction and, if either was correct, used that as the oracle's response. This yielded an overall accuracy of 41%.

Next, we tested the methods against enwik9 as seen in Table 2. With additional training data, the performance of both methods jumped, with Word2Vec's skip gram model improving to an accuracy of 0.64 and DVRS improving to 0.43. While DVRS no longer showed the strong advantage on the semantic categories, nonetheless the concatenation of the two results showed a significant improvement to 0.67.

4 Experiment 2: Impacts of varying model parameters and input data

Following up on the initial experiment, we began to explore how much of the differences came from the structures of the algorithms versus the data available to the models. We varied the size of the context available to both Word2Vec and DVRS and the window size used by Word2Vec. In particular, we varied the parameters available to the best performing combinations from the previous experiment. Given the results of our prior experiment, we focused on concatenation rather than additive combinations.

We trained vectors against two versions of the enwik9 dump, one divided into paragraphs, the other into sentences. For Word2Vec, we varied the window size from 10 to 50, testing against both paragraph and sentence versions. Given the expanded window size, we chose to include the continuous bag of words (CBOW) model for Word2Vec. This is an alternative to the skip gram model which does not take into account word ordering. Given this, it seemed like this model might do better given the larger window size. DVRS structurally makes use of the full context available, so running it against paragraphs and sentences provided an analogous shift in effective window size.

4.1 Results

For this experiment, the results are summarized in Table 3. As seen in the previous experiment, the concatenated models generally did better than the component models. While window size made a slight difference for all the models, the differences in the algorithms seemed more important (with the caveat that more data is required for a definitive statement on this). In particular, the Word2Vec models and DVRS responded in opposite directions to having access to a larger window of data. DVRS performance improved slightly (from 0.407 to 0.409) while the Word2Vec models degraded slightly (for skip grams, from 0.640 to 0.594). This seems natural given that both Word2Vec models make use of sampling. Given that, a larger window simply distributes those samples over a larger and, likely, less meaningful space. Meanwhile, DVRS combines the complete context window to which it has access into a single factor, making larger windows more valuable to it (although at the cost of obscuring more local relations such as syntactic factors).

Nonetheless, as seen with DVRS where, in spite of inferior overall performance, it still proved effective as a concatenative element, we wanted to explore whether Word2Vec-trained vectors with larger windows might prove more effective in an ensemble. The results suggest that this may be the case. In particular, the concatenation of the two best performing Word2Vec models (the skip gram and CBOW models trained on sentences with a window size of 10) performed slightly worse (accuracy 0.655) than models which blended the best individual Word2Vec vectors (skip gram, sentence, window 10) with others (CBOW, paragraph, window 50) trained on a larger window (accuracy 0.664). However, the results here are sufficiently close that it will require more tests on a larger range of data before a general rule can be suggested.

Overall, the best performing concatenations were those where the differences in the two components was greatest. So, within Word2Vec-trained vectors, the skip gram with window 10 trained on sentences with the CBOW model with window 50 trained on paragraphs (0.664). As in the previous experi-

	Vector size	Overall	Semantic	Syntactic
DVRS	300	0.23	0.31	0.15
DVRS	1024	0.27	**0.40**	0.17
Skip gram (SG)	300	**0.30**	0.24	**0.34**
SG	1024	0.25	0.17	0.32
Add DVRS-300, SG-300	300	0.32	0.31	0.33
Concatenate DVRS-300, SG-300	600	**0.39**	**0.38**	0.39
Add DVRS-1024, SG-1024	2048	0.36	0.33	0.38
Concatenate DVRS-1024, SG-1024	2048	0.38	0.36	**0.40**
Concatenate DVRS-1024, SG-300	1324	0.38	**0.38**	0.39
Oracle DVRS-1024, SG-300	1024/300	0.41	0.44	0.39

Table 1: Performance on word analogy problems with vectors trained against the first 10^8 bytes of Wikipedia.

	Vector size	Overall	Semantic	Syntactic
DVRS	300	0.41	0.59	0.26
DVRS	1024	0.43	0.62	0.28
SG	300	**0.64**	**0.69**	**0.60**
SG	1024	0.57	0.60	0.55
Add 300-DVRS, 300-SG	300	0.64	0.72	0.58
Concatenate 300-DVRS, 300-SG	600	**0.67**	**0.74**	**0.60**
Add 1024-DVRS, 1024-SG	1024	0.60	0.66	0.55
Concatenate 1024-DVRS, 1024-SG	2048	0.61	0.68	0.55
Concatenate DVRS-1024, SG-300	1324	0.66	0.73	**0.60**
Oracle DVRS-1024, SG-300	1024/300	0.70	0.79	0.62

Table 2: Performance on word analogy problems with vectors trained against the first 10^9 bytes of Wikipedia.

ments, the best overall result (although marginally so) came from the concatenation of skip gram, sentence, window 10 with DVRS trained on paragraphs (0.671). Finally, even in cases where we were combining vectors from the same model but with different window sizes, we still found a small but consistent improvement in overall performance (for skip grams from 0.640 to 0.662, for CBOW from 0.635 to 0.660, and for DVRS from 0.409 to 0.426).

Care must be taken not to take these results as a claim that a specific combination recipe is correct or preferred. Instead, what our results show convincingly is that the combination of diverse representations can leverage strengths of individual representations, and that the effects of vector combination should be investigated in the context of specific tasks, which we leave as future work.

5 Discussion and Future Work

The question remains of how and why these compositions are working. While we do not claim a final answer to this question, we can point to several factors given these experiments. For the concatenated composition technique, we are left with the two vectors from the original spaces normalized into a single vector. For cosine similarity, the key factor is the dot product. For two vectors x_c and y_c which were formed by concatenating the corresponding vectors x_1 and x_2 from the original spaces, this yields:

$$x_c \cdot y_c = x_1 \cdot y_1 + x_2 \cdot y_2$$

As such, cosine similarity in the concatenated space is determined by a linear combination of the dot products of the component vectors. This provides an intuitive story for some of the behaviors

	Vector size	Overall	Semantic	Syntactic
skip gram (SG), paragraph (para), window 50	200	0.596	0.648	0.554
SG, sentence (sent), win 50	200	0.594	0.648	0.550
SG, sent, win 10	200	**0.640**	**0.682**	**0.607**
CBOW, para, win 50	200	0.603	0.672	0.547
CBOW, sent, win 50	200	0.599	0.661	0.548
CBOW, sent, win 10	200	0.635	0.673	0.604
DVRS, sent	300	0.407	0.590	0.259
DVRS, para	300	0.409	0.592	0.261
concat SG sent win 10, CBOW sent win 10	400	0.655	0.711	0.609
concat SG sent win 10, CBOW para win 50	400	0.664	0.735	0.607
concat SG sent win 10, SG para win 50	400	0.662	0.720	**0.614**
concat CBOW sent win 10, CBOW para win 50	400	0.660	0.727	0.605
concat DVRS para, SG sent win 10	500	**0.671**	**0.744**	0.612
concat DVRS sent, DVRS para	600	0.426	0.616	0.273
concat DVRS sent, CBOW para win 50	500	0.645	0.741	0.566
concat DVRS sent, SG sent win 10	500	0.666	0.739	0.606

Table 3: Variations on window size and data structure with vectors trained against the first 10^9 bytes of Wikipedia.

seen in that a close match with the correct answer in one space will tend to overcome drift in the other. However, a precise accounting of the variations in this behavior is one area where further work is required. In particular, exploring the impact of variations in the weights of this linear combination (easily done simply by weighting one of the vectors prior to concatenation) is an obvious first step. Additionally, it will be interesting to explore the combination of more than two vectors, effectively defining a new semantic space over those bases.

Generally, in the continuing discussion about the relative merits of count-based and prediction-based methods (Baroni et al., 2014), the present work suggests that there may not be a need to choose. By combining both methods through simple compositional functions, we show that it is possible to combine the benefits of both models in a single hybrid representation. Given the extensive work put into the development of distributed representations and the known variations in relative strengths and weaknesses, the benefit of these simple combination schemes is intriguing. We plan to explore the effects of vector combination in downstream tasks.

This work provides several key initial pieces. The first is an existence proof that, even with the most basic approaches and settings, it is possible to improve on the performance of individual models with only minimal increases in system complexity. Second, these experiments demonstrate that the local performance of a given representation is not necessarily a complete representation of its value as a component. In particular, inferior representations may still encode information which proves valuable to an ensemble. Finally, the observed improvements when vectors trained using the same method but with differing window sizes suggests that it may be possible to improve the performance of these algorithms (both Word2Vec models and DVRS) by making use of these observations, perhaps through the use of variable window sizes. In particular, we do not suggest that vector combination is the only way to achieve these improvements. There are multiple routes to incorporating this information within a single method.

One clear next step is to explore optimizing the weights of the components of the combinations in the context of particular tasks. Additionally, given recent discussions over alternative similarity measures (Levy and Goldberg, 2014b), it will be interesting to explore the generalization across spaces where non-linear composition may be required. More generally, the combination of representations may point towards tensor methods where multiple factors are preserved in the tensor structure itself.

Acknowledgments

We thank the anonymous reviewers for insightful suggestions. The effort described here has been partially sponsored by the U.S. Army. Any opinions, content or information presented does not necessarily reflect the position or the policy of the United States Government, and no official endorsement should be inferred.

References

Marco Baroni, Georgiana Dinu, and Germán Kruszewski. 2014. Dont count, predict! a systematic comparison of context-counting vs. context-predicting semantic vectors. In *Proceedings of the 52nd Annual Meeting of the Association for Computational Linguistics*, volume 1, pages 238–247.

Yoshua Bengio, Aaron Courville, and Pascal Vincent. 2013. Representation learning: A review and new perspectives. *Pattern Analysis and Machine Intelligence, IEEE Transactions on*, 35(8):1798–1828.

Scott C. Deerwester, Susan T Dumais, Thomas K. Landauer, George W. Furnas, and Richard A. Harshman. 1990. Indexing by latent semantic analysis. *JASIS*, 41(6):391–407.

Thomas G Dietterich. 2000. Ensemble methods in machine learning. In *Multiple classifier systems*, pages 1–15. Springer.

Michael N Jones and Douglas JK Mewhort. 2007. Representing word meaning and order information in a composite holographic lexicon. *Psychological review*, 114(1):1.

Tao Lei, Yu Xin, Yuan Zhang, Regina Barzilay, and Tommi Jaakkola. 2014. Low-rank tensors for scoring dependency structures. In *Proceedings of the 52nd Annual Meeting of the Association for Computational Linguistics*.

Omer Levy and Yoav Goldberg. 2014a. Dependency-based word embeddings. In *Proceedings of the 52nd Annual Meeting of the Association for Computational Linguistics*, volume 2.

Omer Levy and Yoav Goldberg. 2014b. Linguistic regularities in sparse and explicit word representations. In *Proceedings of the Eighteenth Conference on Computational Natural Language Learning, Baltimore, Maryland, USA, June. Association for Computational Linguistics*.

James L McClelland, David E Rumelhart, PDP Research Group, et al. 1986. Parallel distributed processing. *Explorations in the microstructure of cognition*, 2.

Tomas Mikolov, Kai Chen, Greg Corrado, and Jeffrey Dean. 2013a. Efficient estimation of word representations in vector space. In *Workshop Proceedings of the International Conference on Learning Representations*.

Tomas Mikolov, Wen-tau Yih, and Geoffrey Zweig. 2013b. Linguistic regularities in continuous space word representations. In *Proceedings of the 2013 Conference of the North American Chapter of the Association for Computational Linguistics: Human Language Technologies*, pages 746–751, Atlanta, Georgia, June. Association for Computational Linguistics.

Volkan Ustun, PaulS. Rosenbloom, Kenji Sagae, and Abram Demski. 2014. Distributed vector representations of words in the sigma cognitive architecture. In Ben Goertzel, Laurent Orseau, and Javier Snaider, editors, *Artificial General Intelligence*, volume 8598 of *Lecture Notes in Computer Science*, pages 196–207. Springer International Publishing.

Dependency Link Embeddings: Continuous Representations of Syntactic Substructures

Mohit Bansal
Toyota Technological Institute at Chicago, IL 60637, USA
mbansal@ttic.edu

Abstract

We present a simple method to learn continuous representations of dependency substructures (links), with the motivation of directly working with higher-order, structured embeddings and their hidden relationships, and also to avoid the millions of sparse, template-based word-cluster features in dependency parsing. These link embeddings allow a significantly smaller and simpler set of *unary* features for dependency parsing, while maintaining improvements similar to state-of-the-art, n-ary word-cluster features, and also stacking over them. Moreover, these link vectors (made publicly available) are directly portable as off-the-shelf, dense, syntactic features in various NLP tasks. As one example, we incorporate them into constituent parse reranking, where their small feature set again matches the performance of standard non-local, manually-defined features, and also stacks over them.

1 Introduction

Word representations and more recently, word embeddings, learned from large amounts of text have been quite successful as features in various NLP tasks (Koo et al., 2008; Turian et al., 2010; Collobert et al., 2011; Dhillon et al., 2012; Al-Rfou' et al., 2013; Bansal et al., 2014; Guo et al., 2014; Pennington et al., 2014; Yu and Dredze, 2014; Faruqui et al., 2014; Wang et al., 2015). While these word representations do capture useful, dense relationships among known and unknown words, one still has to work with sparse conjunctions of features on the multiple words involved in the substructure that a task factors on, e.g., head-argument links in dependency parsing. Therefore, most statistical dependency parsers still suffer from millions of such conjoined, template-based, n-ary features on word clusters or embeddings (Koo et al., 2008; Bansal et al., 2014). Some recent work has addressed this issue, via low-rank tensor mappings (Lei et al., 2014), feature embeddings (Chen et al., 2014), or neural network parsers (Chen and Manning, 2014).

Secondly, it would also be useful to learn dense representations directly for the higher-order substructures (that structured NLP tasks factor on) so as to explicitly capture the useful, hidden relationships among these substructures, instead of relying on the sparse word-conjoined relationships.

In this work, we propose to address both these issues by learning simple dependency *link embeddings* on 'head—argument' pairs (as a single concatenated unit), which allows us to work directly with linguistically-intuitive, higher-order substructures, and also fire significantly fewer and simpler features in dependency parsing, as opposed to word cluster and embedding features in previous work (Koo et al., 2008; Bansal et al., 2014), while still maintaining their strong accuracies.

Trained using appropriate dependency-based context in `word2vec`, the fast neural language model of Mikolov et al. (2013a), these link vectors allow a substantially smaller set of *unary* link features (as opposed to n-ary, conjoined features) which provide savings in parsing time and memory. Moreover, unlike conjoined features, link embeddings allow a tractable set of accurate per-dimension features, making the feature set even smaller and the feature-generation process orders of magnitude faster (than

Proceedings of NAACL-HLT 2015, pages 102–108,
Denver, Colorado, May 31 – June 5, 2015.

hierarchical clustering features).

At the same time, these link embedding features maintain dependency parsing improvements similar to the complex, template-based features on word clusters and embeddings by previous work (Koo et al., 2008; Bansal et al., 2014) (up to 9% relative error reduction), and also stack statistically significantly over them (up to an additional 5% relative error reduction).

Another advantage of this approach (versus previous work on feature embeddings or special neural networks for parsing) is that these link embeddings can be imported as off-the-shelf, dense, syntactic features into various other NLP tasks, similar to word embedding features, but now with richer, structured information, and in tasks where plain word embeddings have not proven useful . As an example, we incorporate them into a constituent parse reranker and see improvements that again match state-of-the-art, manually-defined, non-local reranking features and stack over them statistically significantly. We make our link embeddings publicly available[1] and hope that they will prove useful in various other NLP tasks in future work, e.g., as dense, syntactic features in sentence classification or as linguistically-intuitive, initial units in vector-space composition.

2 Dependency Link Embeddings

To train the link embeddings, we use the speedy, skip-gram neural language model of Mikolov et al. (2013a; 2013b) via their toolkit `word2vec`.[2] We use the original skip-gram model and simply change the context tuple data on which the model is trained, similar to Bansal et al. (2014) and Levy and Goldberg (2014). The goal is to learn similar embeddings for links with similar syntactic contextual properties like label, signed distance, ancestors, etc.

To this end, we first parse the BLLIP corpus (minus the PTB portion)[3] using the baseline MSTParser (McDonald et al., 2005b). Next, for each predicted link, we create a tuple, consisting of the parent-child pair p—c (concatenated as a single unit, same as p_c) and its various properties such as the link's dependency relation label l, the grandparent dependency relation label gl, and the signed, binned distance d:

$$\text{“}d_{\text{<D>}} \quad gl_{\text{<GL>}} \quad p\text{—}c \quad l_{\text{<L>}} \quad d_{\text{<D>}}\text{”}, \qquad (1)$$

We then run the skip-gram model on the the above context tuples (Eq. 1) with a window-size of 2, dimension-size of 100, and a min-count cutoff of 4 to give us a vocabulary of around 92K.[4] We also tried other context settings, e.g., where we add more lexicalized, link-based context to the tuple such as the neighboring grandparent-parent link gp—p:

$$\text{“}gl_{\text{<GL>}} \quad gp\text{—}p \quad p\text{—}c \quad d_{\text{<D>}} \quad l_{\text{<L>}}\text{”}, \qquad (2)$$

but the setting in Eq. 1 performs slightly better (based on the development set).

N.Y.–Yonkers, Md.–Columbia, N.Y.–Bronx, Va.–Reston, Ky.–Lexington, Mich.–Kalamazoo, Calif.–Calabasas, ...
boost–revenue, tap–markets, take–losses, launch–fight, reduce–holdings, terminate–contract, identify–bidders, ...
boosting–bid, meeting–schedules, obtaining–order, having–losses, completing–review, governing–industry, ...
says–mean, adds–may, explains–have, contend–has, recalls–had, figures–is, asserted–is, notes–would, ...
would–Based, is–Besides, was–Like, is–From, are–Despite, said–Besides, says–Despite, reported–As, ...
began–Meanwhile, was–Since, are–Often, would–Now, had–During, were–Over, was–Late, have–Until, ...
Catsimatidis–Mr., Swete–Mr., Case–Mr., Montoya–Mr., Byerlein–Mr., Heard–Mr., Leny–Mr., Graham–Mrs., ...
only–1.5, about–170, nearly–eight, approximately–10, almost–15, some–80, Only–two, about–23, roughly–50, ...

Table 1: Example clusters of the link embeddings.

Clusters: Table 1 shows example clusters obtained by clustering link embeddings via MATLAB's `linkage` + `cluster` commands, with 1000 clusters.[5] We can see that these link embeddings are able to capture useful groups and subtle distinctions directly at the link level (without having to work with all pairs of word types), e.g., based on syntactic properties like capitalization, verb form, position in sentence; and based on topics like location, time, finance, etc.

[1] `ttic.edu/bansal`

[2] `https://code.google.com/p/word2vec/`

[3] Same dataset as what was used to train the BROWN clusters in Koo et al. (2008), for comparability.

[4] We add subscripts to all context tokens so as to treat them differently and remove them from the vocabulary after training.

[5] `http://www.mathworks.com/help/stats/linkage.html`, `http://www.mathworks.com/help/stats/cluster.html`

3 Dependency Parsing Experiments

In this section, we will first discuss how we use the link embeddings as features in dependency parsing. Next, we will present empirical results on feature space reduction and on parsing performance on both in-domain and out-of-domain datasets.

3.1 Features

The BROWN cluster features are based on Bansal et al. (2014), who follow Koo et al. (2008) to add 1st and 2nd order features to MSTParser based on prefixes (of length 4, 6, 8, and 12) of the 0-1 hierarchical clustering bit-strings (via the bigram class-based language model of Brown et al. (1992)) of the head and argument, siblings, intermediate words, etc. See McDonald et al. (2005a) and Koo et al. (2008) for the exact feature templates.

For link embeddings, we tried two feature types:

Bucket features: For each dimension of the link vector, we fire a simple indicator feature, where the feature name consists of the dimension index d and the bucketed vector value b at that index (using a bucket of 0.25), i.e., simply $d \wedge b$, as compared to the large list of n-ary feature templates in previous work, which include various conjunctions, in-between and surrounding word information, etc. (see McDonald et al. (2005a) and Koo et al. (2008)). We have another feature that additionally includes the signed, bucketed distance of the particular link in the given sentence.

Also note the difference of our unary bucket features from the binary bucket features of Bansal et al. (2014), who had to work with pairwise, conjoined features of the head and the argument. Hence, they used features on conjunctions of the two bucket values from the head and argument word vectors, firing one pairwise feature per dimension, because firing features on all dimension pairs (corresponding to an outer product) led to an infeasible number of features. The result discussion of these feature differences in presented in §3.2.

Bit-string features: We first hierarchically cluster the link vectors via MATLAB's `linkage` function with {*method=ward, metric=euclidean*} to get 0-1 bit-strings (similar to BROWN). Next, we again fire a small set of *unary* indicator features that simply consist of the link's bit-string prefix, the prefix-length, and another feature that adds the signed, bucketed distance of that link in the sentence.[6]

System	Number of features
Baseline	5M
BROWN	13M
Bansal et al. (2014)	30M
Bucket	**15K**
Bit-string	1M

Table 2: Number of features.

System	Dev	Test
Baseline	92.4	91.9
+ BROWN	93.2	92.7
+ Bucket	93.0	92.3
+ Bit-string	92.9	92.6
+ BROWN + Bucket	93.4	93.0
+ BROWN + Bit-string	**93.4**	**93.1**

Table 3: UAS results on WSJ.

3.2 Setup and Results

For all experiments (unless otherwise noted), we follow the 2nd-order MSTParser setup of Bansal et al. (2014), in terms of data splits, parameters, preprocessing, and feature thresholding. *Statistical significance* is reported based on the bootstrap test (Efron and Tibshirani, 1994) with 1 million samples.

First, we compare the **number of features** in Table 2. Our dense, unary, link-embedding based Bucket and Bit-string features are substantially fewer than the sparse, n-ary, template-based features used in the MSTParser baseline, in BROWN, and in the word embedding SKIP_{DEP} result of Bansal et al. (2014). This in turn also improves our parsing speed and memory. Moreover, regarding the **preprocessing time** taken to generate these various feature types, our Bucket features, which just need the fast `word2vec` training, take 2-3 orders of magnitude lesser time than the BROWN features (*15 mins. versus 2.5 days*)[7]; this is also advantageous when

[6] We again used prefixes of length 4, 6, 8, 12, same as the BROWN feature setting. For unknown links' features, we replace the bucket or bit-string prefix with a special 'UNK' string.

[7] Based on a modern 3.50 GHz desktop and 1 thread. The Bit-string features additionally need hierarchical clustering, but are still at least twice as fast as BROWN features.

System	Test Average
Baseline	83.5
+ BROWN	84.2
+ Bucket	84.0
+ Bit-string	83.8
+ BROWN + Bucket	**84.6**
+ BROWN + Bit-string	84.4

Table 4: UAS results on Web treebanks.

	Dev		Test	
Parsing Model	F1	EX	F1	EX
Baseline (1-best)	90.6	39.4	90.2	37.3
Baseline (log $p(t\|w)$)	90.4	38.9	89.9	37.3
+ Config	91.8	43.8	91.1	40.6
+ Bit-string	91.1	40.3	90.9	40.6
+ Config + Bit-string	**92.0**	**43.9**	**91.4**	**42.0**

Table 5: F1 results of constituent reranker on WSJ.

training and parsing with representations of new domains or languages.

Table 3 shows the main UAS (unlabeled attachment score) results on **WSJ**, where each '+ X' row denotes adding type X features to the MSTParser baseline. All the final test improvements, i.e., Bucket (92.3) and Bit-string (92.6) w.r.t. Baseline (91.9), and BROWN + Bucket (93.0) and BROWN + Bit-string (93.1) w.r.t. BROWN (92.7), are *statistically significant* at $p < 0.01$. Moreover, the Bit-string result (92.6) is the same, i.e., has no statistically significant difference from the BROWN result (92.7), and also from the Bansal et al. (2014) SKIP$_{\text{DEP}}$ result (92.7). Therefore, the main contribution of these link embeddings is that their significantly simpler, smaller, and faster set of unary features can match the performance of complex, template-based BROWN features (and of the dependency-based word embedding features of Bansal et al. (2014)), and also stack over them. We also get similar trends of improvements on the labeled attachment score (LAS) metric.[8]

Moreover, unlike Bansal et al. (2014), our Bucket features achieve statistically significant improvements, most likely because they fired D pairwise, conjoined features, one per dimension d, consisting of the two bucket values from the head and argument word vectors. This would disallow the classifier to learn useful linear combinations of the various dimensions. Firing D^2 features on all dimension pairs (corresponding to an outer product) would lead to an infeasible number of features. On the other hand, we have a single vector for head+argument, allowing us to fire just D features (one per dimension) and still learn useful dimension combinations in linear space.

[8]Note that one can achieve even stronger results by tuning separate prefix lengths for the Bit-string versus the BROWN + Bit-string cases.

We also report out-of-domain performance, in Table 4, on the **Web** treebank (Petrov and McDonald, 2012) test sets, directly using the WSJ-trained models. Again, both our Bucket and Bit-string link-embedding features achieve decent improvements over Baseline and they stack over BROWN, while using much fewer features. Moreover, one can hopefully achieve bigger gains by training link embeddings on Web or Wikipedia data (since BLLIP is news-domain).

4 Off-the-shelf: Constituent Parsing

Finally, these link embeddings are also portable as off-the-shelf, dense, syntactic features into other NLP tasks, either to incorporate missing syntactic information, or to replace sparse (n-ary lexicalized or template-based) parsing features, or where word embedding features are not appropriate and one needs higher-order embeddings, e.g., in constituent parsing (see Andreas and Klein (2014)).

Therefore, as a first example, we import our link embedding features into a constituent parse reranker. We follow Bansal and Klein (2011), reranking 50-best lists of the Berkeley parser (Petrov et al., 2006). We first extract dependency links in each candidate constituent tree based on the head-modifier rules of Collins (2000). Next, we simply fire our Bit-string features on each link, where the feature again consists of just the prefix bit-string, the prefix length, and the signed, bucketed link distance.[9]

Table 5 shows these reranking results, where 1-best and log $p(t|w)$ are the two Berkeley parser baselines, and where Config is the state-of-the-art, non-local, configurational feature set of Huang (2008),

[9]Based on development set tuning, we use prefixes 4, 6, 8, and then gaps of 4 up to the full-length for '+ Bit-string' and prefixes 4, 6, 8, 12, 16, and full-length for '+ Config + Bit-string'.

which in turn is a simplified merge of Charniak and Johnson (2005) and Collins (2000) (here configurational). Again, all our test improvements are *statistically significant* at $p < 0.01$: Bit-string (90.9) over both the baselines (90.2, 89.9); and Config + Bit-string (91.4) over Config (91.1). Moreover, the Bit-string result (90.9) is the same (i.e., no statistically significant difference) as the Config result (91.1). Therefore, we can again match the improvements of complex, manually-defined, non-local reranking features with a much smaller set of simple, dense, off-the-shelf, link-embedding features, and also complement them statistically significantly.

5 Related Work

As mentioned earlier, there has been a lot of useful, previous work on using word embeddings for NLP tasks such as similarity, tagging, NER, sentiment analysis, and parsing (Turian et al., 2010; Collobert et al., 2011; Dhillon et al., 2012; Huang et al., 2012; Al-Rfou' et al., 2013; Hisamoto et al., 2013; Andreas and Klein, 2014; Bansal et al., 2014; Guo et al., 2014; Pennington et al., 2014; Wang et al., 2015), inter alia.

In related work, Bansal et al. (2014) also use dependency context to tailor word embeddings to dependency parsing. However, their embedding features are still based on the sparse set of n-ary, word-based templates from previous work (McDonald et al., 2005a; Koo et al., 2008). Our structured link embeddings achieve similar improvements as theirs (and better in the case of direct, per-dimension bucket features) with a substantially smaller and simpler (unary) set of features that are aimed to directly capture hidden relationships between the substructures that dependency parsing factors on. Moreover, we hope that similar to word embeddings, these link embeddings will also prove useful when imported into various other NLP tasks as dense, continuous features, but now with additional syntactic information.

There has also been some recent, useful work on reducing the sparsity of features in dependency parsing, e.g., via low-rank tensors (Lei et al., 2014) and via neural network parsers that learn tag and label embeddings (Chen and Manning, 2014). In related work, Chen et al. (2014) learn dense feature embeddings for dependency parsing; however, they still work with the large number of manually-defined feature templates from previous work and train embeddings for all those templates, with an aim to discover hidden, shared information among the large set of sparse features. We get similar improvements with a much smaller and simpler set of unary link features; also, our link embeddings are more portable to other NLP tasks than template-based embeddings specific to dependency parsing.

Other work includes learning distributed structured output via dense label vectors (Srikumar and Manning, 2014), learning bilexical operator embeddings (Madhyastha et al., 2014), and learning joint word embeddings and composition functions based on predicate-argument compositionality (Hashimoto et al., 2014).

Our main goal is to directly learn embeddings on linguistically-intuitive units like dependency links, so that they can be used as non-sparse, unary features in dependency parsing, and also as off-the-shelf, dense, syntactic features in other NLP tasks (versus more intrinsic approaches based on feature embeddings or neural network parsers, which are harder to export).

6 Conclusion and Future Work

We presented dependency link embeddings, which provide a small, simple set of unary features for dependency parsing, while maintaining statistically significant improvements, similar and complementary to sparse, n-ary, word-cluster features. These link vectors are also portable as off-the-shelf syntactic features in other NLP tasks; we import them into constituent parse reranking, where they again match and stack over state-of-the-art, non-local reranking features. We release our link embeddings (available at `ttic.edu/bansal`) and hope that these will prove useful in various other NLP tasks, e.g., as dense, syntactic features in sentence classification or as linguistically-intuitive, initial units in vector-space composition.

In future work, it will be useful to try obtaining stronger parsing accuracies via newer, better representation learning tools, e.g., GloVe (Pennington et al., 2014), and by training on larger quantities of automatically-parsed data. It will also be useful to perform intrinsic evaluation of these link embeddings on appropriate syntactic datasets and metrics, and extrinsic evaluation via various other NLP tasks such as sentence classification. Finally, it will be interesting to try parsers or frameworks where we can directly employ the embeddings as features, instead of bucketing or clustering them.

Acknowledgments

I would like to thank Kevin Gimpel, Ryota Tomioka, and the anonymous reviewers for their useful comments.

References

Rami Al-Rfou', Bryan Perozzi, and Steven Skiena. 2013. Polyglot: Distributed word representations for multilingual NLP. In *Proceedings of CoNLL*.

Jacob Andreas and Dan Klein. 2014. How much do word embeddings encode about syntax? In *Proceedings of ACL*.

Mohit Bansal and Dan Klein. 2011. Web-scale features for full-scale parsing. In *Proceedings of ACL*.

Mohit Bansal, Kevin Gimpel, and Karen Livescu. 2014. Tailoring continuous word representations for dependency parsing. In *Proceedings of ACL*.

Peter F. Brown, Peter V. Desouza, Robert L. Mercer, Vincent J. Della Pietra, and Jenifer C. Lai. 1992. Class-based N-gram models of natural language. *Computational Linguistics*, 18(4):467–479.

E. Charniak and M. Johnson. 2005. Coarse-to-fine n-best parsing and maxent discriminative reranking. In *Proc. of ACL*.

Danqi Chen and Christopher D Manning. 2014. A fast and accurate dependency parser using neural networks. In *Proceedings of EMNLP*.

Wenliang Chen, Yue Zhang, and Min Zhang. 2014. Feature embedding for dependency parsing. In *Proceedings of COLING*.

M. Collins. 2000. Discriminative reranking for natural language parsing. In *Proc. of ICML*.

Ronan Collobert, Jason Weston, Léon Bottou, Michael Karlen, Koray Kavukcuoglu, and Pavel Kuksa. 2011. Natural language processing (almost) from scratch. *Journal of Machine Learning Research*, 12:2493–2537.

Paramveer Dhillon, Jordan Rodu, Dean P. Foster, and Lyle H. Ungar. 2012. Two Step CCA: A new spectral method for estimating vector models of words. In *Proceedings of ICML*.

Bradley Efron and Robert J. Tibshirani. 1994. *An introduction to the bootstrap*, volume 57. CRC press.

Manaal Faruqui, Jesse Dodge, Sujay K Jauhar, Chris Dyer, Eduard Hovy, and Noah A Smith. 2014. Retrofitting word vectors to semantic lexicons. In *Proceedings of Deep Learning and Representation Learning Workshop, NIPS*.

Jiang Guo, Wanxiang Che, Haifeng Wang, and Ting Liu. 2014. Revisiting embedding features for simple semi-supervised learning. In *Proceedings of the 2014 Conference on Empirical Methods in Natural Language Processing (EMNLP)*, pages 110–120.

Kazuma Hashimoto, Pontus Stenetorp, Makoto Miwa, and Yoshimasa Tsuruoka. 2014. Jointly learning word representations and composition functions using predicate-argument structures. In *Proceedings of EMNLP*.

Sorami Hisamoto, Kevin Duh, and Yuji Matsumoto. 2013. An empirical investigation of word representations for parsing the web. In *Proceedings of ANLP*.

Eric H. Huang, Richard Socher, Christopher D. Manning, and Andrew Y. Ng. 2012. Improving Word Representations via Global Context and Multiple Word Prototypes. In *Proceedings of ACL*.

L. Huang. 2008. Forest reranking: Discriminative parsing with non-local features. In *Proc. of ACL*.

Terry Koo, Xavier Carreras, and Michael Collins. 2008. Simple semi-supervised dependency parsing. In *Proceedings of ACL*.

Tao Lei, Yu Xin, Yuan Zhang, Regina Barzilay, and Tommi Jaakkola. 2014. Low-rank tensors for scoring dependency structures. In *Proceedings of ACL*.

Omer Levy and Yoav Goldberg. 2014. Dependency-based word embeddings. In *Proceedings of ACL*.

Pranava Swaroop Madhyastha, Xavier Carreras, and Ariadna Quattoni. 2014. Learning task-specific bilexical embeddings. In *Proceedings of COLING*.

R. McDonald, K. Crammer, and F. Pereira. 2005a. Online large-margin training of dependency parsers. In *Proc. of ACL*.

R. McDonald, F. Pereira, K. Ribarov, and J. Hajič. 2005b. Non-projective dependency parsing using spanning tree algorithms. In *Proc. of HLT-EMNLP*.

Tomas Mikolov, Kai Chen, Greg Corrado, and Jeffrey Dean. 2013a. Efficient estimation of word representations in vector space. In *Proceedings of ICLR*.

Tomas Mikolov, Ilya Sutskever, Kai Chen, Greg Corrado, and Jeffrey Dean. 2013b. Distributed representations of words and phrases and their compositionality. In *Proceedings of NIPS*.

Jeffrey Pennington, Richard Socher, and Christopher D Manning. 2014. Glove: Global vectors for word representation. In *Proceedings of the Empiricial Methods in Natural Language Processing (EMNLP 2014)*, volume 12.

Slav Petrov and Ryan McDonald. 2012. Overview of the 2012 shared task on parsing the web. In *Notes of the First Workshop on Syntactic Analysis of Non-Canonical Language (SANCL)*.

S. Petrov, L. Barrett, R. Thibaux, and D. Klein. 2006. Learning accurate, compact, and interpretable tree annotation. In *Proc. of COLING-ACL*.

Vivek Srikumar and Christopher D Manning. 2014. Learning distributional representations for structured output prediction. In *Proceedings of NIPS*.

Joseph Turian, Lev-Arie Ratinov, and Yoshua Bengio. 2010. Word representations: A simple and general method for semi-supervised learning. In *Proceedings of ACL*.

Ling Wang, Chris Dyer, Alan Black, and Isabel Trancoso. 2015. Two/too simple adaptations of word2vec for syntax problems. In *Proceedings of NAACL-HLT*.

Mo Yu and Mark Dredze. 2014. Improving lexical embeddings with semantic knowledge. In *Proceedings of the 52nd Annual Meeting of the Association for Computational Linguistics*, volume 2, pages 545–550.

DeepNL: a Deep Learning NLP pipeline

Giuseppe Attardi
Dipartimento di Informatica
Università di Pisa
Pisa, Italy
attardi@di.unipi.it

Abstract

We present the architecture of a deep learning pipeline for natural language processing. Based on this architecture we built a set of tools both for creating distributional vector representations and for performing specific NLP tasks. Three methods are available for creating embeddings: feedforward neural network, sentiment specific embeddings and embeddings based on counts and Hellinger PCA. Two methods are provided for training a network to perform sequence tagging, a window approach and a convolutional approach. The window approach is used for implementing a POS tagger and a NER tagger, the convolutional network is used for Semantic Role Labeling. The library is implemented in Python with core numerical processing written in C++ using parallel linear algebra library for efficiency and scalability.

1 Introduction

Distributional Semantic Models (DSM) that represent words as vectors of weights over a high dimensional feature space (Hinton et al., 1986), have proved very effective in representing semantic or syntactic aspects of lexicon. Incorporating such representations has allowed improving many natural language tasks. They also reduce the burden of feature selection since these models can be learned through unsupervised techniques from text.

Deep learning algorithms for NLP tasks exploit distributional representation of words. In tagging applications such as POS tagging, NER tagging and Semantic Role Labeling (SRL), this has proved quite effective in reaching state of art accuracy and reducing reliance on manually engineered feature selection (Collobert et al, 2011).

Word embeddings have been exploited also in constituency parsing (Collobert, 2011) and dependency parsing (Chen and Manning, 2014).

A further benefit of a deep learning approach is to allow performing multiple tasks jointly, and therefore reducing error propagation as well as improving efficiency.

This paper presents DeepNL, an NLP pipeline based on a common Deep Learning architecture: it consists of tools for creating embeddings, and tools that exploit word embeddings as features. The current release includes a POS tagger, a NER, an SRL tagger and a dependency parser.

Two methods are supported for creating embeddings: an approach that uses neural network and one using Hellinger PCA (Lebret and Collobert 2014).

2 NLP Toolkits

A short survey of NLP toolkits is presented by Krithika and Akondi (2014).

NLTK is among the most well-known and comprehensive NLP toolkits: it is written in Python and provides a number of basic processing facilities (tokenization, splitting, statistical analysis of corpora, etc.) as well as machine learning algorithms for classification and clustering. Currently it does not provide any tool based on word embeddings, however it can be interfaced to SENNA[1] or it can be used in conjunction with Gensim[2] which provides several algorithms for performing unsupervised semantic modeling from plain text, including word embeddings, random indexing, LDA (Latent Dirichlet Allocation).

The Stanford NLP Toolkit (Manning et al., 2014) is written in Java and provides tools for tokenization, sentence splitting, POS tagging, NER, parsing, sentiment analysis and temporal expression tagging. As a recent inclusion, it pro-

[1] http://ronan.collobert.com/senna/
[2] http://radimrehurek.com/gensim/

Proceedings of NAACL-HLT 2015, pages 109–115,
Denver, Colorado, May 31 – June 5, 2015.

vides a dependency parser based on neural network and word embeddings (Chen et al., 2014).

OpenNLP[3] is a machine learning library written in Java that supports the most common NLP tasks, such as tokenization, sentence segmentation, POS tagging, named entity extraction, chunking, parsing, and coreference resolution.

Typically each tool built with these libraries uses a different approach or an most suitable algorithm for the task: for example Sanford NLP uses Conditional Random Fields for NER while the POS tagger uses MaxEntropy and both require a set of rich features that need to be manually engineered.

DeepNL differs from these toolkits since it is based on a common deep learning architecture: all tools exploit the same core neural network and use mostly just word embeddings as features. For example the POS tagger and the NER tagger have an identical structure, and they differ only in the way they read/write documents and in the configuration of the discrete features used: the POS tagger uses word suffixes while the NER uses gazetteer dictionaries. Embeddings are used as features, providing a continuous rather than discrete representation of text.

The ability of creating suitable embeddings for various tasks is critical for the proper working of the tools in DeepNL; hence the toolkit integrates algorithms for creating word embeddings from text, either in unsupervised or supervised fashion.

3 Building Word Embeddings

Word embeddings provide a low dimensional vector space representation for words, where values in each dimension may represent syntactic or semantic properties.

DeepNL provides two methods for building embeddings, one is based on the use of a neural language model, as proposed by (Turian and Bengio; Collobert et al., 2011; Mikolov et al., 2010) and one based on spectral method as proposed by Lebret and Collobert (2013).

The neural language method can be hard to train and the process is often quite time consuming, since several iterations are required over the whole training set. Some researchers provide precomputed embeddings for English[4]. The Polyglot project (Al-Rafou et al., 2013) makes available embeddings for several languages, built from the plain text of Wikipedia in the respective language, and the Python code for computing them[5], that supports GPU computations by means of Theano[6].

Mikolov et al. (2013) developed an alternative solution for computing word embeddings, which significantly reduces the computational costs. They propose two log-linear models, called bag of words and skip-gram model. The bag-of-word approach is similar to a feed-forward neural network language model and learns to classify the current word in a given context, except that instead of concatenating the vectors of the words in the context window of each token, it just averages them, eliminating a network layer and reducing the data dimensions. The skip-gram model tries instead to estimate context words based on the current word. Further speed up in the computation is obtained by exploiting a mini-batch Asynchronous Stochastic Gradient Descent algorithm, splitting the training corpus into partitions and assigning them to multiple threads. An optimistic approach is also exploited to avoid synchronization costs: updates to the current weight matrix are performed concurrently, without any locking, assuming that updates to the same rows of the matrix will be infrequent and will not harm convergence.

The authors published single-machine multi-threaded C++ code for computing the word vectors[7]. A reimplementation of the algorithm in Python is included in the Genism library (Řehůřek and Petr Sojka, 2010). In order to obtain comparable speed to the C++ version, they use Cython for interfacing a coding in C of the core function for training the network on a single sentence, which in turn exploits the BLAS library for algebraic computations.

The DeepNL implementation is written in Cython[8] and uses C++ code which exploits the Eigen[9] library for efficient parallel linear algebra computations. Data is exchanged between Numpy arrays in Python and Eigen matrices by means of Eigen Map types. On the Cython side, a pointer to the location where the data of a Numpy array is stored is obtained with a call like:

[3] http://opennlp.apache.org/
[4] http://ronan.collobert.com/senna/
http://metaoptimize.com/projects/wordreprs/
http://www.fit.vutbr.cz/~imikolov/rnnlm/
http://ai.stanford.edu/~ehhuang/

[5] https://bitbucket.org/aboSamoor/word2embeddings
[6] http://deeplearning.net/software/theano/
[7] https://code.google.com/p/word2vec
[8] http://docs.cython.org/
[9] http://eigen.tuxfamily.org/

```
<FLOAT_t*>np.PyArray_DATA(self.nn.hid
den_weights)
```

and passed to a C++ method. On the C++ side this is turned into an Eigen matrix, with no computational costs due to conversion or allocation, with the code:

```
Map<Matrix> hidden_weights(
hidden_weights, numHidden, numInput)
```

which interprets the pointer to a double as a matrix with `numHidden` rows and `numInput` columns. Since Eigen by default uses column-major order while Numpy uses row-major order, the class `Matrix` above is declared as:

```
typedef Eigen::Matrix<double, Eig-
en::Dynamic, Eigen::Dynamic, Eig-
en::RowMajor> Matrix;
```

3.1 Word Embeddings through Hellinger PCA

Lebret and Collobert (2013) have shown that embeddings can be efficiently computed from word co-occurence counts, applying Principal Component Analysis (PCA) to reduce dimensionality while optimizing the Hellinger similarity distance.

Levy and Goldberg (2014) have shown similarly that the skip-gram model by Mikolov et al.(2013) can be interpreted as implicitly factorizing a word-context matrix, whose values are the pointwise mutual information (PMI) of the respective word and context pairs, shifted by a global constant.

DeepNL provides an implementation of the Hellinger PCA algorithm using Cython and the LAPACK library SSYEVR from Scipy[10].

Cooccurrence frequencies are computed by counting the number of times each context word $w \in \mathcal{D}$ occurs after a sequence of T words:

$$p(w|T) = \frac{p(w,T)}{p(T)} = \frac{n(w,T)}{\sum_n n(w,T)}$$

where $n(w, T)$ is the number of times word w occurs after a sequence of T words. The set $\mathcal{D}$ of context word is normally chosen as the the subset of the top most frequent words in the vocabulary $\mathcal{V}$.

The word co-occurrence matrix C of size $|\mathcal{V}| \times |\mathcal{D}|$ is built. The coefficients of C are square rooted and then its transpose is multiplied by it to obtain a symmetric square matrix of size $|\mathcal{V}| \times |\mathcal{V}|$, to which PCA is applied to obtain the desired dimensionality reduction.

[10] https://docs.scipy.org/doc/scipy-0.15.1/reference/generated/scipy.linalg.lapack.ssyevr.html

3.2 Sentiment Specific Word Embeddings

For the task of sentiment analysis, semantic similarity is not appropriate, since antonyms end up at close distance in the embeddings space. One needs to learn a vector representation where words of opposite polarity are further apart.

Tang et al. (2014) propose an approach for learning sentiment specific word embeddings, by incorporating supervised knowledge of polarity in the loss function of the learning algorithm. The original hinge loss function in the algorithm by Collobert et al. (2011) is:

$$\mathcal{L}_{CW}(x, x^c) = max(0, 1 - f_\theta(x) + f_\theta(x^c))$$

where x is an ngram and x^c is the same ngram corrupted by changing the target word with a randomly chosen one, $f_\theta(\cdot)$ is the feature function computed by the neural network with parameters θ. The sentiment specific network outputs a vector of 2 dimensions, one for modeling the generic syntactic/semantic aspects of words and the second for modeling polarity.

A second loss function is introduced as objective for minimization:

$$\mathcal{L}_{SS}(x, x^c) = max(0, 1 - \delta_s(x) f_\theta(x)_1 + \delta_s(x) f_\theta(x^c)_1)$$

where δ_s is an indicator function reflecting the sentiment polarity of a sentence,

$$\delta_s(x) = \begin{cases} 1 \; if \; f^g(x) = [1,0] \\ 0 \; if \; f^g(x) = [0,1] \end{cases}$$

where $f^g(x)$ is the gold distribution for ngram x. The overall hinge loss is a linear combination of the two:

$$\mathcal{L}(x, x^c) = \alpha \, \mathcal{L}_{CW}(x, x^c) + (1 - \alpha) \, \mathcal{L}_{SS}(x, x^c)$$

The gradient for the output layer is given by the formula:

$$\begin{pmatrix} \frac{\partial \mathcal{L}}{\partial f_\theta(x)} \\ \frac{\partial \mathcal{L}}{\delta f_\theta(x^c)} \end{pmatrix}_0 = \begin{cases} \begin{pmatrix} -1 \\ 1 \end{pmatrix} \; if \; \mathcal{L}_{CW}(x, x^c) > 0 \\ \begin{pmatrix} 0 \\ 0 \end{pmatrix} \; \text{otherwise} \end{cases}$$

$$\begin{pmatrix} \frac{\partial \mathcal{L}}{\partial f_\theta(x)} \\ \frac{\partial \mathcal{L}}{\delta f_\theta(x^c)} \end{pmatrix}_1 = \begin{cases} \begin{pmatrix} 1 \\ -1 \end{pmatrix} \; if \; \mathcal{L}_{SS}(x, x^c) > 0 \\ \begin{pmatrix} 0 \\ 0 \end{pmatrix} \; \text{otherwise} \end{cases}$$

DeepNL provides an algorithm for training polarized embeddings, performing gradient descent using an adaptive learning rate according to the AdaGrad method (Duchi et al, 2011). The algorithm requires a training set consisting of sentences annotated with their polarity, for example a corpus of tweets. The algorithm builds embeddings for both unigrams and ngrams at the same time, by performing variations on a training sentence replacing not just a single word, but a sequence of words with either another word or another ngram.

4 Deep Learning Architecture

DeepNL adopts a multi layer neural network architecture, as proposed in (Collobert et al., 2011):

1. Lookup layer. It maps word feature indices to a feature vector, as described below.
2. Linear layer. Fully connected network layer, represented by matrix M_1 and input bias b_1.
3. Activation layer (e.g. hardtanh)
4. Linear layer. Fully connected network layer, represented by matrix M_2 and input bias b_2
5. Softmax layer. Computes the softmax of the output values, producing a probability distribution of the outputs.

Overall, the network computes the following function:

$$f(x) = \mathrm{softmax}(M_2\, a(M_1\, x + b_1) + b_2)$$

where $M_1 \in \mathbb{R}^{h \times d}$, $b_1 \in \mathbb{R}^d$, $M_2 \in \mathbb{R}^{o \times h}$, $b_2 \in \mathbb{R}^o$, are the parameters, with d the dimension of the input, h the number of hidden units, o the number of output classes, $a(\cdot)$ is the activation function.

4.1 Lookup layer

The first layer of the network transforms the input into a feature vector representation. Individual words are represented by a tuple of K discrete features, $w \in \mathcal{D}^1 \times \ldots \times \mathcal{D}^k$, where $\mathcal{D}^k$ is the dictionary for the k-th feature.

Each feature has its own *lookup table* $LT_{W^k}(\cdot)$, with a matrix of parameters to be learned $W^k \in \mathbb{R}^{d^k \times |\mathcal{D}^k|}$, where $\mathcal{D}^k$ is the dictionary for the k-th feature and d^k is a user specified vector size. The *lookup table* layer $LT_{W^k}(\cdot)$ associates a vector of weights to each discrete feature $f \in \mathcal{D}^k$:

$$LT_{W^k}(f) = \langle W^k \rangle_f^1$$

where $\langle W^k \rangle_f^1 \in \mathbb{R}^{d_k}$ is the fth column of W and d_k is the word vector size (a hyper-parameter to be chosen by the user).

The feature vector for word w becomes the concatenation of the vectors for all features:

$$LT_{W^1}(w_1) LT_{W^2}(w_2) \cdots LT_{W^K}(w_k)$$

This vector of features for word w, is passed as input to the network. W^k, M_1, b_1, M_2 and b_2 are the parameters to be learned by backpropagation.

4.2 Feature Extractors

The library has a modular architecture that allows customizing a network for specific tasks, in particular its first layer, by supplying extractors for various types of features.

An extractor is defined as a class that inherits from an abstract class with the following interface:

```
class Extractor(object):
   def extract(self, tokens)
   def lookup(self, feature)
   def save(self, file)
   def load(self, file)
```

Method `extract`, applied to a list of tokens, extracts features from each token and returns a list of IDs for those features. The argument is a list of tokens rather than a single token, since features might depend on consecutive tokens. For instance a gazetteer extractor needs to look at a sequence of tokens to determine whether they are mentioned in its dictionary.

Method `lookup` returns the vector of weights for a given feature. Methods `save/load` allow saving and reloading the `Extractor` data to/from disk.

Extractors currently include an `Embeddings` extractor, implementing the word lookup feature, a `Caps`, `Prefix` and `Postfix` extractors for dealing with capitalization and prefix/postfix features, a `Gazetteer` extractor for dealing with the gazetteers typically used in a NER, and a customizable `AttributeFeature` extractor that extracts features from the state of a Shift/Reduce dependency parser, i.e. from the tokens in the stack or buffer as described for example in Nivre (2007).

5 Sequence Taggers

For sequence tagging, two approaches were proposed in Collobert at al. (2011), a window approach and a sentence approach. The window approach assumes that the tag of a word depends mainly on the neighboring words, and is suitable for tasks like POS and NE tagging. The sentence approach assumes that the whole sentence must be taken into account by adding a convolution layer after the first lookup layer and is more suitable for tasks like SRL.

We can train a neural network to maximize the log-likelihood over the training data. Denoting by θ the trainable parameters, including the network and the transition scores, we want to maximize the following log-likelihood with respect to θ:

$$\sum_{(x,t)\in T} \log p(t|x,\theta)$$

where x are all training sentences and t their corresponding tag sequence.

The score $s(x, t, \theta)$ of a sequence of tags t for a sentence x, with parameters θ, is given by the sum of the transition scores and the tag scores:

$$s(x,t,\theta) = \sum_{i=1}^{n} \left(T(t_{i-1}, t_i) + f_\theta(x_i, t_i)\right)$$

where $T(i, j)$ is the score for the transition from tag i to tag j, and $f_\theta(t_i, x_i)$ is the output of the network at word x_i for tag t_i. The probability of a sequence y for sentence x can be expressed as:

$$p(y|x,\theta) = \frac{e^{s(x,y,\theta)}}{\sum_t e^{s(x,t,\theta)}}$$

If we define:

$$\operatorname*{logadd}_i x_i = \log \sum_i e^{x_i}$$

the log of the conditional probability of the correct sequence y is given by:

$$\log p(y|x,\theta) = s(x,y,\theta) - \operatorname*{logadd}_t s(x,t,\theta)$$

The probability can be computed iteratively by defining:

$$\partial_i(a) = \operatorname*{logadd}_{t_i=a} s(x_1^i, t_1^i, \theta)$$

$$= \operatorname*{logadd}_b(\partial_{i-1}(b) + T(b,a)) + f_\theta(a,i) \ \forall a$$

and finally

$$\operatorname*{logadd}_t s(x,t,\theta) = \operatorname*{logadd}_a \delta_{|x|}(a)$$

In order to avoid numeric overflows, the function logadd must be computed carefully, i.e. by subtracting the maximum value to the coefficients before performing exponentiation and then re-adding the maximum.

The computation of the gradients can be performed at once for the whole sequence exploiting matrix operations whose computation can be optimized and parallelized using suitable linear algebra libraries. We implemented two versions of the network trainer, one in Python using NumPy[11] and one in C++ using Eigen[12].

Here for example is the Python code for computing the δ in the above equation:

```
delta = scores
delta[0] += transitions[-1]
tr = transitions[:-1].T
for i in xrange(1, len(delta)):
  # sum by rows
  logadd = logsumexp(delta[i-1]+tr,
1)
  delta[token] += logadd
```

The array `scores[i, j]` contains the output of the neural network for the `i`-th element of the sequence and for tag `j`, `delta[i, j]` represents the sum of all scores ending at the `i`-th token with tag `j`; `transitions[i, j]` contains the current estimate of the probability of a transition from tag `i` to tag `j`.

6 Experiments

We tested the DeepNL sequence tagger on the CoNLL 2003 challenge[13], a NER benchmark based on Reuters data. The tagger was trained with three types of features: the word embeddings from SENNA, a "caps" feature telling whether a word is in lowercase, uppercase, title case, or had at least one non-initial capital letter, and a gazetteer feature, based on the list provided by the organizers. The window size was set to 5, 300 hidden variables were used and training was iterated for 40 epochs. In the following table we report the scores compared with the system by Ando et al. (2005) which uses a semi-supervised approach and with the results by the released version of SENNA[14]:

[11] http://www.numpy.org/
[12] http://eigen.tuxfamily.org/
[13] http://www.cnts.ua.ac.be/conll2003/ner/
[14] http://ml.nec-labs.com/senna/

System	F1
Ando et al. 2005	89.31
SENNA	89.51
DeepNL	89.38

Table 1. Performance on the NER task, using the CoNLL 2003 benchmark.

The slight difference with SENNA might be explained by the use of different gazetteers.

The same sequence tagger can be used for POS tagging. In this case the discrete features used are the same capitalization feature as for the NER and a suffix feature, which denotes whether a token ends with one of the 455 most frequent suffixes of length one or two characters in the training corpus.

Table 2 presents the results achieved by the POS tagger trained on the Penn Treebank, compared with the results of the reference system by Tuotanova et al. (2003), which uses rich features, and with the original SENNA implementation.

System	Precision
Toutanova et al. 2003	97.24
SENNA	97.28
DeepNL	97.12

Table 2. Performance on the POS task, using the Penn Treebank, sections 0-18 for training, sections 22-24 for testing.

Both these experiments confirm that word embeddings can replace the use of complex manually engineered features for typical natural language processing tasks.

7 Dependency Parsing

We have adapted to the use of embeddings our original transition based dependency parser DeSR (Attardi et al., 2009), that was already based on a neural network. The parser uses the neural network to decide which action to perform at each step in the analysis of a sentence. Looking at a short context of past analyzed tokens and next input tokens, it must decide whether the two current focus tokens can be connected by a dependency relation. In this case it performs a reduction, creating the dependency, otherwise it advances on the input. The original implementation used a large set of discrete features to represent the current context.

The deep learning version of the parser exploits word embedding as features and also creates a dense vector representation for the remaining discrete features. A specific extractor (`AttributeExtractor`) was built for this purpose.

8 Conclusions

We have presented the architecture of DeepNL, a library for building NLP applications based on a deep learning architecture. The implementation is written in Python/Cython and uses C++ linear algebra libraries for efficiency and scalability, exploiting multithreading or GPUs where available.

The implementation of DeepNL is available on GitHub[15].

The availability of a library that allows creating embeddings and training a deep learning architecture using them might contribute to the development of further tools for linguistic analysis.

For example we are planning to build a classifier for performing identification of affirmative, negative or speculative contexts in sentences.

We are also considering additional ways of creating embeddings, for example to generate context sensitive embeddings that could provide word representations that disambiguate among word senses.

Acknowledgements

Partial support for this work was provided by project RIS (POR RIS of the Regione Toscana, CUP n° 6408.30122011.026000160).

References

R. Al-Rfou, B. Perozzi, and S. Skiena. 2013. Polyglot: Distributed Word Representations for Multilingual NLP. arXiv preprint arXiv:1307.1662.

R. K. Ando, T. Zhang, and P. Bartlett. 2005. A framework for learning predictive structures from multiple tasks and unlabeled data. Journal of Machine Learning Research, 6:1817–1853.

G. Attardi, F. Dell'Orletta, M. Simi, J. Turian. 2009. Accurate Dependency Parsing with a Stacked Multilayer Perceptron. In *Proc. of Workshop Evalita 2009*, ISBN 978-88-903581-1-1.

Danqi Chen and Christopher D. Manning. 2014. Fast and Accurate Dependency Parser using Neural Networks. In: *Proc. of EMNLP 2014.*

R. Collobert et al. 2011. Natural Language Processing (Almost) from Scratch. *Journal of Machine Learning Research*, 12, 2461–2505.

[15] https://github.com/attardi/deepnl

R. Collobert and J. Weston. 2008. A unified architecture for natural language processing: Deep neural networks with multitask learning. In *ICML*, 2008.

R. Collobert. 2011. Deep Learning for Efficient Discriminative Parsing. In AISTATS, 2011.

P. S. Dhillon, D. Foster, and L. Ungar. 2011. Multiview learning of word embeddings via CCA. In *Advances in Neural Information Processing Systems* (NIPS), volume 24.

John Duchi, Elad Hazan, and Yoram Singer. 2011. Adaptive subgradient methods for online learning and stochastic optimization. *The Journal of Machine Learning Research*.

S. Hartmann, G. Szarvas, and I. Gurevych. 2011. Mining Multiword Terms from Wikipedia, in M.T. Pazienza & A. Stellato (Eds.): Semi-Automatic Ontology Development: Processes and Resources, pp. 226-258, Hershey, PA, USA: IGI Global.

G.E. Hinton, J.L. McClelland, D.E. Rumelhart. Distributed representations. 1986. In: Parallel distributed processing: Explorations in the microstructure of cognition. Volume 1: Foundations, MIT Press, 1986.

L.B. Krithika and Kalyana Vasanth Akondi. 2014. Survey on Various Natural Language Processing Toolkits. World Applied Sciences Journal 32 (3): 399-402.

Rémi Lebret and Ronan Collobert. 2013. Word Embeddings through Hellinger PCA. *Proc. of EACL 2013*.

Omer Levy and Yoav Goldberg. 2014. Neural Word Embeddings as Implicit Matrix Factorization. In *Advances in Neural Information Processing Systems* (NIPS), 2014.

Christopher D. Manning and Hinrich Schütze. 1999. *Foundations of Statistical Natural Language Processing*. The MIT Press. Cambridge, Massachusetts.

Manning, Christopher D., Surdeanu, Mihai, Bauer, John, Finkel, Jenny, Bethard, Steven J., and McClosky, David. 2014. The Stanford CoreNLP Natural Language Processing Toolkit. In *Proceedings of 52nd Annual Meeting of the Association for Computational Linguistics: System Demonstrations*, pp. 55-60.

T. Mikolov, M. Karafiat, L. Burget, J. Cernocky, and Sanjeev Khudanpur. 2010. Recurrent neural network based language model.

Tomas Mikolov, Kai Chen, Greg Corrado, and Jeffrey Dean. 2013. Efficient Estimation of Word Representations in Vector Space. In *Proceedings of Workshop at ICLR*, 2013.

J. Nivre. 2007. Incremental non-projective dependency parsing, *Proceedings of Human LanguageTechnologies: The Annual Conference of the North American Chapter of the Association for Computational Linguistics* (*NAACL HLT*), Rochester, NY, pp. 396–403.

Radim Řehůřek and Petr Sojka. 2010. Software Framework for Topic Modelling with Large Corpora. In *Proceedings of the LREC 2010 Workshop on New Challenges for NLP Frameworks*, ELRA, Valletta, Malta, pp. 45–50.

K. Toutanova, D. Klein, C. D. Manning, and Y. Singer. 2003. Feature-rich part-of-speech tagging with a cyclic dependency network. In *Conference of the North American Chapter of the Association for Computational Linguistics & Human Language Technologies* (*NAACL-HLT*).

A Vector Space Approach for Aspect Based Sentiment Analysis

Abdulaziz Alghunaim, Mitra Mohtarami, Scott Cyphers, James Glass
MIT Computer Science and Artificial Intelligence Laboratory
Cambridge, MA 02139, USA
azizkag@mit.edu, {mitra, cyphers, glass}@csail.mit.edu

Abstract

Vector representations for language has been shown to be useful in a number of Natural Language Processing tasks. In this paper, we aim to investigate the effectiveness of word vector representations for the problem of *Aspect Based Sentiment Analysis*. In particular, we target three sub-tasks namely *aspect term extraction*, *aspect category detection*, and *aspect sentiment prediction*. We investigate the effectiveness of vector representations over different text data and evaluate the quality of domain-dependent vectors. We utilize vector representations to compute various vector-based features and conduct extensive experiments to demonstrate their effectiveness. Using simple vector based features, we achieve F1 scores of 79.91% for aspect term extraction, 86.75% for category detection, and the accuracy 72.39% for aspect sentiment prediction.

1 Introduction

Natural language representation in continuous vector space has been successfully used in many NLP tasks (Al-Rfou et al., 2013; Bansal et al., 2014; Bowman et al., 2014; Boyd-Graber et al., 2012; Chen and Rudnicky, 2014; Guo et al., 2014; Iyyer et al., 2014; Levy and Goldberg, 2014; Mikolov et al., 2013c). Previous research attempted to employ vector representations to present the *syntactic* and *semantic* information in textual content. In this paper, we aim to investigate the effectiveness of vector space representations for *Aspect Based Sentiment Analysis* in which we aim to capture both *semantic* and *sentiment* information encoded in user generated content such as product reviews.

Sentiment analysis or *opinion mining* deals with computational analysis of people's opinions, sentiments, attitudes and emotions towards target entities such as products, organizations, individuals, topics and their attributes (Liu, 2012). The majority of early approaches to this research problem (Pang et al., 2002; Pang and Lee, 2005; Baccianella et al., 2009) attempted to detect the overall sentiment of a sentence, paragraph, or text span regardless of the entities (e.g., *restaurants*) and their aspects (e.g., *food*, *service*) expressed in context. However, only considering overall sentiments fails to capture the sentiments over the aspects on which an entity can be reviewed (Lu et al., 2011). For example, although the restaurant review shown in Table 1 might express an overall positive sentiment, it additionally expresses a positive sentiments toward the restaurant's food and service, as well as negative sentiment toward the restaurant's ambiance. To achieve this aim, aspect based sentiment analysis attempts to extract the aspects (or semantic labels) of given target entities and the sentiment expressed towards each aspect (Hu and Liu, 2004; Liu, 2012). For this purpose, three sub-tasks need to be addressed: (1) *aspect term extraction*, (2) *aspect category detection*, and (3) *aspect sentiment prediction*. We briefly describe these sub-tasks here:

Aspect term extraction identifies aspect terms (or semantic labels) appeared in a given text about a target entity. For instance, in the review in Table 1, the aspects are "orecchiette with sausage and

Proceedings of NAACL-HLT 2015, pages 116–122,
Denver, Colorado, May 31 – June 5, 2015.

Our agreed favorite is the ***orecchiette with sausage and chicken*** *and usually the* ***waiters*** *are kind enough to split the* ***dish*** *in half so you get to sample both* ***meats****. But, the* ***music*** *which is sometimes a little too heavy for my taste.*

Table 1: An example of restaurant review.

chicken", "waiters", "dish", "meats" and "music", and the target entity is "restaurant". Multi-word aspect terms are treated as single aspect, like "orecchiette with sausage and chicken" in the example.

Aspect category detection identifies (latent) aspect categories available in a given text. Aspect categories are coarser than aspect terms, and they do not necessarily occur as terms in the text. For example, the review in Table 1 contains the latent aspect categories "food", "service", and "ambiance". Aspect categories are often considered as predefined categories (e.g., "price", "food") with respect to the target entities.

Aspect sentiment prediction identifies the sentiment toward aspect terms as *positive*, *negative*, *neutral*, or *conflict* (i.e., both positive and negative) for a given set of aspect terms in a text. For example, in the review in Table 1, the aspects "orecchiette with sausage and chicken" and "waiters" are positive, while "music" is negative, and "dish" and "meats" are neutral.

To tackle the above problems and investigate the utility of vector representation models for aspect based sentiment analysis, we present a supervised approach in which vector representations of aspect terms and categories are effectively utilized for aspect based sentiment analysis. Our approach outperforms the baselines and provides significant performance using the simple vector-based features as compared to previous approaches using different text-based features (Pontiki et al., 2014).

The remainder of this paper describes our approach (Section 2), followed by experimental results and analysis (Section 3), and finally conclusion.

2 Method

Distributed vector representations, described by Schütze (Schütze, 1992a; Schütze, 1992b), associate similar vectors with similar words and phrases. These vectors provide useful information for the learning algorithms to achieve better performance in Natural Language Processing tasks (Mikolov et al., 2013c). Most approaches to computing vector representations use the observation that similar words appear in similar contexts (Firth, 1957; Sahlgren, 2006; Mikolov, 2012; Socher, 2014).

To compute the vector representations of words, we use the skip-gram model of `Word2Vec` (Mikolov, 2014; Mikolov et al., 2013a; Mikolov et al., 2013b; Mikolov et al., 2013d). The Skip-gram model aims to find word representations that are useful for predicting the surrounding words in a sentence or document (Mikolov et al., 2013b). The model needs a large amount of unstructured text data for training the word vector representations.

When training the skip-gram model we use the GoogleNews dataset (Mikolov, 2014) that contains 3 million unique words and about 100 billion tokens. In addition, to account for the effect of domain information on the quality of word representations, we employ a dataset of restaurant reviews[1] from Yelp that contains 131,778 unique words and about 200 million tokens. We constructed 300-dimensional word vectors for all these words.

We propose to utilize word vector representations to compute vector-based features for the three subtasks of aspect based sentiment analysis. We employ these features in a supervised learning setting to address the above tasks. Our data (reviews) are first analyzed by Stanford tokenizer (Manning et al., 2010), POS-tagger (Toutanova et al., 2003) and dependency-tree extractor (de Marneffe and Manning, 2008). Then, the pre-processed data and word representations are used to compute task-specific features as explained in the following subsections.

2.1 Aspect Term Extraction

The objective of this sub-task is to extract aspect terms from reviews with respect to a target entity (e.g, restaurant) as explained in Section 1. This task can be considered as part of Semantic Role Labeling (SRL). Previous research has shown that Conditional Random Fields (CRFs) (Lafferty et al., 2001)

[1]This dataset is available on: `http://www.yelp.com/dataset_challenge`.

and sequence tagging with Structural Support Vector Machines (SVM-HMM) (Altun et al., 2003) are effective for the SRL task (Cohn and Blunsom, 2005). As such, we employ CRFsuite (Okazaki, 2007) and SVM-HMM (Altun et al., 2003) with word vector representations as features to label the token sequence with respect to two possible tags: "Aspect" and "Not-Aspect", where an aspect can be multiword. To the best of our knowledge, this is the first attempt of solving the problem of aspect term extraction using CRFsuite or SVM-HMM with vector representations as features. Furthermore, in addition to the above vector features, we employ the POS-tags information as an extra feature. This is mainly because "nouns" are strong candidates to be aspects (Blinov and Kotelnikov, 2014; Pontiki et al., 2014). However, this feature is more effective for the single term aspects as we will discuss in Section 3.

2.2 Aspect Category Detection

The objective of this sub-task is to detect the aspect categories expressed in a sentence with respect to a given set of categories (e.g., *food, service, price, ambience, anecdotes/miscellaneous*) as explained in Section 1. Since a sentence can contain several categories, we employ multi-label one-vs-all Support Vector Machines (SVMs) in conjunction with the following vector-based features for a given sentence:

Normalized Average Vector (NAV) is obtained by averaging the vector representations of the words in the sentence. That is, given a sequence of words $S = w_1, w_2, ..., w_n$, the normalized average vector is computed as follows:

$$NAV = \frac{\frac{1}{N}\sum_{i=1}^{N} v_i}{\left|\frac{1}{N}\sum_{i=1}^{N} v_i\right|} \tag{1}$$

where N is the number of words, v_i is the vector representation of w_i in the sentence, and $|x|$ means the $L2 - norm$ of x. In addition, we only consider adjectives, adverbs, nouns, and verbs to compute the NAV. This is because these word types capture most semantic and sentiment information in a sentence.

Token Numbers (TN) is number of words in sentence that used to compute NAV. Although NAV is effective for this task, some information like TN is missing during the averaging process.

Category Similarities (CS) are computed for each predefined aspect category. To compute CS, we first identify a set of words (called *seeds*) for each category by selecting top 20 nearest word vectors to the vector of category name. Then, for each category, we compute the cosine similarity between its seed vectors and the word vectors of the input sentence. We consider the maximum cosine similarity as a feature representing the similarity between the category and the input sentence.

2.3 Aspect Sentiment Prediction

The objective of this task is to predict the sentiments for a given set of aspects in a sentence as positive, negative, neutral and conflict (i.e., both positive and negative) as explained in Section 1. For this task, we apply one-vs-all SVM and the following vector-based features for a given aspect:

Average Dependency Vector (ADV) is obtained by averaging the vector representations of the *dependency words* (DW) for the aspect. We define dependency words for an aspect as the words that modify or modified by the aspect in dependency tree of the input sentence.

Rating Vectors (RV) are the same as ADV features but they are computed using the vector representations trained on different subsets of our data. We have five subsets, each subset contains only reviews with a specific review rating. Ratings range from 1 (strong negative) to 5 (strong positive). Previous researches showed the impact of the word (w) distribution over different ratings (r) to compute the sentiment of the word (i.e., $P(r|w)$) (de Marneffe et al., 2010) and construct opinion lexicon (Amiri and Chua, 2012). Using this feature, we can investigate the distribution of words and their vector representations in different ratings.

Positive/Negative Similarities (PNS) are obtained by computing the highest cosine similarity between DW vectors and the vectors of a set of positive/negative sentiment words. The sentiment words are automatically computed by selecting top 20 of nearest neighbor word vectors to the vectors of the word "excellent" for positive and "poor" for negative seeds. Furthermore, the difference between the positive and negative similarities is used as an additional feature.

Categories	food	srvc.	price	amb.	misc.	**Total**
Train	1,232	597	321	431	1,132	**3,713**
Test	418	172	83	118	234	**1,025**

Table 2: Category distributions over the dataset.

3 Evaluation and Results

We evaluate our vector-based approach on the aspect term extraction, aspect category detection, and aspect sentiment prediction tasks. We use the restaurant review dataset provided by (Pontiki et al., 2014; Ganu et al., 2009) that contains 3,041 training and 800 test sentences. The training dataset contains 3,693 aspects and 3,713 categories, and test dataset contains 1,134 aspects and 1,025 categories. In the dataset, the predefined aspect categories are *food, service, price, ambiance, anecdotes/miscellaneous*, and Table 2 shows the distributions of these categories over the dataset.

Aspect Term Extraction The results of our vector-based approach for this task are shown in Table 3. As explained in Section 2.1, we employ CRFs and SVM-HMM for this task. As features we utilize POS-tags of aspect terms and their vector representations computed by `word2vec` trained on Yelp (Y) or GoogleNews (G) data. Their corresponding results are shown in the fourth and fifth rows of the table. These results indicate the vector representations trained on Yelp data leads to a high performance in both SVM and CRF. This is while the GoogleNews dataset contains a larger vocabulary of around 3M words as compared to the Yelp data with around 100K words. This implies the effectiveness of the domain in the quality of word representations.

To evaluate the effectiveness of the vector-based features, we repeat our experiments with only POS-tags of the aspect terms. The performance is significantly dropped, as shown in the third row of the table. Although the nouns can be strong candidates for aspects (Blinov and Kotelnikov, 2014), the majority of aspects, like multi-word aspects cannot be captured by only considering their POS-tags.

The first cell of Table 3 shows the F1 performance of 47.15% produced by our baseline (Pontiki et al., 2014). The baseline creates a dictionary of aspect terms from the training data, and then a given sequence of words are tagged as aspects by looking up the dictionary. This approach cannot handle the out of vocabulary aspects.

Baseline-F1 = 65.65	SVM (C = 0.1)		
Features	Precision	Recall	F1
NAV (Y)	89.02	80.68	84.64
NAV + TN (Y)	90.42	81.07	85.49
NAV + TN + CS (Y)	91.18	82.73	**86.75**
NAV + TN + CS (G)	91.51	81.07	85.98

Table 4: Results for the aspect category detection task.

Aspect Category Detection The results of our vector-based approach for this task are shown in Table 4. As explained in Section 2.2, SVMs are applied to this task with a combination of *Normalized Average Vector* (NAV), *Token Numbers* (TN) and *Category Similarities* (CS) features for a given sentence. These features employ the `word2vec` trained on Yelp (Y) or GoogleNews (G) to obtain the vector representations. Their corresponding results are shown in the fifth and sixth rows of the table. The results imply the impact of our vector-based features that lead to the highest performance using the Yelp data.

To evaluate the effectiveness of above vector-based features, we repeat our experiments with different combination of them. It leads to the lower performances by using NAV and TN and ignoring the CS, as shown in the forth row of Table 4., and by using NAV and ignoring both CS and TN, as shown in the third row of the table.

The first cell of Table 4 shows an F1 performance of 65.65% obtained by the baseline (Pontiki et al., 2014). Given a sentence, the baseline first retrieves a set of K similar sentences from the training data. The similarity of two sentences is then determined by computing the Dice Coefficient between the sets of distinct words in the two sentences (Pontiki et al., 2014). Finally, the input sentence is tagged by the most frequent aspect categories appeared in the K retrieved sentences. The limitation of this approach is that it employs the text-based similarity measure to measure the semantic similarity between the sentences. However, the results in the table shows that the vector-based features can better capture the semantic similarity between the sentences as compared to the text-based features.

Baseline-F1 = 47.15	CRF Suite			SVM HMM		
Features	Precision	Recall	F1	Precision	Recall	F1
POS-tags	44.09	9.87	16.13	44.58	9.43	15.57
POS-tags + `word2vec` (Y)	82.38	72.57	77.16	77.33	78.83	**78.08**
POS-tags + `word2vec` (G)	82.69	74.16	**78.19**	76.88	74.51	75.68

Table 3: Results for the aspect term extraction task.

Baseline-Accuracy = 64.28	SVM (C = 0.1)			
Features	Pos-F1	Neg-F1	Neu-F1	Accuracy
ADV (Y)	82.70	52.30	31.39	71.34
RV (Y)	83.26	51.79	32.85	71.95
RV + PNS (Y)	83.48	53.29	32.97	**72.39**

Table 5: Results for the aspect sentiment prediction task.

Aspect Sentiment Prediction The results of our approach for this task are shown in Table 5. The SVMs are applied to this task and the parameter C for SVMs is optimized through cross-validation on training data. The third row of the table shows the results when we use the *Average Dependency Vector* (ADV) computed based on `word2vec` trained on the whole Yelp (Y) data. As explained in Section 2.3, to investigate the distribution of words (Amiri and Chua, 2012) and their vector representations over different ratings, we present *Rating Vectors* (RV). RV features include 4 ADVs in which four vector representations for a word are computed on Yelp reviews with ratings 1, 2, 4, and 5, respectively. Reviews with the rating 3 are not considered, because they are mostly of neutral or conflict orientation. Using RV results in a better performance, as shown in the fourth row of Table 5. However, there is not a significant difference between the results of experiments with RV and ADV. The reason is that most of the reviews in the Yelp data have positive ratings (i.e., ratings 4 and 5) and as such the distributions of words does not dramatically changed as compared to the whole review data.

The highest performance is achieved when we use the combination of RV and *Positive/Negative Similarities* (PNS) features, as shown in the fifth row of the Table 5. Since the vector representations for some positive and negative words (e.g., good and bad) are similar, PNS feature provides more information for a classifier to distinguish between these vectors by defining a set of positive and negative vectors, as explained in Section 2.3.

The first cell of Table 5 shows a performance of 64.28% obtained by our baseline (Pontiki et al., 2014). The baseline tags a given aspect in a test sentence by the most frequent sentiment for the aspect in top K similar training sentences to the test sentence. In addition, for the out of vocabulary aspects, the majority sentiment over all aspects in training data will be assigned.

4 Related Work

Previous works on aspect based sentiment analysis (Liu, 2012; Pang and Lee, 2008) attempted to tackle sentiment and semantic labeling using different approaches such as sequence labeling (Choi and Cardie, 2010; Yang and Cardie, 2013), syntactic patterns (Zhao et al., 2012; Xu et al., 2013; Zhou et al., 2013), topic models (Lu et al., 2011). While some works first separate the semantic and sentiment information and then label them (Mei et al., 2007; Zhao et al., 2010), some other previous works presented joint models for joint semantic and sentiment labeling (Lin and He, 2009; Jo and Oh, 2011).

Vector representations for words and phrases has been found useful for many NLP tasks (Al-Rfou et al., 2013; Bansal et al., 2014; Bowman et al., 2014; Boyd-Graber et al., 2012; Chen and Rudnicky, 2014; Guo et al., 2014; Iyyer et al., 2014; Levy and Goldberg, 2014). Given the success of the previous works the effectiveness of recursive neural networks in relating semantically similar words, in this research, we investigated the impact of word representations techniques for aspect based sentiment analysis. In particular, we aimed to employ vector-based features using word representations to capture both semantic and sentiment information.

5 Conclusion

In summary, we employed vector representations of words to tackle the problem of *Aspect Based Sentiment Analysis*. We introduced several effective vector-based features and showed their utility in addressing the aspect term extraction, aspect category detection, and aspect sentiment prediction sub-tasks. Our vector space approach using these features performed well compared to the baselines. To further improvement, these vector-based features can be combined with text-based features used typically for each sub-task.

Acknowledgments

This research was supported in part by the Qatar Computing Research Institute (QCRI). In addition, we would like to thank Maria Pontiki from the Institute for Language and Speech Processing for providing us access to the database.

References

Rami Al-Rfou, Bryan Perozzi, and Steven Skiena. 2013. Polyglot: Distributed word representations for multilingual NLP. *CoRR*, abs/1307.1662.

Yasemin Altun, Ioannis Tsochantaridis, and Thomas Hofmann. 2003. Hidden markov support vector machines.

Hadi Amiri and Tat-Seng Chua. 2012. Mining slang and urban opinion words and phrases from cqa services: An optimization approach. In *WSDM*, pages 193–202, New York, NY, USA. ACM.

Stefano Baccianella, Andrea Esuli, and Fabrizio Sebastiani. 2009. Multi-facet rating of product reviews. In *ECIR*, pages 461–472, Berlin, Heidelberg. Springer-Verlag.

Mohit Bansal, Kevin Gimpel, and Karen Livescu. 2014. Tailoring continuous word representations for dependency parsing. In *ACL*, pages 809–815, Baltimore, MD, USA.

Pavel Blinov and Eugeny Kotelnikov. 2014. Blinov: Distributed representations of words for aspect-based sentiment analysis at semeval 2014. In *Proceedings of the 8th International Workshop on Semantic Evaluation (SemEval 2014)*, pages 140–144. Association for Computational Linguistics.

Samuel R. Bowman, Christopher Potts, and Christopher D. Manning. 2014. Recursive neural networks for learning logical semantics. *CoRR*, abs/1406.1827.

Jordan L. Boyd-Graber, Brianna Satinoff, He He, and Hal Daumé III. 2012. Besting the quiz master: Crowdsourcing incremental classification games. In *EMNLP-CoNLL 2012, July 12-14, 2012, Jeju Island, Korea*, pages 1290–1301.

Yun-Nung Chen and Alexander I. Rudnicky. 2014. Dynamically supporting unexplored domains in conversational interactions by enriching semantics with neural word embeddings. In *Proceedings of the 2014 Spoken Language Technology Workshop, December 7-10, 2014, South Lake Tahoe, Nevada, USA*, pages 590–595.

Yejin Choi and Claire Cardie. 2010. Hierarchical sequential learning for extracting opinions and their attributes. In *Proceedings of the ACL 2010 Conference Short Papers*, pages 269–274, Stroudsburg, PA, USA.

Trevor Cohn and Philip Blunsom. 2005. Semantic role labelling with tree conditional random fields. In *In Proceedings of CoNLL-2005*, pages 169–172.

Marie-Catherine de Marneffe and Christopher D. Manning. 2008. The stanford typed dependencies representation. In *Coling 2008: Proceedings of the Workshop CrossParser*, pages 1–8, Stroudsburg, PA, USA.

Marie-Catherine de Marneffe, Christopher D. Manning, and Christopher Potts. 2010. "was it good? it was provocative." learning the meaning of scalar adjectives. In *ACL*, pages 167–176, Stroudsburg, PA, USA.

John Firth. 1957. A synopsis of linguistic theory, 1930-1955. *Studies in Linguistic Analysis*, pages 1–32.

Gayatree Ganu, Nomie Elhadad, and Amlie Marian. 2009. Beyond the stars: Improving rating predictions using review text content.

Daniel (Zhaohan) Guo, Gokhan Tur, Wen-tau Yih, and Geoffrey Zweig. 2014. Joint semantic utterance classification and slot filling with recursive neural networks. pages 554–559.

Minqing Hu and Bing Liu. 2004. Mining and summarizing customer reviews. In *Proceedings of the Tenth ACM SIGKDD International Conference on Knowledge Discovery and Data Mining*, KDD '04, pages 168–177, New York, NY, USA. ACM.

Mohit Iyyer, Jordan L. Boyd-Graber, Leonardo Max Batista Claudino, Richard Socher, and Hal Daumé III. 2014. A neural network for factoid question answering over paragraphs. In *Proceedings of the 2014 Conference on Empirical Methods in Natural Language Processing, EMNLP*

2014, October 25-29, 2014, Doha, Qatar, A meeting of SIGDAT, a Special Interest Group of the ACL, pages 633–644.

Yohan Jo and Alice H. Oh. 2011. Aspect and sentiment unification model for online review analysis. In *WSDM*, pages 815–824, New York, NY, USA. ACM.

John D. Lafferty, Andrew McCallum, and Fernando C. N. Pereira. 2001. Conditional random fields: Probabilistic models for segmenting and labeling sequence data. In *ICML*, pages 282–289, San Francisco, CA, USA. Morgan Kaufmann Publishers Inc.

Omer Levy and Yoav Goldberg. 2014. Dependency-based word embeddings. In *Proceedings of the 52nd Annual Meeting of the Association for Computational Linguistics, ACL 2014, June 22-27, 2014, Baltimore, MD, USA, Volume 2: Short Papers*, pages 302–308.

Chenghua Lin and Yulan He. 2009. Joint sentiment/topic model for sentiment analysis. In *CIKM*, pages 375–384, New York, NY, USA. ACM.

Bing Liu. 2012. Sentiment analysis and opinion mining.

Bin Lu, Myle Ott, Claire Cardie, and Benjamin K. Tsou. 2011. Multi-aspect sentiment analysis with topic models. In *ICDMW*, pages 81–88, Washington, DC, USA. IEEE Computer Society.

Christopher Manning, Tim Grow, Teg Grenager, Jenny Finkel, and John Bauer. 2010. `StanfordTokenizer`. `http://nlp.stanford.edu/software/tokenizer.shtml`.

Qiaozhu Mei, Xu Ling, Matthew Wondra, Hang Su, and ChengXiang Zhai. 2007. Topic sentiment mixture: Modeling facets and opinions in weblogs. In *WWW*, pages 171–180, New York, NY, USA. ACM.

Tomas Mikolov, Kai Chen, Greg Corrado, and Jeffrey Dean. 2013a. Efficient estimation of word representations in vector space. *CoRR*, abs/1301.3781.

Tomas Mikolov, Ilya Sutskever, Kai Chen, Greg Corrado, and Jeffrey Dean. 2013b. Distributed representations of words and phrases and their compositionality. *CoRR*, abs/1310.4546.

Tomas Mikolov, Ilya Sutskever, Kai Chen, Gregory S. Corrado, and Jeffrey Dean. 2013c. Distributed representations of words and phrases and their compositionality. In *Advances in Neural Information Processing Systems 26: 27th Annual Conference on Neural Information Processing Systems 2013. Proceedings of a meeting held December 5-8, 2013, Lake Tahoe, Nevada, United States.*, pages 3111–3119.

Tomas Mikolov, Wen-tau Yih, and Geoffrey Zweig. 2013d. Linguistic regularities in continuous space word representations. In *NAACL*, pages 746–751.

Tomàš Mikolov. 2012. *Statistical Language Models Based on Neural Networks*. Ph.D. thesis, Brno University of Technology.

Tomas Mikolov. 2014. `Word2Vec`. `https://code.google.com/p/word2vec/`.

Naoaki Okazaki. 2007. Crfsuite: a fast implementation of conditional random fields (crfs).

Bo Pang and Lillian Lee. 2005. Seeing stars: Exploiting class relationships for sentiment categorization with respect to rating scales. In *ACL*, pages 115–124, Stroudsburg, PA, USA. Association for Computational Linguistics.

Bo Pang and Lillian Lee. 2008. Opinion mining and sentiment analysis. *Found. Trends Inf. Retr.*, 2(1-2):1–135, January.

Bo Pang, Lillian Lee, and Shivakumar Vaithyanathan. 2002. Thumbs up?: Sentiment classification using machine learning techniques. In *EMNLP*, pages 79–86, Stroudsburg, PA, USA.

Maria Pontiki, Dimitris Galanis, John Pavlopoulos, Harris Papageorgiou, Ion Androutsopoulos, and Suresh Manandhar. 2014. Semeval-2014 task 4: Aspect based sentiment analysis. In *SemEval*, pages 27–35. Association for Computational Linguistics.

Magnus Sahlgren. 2006. *The Word-Space Model*. Ph.D. thesis, Stockholm University.

H. Schütze. 1992a. Dimensions of meaning. In *Proceedings of Supercomputing '92*, pages 787–796.

Hinrich Schütze. 1992b. Word space. In *NIPS*, pages 895–902.

Richard Socher. 2014. *Recursive Deep Learning for Natural Language Processing and Computer Vision*. Ph.D. thesis, Stanford University.

Kristina Toutanova, Dan Klein, Christopher D. Manning, and Yoram Singer. 2003. Feature-rich part-of-speech tagging with a cyclic dependency network. In *NAACL-HLT*, pages 173–180, Stroudsburg, PA, USA. Association for Computational Linguistics.

Liheng Xu, Kang Liu, Siwei Lai, Yubo Chen, and Jun Zhao. 2013. Mining opinion words and opinion targets in a two-stage framework. In *ACL*, pages 1764–1773, Sofia, Bulgaria.

Bishan Yang and Claire Cardie. 2013. Joint inference for fine-grained opinion extraction. In *ACL*, pages 1640–1649, Sofia, Bulgaria.

Wayne Xin Zhao, Jing Jiang, Hongfei Yan, and Xiaoming Li. 2010. Jointly modeling aspects and opinions with a maxent-lda hybrid. In *Proceedings of EMNLP*, pages 56–65, Stroudsburg, PA, USA.

Yanyan Zhao, Bing Qin, and Ting Liu. 2012. Collocation polarity disambiguation using web-based pseudo contexts. In *EMNLP-CoNLL*, pages 160–170, Stroudsburg, PA, USA.

Xinjie Zhou, Xiaojun Wan, and Jianguo Xiao. 2013. Collective opinion target extraction in Chinese microblogs. In *EMNLP*, pages 1840–1850, Seattle, Washington, USA, October.

Word Embeddings vs Word Types for Sequence Labeling: the Curious Case of CV Parsing

Melanie Tosik[†] **Carsten L. Hansen**[‡] **Gerard Goossen**[‡] **Mihai Rotaru**[‡]

[†]Department of Linguistics
University of Potsdam
tosik@uni-potsdam.de

[‡]Textkernel B.V.
Amsterdam, Netherlands
{hansen,goossen,rotaru}@textkernel.nl

Abstract

We explore new methods of improving Curriculum Vitæ (CV) parsing for German documents by applying recent research on the application of word embeddings in Natural Language Processing (NLP). Our approach integrates the word embeddings as input features for a probabilistic sequence labeling model that relies on the Conditional Random Field (CRF) framework. Best-performing word embeddings are generated from a large sample of German CVs. The best results on the extraction task are obtained by the model which integrates the word embeddings together with a number of hand-crafted features. The improvements are consistent throughout different sections of the target documents. The effect of the word embeddings is strongest on semi-structured, out-of-sample data.

1 Introduction

Curriculum Vitæ (CV) parsing refers to the task of processing and transforming the relevant information contained in a given CV. The goal is to produce structured output detailing the information presented in the document, including personal information, education items, work experience, or further skills.

CV Parsing is used in multiple real world scenarios. Nowadays, job seekers are frequently presented with the option of simply uploading the required documents into an application system, which then automatically processes the data and directly uploads the candidate information into the corresponding databases. Given structured information on the candidate, recruiters are able to quickly search for potential matches, and systems are enabled to generate personalized recommendations that meet the candidate's specific skill set.

CV Parsing poses an interesting challenge to modern Natural Language Processing (NLP) techniques, because the documents consist of a mixture of semi-structured and free form text with a high degree of variance in the data. The semi-structured text often takes the shape of attribute-value pairs. Typical examples with regard to personal information would be

Name: John Doe, or
Phone: 212 / 123-5678.

A considerable portion of CVs contain personal information without any left context, e.g.

John Doe, MD
900 Main Street
New York, NY

Free form text is most often encountered in work experience items, such as

2006–2008 *Software Developer*
Eastman Kodak Company
Rochester, NY

Led a small team, investigated current systems, and created applications.

High variance in the data stems from the fact that we are dealing with CVs from all possible industries and locations, and on any possible skill level. As a result, there will always be unknown words in the

Proceedings of NAACL-HLT 2015, pages 123–128,
Denver, Colorado, May 31 – June 5, 2015.

entities we seek to extract, most commonly when processing names, addresses, jobs, or companies.

While CV Parsing combines many different NLP components, in this paper we will focus on one task in particular: the extraction of two different types of entities from pre-segmented sections, namely the section containing the personal information of the applicant, and his or her work related information.

More precisely, we investigate the contribution of word embeddings versus word type (or *one-hot*) representations as input feature for a sequence labeling model based on Conditional Random Fields (CRF). By using word embeddings instead of word types, the model is able to utilize large amounts of unlabeled data to supplement the supervised training.

We show that using word embeddings as additional input feature to the CRF model greatly improves the overall model performance. Word embeddings also enhance model performance on out-of-sample data, since the model no longer relies on only the fixed observations in the training data.

2 Related work

To our knowledge, the availability of prior research on CV parsing is very limited. Yu et al. (2005) design a cascaded Information Extraction (IE) framework for CV extraction, comparing flat models based on Hidden Markov Models (HMM) and Support Vector Machines (SVM) with a hierarchical hybrid model.

Over the past decade, there has been an increasing research interest in the application of word embeddings to complex tasks in language processing. As input features for different CRF models, word embeddings are already effectively used in a wide range of NLP systems, including Named Entity Recognition (Demir and Ozgur, 2014), chunking and Part-of-Speech Tagging (Huang and Yates, 2009). Turian et al. (2010) evaluate different techniques for inducing word representations and detail significant improvements for supervised NER and chunking systems when also incorporating word embeddings. Wang and Manning (2013) suggest that linear model architectures benefit from a high-dimensional, discrete feature space. Guo et al. (2014) investigate different approaches on transforming skip-gram embeddings (Mikolov et al., 2013) correspondingly, and report higher performance than directly using the word embeddings with supervised NER as evaluation task. We extend previous work by exploring a novel task in NER, as well as directly comparing the effect of using word types versus word embeddings and how this affects the robustness of the model.

3 Task

As indicated above, our task is to extract structured information from the personal and the experience sections of a diverse set of German input CVs. We solve this extraction task by treating it as a conventional NER problem. Unlike most previous NER work that focuses on extracting the standard name/organization/location/other entities, our domain has an extended set of entities.

For personal information, we extract 6 different entities, specifically the full name of the candidate, the contact address, birthday, phone number, nationality, and email address. From the work experience section, we extract 3 entities, namely the job title, job duration, as well as the company and location. Since experience sections of CVs usually contain multiple previous job descriptions, the task is to extract the given information for each of these jobs.

4 Methodology

We first discuss word embeddings in Section 4.1, before we move on to a formal description of the CRF architecture in Section 4.2.

4.1 Word Embeddings

Word embeddings are continuous vector representations induced from unlabeled input text of arbitrary length. Each dimension of the word embedding represents a latent feature of the word. Intuitively, this kind of meaning representation captures useful properties of the word, both semantically and syntactically (Mikolov et al., 2013).

Word embeddings are typically learned using neural networks (Collobert and Weston, 2008) or clustering as underlying predictive model. Turian et al. (2010) provide a comparison of multiple approaches. Recently, Mikolov et al. (2013) proposed a simple and computationally efficient way to learn word embeddings. In the skip-gram model architecture, the hidden layer is replaced by a shared projection layer, and a window of size c surrounding words $w_{t-c}, .., w_{t-1}, w_{t+1}, .., w_{t+c}$ from word w_t is predicted. The training objective is to learn word embeddings which are good predictors for the surrounding words. This is done by maximizing the average log probability over the data:

$$\frac{1}{T}\sum_{t=1}^{T}\sum_{-c\leq j\leq c, j\neq 0} log\ p(w_{t+j}|w_t)$$

In order to avoid a costly computation proportional to the size of the vocabulary, $p(w_{t+j}|w_t)$ is computed using the hierarchical softmax function as an approximation of the softmax functions. Increasing the window size c can improve accuracy at the expense of training time, since it results in more training examples.

4.2 Conditional Random Fields

The Conditional Random Fields (CRF) model is a state-of-the-art sequence labeling method first introduced by Lafferty et al. (2001).

CRFs are a undirected, graphical model trained to maximize a conditional probability distribution given a set of features. The most common graphical structure used with CRF is linear chain. Let $Y = (y_1, ..., y_T)$ denote a sequence of labels and $X = (x_1, ..., x_T)$ denote the corresponding observations sequence. The sequence of labels is the concept we wish to predict (e.g. target phrases, named-entity, POS, etc.). The observations are the words in the input string. Given a linear chain CRF, the conditional probability $p(Y|X)$ is computed as follows:

$$p(Y|X) = \frac{1}{Z_X}\prod_{t=1}^{T} exp\left\{\sum_{k=1}^{K}\lambda_k f_k(y_t, y_{t-1}, x_t)\right\}$$

Z_X is a normalizing constant such that all the terms normalize to one, f_k is a feature function, and λ_k is a feature weight. CRF offers an advantage over generative approaches by relaxing the conditional independence assumption and allowing for arbitrary features in the observation.

For all our experiments we use *CRFsuite*[1], an implementation of CRF for labeling sequential data provided by Okazaki (2007). We choose an appropriate learning algorithm based on accuracy on the development set and use Limited-memory BFGS optimization (Nocedal, 1980).

5 Experimental setup

We start by describing our data sets in Section 5.1. Section 5.2 details the feature set implemented in the models. Section 5.3 provides details on the generating of the word embeddings, and Section 5.4 specifies the model evaluation.

5.1 Data

We use two separate data sets for evaluation: the main set, and an additional out-of-sample set. Table 1 provides an overview of the number of documents and section-specific entities contained in the main set and the out-of-sample dataset.

	Main set			OOS
	Train	Dev	Test	Test
#Docs	1010	233	214	25
#Pers	6736	1634	1388	n/a
#Exp	20687	4569	4410	356

Table 1: Distribution of documents and personal and experience entities over main set and out-of-sample (OOS) dataset.

In total, the main set is comprised of a sample of 1457 annotated German documents. This sample was randomly split into training (1010 documents), development (233 documents), and test partition (214 documents). All sequence labeling models are trained on the training partition. The test partition is used to evaluate the model performance of previously unseen but similar data.

In addition, we evaluate the performance of the same model on an out-of-sample dataset. This is done in order to measure how well the model generalizes to unseen data from an inherently different sample, i.e. CVs from a new domain not included in the original sample. The out-of-sample set is comprised of a sample of 25 annotated German CVs. These documents are only annotated for experience

[1] `http://www.chokkan.org/software/crfsuite/`

entities, but since each document contains an average of 4.4 work experience items, it provides us with approximately 115 examples of each entity.

Personal information entities usually occur only once per document. Experience entities occur at most once per work experience item. Each document contains 5.9 work experience items on average.

5.2 Features

As indicated in Section 4.2, the CRF model learns based on a number of predefined features. The hand-crafted features include mostly simple orthographic features that account for the beginning and end of a line, unknown words, digits, single characters, multi spaces, capitalization, as well as the first and last token of each line. In addition, high frequency token features encode the 200 most frequent words in the training data in a one-hot binary vector. This is done separately for personal and work experience section.

Similarly, we implement a one-hot representation of word types incorporating all tokens that occur at least twice in the training data. Most importantly, we also implement word embeddings of any given word type as one feature per dimension. We use a BIO encoding (Ramshaw and Marcus, 1995) for labels, resulting in 13 labels for the personal section, and 7 labels for the experience section. Each label spans entire tokens.

5.3 Generating Word Embeddings

To generate the word embeddings, we use the open source *word2vec*[2] toolkit. We conduct a number of experiments to determine most suitable parameters settings. We tune the number of latent dimensions on the development set and find 150 dimensions to give us the best results. Except for vector size, we use default parameters. Applying the skip-gram architecture has proven to be robust across trials.

We experiment with various data sources, including the German Wikipedia, different batches of sample CVs, and spidered job postings. Overall best word embeddings for the information extraction tasks are generated from a set of 200K German sample CVs containing approximately 145.5M tokens.

[2]https://code.google.com/p/word2vec/

5.4 Evaluation

We evaluate five models based on three different groups of features (cf. Table 2). The first baseline model uses only the hand-crafted features. We compare this baseline to two models which incorporate either a feature vector for the word types, or a feature vector for the word embeddings, respectively. Finally, we combine the hand-crafted features with word types or word embeddings for two additional models.

Character-based overlap scores are computed for averaged precision, recall, and F1 scores to evaluate the performance of the models on personal and experience sections. We use character-based overlap instead of token-based overlap scores to penalize the incorrect labeling of longer tokens. Recall that our labeling always spans entire tokens.

6 Results

The macro-averaged precision, recall, and F1 scores for the entities in the personal and experience sections, for the different phrase models on the main test partition, are shown in Table 2.

For the personal section, the models using only word types or only word embeddings give the lowest performance. This is due to the fact that personal sections have a semi-structured layout and content words, which are already well captured when using the hand-crafted orthographic features together with the high frequency token feature.

On less structured experience sections, the effect of the word embeddings is much stronger. By using only word embeddings as features for the model, we outperform the hand-crafted feature baseline by 3.9% on average. The best performance is achieved by combining word embeddings and hand-crafted features, resulting in 96.0% averaged F1 score on the personal section, and 84.0% F1 score on the experience section.

We compare the performance of experience entity extraction on the main test partition with its performance on the out-of-sample data. The results are presented in Table 3. Since word embeddings are learned from large amounts of unlabeled data, we verify that word embeddings also enhance the model performance on the out-of-sample data. Indeed, we observe a 10.1% increase in recall on the out-of-

Model	Personal section			[%]	Experience section		
	Prec (avg.)	Rec (avg.)	F1 (avg.)		Prec (avg.)	Rec (avg.)	F1 (avg.)
Hand-crafted features	94.5	94.0	94.3		84.7	69.8	76.4
Word types	94.7	91.2	92.3		85.3	67.7	75.3
Word embeddings	94.9	93.1	93.9		87.0	74.6	80.3
Word types + features	95.2	95.0	95.1		88.4	74.3	80.6
Word embeddings + features	96.3	95.7	96.0		89.6	79.2	84.0

Table 2: Macro-averaged precision, recall, and F1 scores of the phrase models on the main test partition.

Model	Test set			[%]	Out-of-sample set		
	Prec (avg.)	Rec (avg.)	F1 (avg.)		Prec (avg.)	Rec (avg.)	F1 (avg.)
Word types + features	88.4	74.3	80.6		82.3	57.0	65.6
Word embeddings + features	89.6	79.2	84.0		83.3	67.1	73.8

Table 3: Experience phrase model performance on test partition and out-of-sample dataset.

sample data when using word embeddings instead of word types. Using word embeddings also leads to a greater improvement in F1 score on the out-of-sample set (+8.2%) compared with the main test partition (+3.5%). This suggests that the word embeddings increase the robustness of the model towards the lexical variety comprised in CVs from additional industries.

The results support our hypothesis that the observed improvements are mostly due to the Distributional Hypothesis (Firth, 1957), and the enhanced handling of out-of-vocabulary words: by using word embeddings rather than one-hot representations, the models are able to more accurately predict labels on words that did not occur in the training data.

7 Future Work

Based on the limited sets of sample documents at hand, we currently learn word embeddings from much less data than has been suggested in previous related work. Thus, we are planning on investigating the impact of data source and amount of data for word embedding generation.

Since the focus of the work presented was on German documents, we would additionally like to verify that the results generalize to other languages. First initial test runs on Portuguese indicate that similar improvements can be reproduced easily.

It would also be interesting to move beyond the CRF architecture by comparing performances of different sequence labeling methods on the given task.

8 Conclusion

We describe how word embeddings can be successfully applied to the task of CV parsing. Using the skip-gram architecture, we learn word embeddings from a large set of unlabeled German CVs, and implement them as additional feature to our CRF based sequence labeling model.

Results on the personal section show that neither word types, nor word embeddings alone perform well enough to beat the baseline model based on hand-crafted features only. When combining word types or word embeddings with the hand-crafted features, word embeddings outperform the word types.

We observe that the improvements from the word embeddings combined with hand-crafted features carry over to semi-structured and free form work experience text. Applying word embeddings together with hand-crafted features additionally greatly improves the performance on an out-of-sample dataset.

Acknowledgments

We are thankful to Stephen Roller and the anonymous reviewers for their helpful comments and suggestions. We acknowledge valuable discussions with other researchers at Textkernel: Florence Berbain, Lena Bayeva, Chao Li, and Jakub Zavrel.

References

Collobert, R. and J. Weston (2008). A Unified Architecture for Natural Language Processing: Deep Neural Networks with Multitask Learning. In *Proceedings of the 25th International Conference on Machine Learning*, ICML '08, New York, NY, USA, pp. 160–167. ACM.

Demir, H. and A. Ozgur (2014). Improving Named Entity Recognition for Morphologically Rich Languages Using Word Embeddings. In *13th International Conference on Machine Learning and Applications, ICMLA 2014, Detroit, MI, USA, December 3-6, 2014*, pp. 117–122.

Firth, J. (1957). A synopsis of linguistic theory 1930-1955. pp. 1–32.

Guo, J., W. Che, H. Wang, and T. Liu (2014). Revisiting Embedding Features for Simple Semi-supervised Learning. In *Proceedings of the 2014 Conference on Empirical Methods in Natural Language Processing, EMNLP 2014, October 25-29, 2014, Doha, Qatar, A meeting of SIGDAT, a Special Interest Group of the ACL*, pp. 110–120.

Huang, F. and A. Yates (2009). Distributional Representations for Handling Sparsity in Supervised Sequence-labeling. In *Proceedings of the Joint Conference of the 47th Annual Meeting of the ACL and the 4th International Joint Conference on Natural Language Processing of the AFNLP: Volume 1 - Volume 1*, ACL '09, Stroudsburg, PA, USA, pp. 495–503. Association for Computational Linguistics.

Lafferty, J. D., A. McCallum, and F. C. N. Pereira (2001). Conditional Random Fields: Probabilistic Models for Segmenting and Labeling Sequence Data. In *Proceedings of the Eighteenth International Conference on Machine Learning*, ICML '01, San Francisco, CA, USA, pp. 282–289. Morgan Kaufmann Publishers Inc.

Mikolov, T., K. Chen, G. Corrado, and J. Dean (2013). Efficient Estimation of Word Representations in Vector Space. *CoRR abs/1301.3781.*

Mikolov, T., W. Yih, and G. Zweig (2013). Linguistic Regularities in Continuous Space Word Representations. In *Human Language Technologies: Conference of the North American Chapter of the Association of Computational Linguistics, Proceedings, June 9-14, 2013, Westin Peachtree Plaza Hotel, Atlanta, Georgia, USA*, pp. 746–751.

Nocedal, J. (1980). Updating quasi-newton matrices with limited storage. *Mathematics of computation 35*(151), 773–782.

Okazaki, N. (2007). CRFsuite: a fast implementation of Conditional Random Fields (CRFs).

Ramshaw, L. A. and M. P. Marcus (1995). Text Chunking using Transformation-Based Learning. *CoRR cmp-lg/9505040.*

Turian, J. P., L. Ratinov, and Y. Bengio (2010). Word Representations: A Simple and General Method for Semi-Supervised Learning. In *Proceedings of the 48th Annual Meeting of the Association for Computational Linguistics, July 11-16, 2010, Uppsala, Sweden*, pp. 384–394.

Wang, M. and D. C. Manning (2013). Effect of Non-linear Deep Architecture in Sequence Labeling. In *Proceedings of the Sixth International Joint Conference on Natural Language Processing*, pp. 1285–1291. Asian Federation of Natural Language Processing.

Yu, K., G. Guan, and M. Zhou (2005). Resume Information Extraction with Cascaded Hybrid Model. In *Proceedings of the 43rd Annual Meeting on Association for Computational Linguistics*, ACL '05, Stroudsburg, PA, USA, pp. 499–506. Association for Computational Linguistics.

Morpho-syntactic Regularities in Continuous Word Representations: A Multilingual Study

Garrett Nicolai[†] **Colin Cherry**[‡] **Grzegorz Kondrak**[†]

[†]Department of Computing Science
University of Alberta
Edmonton, AB, T6G 2E8, Canada
{nicolai,gkondrak}@ualberta.ca

[‡]National Research Council Canada
1200 Montreal Road
Ottawa, ON, K1A 0R6, Canada
Colin.Cherry@nrc-cnrc.gc.ca

Abstract

We replicate the syntactic experiments of Mikolov et al. (2013b) on English, and expand them to include morphologically complex languages. We learn vector representations for Dutch, French, German, and Spanish with the WORD2VEC tool, and investigate to what extent inflectional information is preserved across vectors. We observe that the accuracy of vectors on a set of syntactic analogies is inversely correlated with the morphological complexity of the language.

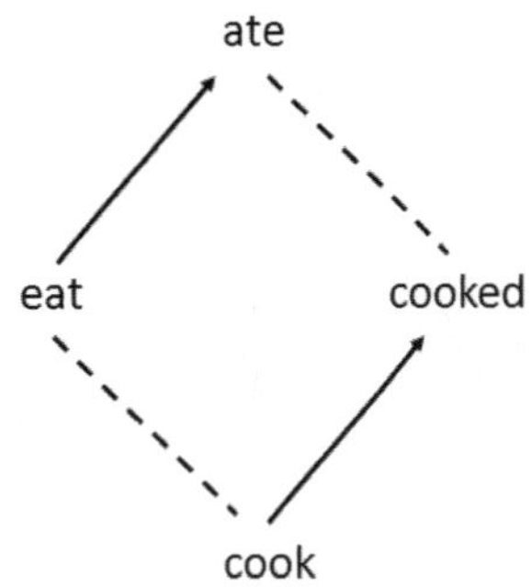

Figure 1: An example of vector offsets.

1 Introduction

Mikolov et al. (2013b) demonstrate that vector representations of words obtained from a neural network language model provide a way of capturing both semantic and syntactic regularities in language. They observe that by manipulating vector offsets between pairs of words, it is possible to derive an approximation of vectors representing other words, such as *queen* $\approx$ *king* $-$ *man* $+$ *woman*. Similarly, an abstract relationship between the present and past tense may be computed by subtracting the base form *eat* from the past form *ate*; the result of composing such an offset with the base form *cook* may turn out to be similar to the vector for *cooked* (Figure 1). They report state-of-the-art results on a set of analogy questions of the form "a is to b as c is to _", where the variables represent various English word forms.

Our work is motivated by two observations regarding Mikolov et al.'s experiments: first, the syntactic analogies that they test correspond to morphological inflections, and second, the tests only evaluate English, a language with little morphological complexity. In this paper, we replicate their syntactic experiments on four languages that are more morphologically complex than English: Dutch, French, German, and Spanish.

2 Replication Experiments

In order to to validate our methodology, we first replicate the results of Mikolov et al. (2013b) on English syntactic analogies.

2.1 Training Corpus for Word Vectors

The vectors of Mikolov et al. (2013b) were trained on 320M tokens of broadcast news data, as described by Mikolov et al. (2011). Since we have no access to this data, we instead train English vectors on a corpus from the Polyglot project (Al-Rfou et al., 2013), which contains tokenized Wikipedia dumps intended for the training of vector-space models. For comparison with the results of Mikolov et al. (2013b), we limit the data to the first 320M lower-cased tokens of the corpus.

Proceedings of NAACL-HLT 2015, pages 129–134,
Denver, Colorado, May 31 – June 5, 2015.

Mikolov et al. (2013b) obtain their best results with vectors of size 1600 that combine several models, but do not elaborate how this composite model was constructed. Instead, we take as a point of reference their second-best model, which employs 640-dimensional vectors produced by a single recursive neural network (RNN) language model.[1]

Rather than use an RNN model to learn our own vectors, we employ the far simpler skip-gram model. Mikolov et al. (2013a) show that higher accuracy can be obtained using vectors derived using this model, which is also far less expensive to train. The skip-gram model eschews a language modeling objective in favor of a logistic regression classifier that predicts surrounding words. The WORD2VEC package includes code for learning skip-gram models from very large corpora.[2] We train 640-dimensional vectors using the skip-gram model with a hierarchical softmax, a context window of 10, sub-sampling of 1e-3, and a minimum frequency threshold of 10.

2.2 Test Set

The test set of Mikolov et al. (2013b) is publicly available[3]. They extract their gold standard inflections, as well as frequency counts, from tagged newspaper text. Their test set was constructed as follows: after tagging 267M words, the 100 most frequent plural nouns, possessive nouns, comparative adjectives, and verbal infinitives were selected. Each was paired with 5 randomly-selected words of the same part-of-speech, and analogy questions were constructed for each word pair. For example, for the pair *people* and *city*, two questions are created: *people*:*person* :: *cities*:*city*, and its mirror: *person*:*people* :: *city*:*cities*.

To solve the analogies in this test set, we apply the word-analogy tool that is included with WORD2VEC. For each analogy $a : b :: c :?$, the tool searches the entire vocabulary for the vector d that is most similar to the vector estimated by performing a linear analogy on the query triplet a, b, c:

$$d = \text{argmax}_{d'} = \cos(d', c + b - a) \quad (1)$$

We calculate accuracy as the percentage of analogies whose answers are correctly predicted, according to an exact match.

The analogies involve nouns, adjectives, and verbs. Nominal analogies consist of comparisons between singular and plural forms, and possessive and nominative forms. Due to the tokenization method used in our training corpus, we are unable to build vectors for English possessives. We therefore modify the nominal test set to only include questions that contain the singular vs. plural distinction. We make no changes to the adjectival and verbal analogy sets. The adjectival set contains analogies between the comparative and the superlative, the comparative and the base, and the superlative and the base. The verbal set includes comparisons between the preterite, the infinitive, and the $3rd$ person singular present, but not the past and present participles.

Test Set	M13	Ours
Adjectives	21.0	18.8
Nouns	40.1	55.2
Verbs	54.8	50.6

Table 1: The results of replicating the experiments of Mikolov et al. (2013b) on English.

2.3 Results

In Table 1, we report two numbers for each part of speech. The first, labeled as M13, is the result of applying the vectors of Mikolov et al. (2013b) to their test set. The results match the results reported in their paper, except for the nominal results, which reflect our modifications described in Section 2.2. The removal of the possessives improves the accuracy from 25.2% reported in the original paper to 40.1%. The second column, labeled as Ours, reports the results for our vectors, which were trained using WORD2VEC on the English data described in Section 2.1.

Our verbal and adjectival vectors obtain slightly lower accuracies than the RNN trained vectors of Mikolov et al. (2013b), but they are not far off. For nouns, however, we obtain higher accuracy than Mikolov et al. The tokenization method that removes possessives from consideration may produce better vectors for singular and plural forms, as it increases the frequency of these types.

[1]The vectors are available at *http://rnnlm.org*.

[2]*https://code.google.com/p/word2vec*.

[3]*http://research.microsoft.com/en-us/projects/rnn*

3 Multilingual Experiments

Our second set of experiments examine to what extent the syntactic regularities are captured by word vectors in four other languages: Dutch, French, German, and Spanish.

3.1 Training Corpora for Word Vectors

As in the previous experiment, our training corpora are from the Polyglot project. We limit each corpus to the first 320M lowercased tokens, except for the Dutch corpus, which has only 180M tokens. Since the WORD2VEC tool cannot handle Unicode, we map all non-ASCII characters to unused ASCII characters. We run WORD2VEC with exactly the same hyper-parameters as in Section 2.1. The English experiments in this section use the same training data and vectors as in Section 2, but we construct a new test set to match our methodology for the other languages.

3.2 Test Sets

In order to make results between multiple languages comparable, we made several changes to the construction of syntactic analogy questions. We follow the methodology of Mikolov et al. (2013b) in limiting analogy questions to the 100 most frequent verbs or nouns. The frequencies are obtained from corpora tagged by TREETAGGER (Schmid, 1994).

We identify inflections using manually constructed inflection tables from several sources. Spanish and German verbal inflections, as well as German nominal inflections, are from a Wiktionary data set introduced by Durrett and DeNero (2013).[4] Dutch verbal inflections and English verbal and nominal inflections are from the CELEX database (Baayen et al., 1995). French verbal inflections are from Verbiste, an online French conjugation dictionary.[5]

Whereas Mikolov et al. create analogies from various inflectional forms, we require the analogies to always include the base dictionary form: the infinitive for verbs, and the nominative singular for nouns. In other words, all analogies are limited to comparisons between the base form and an inflected form. This is to prevent a combinatorial explosion of the number of analogies in languages that contain dozens of different inflection forms. We also create new English test sets using this methodology, in order to ensure a fair cross-lingual comparison. Table 2 shows the number of analogy questions for each language set. Note that the languages are ordered according to increasing morphological complexity.

Set	I	Q	Example
EN-V	5	3096	go:gone see:?
NL-V	9	5136	gaan:gegaan zien:?
DE-V	27	6514	gehen:gegangen sehen:?
FR-V	48	15573	aller:allé voir:?
ES-V	57	22579	ir:ido ver:?
EN-N	2	876	bear:bears lion:?
DE-N	8	1804	Bär:Bären Löwe:?

Table 2: The number of inflectional slots (I) and analogy questions (Q) for each language set.

Following Mikolov et al., we ensure that all analogies contain at least one pair of non-syncretic forms. It would make little sense to include analogies such as "*set* is to *set* as *put* is to *?*" because both verbs in question have the same present and past tense form. However, we do allow analogies which involve syncretic forms for one half of the analogy. For example, either *taken* or *took* is a correct answer to "*play* is to *played* as *take* is to *?*". These types of questions account for an average of 2.8% of analogies, ranging from 0% for English nouns to 8.9% for German verbs.

The number of questions for each language is a function of the number of inflectional forms, but it is not a simple linear relationship. If each English verb had five different inflections, each with sufficient frequency in the training corpus, we would expect 4000 questions for 100 verbs. This is because each verb should ideally be compared to five other verbs, with the base form paired with the other four inflectional forms, in both directions. The actual number of questions is smaller because some forms are identical, while other forms are observed less frequently than our minimum threshold of 10.

[4]We exclude Finnish because of its high morphological complexity and the small size of the corresponding Polyglot corpus.

[5]*http://perso.b2b2c.ca/sarrazip/dev/verbiste.html*

Set	All Inflections		Inflection Subset	
EN-V	52.6	(21.3k)	52.6	(21.3k)
NL-V	37.8	(4.5k)	33.5	(7.0k)
DE-V	29.4	(5.0k)	40.0	(8.9k)
FR-V	25.9	(0.5k)	45.6	(8.6k)
ES-V	22.8	(0.5k)	48.2	(10.6k)
EN-N	52.2	(46.9k)	52.2	(46.9k)
DE-N	28.2	(18.0k)	31.9	(35.6k)

Table 3: Accuracy on analogy questions. The median frequencies of the types involved are provided in brackets.

3.3 Results

We conduct two experiments to quantify the extent that the syntactic regularities observed in English hold in the other languages. In the first experiment, which is referred to as *All Inflections*, we measure the accuracy of vectors on all inflected forms. In the second experiment, named *Inflection Subset*, we attempt to factor out the variation in the number of inflectional forms across languages by considering only the forms that are observed in English (five forms for verbs, and two forms for nouns).

The results of the experiments are in Table 3. In the *All Inflections* column, we see that the overall accuracy decreases as the morphological complexity increases. However, the *Inflection Subset* column reveals an opposite trend: the accuracy is increasing towards the bottom of the table, (although English stands out as a clear exception). Looking across the rows, the accuracy on the inflection subset is higher than on all inflections, except on Dutch. Noun analogies are only tested on two languages, but they seem to follow the same trends as verbs.

The results in Table 3 are not easy to interpret. It appears the lower frequencies of multiple inflected word forms make the task more difficult, which is reflected in the *All Inflections* results. The median frequencies of individual verb forms in French and Spanish are approximately one-tenth of the corresponding numbers in Dutch and German, which in turn are about one-fourth of the English median. However, these ratios are not neatly correlated with the accuracy results in Table 3.

Regarding the contrasting results in the *Inflection Subset* column, we conjecture that a larger number of inflections may make *individual forms* easier to disambiguate. This in turn allows WORD2VEC to learn more precise vectors for each word type. The median frequencies of the forms in the inflection subset tend to be higher than the corresponding values computed for all inflections, but there is a substantial variation between different languages. Dutch, in particular, sees a similar increase in median frequency to German, but while German accuracy increases, Dutch decreases. We conclude that although frequency is an important factor when performing syntactic analogies with vectors, there must be other factors contributing to these results.

It is perhaps unsurprising that English is the winner on its own inflection set. However, another reason that English does not follow the trend in the *Inflection Subset* column may be related to the frequencies of its small set of wordforms, which are uniformly higher than in other languages. The experiments that we describe in the next section provide additional insights into these results.

4 Hyper-Parameter Experiments

In this section, we describe experiments that quantify how the quality of the vectors is affected by the window size and the amount of training data.

4.1 Window size

First, we investigate the role that the window size has on the accuracy of learned vectors. We expect that larger window sizes may create more topic-oriented vectors, while small windows result in vectors that capture syntactic information (Turney, 2012). While all experiments in Section 3 used a window size of 10, the languages have different syntactic and morphological patterns, and some of the results observed in Section 3 may simply be a side effect of better or worse window sizes for particular languages. We run an experiment that tests window sizes of 1, 3, 5 and 10, calculating the analogy accuracy for each language and each window size.

Figure 2 shows the results for varying window sizes. While no single window size is best for all languages, we observe that the morphologically complex languages perform better with larger windows. One benefit that larger window sizes may provide is access to more information during vector training,

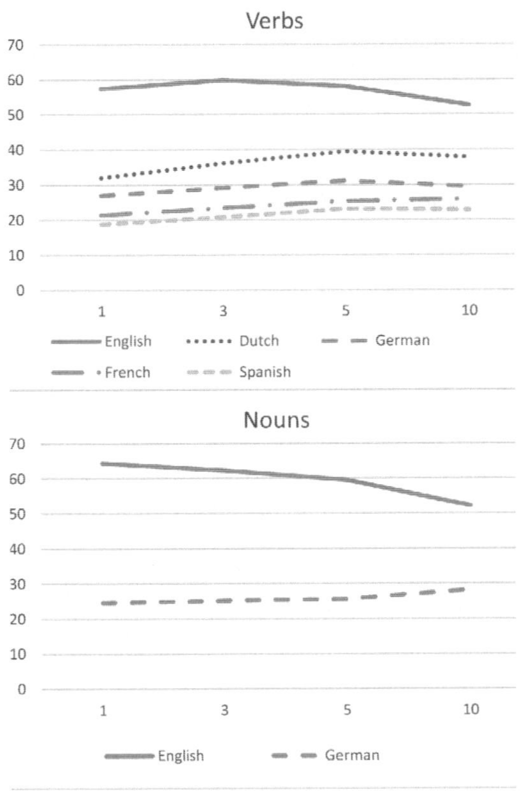

Figure 2: Accuracy for different context windows.

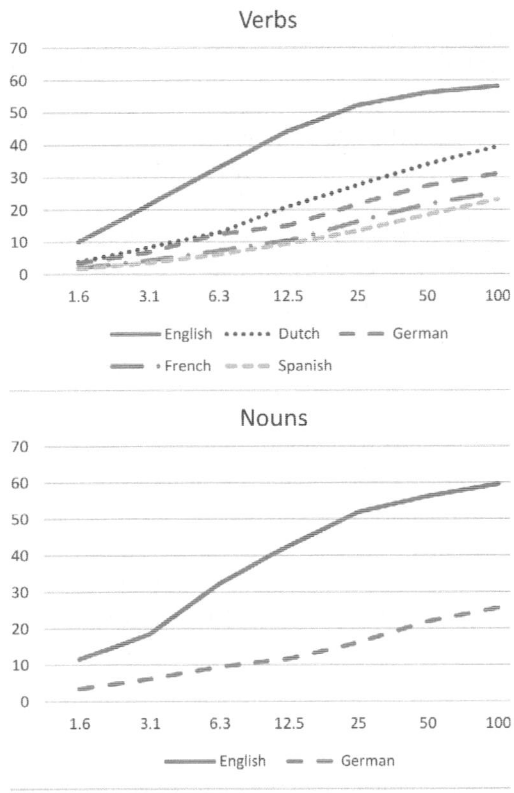

Figure 3: Learning curves.

which may be important when each type is observed less frequently. Our next experiment directly investigates the impact of the training data size.

4.2 Learning curves

In this section, we investigate how varying the size of the vector training data affects the vector accuracy. We progressively subsample the training data: starting with the complete training set, we construct a 50% subsample by selecting each sentence for inclusion with probability 0.5. We then iterate this process, each time sampling roughly 50% of the sentences from the previously created subsample, until we have a subsample that is only 1.6% of the original training data. This gives us training sets with approximately 1.6, 3.1, 6.3, 12.5, 25, 50, and 100% of the full corpora. We set the window size to 5 for this experiment; the other hyper-parameters are the same as those in Section 2.1.

The learning curves for verbs and nouns are shown in Figure 3. We see that the trends observed in Section 3 hold regardless of the amount of data that is used for training: namely, the accuracy of the vectors is inversely correlated with the number of inflection slots in a given language set. Secondly, while the English curves are beginning to level off, the curves for the other languages continue to rise, even as we reach 100% of our data. This suggests that there would be little gain in adding more English data, but a potential gain to be seen by adding more data to the other languages. This seems to support our hypothesis that the sparsity of the data is at least partially responsible for the lower accuracies on the morphologically complex languages.

5 Conclusion

The results of our experiments show that it is possible to learn vectors that preserve morphological information even for languages with complex inflectional systems. The accuracy of vectors on a set of syntactic analogies in four tested languages is lower than in English, and it appears to be inversely proportional to morphological complexity, as measured by the number of inflections in the language. When we limit our test set to the small set of inflections common across languages, we see improvements in the accuracy, which positively correlate with the complexity of the language. This suggests that for frequently observed phenomena, morphological complexity may be an advantage, making each type distinct and easier to model. Additional experiments suggest that the accuracy on more complex languages may further improve if more training data is provided.

These results suggest two possible avenues for future work. The first is to build morphologically-aware vectors, such as those of Botha and Blunsom (2014), so that the more morphologically complex languages can make better use of limited training data. The second is to investigate methods that can distinguish syncretic forms in context. For example, it could be possible to modify the joint word-sense and vector induction algorithm of Neelakantan et al. (2014) to focus on syntactic parts-of-speech instead of topical senses.

Acknowledgments

This research was supported by the Natural Sciences and Engineering Research Council of Canada, and the Alberta Innovates – Technology Futures.

References

Rami Al-Rfou, Bryan Perozzi, and Steven Skiena. 2013. Polyglot: Distributed word representations for multilingual NLP. In *Proceedings of the Seventeenth Conference on Computational Natural Language Learning*, pages 183–192, Sofia, Bulgaria, August. Association for Computational Linguistics.

Harald R. Baayen, Richard Piepenbrock, and Leon Gulikers. 1995. *The CELEX Lexical Database. Release 2 (CD-ROM)*. Linguistic Data Consortium, University of Pennsylvania, Philadelphia, Pennsylvania.

Jan A. Botha and Phil Blunsom. 2014. Compositional Morphology for Word Representations and Language Modelling. In *Proceedings of the 31st International Conference on Machine Learning (ICML)*, Beijing, China, jun. *Award for best application paper*.

Greg Durrett and John DeNero. 2013. Supervised learning of complete morphological paradigms. In *HLT-NAACL*, pages 1185–1195.

Tomas Mikolov, Anoop Deoras, Daniel Povey, Lukas Burget, and Jan Cernocky. 2011. Strategies for training large scale neural network language models. In *Automatic Speech Recognition and Understanding (ASRU), 2011 IEEE Workshop on*, pages 196–201. IEEE.

Tomas Mikolov, Kai Chen, Greg Corrado, and Jeffrey Dean. 2013a. Efficient estimation of word representations in vector space. In *Proceedings of Workshop at ICLR, 2013*.

Tomas Mikolov, Wen-tau Yih, and Geoffrey Zweig. 2013b. Linguistic regularities in continuous space word representations. In *HLT-NAACL*, pages 746–751.

Arvind Neelakantan, Jeevan Shankar, Alexandre Passos, and Andrew McCallum. 2014. Efficient nonparametric estimation of multiple embeddings per word in vector space. In *Proceedings of EMNLP*.

Helmut Schmid. 1994. Probabilistic part-of-speech tagging using decision trees. In *Proceedings of the international conference on new methods in language processing*, volume 12, pages 44–49. Citeseer.

Peter D Turney. 2012. Domain and function: A dual-space model of semantic relations and compositions. *Journal of Artificial Intelligence Research*, pages 533–585.

Towards Combined Matrix and Tensor Factorization for Universal Schema Relation Extraction

Sameer Singh
University of Washington
Seattle, WA
sameer@cs.washington.edu

Tim Rocktäschel* **Sebastian Riedel**
University College London
London, UK
{t.rocktaschel,s.riedel}@cs.ucl.ac.uk

Abstract

Matrix factorization of knowledge bases in universal schema has facilitated accurate distantly-supervised relation extraction. This factorization encodes dependencies between textual patterns and structured relations using low-dimensional vectors defined for each entity pair; although these factors are effective at combining evidence for an entity pair, they are inaccurate on rare pairs, or for relations that depend crucially on the entity types. On the other hand, tensor factorization is able to overcome these shortcomings when applied to link prediction by maintaining entity-wise factors. However these models have been unsuitable for universal schema. In this paper we first present an illustration on synthetic data that explains the unsuitability of tensor factorization to relation extraction with universal schemas. Since the benefits of tensor and matrix factorization are complementary, we then investigate two hybrid methods that combine the benefits of the two paradigms. We show that the combination can be fruitful: we handle ambiguously phrased relations, achieve gains in accuracy on real-world relations, and demonstrate that entity embeddings encode entity types.

1 Introduction

Distantly-supervised relation extraction has gained prominence as it utilizes automatically aligned data to train accurate extractors. Universal schema, in particular, has found impressive accuracy gains by (1) treating the distant-supervision as a knowledge-base (KB) containing both *structured* relations such as `bornIn` and surface form relations such as "was born in" extracted from text, and (2) by *completing* the entries in such a KB using joint and compact encoding of the dependencies between the relations (Riedel et al., 2013; Fan et al., 2014; Chang et al., 2014). Matrix factorization is at the core of this completion: Riedel et al. (2013) convert the KB into a binary matrix with entity-pairs forming the rows and relations forming the columns. Factorization of this matrix results in low-dimensional factors for entity-pairs and relations, which are able to effectively combine multiple evidence for each entity pair to predict unseen relations.

An important shortcoming of this matrix factorization model for universal schema is that no information is shared between the rows that contain the same entity. This can significantly impact accuracy on pairs of entities that are not mentioned together frequently, and for relations that depend crucially on fine-grained entity types, such as `schoolAttended`, `nationality`, and `bookAuthor`. On the other hand, tensor factorization for knowledge-base completion maintains per-entity factors that combine evidence from all the relations an entity participates in, to predict its relations to other entities – a task known as link prediction (Nickel et al., 2012; Bordes et al., 2013). These entity factors, as opposed to pairwise factors in matrix factorization, can be quite effective in identifying the latent, fine-grained entity types. Thus, in the light of the above problems of matrix factorization, the use of tensor factorization for universal schema is tempting. However, directly applying tensor factorization to universal schema has not been successful. Strong results were obtained only through a combination with matrix factorization predictions, and the use of predefined type information (Chang et al., 2014).

*First two authors contributed equally to the paper.

Proceedings of NAACL-HLT 2015, pages 135–142,
Denver, Colorado, May 31 – June 5, 2015.

In this paper, we explore the application of matrix and tensor factorization for universal schema data. On simple, synthetic relations, we contrast the representational capabilities of these methods (in § 3.1) and investigate their benefits and shortcomings.We then propose two hybrid tensor and matrix factorization approaches that, by combining their complementary advantages, is able to overcome the shortcomings on synthetic data. We also present improved accuracy on real-world relation extraction data, and demonstrate that the entity embeddings are effective at encoding entity types.

2 Matrix and Tensor Factorization

In this section we introduce universal schemas and various factorization models that can be used to complete knowledge bases of such schemas.

2.1 Universal Schema

A universal schema is defined as the union of all OpenIE-like surface form patterns found in text and fixed canonical relations that exist in a knowledge base (Riedel et al., 2013). The task here is to complete this schema by jointly reasoning over surface form patterns and relations. A successful approach to this joint reasoning is to embed both kinds of relations into the same low-dimensional embedding space, which can be achieved by matrix or tensor factorization methods. We will study such representations for universal schema in this paper.

2.2 Matrix Factorization with Factors over Entity-Pairs

In matrix factorization for universal schema, Riedel et al. (2013) construct a sparse binary matrix of size $|\mathcal{P}| \times |\mathcal{R}|$ whose rows are indexed by entity-pairs $(a, b) \in \mathcal{P}$ and columns by surface form and Freebase relations $s \in \mathcal{R}$. Subsequently, generalized PCA (Collins et al., 2001) is used to find a rank-k factorization, *i.e.*, with relation factors $\mathbf{r} \in \mathbb{R}^{|\mathcal{R}| \times k}$ and entity-pair factors $\mathbf{p} \in \mathbb{R}^{|\mathcal{P}| \times k}$, the probability of a relation s and two entities a and b is:

$$P(s(a, b)) = \sigma(\mathbf{r}_s \cdot \mathbf{p}_{ab}) \quad (1)$$

where σ is the sigmoid function. Using this factorization, similar entity-pairs and relations are embedded close to each other in a k-dimensional vector space. Since this model uses embeddings for pairs of entities, as opposed to per-entity embeddings, we refer to such models as *pairwise* models. Pairwise embeddings are especially suitable when working with universal schema data, since they can represent correlations between surface pattern relations and structured relations compactly. Furthermore, they combine multiple evidences specific to an entity-pair to predict a relation between them. Since the observed data matrix contains only *true* entries, the parameters are learned using Bayesian personalized Ranking (Rendle et al., 2009) that supports implicit feedback.

Riedel et al. (2013) explore a number of variants of this factorization, including a neighborhood model that learns local classifiers, and an entity model that includes entity representations (we revisit this formulation in Section 2.3.4). In the rest of this paper we will only use the basic factorization model (referred to as **Model F**) as the primary pairwise embedding model, however the ideas apply directly to these variants as well.

There are a few shortcomings of models that rely solely on pairwise embeddings. To learn an appropriate representation of an entity-pair, the two entities need to be mentioned together frequently, which is not the case for many entity-pairs of interest. Since predicting relations often relies on the entity types, this lack of ample relational evidence for an entity pair can result in poor estimation of their types, and hence, of their relations. Further, a large number of pairwise relation instances (relative to the number of entities) results in a large number of model parameters, leading to scalability concerns.

2.3 Tensor Factorization with Entity Factors

Instead of using a matrix, it can be natural to represent the binary relations in universal schema as a mode-3 tensor. Here we allocate one mode for relations, one for entities appearing as first argument of relations, and the last mode for entities as second argument. This formulation allows the use of tensor factorization approaches that we will describe here. We use $\mathbf{e}_a \in \mathbb{R}^k$ to refer to the embedding of an entity a. In cases where the position of the entity requires different embeddings, we use $\mathbf{e}_{a,1}$ and $\mathbf{e}_{a,2}$ to represent its occurrence as first and second argument, respectively.

2.3.1 CANDECOMP/PARAFAC-Decomposition

In CANDECOMP/PARAFAC-decomposition (Harshman, 1970) the data tensor is approximated using a finite sum of rank one tensors, *i.e.*,

$$P(s(a,b)) = \sigma\left(\sum_k r_s^{(k)} e_a^{(k)} e_b^{(k)}\right). \quad (2)$$

This decomposition was originally introduced without the logistic function, *i.e.*, in its linear form. However since the additional non-linearity is beneficial for factorizing for binary data (Collins et al., 2001; Bouchard et al., 2015), we use the version above for our relational data.

2.3.2 Tucker2 Decomposition and RESCAL

CP-decomposition is quite restrictive since it does not take advantage of correlations between multiple entities and relations (Nickel et al., 2012). A more expressive factorization is Tucker decomposition (Tucker, 1966), where in its standard formulation, a mode-3 tensor is decomposed into a core tensor and three matrices. However, it is computationally expensive to estimate the core tensor, thus in practice the data tensor is often factorized only along two (instead of three) modes, which is referred to as Tucker2 decomposition. A natural choice for relational data is to keep the relational mode fixed, and thus represent each relation as a $k \times k$ matrix (*e.g.* $\mathbf{R}_s$ for relation s) and entities as k-vectors:

$$P(s(a,b)) = \sigma((\mathbf{R}_s \times \mathbf{e}_{a,1}) \cdot \mathbf{e}_{b,2}). \quad (3)$$

Like PARAFAC, the Tucker2 model was originally introduced in the linear form, however we use the logistic version here. A variant of Tucker2 decomposition that has been applied very successfully in knowledge base completion is RESCAL (Nickel et al., 2012), where each entity in has a single shared embedding irrespective of its argument position. Although a logistic version of RESCAL has also been introduced by Nickel and Tresp (2013), we use the linear form since an open-source implementation of the logistic version is not available.

2.3.3 TransE

Another formulation that is based on entity representations is the translating embeddings model by Bordes et al. (2013). The idea is that if a relation s between two entities a and b holds, that relation's vector representation $\mathbf{r}_s$ should translate the representation $\mathbf{e}_a$ to the second argument $\mathbf{e}_b$, *i.e.*,

$$\text{score}(s(a,b)) = -\|(\mathbf{e}_a + \mathbf{r}_s) - \mathbf{e}_b\|_2. \quad (4)$$

In this work we use a variant of TransE in which different embeddings are learned for an entity for each argument position.

2.3.4 Model E

Furthermore, we isolate the entity factorization in Riedel et al. (2013) by viewing it as tensor factorization. In this model, each relation is assigned an embedding for each of its two arguments, *i.e.*,

$$P(s(a,b)) = \sigma(\mathbf{r}_{s,1} \cdot \mathbf{e}_a + \mathbf{r}_{s,2} \cdot \mathbf{e}_b). \quad (5)$$

Although not explored in isolation by Riedel et al. (2013), model E can be used on its own to predict relations between entities, even if they have not been observed to be in a relation.

3 Combined Tensor and Matrix Factorization for Universal Schema

In the previous section, we provided background on matrix factorization with pairwise factors, followed by a tensor factorization based formulation of universal schema. Although matrix factorization performs well for universal schema (Riedel et al., 2013), it is not robust to sparse data and does not capture latent entity types that can be crucial for accurate relation extraction. On the other hand, although tensor factorization models are able to compactly represent entity types using unary embeddings, they are unable to adequately represent the *pair*-specific information that is necessary for modeling relations. It is worth noting that tensor factorization for universal schema has been proposed by Chang et al. (2014), who also observed that tensor factorization by itself performs poorly (even with additional type constraints), and the predictions need to be combined with matrix factorization to be accurate. In this section we will present the fundamental differences between matrix and tensor factorization, and examine a few hybrid models that can address these concerns.

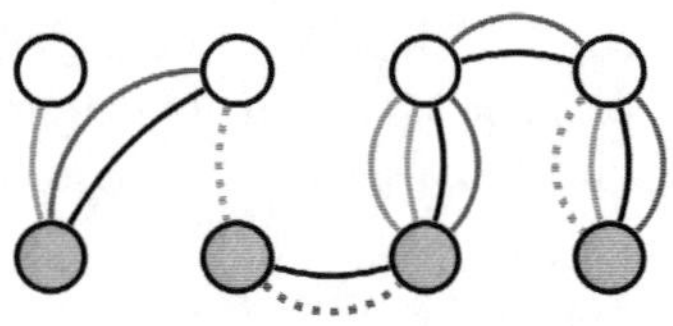

Figure 1: **RGB Relations:** Best viewed in color. **Black** is a sparsely observed relation between *any* pair of entities. **Red** relations correspond to each black edge, and a model that learns this implication can generalize to test instances (red dotted edge). Green relation exists between white and gray entities (we omit many of these edges for clarity), requiring the model to learn latent entity *types*. Finally, Blue relations exist for pairs where *both* a black and green relation is observed.

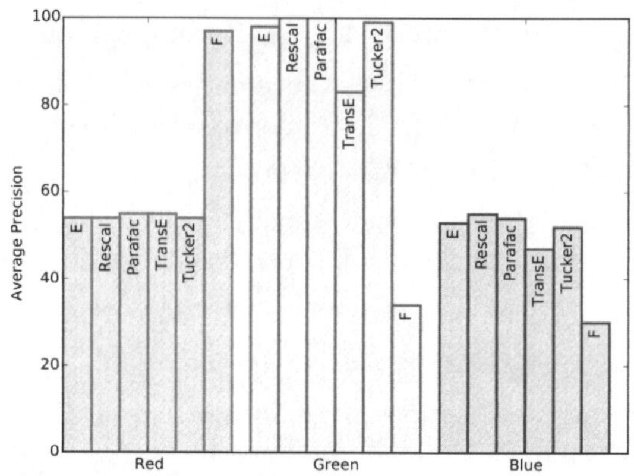

Figure 2: **Matrix versus Tensor Factorization on RGB Data:** illustrating that the tensor factorization approaches (*E*, RESCAL, PARAFAC, *TransE*, and *Tucker2*) are effective only on Green, while matrix factorization (*F*) only on Red. On Blue, both paradigms are unable to generalize.

3.1 Illustration Using Synthetic Relations

As an illustration of the limitations, we present experiments on a simple, synthetic relation extraction task. The generated data consists of entities that belong to one of two types, and the following four types of relations (see Figure 1 for an example): (a) *Black* relations that are observed randomly between any two entities (with probability 0.5), (b) *Red* relations that exist between all pairs for which a *Black* relation exists, similar to a `bornIn` relation corresponding to each observed "X was born in Y" surface pattern, (c) *Green* relations that appear between all pairs of entities of different types, and (d) *Blue* relations that appear between entity pairs that are of different types *and* a Black relation was observed between them. These Blue relation instances represent the relations that often occur in real-data: an ambiguous surface pattern such as "X went to Y" corresponds to `schoolAttended` relation only if the arguments are of certain types. We create such a dataset over 100 entities, and with 5 different sets of such relations (thus 20 total relations, and each entity is assigned 5 of 10 types), and hold out a random 10% of the Red, Green, and Blue relations for evaluation.

These relations target the strengths of the factorization representations. Red relations, as they directly correlate with observed Black instances, should be trivial for matrix factorization.[1] Similarly, Green relations are based on, and clearly define, the latent types of the entities, and thus tensor factorization with entity embeddings should be able to near-perfectly generalize these relations. The converse is more difficult to anticipate; it is unclear how matrix factorization can represent the types needed for Green relations, or whether tensor factorization can encode the Black-Red correspondence. Further, it is not easy to see how any of these approaches will generalize to the Blue relation.

We show the average precision curves on held-out relations for a pairwise embedding approach (matrix factorization *F* from §2.2) and many of the unary embeddings methods from §2.3, with rank 6 in Figure 2. As expected, matrix factorization (*F*) is able to capture the Red relation accurately, however unary embeddings are not able to generalize to it. On the other hand, unary embeddings are able to learn the Green relation which the pairwise approach fail to predict accurately. Blue relations, which most closely model many kinds of relations that occur in text, unfortunately, are not represented well by these approaches that use either unary or pairwise embeddings.

3.2 Hybrid Factorization Models

Since matrix and tensor factorization techniques are quite limited in their representations even on the simple, synthetic data, we now turn to hybrid matrix and

[1] In fact, the set of all Red relations can be represented by rank 2 factors, see Bouchard et al. (2015).

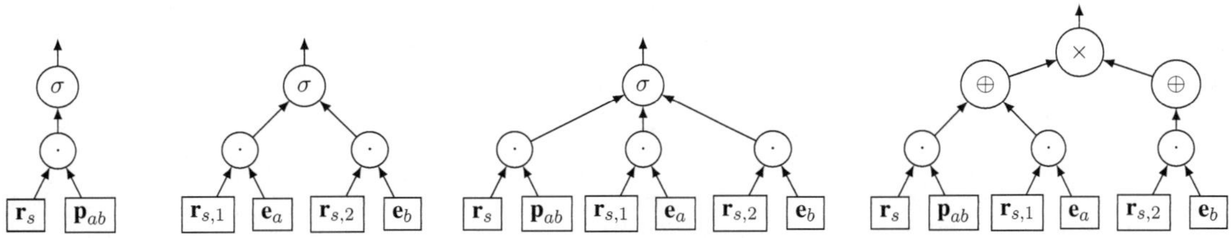

(a) Model F (b) Model E (c) Model FE (d) Model RFE

Figure 3: **Overview of the Models:** Some of the models explored in this work, showing pairwise (*F*) and unary (*E*) models, along with their combinations (*FE* and *RFE*), for computing $P(s(a,b))$.

tensor factorization models that represent entity types for universal schema. We describe two possible combinations, models FE and RFE, summarized in Figure 3. Note that these approaches are distinct from collective factorization (Singh and Gordon, 2008) that can be used when extra entity information is available as unary relations.

3.2.1 Combined Model (FE)

As the direct combination of a pairwise model (Eq. 1) with an entity model (Eq. 5), we consider the FE model from Riedel et al. (2013), *i.e.*, the additive combination of the two:

$$P(s(a,b)) = \sigma(\mathbf{r}_s \cdot \mathbf{e}_{ab} + \mathbf{r}_{s,1} \cdot \mathbf{e}_a + \mathbf{r}_{s,2} \cdot \mathbf{e}_b) \quad (6)$$

Both the matrix factorization model *F* and entity model *E* can de defined as special cases of this model, by setting $\mathbf{r}_{s,1/2}$ or $\mathbf{r}_s$ to zero, respectively.

3.2.2 Rectifier Model (RFE)

A problem with combining the two models additively, as in *FE*, is that one model can easily override the other. For instance, even if the type constraints of a relation are violated, a high score by the pairwise model score might still yield a high prediction for that triplet. To alleviate this shortcoming, we experimented with rectifier units (Nair and Hinton, 2010) so that a score of model *F* or model *E* first needs to reach a certain threshold to influence the overall prediction for a triplet. Specifically, we use the smooth approximation of a rectifier $\oplus(x) = \log(1 + e^x)$ and define the probability for a triplet as follows:

$$P(s(a,b)) = \oplus(\mathbf{r}_s \cdot \mathbf{p}_{ab}) \oplus (\mathbf{r}_{s,1} \cdot \mathbf{e}_a + \mathbf{r}_{s,2} \cdot \mathbf{e}_b)$$

3.3 Parameter Estimation

As by Riedel et al. (2013), we use a Bayesian personalized ranking objective (Rendle et al., 2009) to estimate parameters, *i.e.*, for each observed training fact, we sample an unobserved fact for the same relation, and maximize their relative ranking using AdaGrad. For all models we use $k = 100$ as dimension of latent representations, an initial learning rate of 0.1, and ℓ_2-regularization of all parameters with a weight of 0.01. For CANDECOMP/PARAFAC and RESCAL we use the open-source `scikit-tensor`[2] package with default hyper-parameters.

4 Experiments

In order to evaluate whether the hybrid models are able to effectively combine the benefits of matrix and tensor factorization, we first present experiments on synthetic data in Section 4.1. For a more real-world evaluation, we also experiment with universal schema for distantly-supervised relation extraction in Section 4.2.

4.1 Synthetic RGB Relations

In Section 3.1 we described a simple synthetic data set consisting of multiple *Red*, *Green*, and *Blue* relations constructed in order to illustrate the restrictions in the representation capabilities of matrix and tensor factorization models. Here we revisit the dataset using the proposed combined tensor and matrix factorization approaches to evaluate whether these hybrid models are able to compete with tensor and matrix factorization on the relations they are good at (*Green* and *Red*, respectively), but more importantly, whether the combined approaches can represent the *Blue* rela-

[2] `http://github.com/mnick/scikit-tensor`

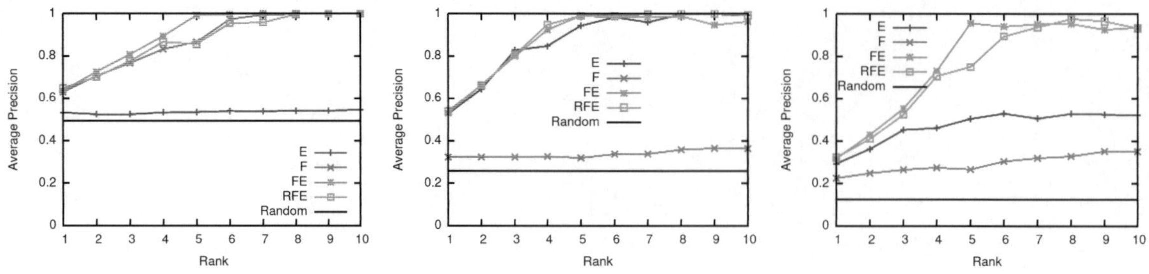

(a) Red (b) Green (c) Blue

Figure 4: **Hybrid Methods on RGB Data:** Average precision as the rank is varied. *FE* and *RFE* perform as well (or better than) tensor factorization on Green and matrix factorization on Red, but importantly, are able to encode the Blue relations that matrix or tensor factorization fail to model.

	R13-F	TR-R13	E	F	RFE	FE
MAP	60	57	56	59	57	62
Weighted MAP	64	61	51	66	60	66

Table 1: **Distantly-Supervised Relation Extraction:** Weighted and unweighted mean average precision for Freebase relations, as achieved by a number of relation extractors, including pairwise (*F*), unary (*E*), and hybrid (*FE* and *RFE*) models.

tions that matrix and tensor factorization approaches fail to generalize to. In Figure 4 we present the average precision on the held-out data as the rank is varied for a number of approaches (we omit the remaining tensor factorization approaches for clarity since they perform similar to RESCAL and Model E). On the *Red* relation (Figure 4a), tensor factorization is close to random, while combined factorization approaches (FE and RFE) are competitive to, and often outperform, matrix factorization (F). Similarly, on the *Green* relation (Figure 4b), the combined approaches perform as well as tensor factorization, while matrix factorization is not much better than random. Finally, on the *Blue* relation on which matrix and tensor factorization fare poorly, the combined approaches are able to obtain high accuracy, in particular achieve close to 90% average precision with only a rank of 5. Although the same rank corresponds to different numbers of parameters for each method, the trend clearly indicates these results do not depend significantly on the number of parameters.

4.2 Universal Schema Relation Extraction

With the promising results shown on synthetic data, we now turn to evaluation on real-world information extraction. In particular, we evaluate the models on universal schema for distantly-supervised relation extraction. Following the experiment setup of Riedel et al. (2013), we instantiate the universal schema matrix over entity pairs and text/Freebase relations for New York Times data, and compare the performance using average precision of the presented models. Table 1 summarizes the performance of our models, as compared to existing approaches (see Riedel et al. (2013) for an overview). In particular, *TR-R13* takes the output predictions of matrix factorization, and combines it with an entity-type aware RESCAL model (Chang et al., 2014).[3] Tensor factorization approaches perform poorly on this data. We present results for Model *E*, but other formulations such as PARAFAC, TransE, RESCAL, and Tucker2 achieved even lower accuracy; this is consistent with the results in Chang et al. (2014). Models that use the matrix factorization (*F, FE, R13-F* and *RFE*) are significantly better, but more importantly, the hybrid appraoch FE achieves the highest accuracy. It is unclear why *RFE* fails to provide similar gains, in particular, performing slightly worse than matrix factorization. Note that we are not introducing a new state-of-art here, the neighborhood model (*NF*) that achieves a higher accuracy is omitted for clarity.

[3]Here, as in Riedel et al. (2013), we only evaluate on entity pairs that are linked to Freebase, thus the performance of Chang et al. (2014) is lower than their reported results.

LG Electronics
Genentech, Industrial and Commercial Bank of China, Broadway Video, Pollack, Bank Hapoalim, Caremark Rx, Mitchell Gold, Tellabs, Cathay Pacific, Eircom
La Stampa
Toronto Star, O Globo, The Daily Telegraph, El Diario, Le Devoir, Politika, The Straits Times, The Day, RedEye, The Globe
Fatherland
Answered Prayers, Age of Innocence, Auntie Mame, House of Meetings, Bergdorf Blondes, Berlin Diary, Clarissa, Eminent Victorians, Darkness Visible, Gossamer

Table 2: **Nearest-Neighbors** for a few randomly-selected entities based on their embeddings, demonstrating that similar entities are close to each other.

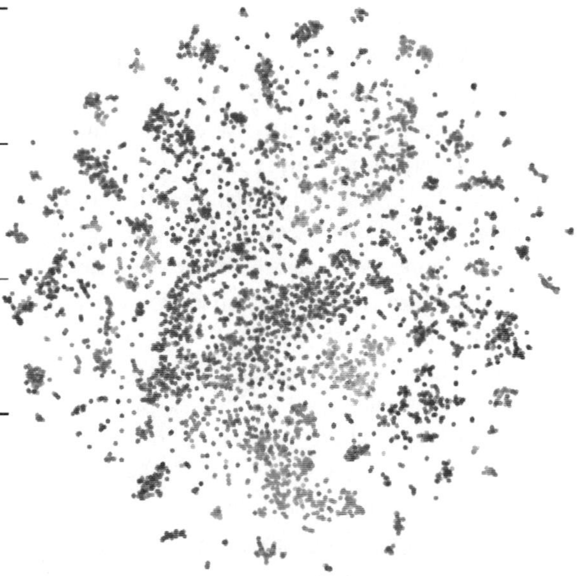

Figure 5: Visualizing entity embeddings, where the colors correspond to their types (**person**, **location**, **organization**, **author**, **actor/musician**, **sports person**, **politician**). Best viewed in color.

4.3 Entity Embeddings and Types

Although the focus of this work is relation extraction, and the models are trained primarily for finding relations, in this section we explore the learned entity embeddings. The low-dimensional entity embeddings have been trained to predict the binary relations that the entity participates in, and thus we expect entities that participate in similar relations to have similar embeddings. To investigate whether the embeddings capture this intuition, we compute similarities of a few randomly selected entities with every other entity using the cosine distance of the *FE* entity embeddings, and show the 10 nearest neighbors in Table 2. The nearest neighbors definitely capture the entity types, for example all the neighbors of "La Stampa" are newspapers in other parts of the world, which is quite impressive considering no explicit type information was available during training. However, the granularity of the types depends on the textual patterns and relations in the schema; for "LG Electronics", the neighbors are mostly generic commercial institutions, perhaps because the observed surface patterns are similar across these types of organizations.

Since the embeddings enable us to compute the similarity between any two entities, we also present a 2D visualization of the entities in the data using the *t-Distributed Stochastic Neighbor Embedding (t-SNE)* (van der Maaten and Hinton, 2008) technique for dimensionality reduction. Further, to investigate whether the embeddings represent correct entity types, we perform an automatic, error-prone alignment of the entity strings to Freebase by finding a prominent entity that has the string as its name, and extract its types. Figure 5 shows the projection for 10 000 randomly selected entities, colored as per their type. We see that the entity embeddings are able to separate most of the coarse level types, as locations are clustered quite separately from the organizations and people, but further, even fine-grained person types occur as distinct collections, for example politicians and sportsmen. There is some cluster overlap as well, especially between the different person types such as authors, actors/musicians, and politicians; it is unclear whether this arises due to incorrect entity linking, inexact two-dimensional projection, entities that belong to multiple types, or from inaccurate embeddings caused by insufficient data.

5 Conclusions and Future Work

Although tensor factorization has been widely used for knowledge-base completion for structured data, it performs poorly on universal schema for relation extraction. Matrix factorization, on the other hand, is appropriate for the task as it is able to compactly represent the correlations between surface pattern and structured KB relations, however learning pairwise factors is not effective for entity pairs with sparse observations or for identifying latent entity types. We illustrate the differences between these matrix and tensor factorization using simple relations, and further, construct an additional relation that none of these approaches are able to model. Motivated by this need for combining their complementary benefits, we explore two hybrid matrix and tensor factorization approaches. Along with being able to model our constructed relations, these approaches also provided improvements on real-world relation extraction. We further provide qualitative exploration of the entity embedding vectors, showing that the embeddings learn fine-grained entity types from relational data.

Our investigations suggest a number of possible avenues for future work. Foremost, we would like to investigate why the hybrid models, which perform significantly better on synthetic data, fail to achieve similar gains on real-world relations. Second, including tensor factorization in the universal schema model enables us to augment the model with external entity information such as observed unary patterns and Freebase types, in order to aid both relation extraction and entity type prediction. Lastly, these hybrid approaches also enable extension of universal schema directly to n-ary relations, allowing a variety of models based on the choice of matrix or tensor representation for each relation.

Acknowledgments

This work was supported in part by Microsoft Research through its PhD Scholarship Programme, an Allen Distinguished Investigator Award, a Marie Curie Career Integration Grant, and in part by the TerraSwarm Research Center, one of six centers supported by the STARnet phase of the Focus Center Research Program (FCRP) a Semiconductor Research Corporation program sponsored by MARCO and DARPA.

References

Antoine Bordes, Nicolas Usunier, Alberto Garcia-Duran, Jason Weston, and Oksana Yakhnenko. 2013. Translating embeddings for modeling multi-relational data. In *Neural Information Processing Systems (NIPS)*.

Guillaume Bouchard, Sameer Singh, and Theo Trouillon. 2015. On approximate reasoning capabilities of low-rank vector spaces. In *AAAI Spring Syposium on Knowledge Representation and Reasoning (KRR): Integrating Symbolic and Neural Approaches*.

Kai-Wei Chang, Wen-tau Yih, Bishan Yang, and Christopher Meek. 2014. Typed tensor decomposition of knowledge bases for relation extraction. In *Empirical Methods in Natural Language Processing (EMNLP)*.

Michael Collins, Sanjoy Dasgupta, and Robert E Schapire. 2001. A generalization of principal components analysis to the exponential family. In *Neural Information Processing Systems (NIPS)*, pages 617–624.

Miao Fan, Deli Zhao, Qiang Zhou, Zhiyuan Liu, Thomas Fang Zheng, and Edward Y. Chang. 2014. Distant supervision for relation extraction with matrix completion. In *Annual Meeting of the Association for Computational Linguistics (ACL)*.

Richard A. Harshman. 1970. Foundations of the PARAFAC procedure: Models and conditions for an "explanatory" multi-modal factor analysis. *UCLA Working Papers in Phonetics*, 16(84).

Vinod Nair and Geoffrey E. Hinton. 2010. Rectified linear units improve restricted boltzmann machines. In *International Conference on Machine Learning (ICML)*.

Maximilian Nickel and Volker Tresp. 2013. Logistic tensor factorization for multi-relational data. In *ICML Workshop - Structured Learning: Inferring Graphs from Structured and Unstructured Inputs (SLG)*.

Maximilian Nickel, Volker Tresp, and Hans-Peter Kriegel. 2012. Factorizing yago: scalable machine learning for linked data. In *Proc. of International Conference on World Wide Web (WWW)*, pages 271–280.

Steffen Rendle, Christoph Freudenthaler, Zeno Gantner, and Lars Schmidt-Thieme. 2009. BPR: Bayesian personalized ranking from implicit feedback. In *Uncertainty in Artificial Intelligence (UAI)*.

Sebastian Riedel, Limin Yao, Andrew McCallum, and Benjamin M Marlin. 2013. Relation extraction with matrix factorization and universal schemas. In *North American Chapter of the Association for Computational Linguistics - Human Language Technologies (NAACL HLT)*, pages 74–84.

Ajit P. Singh and Geoffrey J. Gordon. 2008. Relational learning via collective matrix factorization. In *Knowledge Discovery and Data Mining (KDD)*.

Ledyard R. Tucker. 1966. Some mathematical notes on three-mode factor analysis. *Psychometrika*, 31(3):279–311.

Laurens van der Maaten and Geoffrey E. Hinton. 2008. Visualizing high-dimensional data using t-sne. *Journal of Machine Learning Research*, 9:2579–2605.

Neural word embeddings with multiplicative feature interactions for tensor-based compositions

Joo-Kyung Kim[†], **Marie-Catherine de Marneffe**[‡], **Eric Fosler-Lussier**[†]
[†]Department of Computer Science and Engineering,
[‡]Department of Linguistics,
The Ohio State University, Columbus, OH 43210, USA
kimjook@cse.ohio-state.edu, mcdm@ling.ohio-state.edu,
fosler@cse.ohio-state.edu

Abstract

Categorical compositional distributional models unify compositional formal semantic models and distributional models by composing phrases with tensor-based methods from vector representations. For the tensor-based compositions, Milajevs et al. (2014) showed that word vectors obtained from the continuous bag-of-words (CBOW) model are competitive with those from co-occurrence based models. However, because word vectors from the CBOW model are trained assuming additive interactions between context words, the word composition used for the training mismatches to the tensor-based methods used for evaluating the actual compositions including pointwise multiplication and tensor product of context vectors. In this work, we show whether the word embeddings from extended CBOW models using multiplication or tensor product between context words, reflecting the actual composition methods, can show better performance than those from the baseline CBOW model in actual tasks of compositions with multiplication or tensor-based methods.

1 Introduction

In recent years, there has been a surge of interest in using word vectors for modeling semantics. Mikolov et al. (2013a,b) introduced `word2vec` that includes the continuous bag-of-words (CBOW) model and the skip-gram model.[1] These models have been most widely used for generating word vectors to be used for word related tasks because of their efficient but still effective architectures. The CBOW model takes the mean vector of projections of the context words and use it to predict the target word as the following objective function:[2]

$$\frac{1}{T}\sum_{t=1}^{T}\ln p\left(w_t \middle| \frac{1}{2c}\sum_{-c\leq j\leq c, j\neq 0} p_{t+j}\right), \quad (1)$$

where T is the total number of words in a corpus, w_t is the tth word, p_t is the tth word vector, and c is the half window size.

Milajevs et al. (2014) showed that the word vectors generated from the CBOW model are competitive with those from co-occurrence based models for both simple arithmetic compositions and tensor-based compositions for categorical compositional distributional models (Coecke et al., 2010).[3]

Categorical compositional distributional models represent compositional semantics with algebra of Pregroup by representing each grammatical reduction as a linear map in vector spaces (Coecke et al., 2010; Kartsaklis et al., 2012). For example, *cats like milk* consists of a subject noun, a transitive verb requiring a subject and an object, and an object noun, respectively. In Pregroup grammar, the types of the three words in this example are n, $\left(n^r s n^l\right)$, and n, respectively, where n is a noun, n^r can be combined with a n in the left, n^l can be combined with a n in the right, and s is a declarative statement. Then,

[1]https://code.google.com/p/word2vec

[2]Although sum is used in Mikolov et al. (2013a), the current version of `word2vec` implementation uses mean.

[3]Although Milajevs et al. (2014) described that the skip-gram model was used to generate the word vectors, the CBOW model was actually used in their work.

Proceedings of NAACL-HLT 2015, pages 143–150,
Denver, Colorado, May 31 – June 5, 2015.

they can be reduced to represent the entire phrase with single entity as follows:

$$n\left(n^r s n^l\right) n \rightarrow 1 s n^l n \rightarrow 1 s 1 \rightarrow s \qquad (2)$$

In the reduction, n^r is composed with the left n resulting in an identity element, 1. Then, n^l is composed with the right n resulting in another 1. Because 1 is an identity element, $1s1$ is reduced to s.

Since there is no specification of actual implementation of the composition in categorical compositional distributional models, different composition methods have been introduced; they are reviewed in Section 2. However, there are few studies about the vector representation of single words regarding those compositions.

One issue of using the word vectors from the CBOW model as the constituent vectors for tensor-based composition is that their assumptions of the composition are different. Word embeddings of the CBOW model are trained with an additive context composition, which is the mean of the context projection. However, most tensor-based compositions use point-wise multiplication or tensor product as composition operators. This means that there is a mismatch between the composition method used for the training of the underlying word vectors and the actual composition methods we evaluate.

To alleviate the mismatch, we introduce extensions of the CBOW model with multiplicative interactions between word projections to obtain word embeddings more suitable for the tensor-based compositions. For four datasets, evaluating different types of compositions, we show that those extensions of the CBOW model improve the performance of the actual composition tasks with multiplication or tensor product operations.

2 Tensor-based compositions

Prior to discussing the modification to the CBOW algorithm, we review different composition methods used in the literature (Table 1).

Addition and *Multiplication* are compositions by point-wise addition and multiplication, respectively (Mitchell and Lapata, 2008). They can be done simply without any other information, but they cannot reflect word orders and grammatical structures.

Mitchell and Lapata (2008, 2009) showed that composition by multiplication can be more effective than composition by addition because additive models compose by considering the content altogether whereas multiplicative models focus on the content relevant to the composition by scaling each element of one with the strength of the corresponding element of the other. Using multiplication as the composition method could be unstable in the previous work because multiplication with zero or negative values changes the value abruptly (Mitchell and Lapata, 2009). In our models, however, these instability issues could be alleviated since the training model adapt the constituent word vectors to be proper for the composition by multiplication. Mitchell and Lapata (2010) also showed that the tensor product is effective to represent composition because it allows the interactions between different features in different vectors whereas point-wise multiplication can interact with only the same feature in different vectors. Therefore, we also examine an extension of the CBOW model using tensor product for modeling local context.

There are neural network models using multiplicative interactions in the architectures. Sum-Product Networks use layer-wise multiplicative interactions (Poon and Domingos, 2011; Cheng et al., 2014) and multiplicative recurrent neural networks use multiplication of hidden state outputs from previous time step with the current word projections (Sutskever et al., 2011; Irsoy and Cardie, 2014). These approaches capture multiplicative interactions with hidden layer outputs. Our approach instead utilizes multiplicative interactions in the training of the CBOW model, making the embedded vector spaces more in tune with the compositions of end tasks.

The third to the last composition methods of Table 1 shows tensor-based composition methods for representing phrases consist of subjects, transitive verbs, and objects in categorical compositional distributional models. $\overline{verb} = \sum_i \overrightarrow{Sbj_i} \otimes \overrightarrow{Obj_i}$ represents a verb with the subjects and the objects of the verb across the corpus. The subject and the object of each transitive verb required for calculating $\overline{verb}$ are identified from the dependency tree of PukWaC 1.0 dataset, which consists of web documents in .uk domain crawled with the medium-frequency words from the British National Corpus (BNC) (Burnard,

Method	Phrase	Composition formula	Reference
Addition Multiplication	$w_1 w_2 ... w_n$	$\overrightarrow{w_1} + \overrightarrow{w_2} + ... + \overrightarrow{w_n}$ $\overrightarrow{w_1} \odot \overrightarrow{w_2} \odot ... \odot \overrightarrow{w_n}$	Mitchell and Lapata (2008)
Relational Kronecker	Sbj Verb Obj	$\overline{verb} \odot (\overrightarrow{Sbj} \otimes \overrightarrow{Obj})$ $\widetilde{verb} \odot (\overrightarrow{Sbj} \otimes \overrightarrow{Obj})$	Grefenstette and Sadrzadeh (2011a) Grefenstette and Sadrzadeh (2011b)
Copy sbj. Copy obj.	Sbj Verb Obj	$\overrightarrow{Sbj} \odot (\overline{Verb} \times \overrightarrow{Obj})$ $\overrightarrow{Obj} \odot (\overline{Verb}^{\top} \times \overrightarrow{Sbj})$	Kartsaklis et al. (2012)
Frob. add. Frob. mult. Frob. outer	Sbj Verb Obj	$(\overrightarrow{Sbj} \odot (\overline{Verb} \times \overrightarrow{Obj})) + (\overrightarrow{Obj} \odot (\overline{Verb}^{\top} \times \overrightarrow{Sbj}))$ $(\overrightarrow{Sbj} \odot (\overline{Verb} \times \overrightarrow{Obj})) \odot (\overrightarrow{Obj} \odot (\overline{Verb}^{\top} \times \overrightarrow{Sbj}))$ $(\overrightarrow{Sbj} \odot (\overline{Verb} \times \overrightarrow{Obj})) \otimes (\overrightarrow{Obj} \odot (\overline{Verb}^{\top} \times \overrightarrow{Sbj}))$	Kartsaklis and Sadrzadeh (2014)

Table 1: Tensor-based composition methods (Milajevs et al., 2014).

2007) as the seeds (Baroni et al., 2009; Johansson, 2007).[4] $\widetilde{verb} = \overrightarrow{verb} \otimes \overrightarrow{verb}$ represents a verb as the tensor product of the corresponding verb vector. Those methods consider the relations between transitive verbs and their subjects and objects. Therefore, we can represent their compositions more effectively. Recursive neural tensor networks also use tensor product information in the recursive composition (Socher et al., 2013), but they require training labels and only support binary compositions.

Relational and *Kronecker* represent each phrase by the multiplication of the verb matrix to the tensor product of the subject and the object (Grefenstette and Sadrzadeh, 2011a,b). Although they can represent interactions between subjects and objects as well as the verbs, it is difficult to compose them with other phrases in a uniform way since the result dimensionality is the square of the original vectors. In addition, dealing with large dimensional tensors is not very scalable.

The fifth to the last composition methods use Frobenius operators for the compositions (Kartsaklis et al., 2012), which can resolve the dimensionality issues by maintaining the original dimensionality through matrix-vector multiplication. In *Copy subject*, the verb matrix $\overline{verb}$ is multiplied with the object vector and then composed with the subject vector by point-wise multiplication. *Copy object* is opposite in terms of the positions of the subject and the object. These two methods are different ways of diagonal placement of a plane into a cube (Kartsaklis et al., 2012). The last three methods, *Frobenius addition*, *multiplication*, and *outer product*, represent different combinations of *Copy subject* and *Copy object* (Kartsaklis and Sadrzadeh, 2014).

[4]Available at `http://wacky.sslmit.unibo.it/doku.php?id=corpora`.

3 Extending the CBOW model with multiplicative interactions between word projections

As briefly discussed in the introduction, the CBOW model is an additive model in terms of the composition since the mean of the context word projections is used to predict the target word. As many composition methods in Table 1 use multiplication or tensor product as the composition operators, if these operators are used to compose the contexts in the CBOW model, then the training process can optimize the model to consider their word embeddings to be composed with those multiplicative operations. Therefore, we can train word embeddings that are more suitable for the composition methods that we are evaluating.

In the CBOW model, the point-wise mean of the word projections is used to predict the target word as shown in Equation 1. In addition to the baseline, we experimented with adding different multiplicative terms as shown in Table 2. The added terms are selected to reflect the operations of composition methods in Table 1 and their combinations. In the expressions, p_i is the projection of the ith input context word and c is the size of the context window, which is the number of neighboring words used as the input for each direction.

The second model, *mult*, uses only the multiplication of projections, which best fits to the composition by point-wise multiplication. The third and the

	Type	Expression
1	mean (baseline, Milajevs et al. (2014))	$\sum_{-c\leq i\leq c, i\neq 0} p_i/2c$
2	pointwise multiplication	$\prod_{-c\leq i\leq c, c\neq 0} p_i$
3	mean + pointwise multiplication	mean $+\prod_{-c\leq i\leq c, c\neq 0} p_i$
4	concat{mean, pointwise multiplication}	concat{mean, $\prod_{-c\leq i\leq c, c\neq 0} p_i$}
5	mean + projection of p_{i-1} and p_{i+1}	mean $+W_p$concat$\{p_{i-1}, p_{i+1}\}$
6	projection of tensor product of p_{i-1} and p_{i+1}	$W_{tp}(p_{i-1} \otimes p_{i+1})$
7	mean + projection of tensor product of p_{i-1} and p_{i+1}	mean $+W_{tp}(p_{i-1} \otimes p_{i+1})$

Table 2: Different outputs of the projection layer. p_i is the projection of the ith input context word, c is the size of the context window, and W_p and W_tp are projection matrices.

fourth models evaluate the performance when both the additive and multiplicative interactions are used together since their combination has been shown to be effective (Mitchell and Lapata, 2008). The third model adds the additive terms and multiplicative terms whereas the fourth model concatenates these terms so that they influence the output separately.

In the fifth to the last models, we try to further use the information from p_{i-1} and p_{i+1}, which are the projections of the nearest neighbor words of the ith target word in the training corpus. The fifth model concatenates p_{i-1} and p_{i+1} and project to the original dimension with a projection matrix W_p. This result is added to the baseline model so that information from the nearest words considering the order can be used to estimate the target. W_p is also updated during the training.

In the sixth model, since the tensor-based compositions are used as Table 1 and they can represent multiplicative interactions between different features, we use the tensor product of the projections of (p_{i-1} and p_{i+1}). The tensor product output is also projected to the original dimensionality by multiplying a projection matrix W_{tp}, which is also updated during the training. Although this model can use more powerful interactions of neighbor words, it can only use the information from the nearest neighbor words and it cannot use two word sentences in the training corpus for the training. To deal with these issues, in the last model, we combine the mean with the projection of the tensor product.

4 Experiment results

To evaluate the five different CBOW-based models proposed in Section 3, we use the following datasets: similarity of transitive verbs with multiple senses from Grefenstette and Sadrzadeh (2011a), three-word sentence similarity from Kartsaklis and Sadrzadeh (2014), paraphrase detection from Dolan et al. (2013), and dialog act tagging for the Switchboard corpus (Godfrey et al., 1992) from Stolcke et al. (2000). These are all the datasets evaluated in Milajevs et al. (2014)'s work as well. Each phrase in the first two datasets is fixed as a subject, a transitive verb, and an object whereas the length of each phrase in the last two datasets is arbitrary.

There are several differences between our word vectors and the ones used in Milajevs et al. (2014). First, we use BNC as the training set while Milajevs et al. (2014) use pretrained word vectors from `word2vec` that are trained using GoogleNews dataset. To reduce the size of projection matrices, all the words are lower-cased and words occurring 20 times or less are converted to the words' POS tags. Second, instead of negative sampling, our models use hierarchical softmax as the objective function, where each word is represented as a leaf node of Huffman tree since hierarchical softmax is better for training with infrequent words (Mikolov et al., 2013b). Third, we use gradient clipping for more stable training since gradient can be fluctuating when the projections are multiplied. All the other parameters for the training are the same as those used for Milajevs et al. (2014)'s experiments.

Using the mean as the network combination function can be considered a reimplementation of Milajevs et al. (2014)'s system subject to the changes mentioned above. We trained the CBOW-based models and obtained 300 dimensional word vectors, which are with the same dimensionality used in Mikolov et al. (2013a,b); Milajevs et al. (2014).

Task	Method	(Milajevs et al., 2014)	mean	mult	mean + mult	concat {mean,mult}	mean + nbr_prj	nbr_outer_prj	mean + nbr_outer_prj
Similarity of transitive verbs	Verb only	0.107	0.130	0.014	0.136	0.204	0.187	0.072	**0.250**
	Addition	0.149	0.066	0.012	0.046	-0.030	0.100	0.111	**0.145**
	Multiplication	0.095	0.160	**0.249**	0.058	0.219	0.113	0.050	0.204
	Kronecker	0.117	0.160	0.160	0.121	0.229	0.168	0.047	**0.245**
	Relational	0.362	0.330	0.276	0.319	0.280	0.344	0.316	**0.365**
	Copy sbj.	0.131	0.249	0.064	0.262	0.209	0.262	0.168	**0.290**
	Copy obj.	0.456	0.302	0.361	0.329	**0.382**	0.300	0.371	0.322
	Frob. add.	0.359	0.337	0.293	0.345	0.288	0.349	0.250	**0.355**
	Frob. mult.	0.239	0.270	0.252	0.255	0.189	0.293	0.196	**0.309**
	Frob. outer.	0.375	0.330	0.275	0.339	0.351	0.329	0.293	**0.387**
Sentence similarity	Verb only	0.561	0.528	0.360	0.520	0.531	0.527	0.260	**0.536**
	Addition	0.689	0.728	0.572	0.738	**0.770**	0.722	0.401	0.706
	Multiplication	0.341	0.062	**0.625**	0.178	0.440	0.110	0.269	0.220
	Kronecker	0.561	0.206	**0.623**	0.277	0.501	0.203	0.003	0.457
	Relational	0.618	0.505	**0.665**	0.540	0.527	0.525	0.157	0.574
	Copy sbj.	0.405	0.390	0.453	0.353	0.436	0.396	0.139	**0.454**
	Copy obj.	0.655	0.481	**0.607**	0.487	0.500	0.488	0.190	0.510
	Frob. add.	0.585	0.489	**0.610**	0.407	0.528	0.439	0.210	0.501
	Frob. mult.	0.387	0.211	**0.608**	0.323	0.419	0.335	0.065	0.349
	Frob. outer.	0.622	0.504	**0.664**	0.510	0.544	0.524	0.165	0.569

Table 3: Spearman's ρ on the similarity of transitive verbs with multiple senses (top) and three-word sentence similarity (bottom). The mean column can be considered an implementation of the Milajevs et al. (2014)'s model on the BNC corpus.

4.1 Fixed phrases (three-word)

Table 3 shows the experiment results for the three-word phrases. The first column represents the two evaluation tasks, the second column is the composition methods described in Table 1, and the third column shows the results of neural word embeddings (NWE) from previous work (Milajevs et al., 2014).[5] Bold entries in the table indicate the highest scores among our models.

In the datasets, human annotators rated each phrase pair for semantic similarity (from 1 "no similarity" to 7 "high similarity"). As each unique phrase pair is judged by multiple people, following Milajevs et al. (2014), we took the mean of the ratings to set the rating of each unique pair. Scores in the table entries are Spearman's ρs. A high value of Spearman's ρ in the table means that the similarity of the composed phrases in the vector space is highly correlated with the semantic similarity of the phrases judged by humans. Therefore, if a model shows high scores, it reflects that the model is good at representing the semantics for those short phrases.

[5]The word vectors are available at https://drive.google.com/file/d/0B7XkCwpI5KDYNlNUTTlSS21pQmM/edit.

4.1.1 Similarity of transitive verbs

The top of Table 3 shows the results for the similarity of 199 three-word phrase (subject, transitive verb, and object) pairs introduced in Grefenstette and Sadrzadeh (2011a).[6] In each phrase pair, the transitive verbs are the same but the subjects and the objects are different for each other. We try to identify the senses of a transitive verb with the different contexts. For example, "meet" is a verb with multiple senses. If the given subject is "system" and the object is "specification", "meet" would be semantically closer to "satisfy" than "visit". Then, given "system meets specification" and "system satisfies specification" as a pair, the judge would give a high rating for the similarity of the verbs.

Our results were not consistently better than Milajevs et al. (2014)'s results. However, considering that the model used for the previous work and our baseline (*mean*) are similar CBOW models, the performance difference would mainly due to the different training sets (GoogleNews and BNC). Among our models, adding tensor product result to the mean (*mean+nb_outer_prj*) showed the best performance in most types of compositions. Interestingly, the

[6]Available at http://www.cs.ox.ac.uk/activities/compdistmeaning/GS2011data.txt.

power seems to come from the combination of mean and the tensor product, as both individually perform worse than the combination. For this dataset, as the verbs are the same for both phrases in each pair, the subjects and the objects play important roles for the verb disambiguation. When a transitive verb is an ith word in a sentence denoted as w_i, in many cases, the subject and the object are w_{i-1} and w_{i+1}, respectively. Since tensor product of the $i-1$th word projection and the $i+1$th word projection can represent multiplicative interactions between different features of the two words, considering the tensor product of those projections in the model could be helpful to identify the transitive verbs.

4.1.2 Similarity of three-word phrases

The bottom of Table 3 shows the evaluation results on the similarity of 109 three-word phrase pairs with human judged ratings from (Kartsaklis and Sadrzadeh, 2014).[7] For example, the similarities of two sentences like "programme offer support" and "service provide help" are evaluated.

In this evaluation, considering the interleaved words with tensor product (*mean+nb_outer_prj*) still showed better performance than the baseline (*mean*) for the most composition methods except addition. However, the multiplication only model, *mult*, showed the best performance in most cases except when verb only or addition were used as the composition methods.

4.2 Arbitrary length phrases

The three-word phrases in the previous section are useful for the evaluation of the tensor-based compositions since we do not need to care about the structural variations of the phrases. However, we would be more interested in phrases where the lengths are not fixed. As each phrase can have different length, we cannot use the tensor-based compositions used for the fixed-length phrases. Therefore, we evaluated the composition of each phrase by only using point-wise addition and multiplication.

Table 4 shows the accuracies of classification tasks given arbitrary length phrases as the inputs. The results evaluate whether composition of arbitrary length phrases can be well represented with the word vectors from the proposed models.

4.2.1 Paraphrase detection

The top of Table 4 shows the binary classification accuracies on the Microsoft Research Paraphrase Corpus (Dolan et al., 2013), which consists of arbitrary length phrase pairs. In this dataset, each phrase pair comes with a binary label: 1 if the phrases were judged to be paraphrases, 0 otherwise. The minimum, mean, and maximum lengths of the phrases in the training set are 6, 19.8, and 35, respectively.

With this dataset, we can evaluate if our models work well for representing general phrases. Following the setting of Milajevs et al. (2014)'s work, we trained a linear binary classifier on 2000 phrase pairs and tested on 1726 phrase pairs. The classifier is trained to find the threshold of cosine similarity deciding if two phrases are paraphrases or not.

Comparing to the baseline CBOW model, there were no significant gain in the proposed models for the composition by addition. However, using multiplication of the projections (*mult*) showed significantly better performance when composed by multiplication, and started to show statistical insignificance to additive composition methods when tested by McNemar's test with p-value 0.05.

4.2.2 Dialog act tagging

The bottom of Table 4 shows the classification accuracies of dialog act tagging (Stolcke et al., 2000) on the Switchboard corpus (Godfrey et al., 1992). Switchboard is a collection of about 2400 telephone dialogs among 543 speakers in the United States. Each utterance is assigned one of 42 dialog-act tags, which summarize syntactic, semantic and pragmatic information about the turns (e.g., yes/no question, yes answer, agree).[8] The minimum, mean, and maximum lengths of the phrases in the training set are 0, 34.1, and 549, respectively. Zero length phrases exist because of the preprocessing, and they are ignored.

The task in this section is identifying the dialog act tags from given utterances. Following Milajevs and Purver (2014); Milajevs et al. (2014), we used the first 1115 utterances as the training set and the

[7] Available at `http://www.cs.ox.ac.uk/activities/compdistmeaning/emnlp2013_turk.txt`.

[8] The tags are described in `http://web.stanford.edu/~jurafsky/ws97/manual.august1.html`.

Task	Method	(Milajevs et al., 2014)	mean	mult	mean + mult	concat {mean,mult}	mean + nbr_prj	nbr_outer_prj	mean + nbr_outer_prj
Paraphrase detection	Addition	0.73	0.686	0.665	**0.690**	0.688	0.689	0.684	0.688
	Multiplication	0.42	0.393	**0.652**	0.388	0.587	0.387	0.412	0.371
Dialog act tagging	Addition	0.63	**0.638**	0.636	0.633	0.636	0.636	0.565	0.626
	Multiplication	0.58	0.522	**0.606**	0.593	0.515	0.581	0.573	0.598

Table 4: Accuracies on the paraphrase detection (top) and the dialog act tagging (bottom). The mean column can be considered an implementation of the Milajevs et al. (2014)s model on our training set.

following 19 utterances as the test set. We also concatenated utterances separated by an interruption by the other person (Webb et al., 2005), and we removed disfluency markers and punctuation signs. Once we have the vectors composed by either addition or multiplication for all of the utterances in the training set, the vector dimensionality is reduced to 50 by Singular Value Decomposition (SVD) and a k-nearest-neighbor classifier (k=5) is used to identify the dialog act tags.[9] The baseline (*mean*) model showed the best performance for the composition by addition and the *mult* model was the best for the composition by multiplication, but the differences were insignificant in this case.

The results on both evaluation for arbitrary length phrases support that matching the composition of contexts for the training of constituent word vectors with the actual composition methods shows better or competitive performance.

5 Discussion

We showed the experiment results on seven types of word vectors trained using different composition methods. Overall, we can see that multiplicative interactions in the CBOW models can help representing compositions that are multiplicative in nature.

Using only the multiplication of projections showed significant improvement for all the evaluated datasets when the phrases are composed with multiplications. Because the composition used for the training of word vectors is matching to the actual evaluated compositions, we can think that the word vectors are trained to represent their multiplications properly. One evidence is that the mean of word vectors of the $mult$ model is around 0.12 while the means of the other models are around 0. Since there are fewer negative elements in the word vectors of the $mult$ model, the composition by multiplication produces relatively more positive values. This possibly gives more stable results when used in multiplication-based compositions since fluctuations of the composition by multiplication with negative values is reduced. In the task of transitive verb disambiguation, since the interactions between non-adjacent subjects and objects are important, having their tensor product as a term in the model (*mean+nbr_outer_prj*) was noticeably helpful. In the task of three-word phrase similarity, using the tensor product as a term still showed better performance than using the models of *mean* and *mean+mult* in most cases except when the phrases are composed with addition. Interestingly, however, the model with only multiplication showed the best performance for most of the compositions by multiplication and tensor product.

In summary, for better representation of phrase compositions, we showed that it can be helpful to train the word embedding models by composing the input contexts of the model to be similar to the actual composition methods to be used because the word vectors are adjusted to more properly represent the composition by the composition method used. Specifically, using point-wise multiplication in the training model consistently showed better performance when the actual composition is also multiplication. The *mean+nbr_outer_prj* model, which is with the combination of mean and tensor product also showed better or similar performance for tensor-based composed phrases compared to the *mean* model and the *mean+mult* model.

One issue is that we used the word vectors of targets's neighbors to obtain tensor product terms. Since only the compositions of subjects, verbs, and objects are evaluated, we can expect better performance if only tensor products of subject-object pairs

[9] We used scikit-learn (Pedregosa et al., 2011) to run SVD and k-NN classifiers.

are used as the tensor product terms. As future work, An in-depth analysis of the strengths and weaknesses of each approach would be helpful to gain more insights about the patterns we see in the results.

References

Marco Baroni, Silvia Bernardini, Adriano Ferraresi, and Eros Zanchetta. The WaCky Wide Web: A collection of very large linguistically processed web-crawled corpora. *Language Resources and Evaluation*, 43(3):209–226, 2009.

Lou Burnard, editor. *Reference Guide for the British National Corpus*. Research Technologies Service at Oxford University Computing Services, 2007.

Wei-Chen Cheng, Stanley Kok, Hoai Vu Pham, Hai Leong Chieu, and Kian Ming A. Chai. Language modeling with sum-product networks. In *Proceedings of Interspeech*, 2014.

Bob Coecke, Mehrnoosh Sadrzadeh, and Stephen Clark. Mathematical foundations for a compositional distributional model of meaning. *Linguistic Analysis*, 36:345–384, 2010.

Bill Dolan, Chris Brockett, and Chris Quirk. Microsoft research paraphrase corpus, 2013.

John J Godfrey, Edward C Holliman, and Jane McDaniel. Switchboard: Telephone speech corpus for research and development. In *IEEE International Conference on Acoustics, Speech, and Signal Processing (ICASSP)*, pages 517–520, 1992.

Edward Grefenstette and Mehrnoosh Sadrzadeh. Experimental support for a categorical compositional distributional model of meaning. In *Proceedings of the 2011 Conference on Empirical Methods in Natural Language Processing*, pages 1394–1404, 2011a.

Edward Grefenstette and Mehrnoosh Sadrzadeh. Experimenting with transitive verbs in a discocat. In *Proceedings of the GEMS 2011 Workshop on Geometrical Models of Natural Language Semantics, EMNLP 2011*, pages 62–66, 2011b.

Ozan Irsoy and Claire Cardie. Modeling compositionality with multiplicative recurrent neural networks. *arXiv*, abs/1412.6577, 2014.

Richard Johansson. Dependency Syntax in the CoNLL Shared Task 2008, 2007.

Dimitri Kartsaklis and Mehrnoosh Sadrzadeh. A study of entanglement in a categorical framework of natural language. In *Proceedings of the 11th Workshop on Quantum Physics and Logic (QPL)*, 2014.

Dimitri Kartsaklis, Mehrnoosh Sadrzadeh, and Stephen Pulman. A unified sentence space for categorical distributional-compositional semantics: Theory and experiments. In *Proceedings of 24th International Conference on Computational Linguistics (COLING)*, pages 549–558, 2012.

Tomas Mikolov, Greg Corrado, Kai Chen, and Jeffrey Dean. Efficient Estimation of Word Representations in Vector Space. In *International Conference on Learning Representations (ICLR) workshop*, 2013a.

Tomas Mikolov, Ilya Sutskever, Kai Chen, Greg S Corrado, and Jeffrey Dean. Distributed representations of words and phrases and their compositionality. In *Advances in Neural Information Processing Systems (NIPS)*, pages 3111–3119, 2013b.

Dmitrijs Milajevs and Matthew Purver. Investigating the contribution of distributional semantic information for dialogue act classification. In *Proceedings of the 2nd Workshop on Continuous Vector Space Models and their Compositionality (CVSC)*, pages 40–47, 2014.

Dmitrijs Milajevs, Dimitri Kartsaklis, Mehrnoosh Sadrzadeh, and Matthew Purver. Evaluating neural word representations in tensor-based compositional settings. In *Proceedings of the Conference on Empirical Methods in Natural Language Processing (EMNLP)*, pages 708–719, 2014.

Jeff Mitchell and Mirella Lapata. Vector-based models of semantic composition. In *Proceedings of ACL-08: HLT*, pages 236–244, 2008.

Jeff Mitchell and Mirella Lapata. Language models based on semantic compositon. In *Proceedings of the 2009 Conference on Empirical Methods in Natural Language Processing (EMNLP)*, pages 430–439, 2009.

Jeff Mitchell and Mirella Lapata. Composition in distributional models of semantics. *Cognitive science*, 34:1388–1429, 2010.

F. Pedregosa, G. Varoquaux, A. Gramfort, V. Michel, B. Thirion, O. Grisel, M. Blondel, P. Prettenhofer, R. Weiss, V. Dubourg, J. Vanderplas, A. Passos, D. Cournapeau, M. Brucher, M. Perrot, and E. Duchesnay. Scikit-learn: Machine learning in Python. *Journal of Machine Learning Research*, 12:2825–2830, 2011.

Hoifung Poon and Pedro Domingos. Sum-product networks: A new deep architecture. In *Proceedings of Uncertainty in Artificial Intelligence (UAI)*, 2011.

Richard Socher, Alex Perelygin, Jean Wu, Jason Chuang, Chris Manning, Andrew Ng, and Chris Potts. Recursive deep models for semantic compositionality over a sentiment treebank. In *Proceedings of the 2013 Conference on Empirical Methods in Natural Language Processing (EMNLP)*, pages 1631–1642, 2013.

Andreas Stolcke, Klaus Ries, Noah Coccaro, Elizabeth Shriberg, Rebecca Bates, Daniel Jurafsky, Paul Taylor, Carol Van Ess-Dykema, Rachel Martin, and Marie Meteer. Dialogue act modeling for automatic tagging and recognition of conversational speech. *Computational Linguistics*, 26(3):339–373, 2000.

Ilya Sutskever, James Martens, and Geoffrey E Hinton. Generating text with recurrent neural networks. In *Proceedings of the 28th International Conference on Machine Learning (ICML)*, pages 1017–1024, 2011.

Nick Webb, Mark Hepple, and Yorick Wilks. Dialogue act classification based on intra-utterance features. In *Proceedings of the AAAI Workshop on Spoken Language Understanding*, 2005.

Bilingual Word Representations with Monolingual Quality in Mind

Minh-Thang Luong **Hieu Pham** **Christopher D. Manning**
Computer Science Department, Stanford University, Stanford, CA, 94305
{lmthang, hyhieu, manning}@stanford.edu

Abstract

Recent work in learning bilingual representations tend to tailor towards achieving good performance on bilingual tasks, most often the crosslingual document classification (CLDC) evaluation, but to the detriment of preserving clustering structures of word representations monolingually. In this work, we propose a joint model to learn word representations from scratch that utilizes both the context coocurrence information through the monolingual component and the meaning equivalent signals from the bilingual constraint. Specifically, we extend the recently popular skipgram model to learn high quality bilingual representations efficiently. Our learned embeddings achieve a new state-of-the-art accuracy of 80.3 for the German to English CLDC task and a highly competitive performance of 90.7 for the other classification direction. At the same time, our models outperform best embeddings from past bilingual representation work by a large margin in the monolingual word similarity evaluation.[1]

1 Introduction

Distributed word representations have been key to the recent success of many neural network models in tackling various NLP tasks such as tagging, chunking (Collobert et al., 2011), sentiment analysis (Maas et al., 2011; Socher et al., 2013b), and parsing (Socher et al., 2013a; Chen and Manning, 2014). So far, most of the focus has been spent on monolingual problems despite the existence of a wide variety of multilingual NLP tasks, which include not only machine translation (Brown et al., 1993), but also noun bracketing (Yarowsky and Ngai, 2001), entity clustering (Green et al., 2012), and bilingual NER (Wang et al., 2013). These multilingual applications have motivated recent work in training bilingual representations where similar-meaning words in two languages are embedded close together in the same high-dimensional space. However, most bilingual representation work tend to focus on learning embeddings that are tailored towards achieving good performance on a bilingual task, often the cross-lingual document classification (CLDC) task, but to the detriment of preserving clustering structures of word representations monolingually.

In this work, we demonstrate that such a goal of learning representations of high quality both bilingually and monolingually is achievable through a joint learning approach. Specifically, our joint model utilizes both the context concurrence information present in the monolingual data and the meaning equivalent signals exhibited in the parallel data. The key for our approach to work is in designing a bilingual constraint consistent with monolingual components in our joint objective. To that end, we propose a novel bilingual skipgram model that extends the recently proposed skipgram approach (Mikolov et al., 2013a) to the bilingual context. Our model is efficient to train and achieves state-of-the-art performance in the CLDC task for the direction from German to English. At the same time, we demonstrate that our model well preserves the monolingual clustering structures in each language both quantitatively through the word similarity task and qualitatively through our detailed analysis.

2 Background

2.1 Monolingual Models

Existing approaches to distributed word representation learning divide into two categories: (a) neu-

[1]All our code, data, and embeddings are publicly available at http://stanford.edu/~lmthang/bivec.

Proceedings of NAACL-HLT 2015, pages 151–159,
Denver, Colorado, May 31 – June 5, 2015.

ral probabilistic language models and (b) margin-based ranking models. The former specify either exactly or approximately distributions over all words w in the vocabulary given a context h, and representatives of that approach include (Bengio et al., 2003; Morin, 2005; Mnih and Hinton, 2009; Mikolov et al., 2010; Mikolov et al., 2011). The later eschew the goal of training a language model and try to assign high scores for probable words w given contexts h and low scores for unlikely words $\tilde{w}$ for the same contexts. Work in the later trend includes (Collobert and Weston, 2008; Huang et al., 2012; Luong et al., 2013).

Recently, Mikolov et al. (2013a) introduced the *skipgram* (SG) approach for learning solely word embeddings by reversing the prediction process, that is, to use the current word to infer its surrounding context, as opposed to using preceding contexts to predict subsequent words in traditional language model approaches. SG models greatly simplify the standard neural network-based architecture to only contain a linear projection input layer and an output softmax layer, i.e., there is no non-linear hidden layer. Despite its simplicity, SG models can achieve very good performances on various semantic tasks while having an advantage of fast training time.

We adapt SG models in our bilingual approach. Specifically, we follow Mikolov et al. (2013c) to use the *negative sampling* (NS) technique so as to avoid estimating the computationally expensive normalization terms in the standard softmax. Negative sampling is a simplified version of the noise contrastive estimation method (Gutmann and Hyvärinen, 2012), which attempts to differentiate data from noise by means of logistic regression. Specifically, in the SG-NS model, every word w has two distributed representations: the *input* vector $\boldsymbol{x}_w^{(i)}$ and the *output* one $\boldsymbol{x}_w^{(o)}$. For NS to work, one needs to define a scoring function to judge how likely a word w_n is likely to be a neighbor word of the current word w. We use a simple scoring function (Mikolov et al., 2013c) as follows, $score(w, w_n) = \boldsymbol{x}_w^{(i)\top} \boldsymbol{x}_{w_n}^{(o)}$. In our evaluation, we consider the embedding of a word as the sum of its input and output vectors.

2.2 Bilingual Models

Before delving further into comparing our models with those of others, let us first categorize different approaches to training bilingual word representations to three schemes: bilingual mapping, monolingual adaptation, and bilingual training.

In *Bilingual Mapping*, word representations are first trained on each language independently and a mapping is then learned to transform representations from one language into another. The advantage of this method lies in its speed as no further training of word representations is required given available monolingual representations. Representatives for this approach includes the recent work by Mikolov et al. (2013b) which utilizes a set of meaning-equivalent pairs (translation pairs) obtained from Google Translate to learn the needed linear mapping.

Monolingual Adaptation, on the other hand, assumes access to learned representations of a source language. The idea is to bootstrap learning of target representations from well trained embeddings of a source language, usually a resource-rich one like English, with a bilingual constraint to make sure embeddings of semantically similar words across languages are close together. In this scheme, the recent work by Zou et al. (2013) considers the unsupervised alignment information derived over a parallel corpus to enforce such a bilingual constraint.

Bilingual Training, unlike the previous schemes which fix pretrained representations on either one or both sides, attempts to jointly learn representations from scratch. To us, this is an interesting problem to attest if we can simultaneously learn good vectors for both languages. Despite there has been an active body of work in this scheme such as (Klementiev et al., 2012; Hermann and Blunsom, 2014; Kočiský et al., 2014; Chandar A P et al., 2014; Gouws et al., 2014), none of these work has carefully examined the quality of their learned bilingual embeddings using monolingual metrics. In fact, we show later in our experiments that while the existing bilingual representations are great for their cross-lingual tasks, they perform poorly monolingually.

3 Our Approach

We hypothesize that by allowing the joint model to utilize both the cooccurrence context information within a language and the meaning-equivalent signals across languages, we can obtain better word vectors both monolingually and bilingually. As such, we examine the following general joint objective similar to (Klementiev et al., 2012; Gouws et al., 2014):

$$\alpha(Mono_1 + Mono_2) + \beta Bi \quad (1)$$

In this formulation, each monolingual model, $Mono_1$ and $Mono_2$, aims to capture the clustering structure of each language, whereas the bilingual component, Bi, is used to tie the two monolingual spaces together. The α and β hyperparameters balance out the influence of the mono components over the bilingual one. When $\alpha = 0$, we arrive at the model proposed in (Hermann and Blunsom, 2014), whereas $\alpha = 1$ results in (Klementiev et al., 2012; Gouws et al., 2014) as well as our approach. Their models and ours, however, differ in terms of the choices of monolingual and bilingual components detailed next.

3.1 Model Choices

In terms of the monolingual component, any model listed in Section 2.1 can be a good candidate. Specifically, Klementiev et al. (2012) uses a neural probabilistic language model architecture, whereas Gouws et al. (2014) adapts the skipgram model trained with negative sampling.

When it turns to capturing bilingual constraints, these work generally use a different type of objectives for their bilingual models compared to the monolingual ones. For example, Klementiev et al. (2012) transforms the bilingual constraints into a multitask learning objective, whereas Gouws et al. (2014) minimizes the L_2-loss between the bag-of-word vectors of parallel sentences.[2]

In contrast to the existing approaches, we use the same type of models for both of our monolingual and bilingual constraints. Specifically, we adapt the skipgram model with negative sampling (SG-NS) to the bilingual context. Such a consistent choice of architectures results in a natural and effective way of building bilingual models from existing monolingual models (see §2.1).

In our case, we extend the *word2vec* software[3], an efficient implementation of the SG-NS, to build our fast code for bilingual representation learning. More importantly, we emperically show that our method is effective in learning representations both monolingually and bilingually as compared to existing approaches which use different architectures for monolingual and bilingual constraints.

[2]Hermann and Blunsom (2014) also uses a similar L_2-loss. Chandar A P et al. (2014) optimizes for the autoencoder reconstruction loss between sentence pairs, while Kočiský et al. (2014) defines an energy function for the translation probabilities between words across languages.

[3]`https://code.google.com/p/word2vec/`

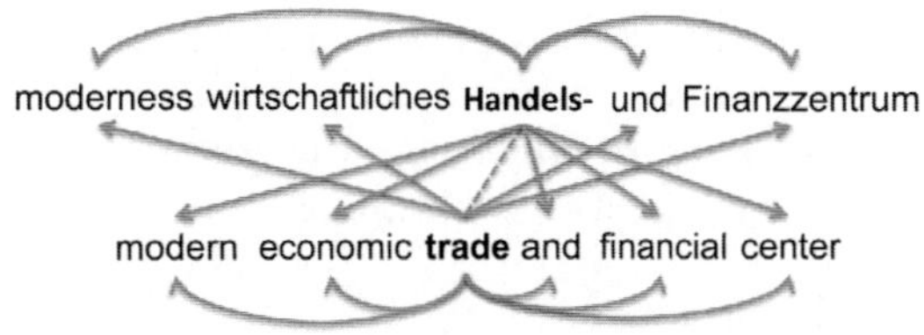

Figure 1: **Bilingual Skipgram Model** – besides predicting within languages, the model also predicts cross-lingually based on the alignment information. Glosses for German text are: *modern economy trading [finance center].*

3.2 Bilingual Skipgram Model (*BiSkip*)

The motivation behind our proposed *bilingual skipgram* (BiSkip) model is to be able to predict words crosslingually rather than just monolingually as in the standard skipgram model. Imagine if we know that the word *trade* is aligned to and has the same meaning as the German word *Handels-* as in Figure 1, we can simply substitute *trade* and use *Handels-* to predict the surrounding words such as *financial* and *economic*.

Concretely, given an alignment link between a word w_1 in a language l_1 and a word w_2 in another language l_2, the BiSkip model uses the word w_1 to predict neighbors of the word w_2 and vice versa. That has the effect of training a single skipgram model with a joint vocabulary on parallel corpora in which we enrich the training examples with pairs of words coming from both sides instead of just from one language. Alternatively, one can also think of this BiSkip model as training four skipgram models jointly which predict words between the following pairs of languages: $l_1 \rightarrow l_1$, $l_2 \rightarrow l_2$, $l_1 \rightarrow l_2$, and $l_2 \rightarrow l_1$.

In our work, we experiment with two variants of our models: (a) *BiSkip-UnsupAlign* where we utilize unsupervised alignment information learned by the Berkeley aligner (Liang et al., 2006) and (b) *BiSkip-MonoAlign* where we simply assume monotonic alignments between words across languages. For the former, if a word is unaligned but at least one of its immediate neighbors is aligned, we will use either the only neighbor alignment or an average of the two neighbor alignments. For the latter, each source word at position i is aligned to the target word at position $[i * T/S]$ where S

and T are the source and target sentence lengths. These two variants are meant to attest how important unsupervised alignment information is in learning bilingual embeddings.

4 Experiments

4.1 Data

We train our joint models on the parallel Europarl v7 corpus between German (de) and English (en) (Koehn, 2005), which consists of 1.9M parallel sentences (49.7M English tokens and 52.0M German tokens). After lowercasing and tokenizing we map each digit into 0, i.e. 2013 becomes 0000. Other rare words occurring less than 5 times are mapped to <unk>. The resulting vocabularies are of size 40K for English and 95K for German.

4.2 Training

We use the following settings as described in (Mikolov et al., 2013c): stochastic gradient descent with a default learning rate of 0.025, negative sampling with 30 samples, skipgram with context window of size 5, and a subsampling rate[4] of value $1e\text{-}4$. All models are trained for 10 epochs and the learning rate is decayed to 0 once training is done. We set the hyperparameters in Eq. (1) to 1 for α and 4 for β in our experiments.

4.3 Evaluation Tasks

We evaluate our models on two aspects: (a) monolingually with a word similarity task and (b) bilingually through a cross-lingual document classification setup.

4.3.1 Word Similarity

This task measures the semantic quality of the learned word vectors monolingually over various word similarity datasets which have been used in papers on word embedding learning lately. For each dataset, we report a Spearman's rank correlation coefficient between similarity scores given by the learned word vectors and those rated by humans. For English, we utilize the following publicly available datasets: WordSim353 (353 pairs), *MC* (30 pairs), *RG* (65 pairs), SCWS (1762 pairs), and RW (2034 pairs). See (Luong et al., 2013) for more information about these datasets.

To evaluate the semantic quality of German embeddings, we devise our own version of the WordSim353 *German counterpart*. Our procedure is as follows: we first used Google Translate to get German translations for the 437 distinct tokens in the English WordSim353. We then asked two German speakers to help us verify these translations, out of which, we fixed 23 translation pairs.

4.3.2 Cross-lingual Document Classification

To judge the bilingual aspect of our models, we follow (Klementiev et al., 2012) in using a cross-lingual document classification task: train with 1000 and test on 5000 RCV-labeled documents.[5] In this setup, a multi-class classifier is trained using the averaged perceptron algorithm. The feature vector for each document is the averaged vector of words in the document weighted by their idf values. A classification model trained on one language is then applied directly to classify new documents in another language without retraining. This is an example of transfer learning of models from a resource-rich language into a resource-poor one. The premise for such a setup to work is because word vectors in these languages are embedded in the same space, so document feature vectors are constructed consistently across these two languages and trained weights can be reused.

5 Results

In this section, we present results of our joint models trained on the Europarl corpus. Our first focus is on the CLDC evaluation where we compare performances achieved by our BiSkip models over the best CLDC results from past work. Specifically, we utilize the best set of embeddings from each of the following bilingual work: (a) *multitask* learning model (Klementiev et al., 2012), (b) bilingual without alignment model (Gouws et al., 2014), (c) *distributed word alignment* model (Kočiský et al., 2014), (d) *autoencoder* model (Chandar A P et al., 2014), and (e) *compositional* model (Hermann and Blunsom, 2014).

The above models are compared against our two *BiSkip* models, one utilizing the unsupervised alignments (*UnsupAlign*) and one assuming monotonic alignments (*MonoAlign*); we trained both 40- and 128-dimensional vectors to be comparable with existing embeddings. Simultane-

[4] Smaller values mean frequent words are discarded more often, see (Mikolov et al., 2013c) and the word2vec code for more details.

[5] Our experiments are based on the same code and data split provided by the authors.

Models	Dim	Data	Word Similarity						CLDC	
			de	en					en→de	de→en
			WS353	WS353	MC	RG	SCWS	RW		
Existing best models										
I-Matrix	40	Europarl+RCV	23.8	13.2	18.6	16.4	19.0	07.3	77.6	71.1
BilBOWA	40	Europarl+RCV	_	_	_	_	_	_	86.5	75.0
DWA	40	Europarl	_	_	_	_	_	_	83.1	75.4
BAE-cr	40	Europarl+RCV	34.6	39.8	32.1	24.8	29.3	20.5	**91.8**	74.2
CVM-Add	128	Europarl	28.3	19.8	21.5	24.0	28.9	13.6	86.4	74.7
Our BiSkip models										
MonoAlign	40	Europarl	43.8	41.0	33.9	32.2	39.5	24.4	86.4	75.6
	128	Europarl	45.9	46.0	30.4	27.1	**43.4**	**25.3**	89.5	78.4
UnsupAlign	40	Europarl	43.0	40.2	31.7	32.1	37.6	23.1	87.6	77.8
	128	Europarl	45.5	45.8	36.6	32.3	42.3	*24.6*	88.9	77.4
	256	Europarl	*46.7*	*47.3*	*37.9*	**35.1**	43.2	24.5	88.4	**80.3**
	512	Europarl	**47.4**	**49.3**	**45.7**	**35.1**	**43.4**	24.0	*90.7*	*80.0*

Table 1: **German (de) - English (en) bilingual embeddings** – results of various models in terms of both the *monolingual* (word similarity) and *bilingual* (cross-lingual document classification) tasks. Spearman's rank correlation coefficients are reported for word similarity tasks, whereas accuracies on 1000 RCV-labeled documents are used for CLDC. We compare our *BiSkip* embeddings to the best ones from past work: multitask *I-Matrix* (Klementiev et al., 2012), bilingual without alignment *BilBOWA* (Gouws et al., 2014), distributed word alignment *DWA* (Kočiský et al., 2014), autoencoder *BAE-cr* (Chandar A P et al., 2014), and compositional *CVM-Add* (Hermann and Blunsom, 2014). Numbers in boldface highlight the best scores per metric. We italicize the second best results and mark _ for models where we do not have access to the trained embeddings.

ously, we test if these learned bilingual embeddings still preserve the clustering properties monolingually in terms of their performance on the word similarity datasets.

At 40 dimensions, both our BiSkip embeddings outperform those produced by the model in (Klementiev et al., 2012) over all aspects. Our MonoAlign model also surpasses the CLDC performances of the BilBOWA model (Gouws et al., 2014). These two models we are comparing to are most similar to ours in terms of the joint objective, i.e. with two monolingual language models and a bilingual component.

The fact that the embeddings in (Klementiev et al., 2012) perform poorly on the monolingual aspects, i.e. the word similarity tasks, supports one of our early observations that it is important to design a bilingual component that is consistent with the monolingual models (§3.1). Otherwise, the model will make a tradeoff between obtaining good performance for bilingual tasks over monolingual tasks as seems to be the case for the embeddings produced by the multitask learning model.

Our 40-dimensional embeddings also rival those trained by much more complex models than ours such as the autoencoder model BAE-cr (Chandar A P et al., 2014). It is worthwhile to mention that beside the Europarl corpus, the autoencoder model was also trained with the RCV documents on which the CLDC classifiers were built, which is an advantage over our model. Despite this, our MonoAlign representations outperform the embeddings in (Chandar A P et al., 2014) over all word similarity datasets and $\text{CLDC}_{de \rightarrow en}$.

Larger dimensions – When learning higher dimensional embeddings, which is an advantage of our joint models as it is very fast to train compared to other methods, the results across all metrics well correlate with the embedding sizes as we increase from 40, 128, 256, to 512. Our 256- and 512-dimensional embeddings trained with unsupervised alignments produce strong results, significantly better than all other models in terms of the word similarity datasets and achieve *state-of-the-art performance* in terms of the $\text{CLDC}_{de \rightarrow en}$ with an accuracy of 80.3. For $\text{CLDC}_{en \rightarrow de}$, our model reaches a very high score of 90.7, close to the best published result of 91.8 produced by the autoencoder model.[6]

[6]The 256- and 512-dimensional MonoAlign models do

	january		microsoft		distinctive		
	en	*de*	*en*	*de*	*en*	*de*	*gloss*
BiSkip	january	januar	microsoft	microsoft	distinctive	unverwechselbare	distinctive
	july	februar	ibm	ibm	character	darbietet	presents
	december	juli	linux	walt	features	eigenheit	peculiarity
	october	dezember	ipad	mci	individualist	unschtzbarer	invaluable
	march	november	blockbuster	linux	patrimony	charakteristische	characteristic
	february	jahres	doubleclick	kurier	diplomacies	identittsstiftende	identity
	april	oktober	yahoo	setanta	splendour	christlich-jdischen	christian-jewish
	november	april	rupert	yahoo	vocations	identittsfindung	identity-making
	september	august	alcatel	warner	multi-faith	zivilisationsprojekt	civilization project
	august	juni	siemens	rhne-poulenc	characteristics	ost-west-konflikt	east-west conflict
Autoencoder	january	januar	microsoft	microsoft	distinctive	rang	rank
	march	mrz	cds	cds	asset	wiederentdeckung	rediscovery
	october	oktober	insider	warner	characteristic	echtes	real
	july	juli	ibm	tageszeitungen	distinct	bestimmend	determining
	december	dezember	acquisitions	ibm	predominant	typischen	typical
	1999	jahres	shareholding	telekommun*	characterise	bereichert	enriched
	june	juni	warner	handelskammer	derive	sichtbaren	visible
	month	1999	online	exchange	par	band	band
	year	jahr	shareholder	veranstalter	unique	ausgeprgte	pronounced
	september	jahresende	otc	geschftsfhrer	embraces	vorherrschende	predominant

Table 2: **Nearest neighbor words** – shown are the top 10 nearest English (en) and German (de) words for each of the following words in the list {*january, microsoft, distinctive*} as measured by the Euclidean distances given a set of embeddings. We compare our learned vectors (BiSkip-UnsupAlign, $d = 128$) with those produced by the autoencoder model (Chandar A P et al., 2014). For the word *distinctive*, we provide Google Translate glosses for German words. The word *telekommunikationsunternehmen* is truncated into telekommun*.

Alignment effects – It is interesting to observe that the 40- and 80-dimensional *MonoAlign* models with a simple monotonic alignment assumption can rival the *UnsupAlign* models, which uses unsupervised alignments, in many metrics. Overall, all our models are superior to the DWA approach (Kočiský et al., 2014) which learns distributed alignments and embeddings simultaneously.

Word similarity results – It is worthwhile to point out that this work does not aim to be best in terms of the word similarity metrics. Past work such as (Pennington et al., 2014; Faruqui and Dyer, 2014) among many others, have demonstrated that higher word similarity scores can be achieved by simply increasing the vocabulary coverage, training corpus size, and the embedding dimension. Rather, we show that our model can learn bilingual embeddings that are naturally better than those of existing approaches monolingually.

6 Analysis

Beside the previous quantitative evaluation, we examine our learned embeddings qualitatively in this section through the following methods: (a) nearest neighbor words and (b) embedding visualization.

not yield consistent improvements across metrics, so we exclude them for clarity.

6.1 Nearest Neighbor Words

For the former method, we follow (Chandar A P et al., 2014) to find, for each English word, a list of top 10 English and German words closest to it based on Euclidean distance in a learned bilingual space. Our list of words include {*january, microsoft, distinctive*}, in which the first two choices are made by the previous work. We compare our learned embeddings using the BiSkip-UnsupAlign model ($d = 128$) with those produced by the autoencoder model in (Chandar A P et al., 2014).

Examples in Table 2 demonstrate that our learned representations are superior in two aspects. Bilingually, our embeddings succeed in selecting the 1-best translations for all words in the list, whereas the other model fails to do so for the word *distinctive*. Monolingually, our embeddings possess a clearly better clustering structure. For example, all months are clustered together, around the word *january*, whereas that is not the case for the other embeddings with the occurrences of {*1999, month, year*} in the top 10 list. Our embeddings also find very relevant neighbor words for the word *microsoft* such as {*ibm, yahoo, etc.*}.

We also examine the BiSkip-MonoAlign model

Figure 2: Bilingual Embeddings of German and English words about banking and financial

in this aspect. Overall, the BiSkip-MonoAlign model exhibits very similar monolingual properties as in the BiSkip-UnsupAlign one, i.e., it clusters all months together and even places {*google, patents, merger, software, copyright*} as closest words to *microsoft*. On the other hand, the BiSkip-MonoAlign fails to find correct translations for the word *distinctive*, emphasizing the fact that knowledge about word alignment does offer the BiSkip-UnsupAlign model an advantage.

6.2 Embedding Visualization

In this section, we visualize embeddings of the German and English words in banking and financial context. The two-dimensional visualizations of word vectors are produced using the t-SNE algorithm (van der Maaten and Hinton, 2008). Figure 2 shows that English-German words with similar meanings are close to each other, e.g., "*managers*" and "*managern*". Monolingually, German compound words, such as "*welthandelsorganisation*" and "*investitionsbank*", also appears next to each other. These observations further demonstrate the ability of our models to learn representations well both bilingually and monolingually.

7 Related Work

We have previously discussed in Section 2 models directly related to our work. In this section, we survey other approaches in learning monolingual and bilingual representations.

Current work in dimensionality reduction of word representations can be broadly grouped into three categories (Turian et al., 2010): (a) distributional representations learned from a co-occurrence matrix of words and contexts (documents, neighbor words, etc.) using techniques such as LSA (Dumais et al., 1988) or LDA (Blei et al., 2003), (b) clustering-based representations, e.g., Brown et al. (1992)'s hierarchical clustering algorithm which represents each word as a binary path through the cluster hierarchy, and (c) distributed representations, where each word is explicitly modeled by a dense real-valued vector and directly induced by predicting words from contexts or vice versa as detailed in Section 2.1.

Moving beyond monolingual representations, work in constructing bilingual vector-space models divides into two main streams: (a) those that make use of comparable corpora and (b) those that only require unaligned or monolingual text. The former includes various extensions to standard techniques such as bilingual latent semantic models (LSA) (Tam and Schultz, 2007; Ruiz and Federico, 2011) or bilingual/multilingual topic models (LDA) (Zhao and Xing, 2007; Ni et al., 2009; Mimno et al., 2009; Vulic et al., 2011). In this work, the general assumption is that aligned documents share identical topic distributions. The latter stream, which eschews the use of comparable data, generally requires a small initial lexicon which is extracted either manually or automatically (e.g., cognates, string edit distances, etc.). Representatives of this strand include work that extends CCA (Haghighi et al., 2008; Boyd-Graber and Blei, 2009), mapping representations of words in different languages into the same space, as well as work that follows a bootstrapping style to iteratively enlarge the initial lexicon (Peirsman and Padó, 2010; Vulić and Moens, 2013).

8 Conclusion

This work proposes a novel approach that jointly learns bilingual representations from scratch by utilizing both the context concurrence information in the monolingual data and the meaning-equivalent signals in the parallel data. We advocate a new standard in training bilingual embeddings, that is, to be good in not only gluing representations bilingually but also preserving the clustering structures of words in each language.

We provide a key insight to train embeddings that meet the above two criteria, that is, to design a bilingual constraint that is consistent with the monolingual models in our joint objective. Our learned representations are superior to the best embeddings from past bilingual work in two tasks: (a) the crosslingual document classification one in which we achieve a new state-of-the-art performance for the direction from German to English, and (b) the word similarity evaluation where we outperform other embeddings by a large margin over all datasets. We also evaluate the learned vectors qualitatively by examining nearest neighbors of words and visualizing the representations.

Lastly, it would be interesting to extend our method to multiple languages as in (Hermann and Blunsom, 2014) and to be able to train on a large amount of monolingual data similar to (Gouws et al., 2014).

Acknowledgment

We gratefully acknowledge support from a gift from Bloomberg L.P. and from the Defense Advanced Research Projects Agency (DARPA) Broad Operational Language Translation (BOLT) program under contract HR0011-12-C-0015 through IBM. Any opinions, findings, and conclusions or recommendations expressed in this material are those of the author(s) and do not necessarily reflect the view of DARPA, or the US government. We also thank members of the Stanford NLP Group as well as the annonymous reviewers for their valuable comments and feedbacks.

References

Y. Bengio, R. Ducharme, P. Vincent, and C. Janvin. 2003. A neural probabilistic language model. *JMLR*, 3:1137–1155.

David M. Blei, Andrew Y. Ng, and Michael I. Jordan. 2003. Latent dirichlet allocation. *JMLR*, 3:993–1022.

Jordan Boyd-Graber and David M. Blei. 2009. Multilingual topic models for unaligned text. In *UAI*.

Peter F. Brown, Peter V. deSouza, Robert L. Mercer, Vincent J. Della Pietra, and Jenifer C. Lai. 1992. Class-based n-gram models of natural language. *CL*, 18(4):467–479.

Peter F. Brown, Vincent J. Della Pietra, Stephen A. Della Pietra, and Robert L. Mercer. 1993. The mathematics of statistical machine translation: Parameter estimation. *CL*, 19(2):263–311, June.

Sarath Chandar A P, Stanislas Lauly, Hugo Larochelle, Mitesh Khapra, Balaraman Ravindran, Vikas C Raykar, and Amrita Saha. 2014. An autoencoder approach to learning bilingual word representations. In *NIPS*.

Danqi Chen and Christopher D Manning. 2014. A fast and accurate dependency parser using neural networks. In *EMNLP*.

R. Collobert and J. Weston. 2008. A unified architecture for natural language processing: deep neural networks with multitask learning. In *ICML*.

R. Collobert, J. Weston, L. Bottou, M. Karlen, K. Kavukcuoglu, and P. Kuksa. 2011. Natural language processing (almost) from scratch. *JMLR*, 12:2493–2537.

S. T. Dumais, G. W. Furnas, T. K. Landauer, S. Deerwester, and R. Harshman. 1988. Using latent semantic analysis to improve access to textual information. In *CHI*.

Manaal Faruqui and Chris Dyer. 2014. Improving vector space word representations using multilingual correlation. In *EACL*.

Stephan Gouws, Yoshua Bengio, and Greg Corrado. 2014. Bilbowa: Fast bilingual distributed representations without word alignments. In *NIPS Deep Learning Workshop*.

Spence Green, Nicholas Andrews, Matthew R. Gormley, Mark Dredze, and Christopher D. Manning. 2012. Entity clustering across languages. In *NAACL*.

Michael Gutmann and Aapo Hyvärinen. 2012. Noise-contrastive estimation of unnormalized statistical models, with applications to natural image statistics. *JMLR*, 13:307–361.

Aria Haghighi, Percy Liang, Taylor Berg-Kirkpatrick, and Dan Klein. 2008. Learning bilingual lexicons from monolingual corpora. In *ACL*.

Karl Moritz Hermann and Phil Blunsom. 2014. Multilingual Models for Compositional Distributional Semantics. In *ACL*.

E. H. Huang, R. Socher, C. D. Manning, and A. Y. Ng. 2012. Improving word representations via global context and multiple word prototypes. In *ACL*.

Alexandre Klementiev, Ivan Titov, and Binod Bhattarai. 2012. Inducing crosslingual distributed representations of words. In *COLING*.

Philipp Koehn. 2005. Europarl: A Parallel Corpus for Statistical Machine Translation. In *MT Summit*.

Tomáš Kočiský, Karl Moritz Hermann, and Phil Blunsom. 2014. Learning Bilingual Word Representations by Marginalizing Alignments. In *ACL*.

P. Liang, B. Taskar, and D. Klein. 2006. Alignment by agreement. In *NAACL*.

Minh-Thang Luong, Richard Socher, and Christopher D. Manning. 2013. Better word representations with recursive neural networks for morphology. In *CoNLL*.

Andrew L. Maas, Raymond E. Daly, Peter T. Pham, Dan Huang, Andrew Y. Ng, and Christopher Potts. 2011. Learning word vectors for sentiment analysis. In *NAACL-HLT*.

Tomas Mikolov, Martin Karafiát, Lukas Burget, Jan Cernocký, and Sanjeev Khudanpur. 2010. Recurrent neural network based language model. In *Interspeech*.

Tomas Mikolov, Stefan Kombrink, Lukas Burget, Jan Cernocký, and Sanjeev Khudanpur. 2011. Extensions of recurrent neural network language model. In *ICASSP*.

Tomas Mikolov, Kai Chen, Greg Corrado, and Jeffrey Dean. 2013a. Efficient estimation of word representations in vector space. In *ICLR*.

Tomas Mikolov, Quoc V. Le, and Ilya Sutskever. 2013b. Exploiting similarities among languages for machine translation. *CoRR*, abs/1309.4168.

Tomas Mikolov, Ilya Sutskever, Kai Chen, Greg Corrado, and Jeffrey Dean. 2013c. Distributed representations of words and phrases and their compositionality. In *NIPS*.

David Mimno, Hanna M. Wallach, Jason Naradowsky, David A. Smith, and Andrew McCallum. 2009. Polylingual topic models. In *EMNLP*.

Andriy Mnih and Geoffrey Hinton. 2009. A scalable hierarchical distributed language model. In *NIPS*.

Frederic Morin. 2005. Hierarchical probabilistic neural network language model. In *AISTATS*.

Xiaochuan Ni, Jian-Tao Sun, Jian Hu, and Zheng Chen. 2009. Mining multilingual topics from wikipedia. In *WWW*.

Yves Peirsman and Sebastian Padó. 2010. Cross-lingual induction of selectional preferences with bilingual vector spaces. In *NAACL-HLT*.

Jeffrey Pennington, Richard Socher, and Christopher Manning. 2014. Glove: Global vectors for word representation. In *EMNLP*.

Nick Ruiz and Marcello Federico. 2011. Topic adaptation for lecture translation through bilingual latent semantic models. In *WMT*.

Richard Socher, John Bauer, Christopher D. Manning, and Andrew Y. Ng. 2013a. Parsing With Compositional Vector Grammars. In *ACL*.

Richard Socher, Alex Perelygin, Jean Wu, Jason Chuang, Christopher D. Manning, Andrew Y. Ng, and Christopher Potts. 2013b. Recursive deep models for semantic compositionality over a sentiment treebank. In *EMNLP*.

Yik-Cheung Tam and Tanja Schultz. 2007. Bilingual LSA-based translation lexicon adaptation for spoken language translation. In *Interspeech*.

J. Turian, L. Ratinov, and Y. Bengio. 2010. Word representations: a simple and general method for semi-supervised learning. In *ACL*.

Ivan Vulić and Marie-Francine Moens. 2013. A study on bootstrapping bilingual vector spaces from non-parallel data (and nothing else). In *EMNLP*.

Ivan Vulic, Wim De Smet, Marie-Francine Moens, and KU Leuven. 2011. Identifying word translations from comparable corpora using latent topic models. In *ACL-HLT*.

Mengqiu Wang, Wanxiang Che, and Christopher D. Manning. 2013. Joint word alignment and bilingual named entity recognition using dual decomposition. In *ACL*.

David Yarowsky and Grace Ngai. 2001. Inducing multilingual pos taggers and np bracketers via robust projection across aligned corpora. In *NAACL*.

Bing Zhao and Eric P. Xing. 2007. HM-BiTAM: Bilingual Topic Exploration, Word Alignment, and Translation. In *NIPS*.

Will Y. Zou, Richard Socher, Daniel Cer, and Christopher D. Manning. 2013. Bilingual word embeddings for phrase-based machine translation. In *EMNLP*.

Distributed Word Representations Improve NER for e-Commerce

Mahesh Joshi
mahesh.joshi@ebay.com

Ethan Hart
ejhart@ebay.com

Mirko Vogel
miavogel@ebay.com

Jean-David Ruvini
Jean-David.Ruvini@ebay.com

eBay Inc.
2065 Hamilton Ave
San Jose, CA, 95125, USA

Abstract

This paper presents a case study of using distributed word representations, `word2vec` in particular, for improving performance of Named Entity Recognition for the e-Commerce domain. We also demonstrate that distributed word representations trained on a smaller amount of in-domain data are more effective than word vectors trained on very large amount of out-of-domain data, and that their combination gives the best results.

1 Introduction

On-line commerce has gained a lot of popularity over the past decade. Large on-line C2C marketplaces like eBay, Alibaba, and Amazon feature a very large and long-tail inventory with millions of *items* (product offers) entered into the marketplace every day by a large variety of sellers.

To manage items effectively and provide the best user experience, it is critical for these marketplaces to structure their inventory into descriptive name-value pairs (called *properties*) and ensure that items of the same kind (digital cameras, for instance) are described using a unique set of properties (brand name, model number, zoom, resolution, etc.). This is important for recommendations in merchandising, providing faceted navigation, and assisting business intelligence applications.

While some sellers (generally large, professional retailers) provide rich, structured descriptions of their products (using schemas or global trade item numbers), the vast majority of sellers only provide unstructured natural language descriptions. In the latter case, one solution to the problem of structuring e-commerce inventory is to use techniques such as Named-Entity Recognition (NER) to extract properties from the textual description of the items. The scale at which on-line marketplaces operate makes it impractical to solve this problem manually. [1]

This paper focuses on NER, generally defined as the task of classifying elements of text into predefined categories (often referred to as *entity types* or *entities*). Entities usually include names of persons, organizations, locations, times, and quantities (`CoNLL-2003` dataset), as well as nationalities or religious groups, products (vehicles, weapons, foods, etc.), and titles of books or songs (`Ontonotes 5.0` dataset).

In the e-commerce domain, these entities are item properties such as `brand name`, `color`, `material`, `clothing size`, `golf club type`, `makeup shade code`, `sun protection factor`, etc. Another important specificity of the e-commerce domain with respect to NER is that the sentences are usually much shorter than in other applications and don't exhibit the grammatical structure of natural language.

This paper investigates whether distributed word vectors benefit NER in the e-commerce domain. Distributed word representations based on neural networks from unlabeled text data have proven useful for many natural language tasks, including NER. In fact, Passos et al. (2014) reported results compa-

[1] For instance, in late 2014, eBay.com reported 800 million available items at any given time and more than 25 million sellers. Alibaba.com reported 8.5 million sellers. Amazon.com has not disclosed similar information.

Proceedings of NAACL-HLT 2015, pages 160–167,
Denver, Colorado, May 31 – June 5, 2015.

rable to state-of-the-art for the CoNLL 2003 NER task using such representations. In this paper, we evaluate distributed word vectors with a focus on using in–domain data for their training.

In the remainder of this paper, we first explain the specificity of NER in the e-commerce domain and describe the approach we use for performing the task. In Section 3, we describe our datasets. In Section 4, we describe the setting of the experiments we have conducted and discuss the results in Section 5. Finally, we review related works in Section 6.

2 NER for e-Commerce

The e-commerce domain raises specific challenges for NER. This section describes in detail the task, and the methodology we have chosen to tackle it.

2.1 Description of the task

We consider the task of named entity recognition (NER) on text from the e-commerce domain. The text data associated with an e-commerce item usually consists of two parts: the *title* and the *description*. In the current work, we focus only on item titles since item descriptions are often optional, vary greatly from seller to seller and between marketplaces, and are not shown on the search results page. The item title is a short sentence usually consisting of a sequence of approximately 10 to 35 nouns, adjectives, and numbers. They rarely contain verbs, pronouns, or determiners. The title is mandatory for most marketplaces, as it is indexed by the search engine and searched against by users of the website. Snippets shown in search result pages are generated from the titles of the items in the search result set.

Table 1 shows some examples of item titles (rows 1, 3, 5) from various online marketplaces. These examples show that sellers use capitalization and special characters as visual features in a manner not necessarily consistent with conventional English grammar rules. Besides their limited grammatical structure and the lack of contextual information due to their length, titles also contains typographical errors and abbreviations. While many abbreviations are standard in the e-commerce domain and used across all marketplaces (such as "w/" for "with", "NIB" for "new in box", "BNWT" for "brand new with tag", etc.), some are seller specific and are often difficult to decipher.

Performing NER for e-commerce involves classifying the various tokens in the title of an item into property names (entities) relevant to that item. Table 1 also shows the annotated entities (rows 2, 4, 6) for each of the titles. Section 3 provide details about the e-commerce categories, and the empirically defined entities within each of those categories. Next, we describe the approach that we use for NER.

2.2 Approach

Following current best practices, we approach NER as a sequence labeling problem. We use linear–chain Conditional Random Field (CRF) (Lafferty et al., 2001) which has been shown to achieve the best performance for many applications of NER (Suzuki and Isozaki, 2008; Lin and Wu, 2009; Passos et al., 2014), including NER for the e-commerce domain (Putthividhya and Hu, 2011).

We use a fairly standard set of lexical features used in most NER systems, including character affixes. Our features are detailed in Section 4.

In addition to the lexical features, modern NER systems also attempt to leverage some form of vector representation of the syntactic and semantic properties of the tokens. While discrete word representations derived from word clusters have been shown to be very beneficial to NER (Miller et al., 2004; Lin and Wu, 2009; Ratinov and Roth, 2009; Turian et al., 2010), more and more attention is being paid to distributed word representations since the introduction of efficient algorithms to produce them (Mikolov et al., 2013). Passos et al. (2014), for instance, reported performance comparable to state-of-the-art NER systems using a modified skip–gram model trained to predict membership of words to a domain specific lexicon.

To the best of our knowledge, all the results reported so far for NER used distributed word vectors trained from documents composed in standard, mostly grammatical English (Collobert and Weston, 2008; Turian et al., 2010; Baroni et al., 2014; Passos et al., 2014). However, it is clear that some phrases in the e-commerce domain have a very different meaning than in conventional English. For instance, "adventure time," "baby, the stars shine bright," and "miss me" are a few examples of e-commerce brand names which occur rarely in Wikipedia. In

1:	Apple	iPhone	6	-	16GB	-	Space	Grey	(	Unlocked	)	Smartphone
2:	b	p	p		d		c	c		a		t
3:	Cole	Haan	Men	's	Carter	Grand	Cap	Oxford				
4:	b	b	g	g	p	p		t				
5:	Womens	CRISTINALOVE	SHOULDER	DRESS	-	Size	XL	-	L@@K			
6:		b	t	t			s					

Table 1: Examples of annotated titles for different e-commerce categories from various online marketplaces. Entity types are denoted by the single letters: "a"– "contract," "b"– "brand name," "c"– "color," "d"– "dimension," "g"– "gender," "p"– "product name or number," "t"– "type," "s"– "size."

this paper, we investigate whether useful distributed representations can be learned from fairly unstructured, short, ungrammatical documents such as e-commerce titles and capture enough e-commerce semantics to benefit NER. We also study how they compare to distributed vectors trained from a non e-commerce corpus.

3 Data

To make discovering and browsing the inventory easy, most on-line marketplaces organize their inventory into a category structure similar to a topic hierarchy. eBay and Alibaba hierarchies comprise around 40 top level nodes, called *categories*, and more than 10,000 leaf nodes. The goods from different categories are usually very different in nature as exemplified by eBay categories such as "Antiques," "Clothing, Shoes & Accessories," and "Toys & Hobbies," to name a few.

3.1 Data Selection

The models trained for our experiments focus on a subset of five popular categories, namely Cellphones (CELLPH), Cellphone Accessories (CELLACC), Men's Shoes (MSHOES), Watches (WATCHES), and Women's Clothing (WCLOTH). Our datasets consist of user-defined e-commerce item titles. Table 2 provides statistics about these titles. Titles were tokenized using CoreNLP (Manning et al., 2014).

3.2 Training and testing data

Training and testing data for CRF was produced by manually labeling data. Based on the labeling resources available, we sampled 2,000 titles for most categories. Splitting these samples resulted in the training and test splits shown in Table 3.

category	# titles	# tokens	vocab. size
CELLPH	29M	46M	23K
CELLACC	143M	1.8B	114K
MSHOES	61M	665M	95K
WATCHES	97M	959M	190K
WCLOTH	150M	1.6B	118K

Table 2: Approximate statistics for the in-domain titles (B: billion, M: million, K: thousand). The vocabulary size is based on a minimum count of 50.

category	titles	tokens	vocab
CELLPH	1500 / 500	20776 / 7056	3806 / 1647
CELLACC	1330 / 443	18650 / 6195	4964 / 2261
MSHOES	1485 / 494	19278 / 6373	5424 / 2513
WATCHES	1339 / 495	15735 / 5828	5176 / 2487
WCLOTH	3098 / 500	39196 / 6279	7576 / 2621

Table 3: Training / test data splits (titles, token count, vocabulary size) for each category.

3.3 Entity Types

An important step in preparing the data was determining which properties of the items are most important to each category (concretely, which entities should be targeted). Because items across categories are quite different and can vary greatly in nature, a unique set of entities was used for each category, though several entities are common across categories (e.g. `brand, color`). For example, a title in WCLOTH might contain the properties `brand, type, size, style, color` whereas a title in CELLPH might describe an item by `brand, product name, storage size, contract`. These tags were chosen based on frequently occurring, user-defined properties that are assigned to an item. This set was manually pared down based on how much coverage an entity set could achieve while maintaining a manageable number of entities. While it would be ideal to have a set of entities such that every word in a title is tagged, this does not scale well and makes the annotation task more difficult. Table 4 shows the set of entities used for each category and the distribution of entities over the individual tokens within each category.

3.4 Annotation Procedure

Titles in Table 3 were annotated by two language specialists. Annotators had access to the listing page of the item in question to use as a reference. This page typically includes some pictures as well as a description of the item which may provide information about a particular token and reduce the amount of research required to correctly label a token (e.g. an obscure brand name). The two annotators regrouped after tagging to resolve disagreements between the individually tagged data sets. Agreement scores between the annotators were calculated using unweighted Cohen's Kappa with the following results: CELLPH: .92, CELLACC: .82, MSHOES: .78, WATCHES: .81, WCLOTH: .93. BIO encoding was not used for these datasets, but experimenting with it is important, and we plan do so in future work.

3.5 `word2vec` training data

For training the category–specific in–domain word vector representations, the set of tokenized titles referred to in Table 2 are used for the respective category. Section 4 provides details about the `word2vec` training process.

4 Experiments

We now present our experimental results for NER on e-commerce item titles. The goal of our work is not necessarily to present the best possible results for this task. Instead, our experiments are driven by the following two questions: (1) Are distributed word representations created from highly unstructured data (namely, e-commerce item titles) beneficial for the task of named entity recognition on the same kind of unstructured data? (2) How do distributed word vector representations created from out-of-domain (namely, non e-commerce data) compare with those created from in-domain data?

4.1 Training

We use the CRFsuite package (Okazaki, 2007) for our experiments. Following Turian et al. (2010), we use stochastic gradient descent (SGD) for our training, and allow negative state features and negative transition features. The l_2 regularization hyper–parameter (`c2` for CRFsuite) is tuned using a randomly chosen subset of 30% sentences (item titles) held out as the development set during training. The final model is retrained on the entire training set using the best value of `c2` (which varies depending on the feature configuration). The set of `c2` values we tried is {`0.001, 0.005, 0.01, 0.05, 0.1, 1, 2, 5, 10, 50, 100`}.

feature	comment
w_0, w_{-1}, w_{+1}	current token, tokens in window of 1
$\langle w_{-2}, w_{-1}\rangle$, $\langle w_{+1}, w_{+2}\rangle$	left and right bigram
CLASS(w_{-1}, w_0, w_{+1})	`ALLCAPS`, `Initcap`, `UpperCamelCase`, etc.
$\lvert w_0 \rvert$	length of current token
RELPOS(w_0)	relative position in the item title
AFFIXES(w_{-1}, w_0, w_{+1})	up to 3-character prefixes and suffixes
t_{-1}	tag of the previous token

Table 5: Table shows the features that we use for our baseline.

4.2 Baseline Features

Table 5 shows the features that we use for our baseline. We refer to this feature set by the name **BASE** in our results section.

We also experimented with larger window sizes (two and three) for all of the windowed features listed in Table 5, however, the performance degraded for larger window sizes. We believe this is due to the highly unstructured nature of text in the item titles.

4.3 Distributed Word Vector Features

We explored two different types of sources of text for the generation of distributed word representations for our task. First, we used word vectors trained by Baroni et al. (2014) — in particular, the "best predict vectors" made available by the authors[2]. These are, for our purposes, vectors trained on out-of-domain text corpora. Results using features based on these word vectors are denoted by the name **BASE+GEN**. In our experiments, features based on word vectors are always added on top of

[2]`http://clic.cimec.unitn.it/composes/semantic-vectors.html`

Category	Tag
CELLPH	Product Name 17.8%, Brand 11.3%, Dimension 7.4%, Color 5.2%, Contract 3.8%, Operating System 2.1%, Location 0.4%, no tag 52.0%
CELLACC	Product Name 25.6%, Type 19.4%, Brand 7.3%, Feature 3.8%, Material 2.4%, Color 2.3%, Style 1.2%, Connectivity 1.1%, Pattern 0.6%, Battery Capacity 0.4%, Location 0.4%, Finish 0.3%, Fit 0.3%, Storage Capacity 0.3%, Storage Format 0.2%, Sports Team 0.2%, no tag 34.2%
MSHOES	Product Line 28.2%, Brand 11.4%, Color 8.8%, Size 6.9%, Type 5.6%, Gender 3.9%, Purpose/Occasion/Activity 2.9%, Material 2.2%, Height 1.3%, Style 1.1%, Pattern 0.4%, no tag 27.3%
WATCHES	Product Name 13.8%, Brand 9.3%, Type 7.4%, Feature 5.1%, Gender 4.7%, Material 4.0%, Color 3.1%, Movement 2.9%, Component 2.9%, Style/Purpose/Occasion 2.9%, Size 1.1%, Display Type 0.8%, Location 0.8%, Purity/Quality 0.3%, Shape 0.2%, Closure 0.1%, no tag 40.6%
WCLOTH	Type 16.0%, Brand 8.3%, Size 7.3%, Color 4.0%, Material 3.8%, Purpose/Occasion/Activity 3.2%, Style 2.1, Pattern 1.5%, Location 0.8%, no tag 53.0%

Table 4: The entities targeted by our NER system and their distributions over total tokens for each category.

our baseline features (**BASE**). Second, we used word vectors trained on a large set of in-domain data for each of the five categories, namely e-commerce item titles for the respective categories. The word vectors for each category were trained separately, in order to provide the "purest" form of in–domain data. Results using features based on these word vectors are denoted by the name **BASE+DOM**. Additionally, we also conduct experiments using features based on both the in–domain as well as out–of–domain word vectors. Results using this combined set of word vector features are denoted by **BASE+ALL**.

Word vector features are computed for w_0, w_{-1}, and w_{+1}— that is, for the current token and its two surrounding tokens. Here too, we experimented with larger window sizes, but that resulted in a lower overall performance.

4.4 word2vec

Both the out–of–domain and the in–domain word vectors that we train are trained using the `word2vec` toolkit[3] (Mikolov et al., 2013). Details of how the out–of–domain word vectors were trained is provided by Baroni et al. (2014) — their 400–dimensional word vectors were trained on approximately 2.8 billion tokens using `word2vec`'s continuous bag–of–words (`cbow`) representation, with a window size of five.

Initially, we experimented with several parameter choices for training our `word2vec` models. In particular, we tried the following grid of values: representation: `skip-gram`, continuous bag–of–words (`cbow`); context window size: {`2, 5`}, down–sampling parameter: {`1e-3, 1e-4, 1e-5`}; hierarchical softmax: {`off, on`}; # of negative samples: {`5, 10`}; word frequency cutoff: {`10, 50`}; and word vector dimensionality: {`50, 100, 200, 300, 400, 500`}. Based on this parameter sweep, we found that the following parameters worked best overall for our task: representation: skip-gram, context window size: `2`, down–sampling parameter: `1e-3`, hierarchical softmax: `off`, # negative samples: `10`, word frequency cutoff: `50`. These are the settings we use for all the results reported in this paper. As for the word vector dimensionality, we tuned it based on our validation set (similar to the `c2` parameter for CRFsuite), using the following set of values: {`50, 100, 200, 300, 400, 500`}). In our results we will report the best word vector dimensionality when features based on in–domain word vectors are used.

The `skip-gram` representation worked better in our experiments for capturing semantics of the word co-occurrences in the item titles. This is consistent with the comparative analysis published by Mikolov et al. (2013) between `skip-gram` and `cbow` models — the `cbow` models were found to be better for syntactic tasks while the `skip-gram` models were better for semantic tasks. A narrower context window is better for our highly unstructured data.

5 Results and Discussion

Table 6 shows our complete set of results. We report the weighted token–level precision, recall, and F1 score for all our experiments: $F1_{\text{weighted}} =$

[3]`https://code.google.com/p/word2vec`

	config	prec.	rec.	F1	# dims
CELLPH	BASE	.9505	.9497	.9501	NA
	BASE+DOM	.9590	.9590	.9590	100
	BASE+GEN	.9560	.9554	.9557	NA
	BASE+ALL	**.9604**	**.9599**	**.9601**	300
CELLACC	BASE	.8571	.8567	.8569	NA
	BASE+DOM	.8723	.8731	.8727	500
	BASE+GEN	.8648	.8649	.8648	NA
	BASE+ALL	**.8806**	**.8812**	**.8809**	300
MSHOES	BASE	.8248	.8213	.8230	NA
	BASE+DOM	.8491	.8486	.8488	100
	BASE+GEN	.8376	.8338	.8357	NA
	BASE+ALL	**.8581**	**.8550**	**.8565**	200
WATCHES	BASE	.8243	.8210	.8227	NA
	BASE+DOM	.8382	.8384	.8383	200
	BASE+GEN	.8386	.8372	.8379	NA
	BASE+ALL	**.8496**	**.8480**	**.8488**	200
WCLOTH	BASE	.8600	.8619	.8609	NA
	BASE+DOM	.8874	.8882	.8878	400
	BASE+GEN	.8752	.8732	.8742	NA
	BASE+ALL	**.8883**	**.8892**	**.8887**	400

Table 6: Table shows the full set of results (weighted precision, recall, and F1) for each of the five e-Commerce categories we experiment with. The last column shows the best (tuned) `word2vec` dimensionality for the in–domain word vectors.

$\sum_{t \in \{\text{tags}\}} p(t)\text{F1}(t)$, where $p(t)$ is the relative frequency of tag t in the test set and $\text{F1}(t)$ is the F1 score for tag t.

Several trends are clear from the results. First, the combined feature set based on in–domain and out–of–domain word vectors (**BASE+ALL**) gives the best performance for all categories, with a boost of 2+ percentage points over **BASE** for all categories except CELLPH. Second, most of the improvement over the baseline (**BASE**) is achieved by the in–domain word vector features (**BASE+DOM**). Except for the WATCHES category, the out–of–domain word vector features by themselves are less useful compared to the in–domain vectors. This is not entirely surprising. However, it is worth noting for a couple of reasons: (1) The in–domain data we have, as mentioned earlier, is highly unstructured, and it is not obvious that word vectors trained on such data will be meaningful, let alone useful in a quantitative evaluation like the one we have presented. (2) The in–domain data that we use for word vector training is, in most cases, significantly smaller than the dataset used for training the out–of–domain word vectors. While we directly use the word vectors from Baroni et al. (2014) as our out–of–domain vectors (since they have been shown to perform well across a range of semantic relatedness tasks), in the future it might be worth tuning the out–of–domain word vectors specifically for our task.

In order to gain an understanding of where the distributed word representations are useful, we performed an error analysis on the predictions from our various models. Table 7 shows several different item titles where our trained models differed. The table shows, for example, that the **BASE+DOM** model is able to identify "Movistar" as a `brand` correctly, while the **BASE** model is not. This is interesting because "Movistar" does not appear in our training data at all. However, it does have a representation in our `word2vec` model, and thus the **BASE+DOM** model is able to correctly tag it. The **BASE+DOM** model also correctly tags both tokens in "Red Pocket" as a `brand`, unlike the **BASE+GEN** model, which tags them as `color` and `contract` incorrectly. This shows that the in–domain semantic representation for the token "Red" is more useful compared to its out–of–domain representation. Finally, there are also cases where the out–of–domain semantic representation adds value: "TANGERINE", for example, is correctly predicted as a `color` by **BASE+ALL**, but not by **BASE+DOM** because it is not present in our in–domain vectors.

6 Related Work

6.1 Word representations

The problem of modeling the meaning of words in text has been approached in various ways including distributional semantics (see Turney and Pantel (2010), Erk (2012) for surveys), word clustering (Brown et al., 1992; Lin and Wu, 2009), and, more recently, distributed representations (Mnih and Hinton, 2007; Collobert and Weston, 2008).

While word clusters and distributional approaches have been shown to be very effective for NER applications (Miller et al., 2004; Lin and Wu, 2009; Ratinov and Roth, 2009; Turian et al., 2010; Dhillon et al., 2011), direct applications of distributed representations to NER systems did not show benefit over Brown clusters (Turian et al., 2010). However, Passos et al. (2014) recently reported performance

	sample titles
BASE+DOM > BASE	New Samsung Galaxy S3 i9300 Unlocked Movistar (brand, no-tag) Claro (brand, no-tag) Vodafone (brand, no-tag) ATT Fido O2 (brand, product) Fido
	VERTU SUPER (no-tag, product) LUXURY CELLPHONE CONSTELLATION AYXTA (product, no-tag) PINK (color, no-tag) WITH RUBBY KEY NEVER USED
BASE+DOM > BASE+GEN	Brand New Nokia 101 100 Unlocked GSM Cellular Phone Phantom (color, no-tag) Black 2 SIM / w MP3
	iPhone 4S STRAIGHT TALK 32GB White Net10 ATT H2 AIO (brand, product) AirVoice (brand, product) Red (brand, color) Pocket (brand, contract) unlocked
BASE+ALL > BASE+DOM	NEW IN BOX SONY ERICSSON W380a W380 BLACK ORANGE TANGERINE (color, no-tag) UNLOCKED GSM Phone
	NEW Unlocked black BlackBerry Bold 9900 gsm cell phone telus (brand, no-tag) rogers (brand, no-tag) koodoo pda

Table 7: A small sample of errors made by our various models on the CELLPH category. The first column shows the models being compared (">" stands for "better than"). The predictions of the models differ for the underlined tokens. In parentheses, the prediction from the correct model is shown first, followed by the prediction of the incorrect model.

comparable to state-of-the-art NER systems using a modified skip-gram model trained to predict membership of words to a domain specific lexicon.

6.2 E-Commerce

E-commerce has recently garnered attention in the natural language processing research community.

Ghani et al. (2006) and Putthividhya and Hu (2011) also address the problem of structuring items in the e-commerce domain through NER and present experimental results on data similar to ours, but do not leverage word vector representations. Mauge et al. (2012) presents an unsupervised approach for identifying attribute names and values from unstructured natural language listings seen in e-commerce sites. Finally, unrelated to NER, Shen et al. (2012) proposed a method for hierarchical classification of product offers which they validated on eBay data.

7 Conclusions

Distributed word representations have been used successfully for improving performance on several natural language processing tasks in the recent past, including the task of named entity recognition (NER). Much of the work, however, has focused on learning these word representations from corpora that consist of relatively well–formed, grammatical language. Moreover, the NER tasks that used these word representations were also based on similar well–formed language. In this work we explore distributed word representations based on e-commerce domain item titles, which are highly unstructured in nature. We also evaluate our constructed word vectors on the task of NER for these item titles.

Our experiments show the following: (1) It is possible to learn useful (as evaluated quantitatively on an NER task) distributed word representations based on unstructured e-commerce item title data. (2) The word representations that we train on a relatively small amount of in–domain data are, in general, more useful than word representations trained on very large out–of–domain data. (3) The combination of in–domain and out–of–domain word representations gives the best result, adding domain–knowledge where necessary, while also using background general knowledge from out–of–domain representations.

Based on our experiments, there are a couple of interesting questions that may be considered for future research. First, we use the most straightforward way of combining in–domain and out–of–domain knowledge – training these word representations separately and using features based on both of them. Whether it is possible to learn better word representations by considering in–domain and out–of–domain data simultaneously at training time is an open question. Second, in our task formulation, the multiple e-commerce categories were trained separately even though they share some semantic tags. This can be improved upon in the future by considering approaches to multi–task learning.

References

Marco Baroni, Georgiana Dinu, and Germán Kruszewski. 2014. Don't count, predict! a systematic comparison of context-counting vs. context-predicting semantic vectors. In *Proceedings of the 52nd Annual Meeting of the Association for Computational Linguistics (Volume 1: Long Papers)*, pages 238–247.

Peter F. Brown, Peter V. deSouza, Robert L. Mercer, Vincent J. Della Pietra, and Jenifer C. Lai. 1992. Class-based n-gram models of natural language. *Computational Linguistics*, 18(4):467–479.

Ronan Collobert and Jason Weston. 2008. A unified architecture for natural language processing: Deep neural networks with multitask learning. In *Proceedings of the 25th International Conference on Machine Learning*, ICML '08, pages 160–167.

Paramveer Dhillon, Dean P Foster, and Lyle H. Ungar. 2011. Multi-view learning of word embeddings via cca. In J. Shawe-Taylor, R.S. Zemel, P.L. Bartlett, F. Pereira, and K.Q. Weinberger, editors, *Advances in Neural Information Processing Systems 24*, pages 199–207.

Katrin Erk. 2012. Vector space models of word meaning and phrase meaning: A survey. *Language and Linguistics Compass*, 6(10):635–653.

Rayid Ghani, Katharina Probst, Yan Liu, Marko Krema, and Andrew Fano. 2006. Text mining for product attribute extraction. *SIGKDD Explorations*, 8:41–48.

John D. Lafferty, Andrew McCallum, and Fernando C. N. Pereira. 2001. Conditional random fields: Probabilistic models for segmenting and labeling sequence data. In *Proceedings of the Eighteenth International Conference on Machine Learning*, ICML '01, pages 282–289.

Dekang Lin and Xiaoyun Wu. 2009. Phrase clustering for discriminative learning. In *Proceedings of the Joint Conference of the 47th Annual Meeting of the ACL and the 4th International Joint Conference on Natural Language Processing of the AFNLP: Volume 2 - Volume 2*, ACL '09, pages 1030–1038.

Christopher D. Manning, Mihai Surdeanu, John Bauer, Jenny Finkel, Steven J. Bethard, and David McClosky. 2014. The Stanford CoreNLP natural language processing toolkit.

Karin Mauge, Khash Rohanimanesh, and Jean-David Ruvini. 2012. Structuring e-commerce inventory. In *Proceedings of the 50th Annual Meeting of the Association for Computational Linguistics: Long Papers - Volume 1*, pages 805–814.

Tomas Mikolov, Kai Chen, Greg Corrado, and Jeffrey Dean. 2013. Efficient estimation of word representations in vector space. In *Proceedings of Workshop at ICLR*.

Scott Miller, Jethran Guinness, and Alex Zamanian. 2004. Name tagging with word clusters and discriminative training. In Daniel Marcu Susan Dumais and Salim Roukos, editors, *HLT-NAACL 2004: Main Proceedings*, pages 337–342.

Andriy Mnih and Geoffrey Hinton. 2007. Three new graphical models for statistical language modelling. In *Proceedings of the 24th International Conference on Machine Learning*, ICML '07, pages 641–648.

Naoaki Okazaki. 2007. Crfsuite: a fast implementation of conditional random fields (crfs).

Alexandre Passos, Vineet Kumar, and Andrew McCallum. 2014. Lexicon infused phrase embeddings for named entity resolution. In *Proceedings of the Eighteenth Conference on Computational Natural Language Learning (CoNLL 2014)*, pages 78–86.

Duangmanee Putthividhya and Junling Hu. 2011. Bootstrapped named entity recognition for product attribute extraction. In *EMNLP*, pages 1557–1567.

Lev Ratinov and Dan Roth. 2009. Design challenges and misconceptions in named entity recognition. In *Proceedings of the Thirteenth Conference on Computational Natural Language Learning*, CoNLL '09, pages 147–155.

Dan Shen, Jean-David Ruvini, and Badrul Sarwar. 2012. Large-scale item categorization for e-commerce. In *CIKM*, pages 595–604.

Jun Suzuki and Hideki Isozaki. 2008. Semi-supervised sequential labeling and segmentation using giga-word scale unlabeled data. In *Proceedings of ACL-08: HLT*, pages 665–673.

Joseph Turian, Lev-Arie Ratinov, and Yoshua Bengio. 2010. Word representations: A simple and general method for semi-supervised learning. In *Proceedings of the 48th Annual Meeting of the Association for Computational Linguistics*, pages 384–394.

Peter D. Turney and Patrick Pantel. 2010. From frequency to meaning: Vector space models of semantics. *Journal of Artificial Intelligence Research*, 37(1):141–188.

Semantic Information Extraction for Improved Word Embeddings

Jiaqiang Chen
IIS, Tsinghua University
Beijing, China
cjq0707@gmail.com

Gerard de Melo
IIIS, Tsinghua University
Beijing, China
gdm@demelo.org

Abstract

Word embeddings have recently proven useful in a number of different applications that deal with natural language. Such embeddings succinctly reflect semantic similarities between words based on their sentence-internal contexts in large corpora. In this paper, we show that information extraction techniques provide valuable additional evidence of semantic relationships that can be exploited when producing word embeddings. We propose a joint model to train word embeddings both on regular context information and on more explicit semantic extractions. The word vectors obtained from such an augmented joint training show improved results on word similarity tasks, suggesting that they can be useful in applications that involve word meanings.

1 Introduction

In recent years, the idea of embedding words in a vector space has gained enormous popularity. This success of such *word embeddings* as semantic representations has been driven in part by the development of novel methods to efficiently train word vectors from large corpora, such that words with similar contexts end up having similar vectors. While it is indisputable that context plays a vital role in meaning acquisition, it seems equally plausible that some contexts would be more helpful for this than others. Consider the following sentence, taken from Wikipedia, a commonly used training corpus for word representation learning:

> Although Roman political authority in the West was lost, Roman culture would last in most parts of the former Western provinces into the 6th century and beyond.

In this example sentence, the token "parts" does not seem to bear any particularly close relationship with the meaning of some of the other tokens, e.g. "Roman" and "culture". In contrast, the occurrence of an expression such as "Greek and Roman mythology" in a corpus appears to indicate that the two tokens "Roman" and "Greek" likely share certain commonalities. There is a large body of work on *information extraction* techniques to discover text patterns that reflect semantic relationships (Hearst, 1992; Tandon and de Melo, 2010).

In this paper, we propose injecting semantic information into word embeddings by training them not just on general contexts but paying special attention to stronger semantic connections that can be discovered in specific contexts on the Web or in corpora. In particular, we investigate mining information of this sort from enumerations and lists, as well as from definitions. Our training procedure can exploit any source of knowledge about pairs of words being strongly coupled to improve over word embeddings trained just on generic corpus contexts.

2 Background and Related Work

Words are substantially discrete in nature, and thus, traditionally, the vast majority of natural language processing tools, both rule-based and statistical,

This research was partially funded by China 973 Program Grants 2011CBA00300, 2011CBA00301, and NSFC Grants 61033001, 61361136003, 20141330245.

Proceedings of NAACL-HLT 2015, pages 168–175,
Denver, Colorado, May 31 – June 5, 2015.

have regarded words as distinct atomic symbols. Even methods that rely on vectors typically made use of so-called "one-hot" representations, which allocate a separate dimension in the vector space for every content word in the vocabulary. Such representations suffer from two problems. First, vectors for two distinct word forms have distinct vectors without any overlap, which means that the vector similarities for any two distinct individual word forms will fail to reflect any possible syntactic or semantic similarities between them. Second, the vector space dimensionality is proportional to the vocabulary size, which can be very large. For instance, the Google 1T corpus has 13M distinct words.

To address these two problems, other representations have been proposed. Brown clustering (Brown et al., 1992) organizes words into a binary tree based on the contexts in which they occur. Latent Semantic Analysis and Indexing (LSA/LSI) use singular value decomposition (SVD) to identify the relationships between words in a corpus. Latent Dirichlet Analysis (LDA) (Blei et al., 2003), a generative graphical model, views each document as a collection of topics and assigns each word to these topics.

Recently, neural networks have been applied to learn word embeddings in dense real-valued vector spaces. In training, such an approach may combine vector space semantics with predictions from probabilistic models. For instance, Bengio et al. (2003) present a neural probabilistic language model that uses the n-gram model to learn word embeddings. The network tries to use the first $n-1$ words to predict the next one, outperforming n-gram frequency baselines. Collobert et al. (2011) use word embeddings for traditional NLP tasks: POS tagging, named entity recognition, chunking, and semantic role labeling. Their pairwise ranking approach tries to maximize the difference between scores from text windows in a large training corpus and corresponding randomly generated negative examples. However, the training for this took about one month. The next breakthrough came with Mikolov et al. (2013a), who determined that, for the previous models, most of the complexity is caused by the non-linear hidden layer. The authors thus investigated simpler network architectures to efficiently train the vectors at a much faster rate and thus also at a much larger scale. Their word2vec[1] implementation provides two architectures, the CBOW and the Skip-gram models. CBOW also relies on a window approach, attempting to use the surrounding words to predict the current target word. However, it simplifies the hidden layer to be just the average of surrounding words' embeddings. The Skip-gram model tries to do the opposite. It uses the current word to predict the surrounding words. Both architectures can be trained in just a few hours, while obtaining state-of-the-art embeddings.

Distributed word representations now have been applied to numerous natural language processing tasks. For instance, they have been used for sentiment analysis (Socher et al., 2013), paraphrase detection (Socher et al., 2011), machine translation (Devlin et al., 2014), relation extraction (Chang et al., 2014), and parsing, just to name a few. Some of these works use neural network models, e.g. recursive neural networks, auto-encoders, or convolutional neural networks. Others use word embeddings directly as features for clustering or classification with alternative machine learning algorithms.

There have been other proposals to adapt the word2vec model. Similar to previous work on semantic spaces based on dependency parse relations (Padó and Lapata, 2007), Levy and Goldberg (2014) rely on dependency parsing to create word embeddings. These are able to capture contextual relationships between words that are further apart in the sentence while simultaneously filtering out some words that are not directly related to the target word. Further analysis revealed that their word embeddings capture more functional but less topical similarity. Faruqui et al. (2015) apply post-processing steps to existing word embeddings in order to bring them more in accordance with semantic lexicons such as PPDB and FrameNet. Wang et al. (2014) train embeddings jointly on text and on Freebase, a well-known large knowledge base. Their embeddings are trained to preserve relations between entities in the knowledge graph. Rather than using structured knowledge sources, our work focuses on improving word embeddings using textual data by relying on information extraction to expose particularly valuable contexts in a text corpus.

[1] `https://code.google.com/p/word2vec/`

3 Joint Model

Our model simultaneously trains the word embeddings on generic contexts from the corpus on the one hand and semantically significant contexts, obtained using extraction techniques, on the other hand. For the regular general contexts, our approach draws on the word2vec CBOW model (Mikolov et al., 2013a) to predict a word given its surrounding neighbors in the corpus.

At the same time, our model relies on our ability to extract semantically salient contexts that are more indicative of word meanings. Our algorithm assumes that these have been transformed into a set of word pairs known to be closely related. These pairs of related words are used to modify the word embeddings by jointly training them simultaneously with the word2vec model for regular contexts. Due to this more focused information, we expect the final word embeddings to reflect more semantic information than embeddings trained only on regular contexts.

Given an extracted pair of semantically related words, the intuition is that the embeddings for the two words should be pulled together. We formalize this intuition with following objective:

$$\frac{1}{T}\sum_{t=1}^{T}\sum_{w_{\mathrm{r}}} \log p(w_{\mathrm{r}}|w_{\mathrm{t}})$$

Here, w_{r} is a word related to another word w_{t} according to the extractions, and T is the vocabulary size.

Thus, given a word w_{t}, we try to maximize the probability of finding its related words w_{r}. Traditionally, the softmax function is used for the probability function. Its time complexity is proportional to the vocabulary size. Here, we use negative sampling as a speed-up technique (Mikolov et al., 2013b). This is a simplified version of Noise Contrastive Estimation (NCE) (Mnih and Teh, 2012), which reduces the problem of determining the softmax to that of binary classification, discriminating between samples from the data distribution and negative samples.

In the training procedure, this amounts to simply generating k random negative samples for each extracted word pair. That is, we replace w_{r} with random words from the vocabulary. For the negative samples, we assign the label $l = 0$, while for the original word pairs, $l = 1$. Now, for each word pair we try to minimize its loss function:

$$Loss = -l \cdot \log f - (1-l) \cdot \log(1-f)$$

$$f = \sigma(v_{w_{\mathrm{t}}}^{T} \cdot v_{w_{\mathrm{r}}})$$

Here, $\sigma(\cdot)$ is the sigmoid function $\sigma(x) = \frac{1}{1+e^{-x}}$ and $v_{w_{\mathrm{t}}}$, $v_{w_{\mathrm{r}}}$ refer to the vectors for the two words w_{t} and w_{r}. We use stochastic gradient descent to optimize this function. The formulae for the gradient are easy to compute:

$$\frac{\partial Loss}{\partial v_{w_{\mathrm{r}}}} = -(l-f)\, v_{w_{\mathrm{t}}}$$

$$\frac{\partial Loss}{\partial v_{w_{\mathrm{t}}}} = -(l-f)\, v_{w_{\mathrm{r}}}$$

This objective is optimized alongside with the original word2vec CBOW objective. Our overall model combines the two objectives. Training the model in parallel with the word2vec model allows us to inject the extracted knowledge into the word vectors such that they are reflected during the word2vec training rather than just as a post-processing step. Thus the two components are able to mutually influence each other.

Both objectives contribute to the embeddings' ability to capture semantic relationships. Training with the extracted contexts enables us to adjust word embeddings based on concrete evidence of semantic relationships, while the use of general corpus contexts enables us to maintain the advantages of the word2vec model, in particular its ability to benefit from massive volumes of raw corpus data.

4 Information Extraction

Our model can flexibly incorporate semantic relationships extracted using various kinds of information extraction methods. Different kinds of sources and extraction methods can bring different sorts of information to the vectors, suitable for different applications. In our experiments, we investigate two sources: a dictionary corpus from which we extract definitions and synonyms, and a general Web corpus, from which we extract lists. Our model could similarly be used with other extraction methods, or in fact any method to mine pairs of semantically related words.

word w_t	**definition** w_r **for** w_t
Befuddle	to becloud and confuse as with liquor
Befuddled	dazed by alcoholic drink
Befuddled	unclear in mind or intent filled with bewilderment
Befuddled	confused and vague, used especially of thinking
Beg	to ask earnestly for, to entreat, or supplicate for, to beseech
word w_t	**synonym** w_r **for** w_t
Effectual	effectual, efficacious, effective
Effectuality	effectiveness, effectivity, effectualness
Efficacious	effectual
Efficaciousness	efficacy

Table 1: Definitions and synonyms from the GCIDE

player, captain, manager, director, vice-chairman
group, race, culture, religion, organisation, person
Italian, Mexican, Chinese, Creole, French
prehistoric, roman, early-medieval, late-medieval, post-medieval, modern
ballscrews, leadscrews, worm gear, screwjacks, linear, actuator
Cleveland, Essex, Lincolnshire, Northamptonshire, Nottinghamshire, Thames Valley, South Wales

Table 2: Lists of related words extracted from UKWaC

4.1 Definition Extraction

One can safely assume that any large, broad-coverage Web corpus will contain significant occurrences of word definitions, e.g. whenever new terminology is introduced. These can be harvested using broad-coverage Definition Extraction methods (Sierra et al., 2009).

Instead of adopting such generic methods that are intended to operate on arbitrary text, another option, appropriate for Web corpora, is to specifically identify the kinds of Web sources that provide high-quality definitions, e.g. Wiktionary or Wikipedia. In fact, when compiling a Web corpus with the explicit purpose of using it to train word representations, one may reasonably wish to explicitly ensure that it includes dictionaries available on the Web. Obviously, the definitions from a dictionary can provide meaningful semantic relationships between words.

In our experiments, we use the GNU Collaborative International Dictionary of English (GCIDE) as our dictionary corpus, which is derived from an older edition of Webster's Revised Unabridged Dictionary. From this data, we extract the dictionary glosses as genuine definitions as well as synonyms. In the dictionary, they are indexed by the $\langle def \rangle$ and $\langle syn \rangle$ tags. We ignore other embedded tags within the definitions and synonym entries. These provide additional word usage notes and other attributes that are not significant in our work. In total, we obtain 208,881 definition entries. Some words have multiple meanings and thus are part of several entries. We also obtain 10,148 synonym entries, each of which consists of one or more synonyms for a given word. Table 1 shows some examples of this extraction. We can observe that the definition and synonym extractions indeed appear to convey valuable information about semantic proximity of words.

4.2 List Extraction

Lists and enumerations are another promising source of information. Words that occur together within a list are not just semantically connected but often even of the same type. These sorts of contexts thus also have the potential to improve the word embeddings. We extract them from the UKWaC corpus (Baroni et al., 2009), a general broad-coverage corpus crawled from the Web, but limited to the `.uk` domain. After post-crawl cleaning, it contains a total of about 2 billion words. It is annotated with POS and dependency tags, which simplifies our work of extracting high-quality lists.

To extract lists of similar words, we use a simple rule-based method. We first search for continuous appearances of commas, which indicate a possible list of similar things. To filter out noise, we require that the entries in the list be approximately of equal length. The length of each entry should be in the range from 1 to 4. Longer entries are much more likely to be short sentences or clauses, which are not very useful when our aim is to obtain lists of similar words. We also restrict list items to be nouns and adjectives using the POS tags provided with the UKWaC.

Additionally, we rely on special search patterns matching for instance *"include A, B, C, (and) D"*, *"A and(or) B"*, *"cities(or other nouns) like A, B, C, D"*, *"cities(or other nouns) such as A, B, C, (and) D"*, etc. Here, the letters *A*, *B*, and so on, refer to the extracted target words, while other words and punctuation, merely indicating the occurrence of the lists, are removed, e.g. commas or the word *"and"*.

In total, 339,111 lists are extracted from the UKWaC, examples of which are shown in Table 2. We see that although there is some noise, the list extraction also captures semantically meaningful relationships. The words in the lists tend to be of the same or similar type and represent similar or related things.

5 Experiments and Evaluation

In order to investigate the impact of extractions on word embeddings, we conduct an empirical analysis based on semantic relatedness assessments.

5.1 Data

Our model relies on two types of input. For semantically salient contexts, we rely on the data and extraction techniques described above in Section 4 to obtain pairs of related words.

For the regular contexts used by the CBOW model, we rely on a 2010 Wikipedia data set[2]. We normalize the text to lower case and remove special characters. After prepocessing, it contains 1,205,009,210 tokens. We select words appearing at least 50 times and obtain a vocabulary of 220,521 words.

5.2 Training

Having obtained two kinds of extracted word contexts, we use these separately to train word embeddings jointly with the word2vec model. Our training implementation relies on a multi-threaded architecture in which some threads optimize for the original word2vec objective, training on different parts of the corpus. At the same time, alongside with these threads, further threads optimize based on the extracted pairs of words using the objective given earlier. All threads asynchronously update the word embeddings, using stochastic gradient descent steps. Thus, both the raw corpus for the word2vec model and the related word pairs can bring their information to bear on the word embeddings.

We use 20 threads for the CBOW architecture, which runs faster than the Skip-gram model. The window size of the CBOW model is set to 8. We run it for 3 passes over the Wikipedia data set, which is sufficient to achieve good results. We sample 10 random words as negative examples for each instance.

Additional threads are used for the extracted pairs of words. We use 4 threads each for lists and definitions (by splitting definitions) and one thread for synonyms. In each case, the extractions lead to positive pairs of semantically related words. For definitions and synonyms, the word pair consists of a headword and one word from its definition, or of the headword and one of its synonyms. For the list extraction setup, the training word pairs consist of any two words from the same list. For these word pairs, we also randomly sample 10 words as the corresponding negative examples. They update the word embeddings jointly with the CBOW model. This way, the semantic information they contain can be used to adjust the results from word2vec.

We use different learning rates to control each source's contribution to the final word embeddings. We set the initial learning rate for the CBOW threads to be 0.050 and report results for different rates for the other threads, ranging from 0.001 to 0.1.

We stop training the word embeddings in the fol-

[2] `http://nlp.stanford.edu/data/WestburyLab.wikicorp.201004.txt.bz2`

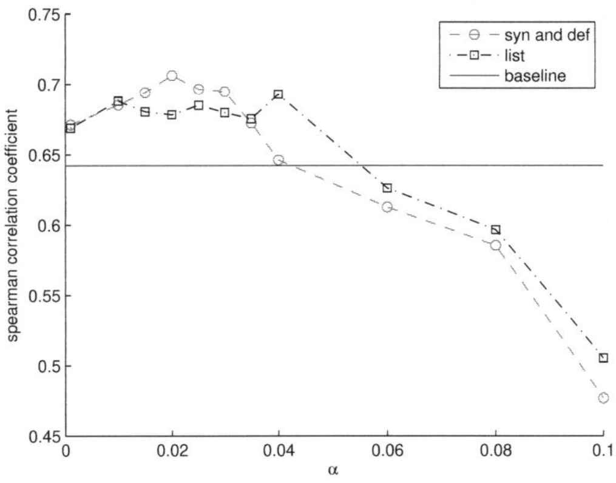

Figure 1: Spearman's ρ for wordsim-353

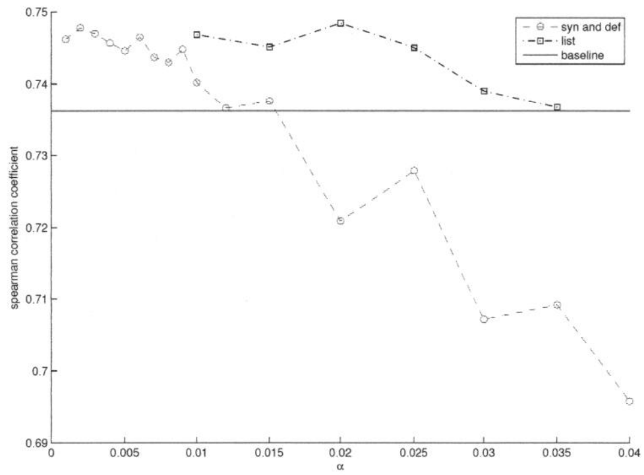

Figure 3: Spearman's ρ for MEN

lowing way to ensure convergence: when all the CBOW threads finish, the other threads are terminated. This is because the extractions are supplementary to the CBOW model, which is the main source to train the word vectors. This mode of operation also ensures that we are always training on both components of the model jointly rather than allowing one component to dominate towards the end. We did also experiment with pre-defined numbers of iterations for the additional threads to control convergence, but the results were not very different.

5.3 Evaluation and Analysis

We use the wordsim-353 (Finkelstein et al., 2001) and MEN (Bruni et al., 2014) datasets to evaluate the semantic similarities reflected in the final word embeddings. Wordsim-353 and MEN are datasets of English word pairs with human-assigned similarity judgements. They are often used to train or test semantic similarity measures of words. We calculate the cosine distance of word embeddings for the word pairs in wordsim-353 and MEN and compare them to the scores from human annotations.

Fig. 1 shows the Spearman's correlation coefficients for the wordsim-353 dataset. Even for a learning rate α as low as 0.001 for the additional threads, we can obtain some improvement over the CBOW baseline (which corresponds to an α setting of 0.0). As α increases, the result gets better. The best result we get for synonyms and definitions is 0.706, while for lists from UKWaC, it is 0.693. The best learning rate for the definitions and synonyms is 0.020, while for the list extractions, it is 0.040. Both lead to noticeably better results than the CBOW baseline's correlation coefficient of 0.642. Note that for large α, the augmentation performs worse than the baseline. This is expected, as an overly high learning rate causes information from the related words to overwhelm the original CBOW model, leading to excessively biased final embeddings.

Fig. 3 plots the results on the MEN dataset. The best-performing learning rate is different from that for wordsim-353. In particular, well-performing learning rates are slightly smaller. For the definitions and synonyms, the best is 0.002, while for the lists, the best learning rate is 0.020. After training jointly, we obtain higher correlation coefficients for the MEN similarity task.

	wordsim-353	MEN
CBOW (baseline)	0.642	0.736
Definitions and synonyms	0.706	0.748
Lists	0.693	0.749

Table 3: Best results for the word similarity tasks

Table 3 provides a summary of the best results that we obtain on the two similarity tasks.[3] It can be seen that we obtain higher correlation coefficients for these tasks. This suggests that the word vectors

[3]Unfortunately, there is no independent tuning set from the same distribution and thus we follow previous work in reporting best results on the final set.

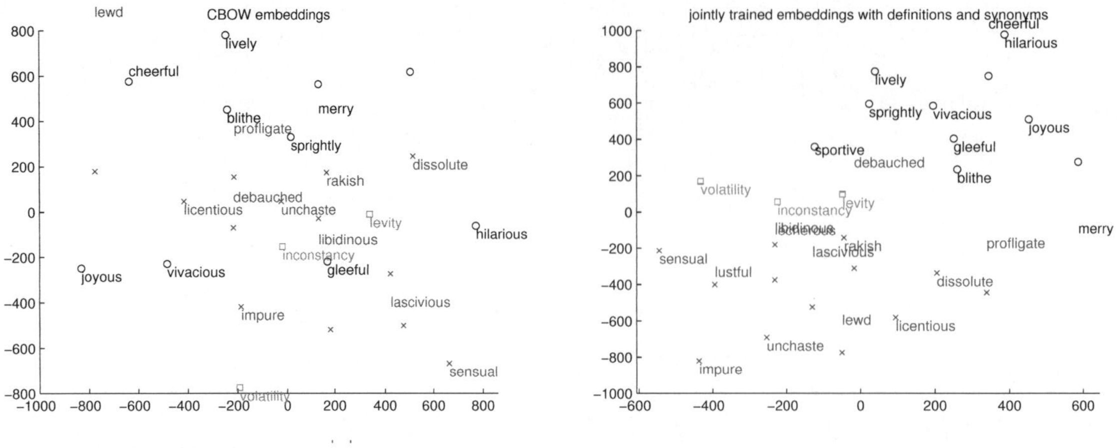

Figure 2: A t-SNE visualization of the word embeddings, comparing the CBOW baseline (left) with that of our joint model (right)

capture more semantic properties of words and thus may be used in applications that benefit from semantic information.

Finally, we plot a sample of the word embeddings obtained from the joint training with definitions and synonyms using t-SNE (van der Maaten and Hinton, 2008). t-SNE is a technique for visualization of high-dimensional datasets using dimensionality reduction. The perplexity of the Gaussian kernel for the t-SNE is set to 15. Figure 2 shows a plot for 26 words: *levity*, *lewd*, and *merry*, and their synonyms. We see that our model successfully distinguishes the different meanings of these words while reflecting semantic relationships.

6 Conclusion

We have presented a way to improve word embeddings by drawing on the idea that certain contexts exhibit more semantically meaningful information than others. Information extraction methods allow us to discover such contexts and mine semantic relationships between words. We focus on word definitions and synonyms, as well as on lists and enumerations. The final word embeddings after joint training show better correlation coefficients in similarity tasks. This suggests that information extraction methods can help word vectors capture more meaning, making them useful for semantic applications and calling for further research in this area.

References

Marco Baroni, Silvia Bernardini, Adriano Ferraresi, and Eros Zanchetta. 2009. The wacky wide web: a collection of very large linguistically processed web-crawled corpora. *Language Resources and Evaluation*, 43(3):209–226.

Yoshua Bengio, Réjean Ducharme, Pascal Vincent, and Christian Janvin. 2003. A neural probabilistic language model. *J. Mach. Learn. Res.*, 3:1137–1155, March.

David M. Blei, Andrew Y. Ng, and Michael I. Jordan. 2003. Latent dirichlet allocation. *J. Mach. Learn. Res.*, 3:993–1022, March.

Peter F. Brown, Peter V. deSouza, Robert L. Mercer, Vincent J. Della Pietra, and Jenifer C. Lai. 1992. Class-based n-gram models of natural language. *Comput. Linguist.*, 18(4):467–479, December.

Elia Bruni, Nam Khanh Tran, and Marco Baroni. 2014. Multimodal distributional semantics. *J. Artif. Int. Res.*, 49(1):1–47, January.

Kai-Wei Chang, Wen-tau Yih, Bishan Yang, and Christopher Meek. 2014. Typed tensor decomposition of knowledge bases for relation extraction. In *Proceedings of the 2014 Conference on Empirical Methods in Natural Language Processing (EMNLP)*, pages 1568–1579. Association for Computational Linguistics.

Ronan Collobert, Jason Weston, Léon Bottou, Michael Karlen, Koray Kavukcuoglu, and Pavel Kuksa. 2011. Natural language processing (almost) from scratch. *J. Mach. Learn. Res.*, 12:2493–2537, November.

Jacob Devlin, Rabih Zbib, Zhongqiang Huang, Thomas Lamar, Richard Schwartz, and John Makhoul. 2014. Fast and robust neural network joint models for statistical machine translation. In *Proceedings of the*

52nd Annual Meeting of the Association for Computational Linguistics (Volume 1: Long Papers), pages 1370–1380, Baltimore, Maryland, June. Association for Computational Linguistics.

Manaal Faruqui, Jesse Dodge, Sujay K. Jauhar, Chris Dyer, Eduard Hovy, and Noah A. Smith. 2015. Retrofitting word vectors to semantic lexicons. In *Proceedings of NAACL*.

Lev Finkelstein, Gabrilovich Evgenly, Matias Yossi, Rivlin Ehud, Solan Zach, Wolfman Gadi, and Ruppin Eytan. 2001. Placing search in context: the concept revisited. In *Proceedings of the Tenth International World Wide Web Conference*.

Marti A. Hearst. 1992. Automatic acquisition of hyponyms from large text corpora. In *COLING*, pages 539–545.

Omer Levy and Yoav Goldberg. 2014. Dependency-based word embeddings. In *Proceedings of the 52nd Annual Meeting of the Association for Computational Linguistics (Volume 2: Short Papers)*, pages 302–308. Association for Computational Linguistics.

Tomas Mikolov, Kai Chen, Greg Corrado, and Jeffrey Dean. 2013a. Efficient estimation of word representations in vector space. *CoRR*, abs/1301.3781.

Tomas Mikolov, Ilya Sutskever, Kai Chen, Greg S Corrado, and Jeff Dean. 2013b. Distributed representations of words and phrases and their compositionality. In C.J.C. Burges, L. Bottou, M. Welling, Z. Ghahramani, and K.Q. Weinberger, editors, *Advances in Neural Information Processing Systems 26*, pages 3111–3119. Curran Associates, Inc.

Andriy Mnih and Yee Whye Teh. 2012. A fast and simple algorithm for training neural probabilistic language models. In *Proceedings of the 29th International Conference on Machine Learning*, pages 1751–1758.

Sebastian Padó and Mirella Lapata. 2007. Dependency-based construction of semantic space models. *Comput. Linguist.*, 33(2):161–199, June.

Gerardo Sierra, Maria Pozzi, and Juan-Manuel Torres, editors. 2009. *WDE '09: Proceedings of the 1st Workshop on Definition Extraction*, Stroudsburg, PA, USA. Association for Computational Linguistics.

Richard Socher, Eric H. Huang, Jeffrey Pennington, Andrew Y. Ng, and Christopher D. Manning. 2011. Dynamic pooling and unfolding recursive autoencoders for paraphrase detection. In John Shawe-Taylor, Richard S. Zemel, Peter L. Bartlett, Fernando C. N. Pereira, and Kilian Q. Weinberger, editors, *NIPS*, pages 801–809.

Richard Socher, Alex Perelygin, Jean Wu, Jason Chuang, Christopher D. Manning, Andrew Y. Ng, and Christopher Potts. 2013. Recursive deep models for semantic compositionality over a sentiment treebank. In *Proceedings of the 2013 Conference on Empirical Methods in Natural Language Processing*, pages 1631–1642, Stroudsburg, PA, October. Association for Computational Linguistics.

Niket Tandon and Gerard de Melo. 2010. Information extraction from web-scale n-gram data. In Chengxiang Zhai, David Yarowsky, Evelyne Viegas, Kuansan Wang, and Stephan Vogel, editors, *Web N-gram Workshop. Workshop of the 33rd Annual International ACM SIGIR Conference on Research and Development in Information Retrieval*, volume 5803, pages 8–15. ACM.

Laurens van der Maaten and Geoffrey E. Hinton. 2008. Visualizing high-dimensional data using t-sne. *Journal of Machine Learning Research*, 9:2579–2605.

Zhen Wang, Jianwen Zhang, Jianlin Feng, and Zheng Chen. 2014. Knowledge graph and text jointly embedding. In *Proceedings of the 2014 Conference on Empirical Methods in Natural Language Processing (EMNLP)*, pages 1591–1601, Doha, Qatar, October. Association for Computational Linguistics.

Named Entity Recognition for Arabic Social Media

Ayah Zirikly
Department of Computer Science
The George Washington University
Washington DC, USA
ayaz@gwu.edu

Mona Diab
Department of Computer Science
The George Washington University
Washington DC, USA
mtdiab@gwu.edu

Abstract

The majority of research on Arabic Named Entity Recognition (NER) addresses the the task for newswire genre, where the language used is Modern Standard Arabic (MSA), however, the need to study this task in social media is becoming more vital. Social media is characterized by the use of both MSA and Dialectal Arabic (DA), with often code switching between the two language varieties. Despite some common characteristics between MSA and DA, there are significant differences between which result in poor performance when MSA targeting systems are applied for NER in DA. Additionally, most NER systems rely primarily on gazetteers, which can be more challenging in a social media processing context due to an inherent low coverage. In this paper, we present a gazetteers-free NER system for Dialectal data that yields an F1 score of 72.68% which is an absolute improvement of $\approx 2-3\%$ over a comparable state-of-the-art gazetteer based DA-NER system.

1 Introduction

Named Entity Recognition (NER) is the task of tagging names with a predefined set of named entity types (e.g. Location, Person) in open-domain text (Nadeau and Sekine, 2007). NER has been shown to improve Information Retrieval performance (Thompson and Dozier, 1997) and Question Answering (QA) performance where (Ferrndez et al., 2007) shows that, on average, questions contain $\approx 85\%$ Named Entities.

In the current world of ubiquitous social media presence, processing informal genre is becoming ever more crucial. One of the prevalent genre in social media in need for text mining is microblog data such as Twitter. Twitter data is characterized by being massive. Off the shelf NER systems trained on formal genre such as newswire fail to process such data, thereby current research in information extraction has been specifically targeting this genre (Ritter et al., 2011). This problem is quite significant in English and is ever more pronounced in lower resourced languages such as Arabic.

Arabic has gained more attention recently due to the increased availability of annotated datasets. Arabic NER systems, as other languages, are domain dependent and mainly trained on news corpora or other well structured data that uses the Modern Standard Arabic (MSA) variety of the language (Benajiba et al., 2007) and (Abdallah et al., 2012). Arabic, in general, poses additional challenges to Natural Language Processing (NLP) tasks, as opposed to other languages, due its rich morphology and highly inflected nature. Moreover, Arabic is also one of those languages that exists in a state of diglossia where multiple forms of the language exist in the same context, the standard formal form, MSA, used in formal settings (education, formal speeches, etc.) and the spoken vernaculars that differ significantly from MSA, known as Dialectal Arabic (DA) that are used pervasively in informal settings such as in social media. Since MSA and DA co-exist, we note that people very often code switch between the two varieties within the same utterance which is reflected in microblog data. Hence NLP systems targeting the Twitter genre needs to account for this phenomenon.

Compared to English NER, here are some example challenges posed for Arabic NER (Abdul-Hamid and Darwish, 2010):

- Lack of capitalization: Capitalization in Latin languages is a strong indicator of Named Entity (NE). However, in Arabic,

Proceedings of NAACL-HLT 2015, pages 176–185,
Denver, Colorado, May 31 – June 5, 2015.

proper nouns are not capitalized, which renders the identification of NEs more complicated;

- Nominal Confusability: Some words can be proper nouns, nouns, or adjectives. For instance, *jamiyolap*[1] which means 'beautiful' can be a proper noun or an adjective. Another example, *jamAl*, which means 'beauty', is a noun but can be a common noun or a proper name;
- Agglutination: Since Arabic exhibits concatenative morphology, we note the pervasive presence of affixes agglutinating to proper nouns as prefixes and suffixes (Shaalan, 2014). For instance, determiners appear as prefixes *Al* as in (*AlqAhrp*, 'Cairo'), likewise with affixival prepositions such as *l*, 'for' (*ldm$q* 'for/to/from Damascus'), as well as prefixed conjunctions such as *w*, 'and', as in (*wAlqds* 'and Jerusalem');
- Absence of Short Vowels (Diacritic Markers): Written MSA, even in newswire, is underspecified for short vowels, aka undiacritized, which results in higher ambiguity that can only be resolved using contextual information (Benajiba et al., 2009). Examples of ambiguity are: *mSr*, may be *miSor* as in 'Egypt' or *muSir* as in 'insistent'; *qTr* may be the name of the country 'Qatar' if vowelized/diacritized as *qaTar*, *qaTor* for 'sugar syrup', *quTor* for 'diameter'.

In addition to the afore mentioned challenges, in general, for Arabic NER in general compared to Latin-based languages, DA NER faces additional issues:

- Lack of annotated data for supervised DA NER;
- Lack of standard orthographies or language academics (Habash et al., 2013): Unlike MSA, the same word in DA can be rewritten in so many forms, e.g. *mAtEyT$, mtEyt$, mA tEyT$*, 'do not cry', are all acceptable variants since there is no one standard;
- Lack of comprehensive Gazetteers: this is a problem facing all NER systems for all languages addressing NER in social media text, since by definition such media has a ubiquitous presence of highly productive names exemplified by the usage of nick names, hence the PERSON class in social media NER will always have a coverage problem;
- Applying NLP tools designed for MSA to DA results in considerably lower performance, thus the need to build resources and tools that specifically target DA (Habash et al., 2012).

The majority of existing NER systems rely on the use of gazetteers to improve the system accuracy (Kazama and Torisawa, 2007), however, large external resources are correlated with higher performance cost. In this paper, we study the impact of word representation and embedding features on Arabic NER performance for Twitter and Dialectal Arabic, and demonstrate that our proposed features show comparable and superior results to other NER systems that use large gazetteers. Our contributions are as follows:

- Show the impact of using word representations and embedding on NER performance;
- Propose a set of features that does not include the use of external resources;
- Produce comparable NER performance to other systems that use large gazetteers.

2 Related Work

Significant amount of work in the area of NER has taken place. In (Nadeau and Sekine, 2007), the authors survey the literature of NER and report on the different sets of used features such as contextual and morphological features. Although more research has been employed in the area of English NER, Arabic NER has been gaining more attention recently. Similar to other languages, several approaches have been used for Arabic NER: Rule-based methods, Statistical Learning methods, and a hybrid of both.

In (Shaalan and Raza, 2009), the authors present rule-based NER system for MSA that comprises gazetteers, local grammars in the form of regular expressions, and a filtering mechanism that mainly focuses on rejecting incorrect NEs based on a blacklist. Their system yields a performance of 87.7% F1 measure for the Person label (PER), 85.9% for Location (LOC), and 83.15% for Organization (ORG) when evaluated against corpora

[1]We use the Buckwalter encoding system to render Arabic. For a reference listing please see http://www.qamus.org/transliteration.htm

developed by the authors. (Elsebai et al., 2009) proposed a rule-based system targeting PER in MSA. It uses the Buckwalter Arabic Morphological Analyser (BAMA) and a set of keywords. The proposed system yields an F-score of 89% when tested on an in-house annotated dataset of 700 news articles extracted from Aljazeera television website.

Although rule based approaches proved successful to some extent, most recent NER research focuses on Statistical Learning techniques due to the shortcomings of rule based approaches in terms of coverage and robustness (Nadeau and Sekine, 2007). For example, (Benajiba et al., 2007) proposes an MSA NER system (ANERsys) based on n-grams and maximum entropy. The authors also introduce ANERCorp corpora and ANERGazet gazetteers. (Benajiba and Rosso, 2008) further modify ANERsys in terms of the underlying machinery to use Conditional Random Fields (CRF) sequence labeling as the statistical learning framework. ANERsys uses the following features: part of speech (POS) tags, Base Phrase Chunks (BPC), gazetteers, and nationality information. The latter feature is included based on the observation that PER occur after mentioning the nationality, in particular in newswire data. In (Benajiba et al., 2008), a different classifier is built for each NE type. The authors study the effect of features on each NE type, then the overall NER system is a combination of the different classifiers that target each NE class label independently. The set of features used is a combination of general features as listed in (Benajiba and Rosso, 2008) and Arabic-dependent (morphological) features. Their system's best performance is 83.5% for ACE 2003, 76.7% for ACE 2004, and 81.31% for ACE 2005, respectively. (Benajiba et al., 2010) presents an Arabic NER system that incorporates lexical, syntactic, and morphological features and augmenting the model with syntactic features derived from noisy data as projected from Arabic-English parallel corpora. The system F-score performance is 81.73%, 75.67%, 58.11% on ACE2005 Broadcast News, Newswire, and Web blogs, respectively. The authors in (Abdul-Hamid and Darwish, 2010) suggest a number of features, some of which we incorporate in our current DA-NER system, namely, the head and trailing 2-grams (L2), 3-grams (L3), and 4-grams (L4) characters in a word. (Abdul-Hamid and Darwish, 2010) produce near state-of-the-art results with the use of generic and language independent features that we use to generate baseline results (BL).
(Shaalan and Oudah, 2014) presents a hybrid approach that targets MSA and produces state-of-the-art results. However, we could not get access to the exact rules employed, we were not able to replicate their results. The rule-based component is identical to their previous proposed rule-based system in (Shaalan and Raza, 2009). The features used in their study are a combination of the rule-based rules in addition to morphological, capitalization, POS tag, word length, and dot (i.e. if a word has an adjacent dot) features. All the previous work mentioned above focused on MSA, albeit with variations in genres to the extent exemplified by the ACE data and author generated data. However, unlike the work mentioned above, (Darwish and Gao, 2014) proposed an NER system that specifically targets microblogs as a genre, as opposed to newswire data. Their proposed language-independent system relies on a set of features that is similar to (Abdul-Hamid and Darwish, 2010), with the use of a simple yet effective domain adaptation approach (Daumé et al., 2010) based on a two-pass semi supervised method. Their NER system on Twitter data yields an overall F-score=65.2% (76.7% for LOC, 55.6% for ORG, and 55.8% for PER).
In our prior work, (Zirikly and Diab, 2014), we proposed a small set of annotated DA data and DA-NER system that yields an F-score=70.3%. We used n-gram, gazetteers and an extensive set of morphological features. In our current work, we explore the impact of using word embedding features and how can word representations and embedding replace the use of dictionaries and even generate better performance.

3 Approach

In this paper, we adopt a supervised machine learning approach. Supervised approaches have been shown to outperform unsupervised approaches for the NER task (Nadeau et al., 2006). We use Conditional Random Fields (CRF) sequence labeling as described in (Lafferty et al., 2001). Guided by previous work, for example (Benajiba and Rosso, 2008) demonstrates that CRF yields better results over other supervised machine learning techniques for the task of NER. One of the goals of our empirical investigation is to show the impact of using skip-gram word embedding and word representations on the NER performance, with the potential of these features substituting the use of extensive large gazetteers.

3.1 Baseline

For our baseline system (BL), we reimplemented the features proposed in (Abdul-Hamid and Darwish, 2010) that produced the best results: previous and next word, and leading and trailing +/- (2-4) character ngrams. These features are chosen as a preferred set for the baseline since they are directly applicable to DA, as none of the features rely on the availability of morphological or syntactic analyzers. This baseline is also adapted from (Darwish and Gao, 2014). We opted for this baseline as opposed to (Darwish and Gao, 2014)'s NER system since they use Wikipedia gazetteers (WikiGaz) for their NER system.[2] However, we report the results of applying their features using exact match against the gazetteers' entries in Section 4.3.

3.2 Our NER Features

In addition to the features employed in the baseline BL, we introduce the following additional features in our NER system:

- **Lexical Features**: character n-gram features, the leading and trailing character bigrams (L2), trigrams (L3), and quadrigrams (L4);

- **Contextual Features** (CTX): The surrounding undiacritized words of a context window $= \pm 1$;(W-1,W0,W1);

- **Gazetteers** (GAZ): Although our work mainly targets NER systems without the use of external sources, but we added GAZ features for comparison purposes. The gazetteer used is the union of: i) ANERGaz: proposed by (Benajiba and Rosso, 2008), which contains 2183 LOC, 402 ORG, and 2308 PER; and ii) WikiGaz: large Wikipedia gazetteer (Darwish and Gao, 2014), which contains 50141 LOC, 17092 ORG, and 65557 PER. We followed this strategy for text matching against gazetteer entries:
  - Exact match (EM-GAZ): For more efficient search, we use Aho-Corasick Algorithm (Aho and Corasick, 1975) that has linear running time in terms of the input length plus the number of matching entries in a gazetteer. When a word sequence matches an entry in the gazetteer;
  - Partial match(PM-GAZ): This feature is created to handle the case of compound gazetteer entries. If the token is part of the compound name then this feature is set to true. For example, if the gazetteer entry is *yAsr ErfAt* 'Yasser Arafat' and the input text is *yAsr BrkAt* then PM-GAZ for the token *yAsr* will be set to true. This is particularly useful in persons names;
  - Levenshtein match (LVM-GAZ): We use Levenshtein distance (Levenshtein, 1966) to compare the similarity between the input and a gazetteer entry. This is based on the observation that social media data might contain non-standard spelling of words since it contains the DA variety.

- **Morphological Features**: The morphological features that we employ in our feature set are generated by MADAMIRA (Pasha et al., 2014). The set comprises the following:
  - Part of Speech (POS) tags: We use POS tags generated from MADAMIRA within a window of ± 1 (POS-1, POS0, POS1);
  - Capitalization (CAPS): In order to circumvent the lack of capitalization in Arabic, we check the capitalization of the translated NE which could indicate that a word is an NE (Benajiba et al., 2008). This feature is dependent on the English gloss generated by MADAMIRA. This feature is set to true when the gloss starts with a capital letter;
  - Aspect (ASP), person (PERS), proclitics0 (PROC0), proclitics1 (PROC1), proclitics2 (PROC2), proclitics3 (PROC3), enclitics0 (ENC0); detailed description for these features is provided in Table 1;

[2] Though the authors kindly gave us access to the actual gazetteer, we were unable to replicate their results since the gazetteer matching method is not detailed in their paper.

Feature	Feature Values
Aspect	Verb aspect: Command, Imperfective, Perfective, Not applicable
Person	Person Information: 1st, 2nd, 3rd, Not applicable
Proclitic3	Question proclitic: No proclitic, Not applicable, Interrogative particle
Proclitic2	Conjunction proclitic: No proclitic, Not applicable, Conjunction *f*, Connective particle *f*, Response conditional *f*, Subordinating conjunction *f*, Conjunction *w*, Particle *w*, Subordinating conjunction *w*
Proclitic1	Preposition proclitic: No proclitic, Not Applicable, Interrogative *i$*, Particle *b*, Preposition *b*, Progressive verb particle *b*, Preposition *E*, Preposition *ElY*, Preposition *fy*, Demonstrative *hA*, Future marker *H*, Preposition *k*, Emphatic particle *l*, Preposition *l*, Preposition *l* + preposition *b*, Emphatic *l* + future marker *H*, Response conditional *l* + future marker *H*, Jussive *l*, Preposition *l*, Preposition *mn*, Future marker *s*, Preposition *t*, Particle *w*, Preposition *w*, Vocative *w*, vocative *yA*
Proclitic	Article proclitic: No proclitic, Not Applicable, Demonstrative particle *A*, Determiner, Determiner *Al* + negative particle *mA*, Negative particle *lA*, Negative particle *mA*, Negative particle *mA*, Particle *mA*, relative pronoun *mA*
Enclitics	Pronominals: No enclitic, Not applicable, 1st person plural/singular, 2nd person dual/plural, 2nd person feminine plural/singular, 2nd person masculine plural/singular, 3rd person dual/plural, 3rd person feminine plural/singular, 3rd person masculine plural/singular, Vocative particle, Negative particle *lA*, Interrogative pronoun *mA*, Interrogative pronoun *mA*, Interrogative pronoun *mn*, Relative pronoun *mn, m, mA*, Subordinating conjunction *m, mA*.

Table 1: Morphological Features

  - isNum: Binary feature that is set to true if the token is a number;
  - isNoun: Binary feature that is set to true if the token is proper noun (i.e. POS=noun_prop).

- **Brown Clustering IDs** (BC): Brown clustering (Brown et al., 1992) is a hierarchical clustering approach that maximizes the mutual information of word bigrams. Word representations, especially Brown Clustering, have been shown to improve the performance of NER system when added as a feature (Turian et al., 2010). In this work, we use Brown Clustering IDs (BC) of variable prefix lengths (4,5,6,7,10,13 and the full length of the cluster ID) as features resulting in the following set of features BC4, BC5, BC6, BC7, BC10, BC13, and BC, respectively. For example if *AmrykA* 'America' has the brown cluster ID BC=11110010 then BC7=1111001, whereas BC10 and BC13 are empty strings. This feature is based on the observation that semantically similar words will be grouped together in the same cluster and will have a common prefix;

- **Word2vec Cluster IDs** : Word2vec is an algorithm for learning embeddings using a neural network model (Mikolov et al., 2013). Embeddings are represented by a set of latent variables, where each word is represented by a specific instantiation of these variables. In our system, we apply K-means clustering on the word vectors and use the clusters IDs as features.

3.3 Datasets

We use Microblogs and Dialectal weblogs datasets for our experiments:

- Twitter dataset: We use the training and test data split proposed in (Darwish, 2013), where the training dataset contains 3,646 tweets which were randomly selected from tweets that were authored in the period of May 3-12, 2012. The tweets were scraped from Twitter using the query lang:ar. The testing data contains 1,423 tweets that were randomly selected from tweets authored between November 23, 2011 and November 27, 2011. This dataset has also been used in (Darwish and Gao, 2014) for testing. Both datasets are annotated using the Linguistics Data Consortium ACE tagging guidelines;

- Dialectal Arabic dataset (DA-EGY): The annotated data was chosen from a set of web blogs that are manually identified by LDC as Egyptian dialect and contains nearly 40k tokens. The data was annotated by one native Arabic speaker annotator who followed the Linguistics Data Consortium guidelines for tagging. We use the same 80/20 train/test 5-fold cross validation split proposed in (Zirikly and Diab, 2014)

Table 2 shows dataset statistics, namely number of tokens, and the named entity types: PER, LOC, and ORG.

Brown Clustering and word2vec Data In our work, we run brown clustering and word2vec three times based on the data genre: i) Newswire

	#Tokens	#PER	#LOC	#ORG
Twitter-Train	55k	788	713	449
Twitter-Test	26k	464	587	316
DA-EGY	24k	311	155	19

Table 2: Twitter and DA-EGY Evaluation data statistics

(NW): Arabic Gigaword, ANERCorp, and NW data of ACE2005 and ACE2006; ii) Broadcast News (BN): BN data of ACE2005 and ACE2006; iii) Weblogs (WL): Twitter data (training and testing), WL data of ACE2005 and ACE2006, and Arabic Dialect[3]. The number of Brown and word2vec clusters is empirically chosen; the best results achieved are: 500, 200, 200 for brown clustering on NW, BN, and WL respectively, as opposed to: 300,150,150 for word2vec on NW, BN, and WL respectively.

Parametric features values We use the following values for the parametric features:

- CTX features: we set context window = ± 1 for words;
- LM-GAZ: Threshold of the number of deletion, insertion, or modification ≤ 2;
- BC: Length of the prefixes of brown clusters ID is set to 4,5,6,7,10,13, and full length of cluster ID.

3.4 Data Normalization and Preprocessing

Arabic normalization has proven to improve retrieval results (Darwish et al., 2012). We apply the following normalizations on training, testing, BC and word2vec input data: i) Number normalizations: $[0-9] \rightarrow 8$; ii) Hamza normalization: hamza numerous forms are used interchangeably depending on the role of a word in the sentence. For instance, the term "his sky" can be written smA&h, smA'h, or smA}h, where the hamza takes its form based on the term being subject, object, or idafa (construct state indicating possessive), respectively $', >, <, \&, \}, |, \{, `, Y \rightarrow A$; iii) Normalizing elongated words: We remove consecutive repeated letters that occur > 2.

Tools In this work, we use the following tools:

1. MADAMIRA (Pasha et al., 2014): For tokenization preprocessing and morphological features such as gender and POS tags;
2. CRFSuite implementation (Okazaki, 2007).

[3]LDC2012T09

4 Experiments & Discussion

4.1 Features set

The list of feature sets used in our experiments are:

- Feature set1 (FS1): Baseline (BL) features, as proposed in (Abdul-Hamid and Darwish, 2010) with the use of exact match against the Wikipedia gazetteers (WikiGaz) for PER, LOC, and ORG named entity types;
- Feature set2 (FS2): BL features with the use of CAPS (English gloss capitalization) and the current, previous and next POS;
- Feature set3 (FS3): FS2 features in addition to ENC0, PROC0, PROC1, PROC2, PROC3, as demonstrated in Table 1;
- Feature set4 (FS4): FS3 in addition to isNum, isNoun binary features;
- Feature set5 (FS5): FS4 features with the use of word2vec cluster IDs;
- Feature set6 (FS6): FS4 features with the use of BC cluster IDs with different prefixes length;
- Feature set7 (FS7): FS6 features with the use of word2vec cluster IDs;
- Feature set8 (FS8): FS7 features with the use of exact (EM-GAZ) and partial (PM-GAZ) match against WikiGaz gazetteers' entries;
- Feature set9 (FS9): FS8 features in addition to the use of Levenshtein gazetteers' entires match with distance threshold set to 1 (LVM-GAZ1);
- Feature set10 (FS10): FS7 features in addition to the use of Levenshtein gazetteers' entires match with distance threshold set to 2 (LVM-GAZ2);
- Feature set11 (FS11): FS8 features in addition to LVM-GAZ1 and LVM-GAZ2;
- Feature set12 (FS12): FS11 with the use pf ASP and PERS morphological features;
- Feature set13 (FS13): FS7 in addition to ASP and PERS features;
- Feature set14 (FS14): FS6 in addition to ASP and PERS features;
- Feature set15 (FS15): FS5 in addition to ASP and PERS features;

4.2 Evaluation Metrics

We choose precision (PREC), recall (REC), and harmonic F-measure (F1) metrics to evaluate the performance of our NER system over accuracy. This decision is based on the observation that the baseline accuracy is always high as the majority of the words in free text are not named entities.

4.3 Results & Discussion

Twitter Results: Table 3 illustrates results of our NER system performance. We use the weighted macro-average across the three NEs (PER, LOC, ORG) to calculate the overall performance. Although we were not able to replicate (Darwish and Gao, 2014) results with WikiGaz (F1=55% vs. 51.62%), but our proposed features coupled with BC and word2vec surpass their performance yielding an F1=57.84% without the use of any external resources vs. 59.59% with the use of gazetteers.[4] Although word2vec and BC increase F1 $\approx$ 10% over BL, we note that BC impact (+6%) is more significant in comparison to word2vec with only 3% improvement. It is worth mentioning that this is aligned with (Turian et al., 2010) observations that Brown Clustering yields better English NER performance as opposed to word embedding. This is due to Brown Clustering's ability to induce rare words compared to word embedding. We also note that our intuition for using Levenshtein Matching approach, LVM-GAZ, against gazetteers' entries to overcome non-standardization issue in DA shows 0.8% improvement over EX-GAZ and PAR-GAZ. We should note that LVM-GAZ very much depends on the percentage of present DA variety in the data. The results achieved are promising, especially in the area of social media since generating gazetteers that have high coverage is a challenging and expensive task.

When observing the MORPH feature set in more details, we notice that CAPS and POS yield the highest improvement over the baseline, especially in the PER class, this is mainly due to the correct assignment of the Proper Noun POS tag to this class confirming that POS tag is a strong indicator for NE.

We study the impact of applying BC and word2vec on different data genre. We take as an example BC, shown in Figure 1. We note that genre variations impose minimum impact on word representations, thus we can induce that word2vec and BC presents robust and domain-independent features.

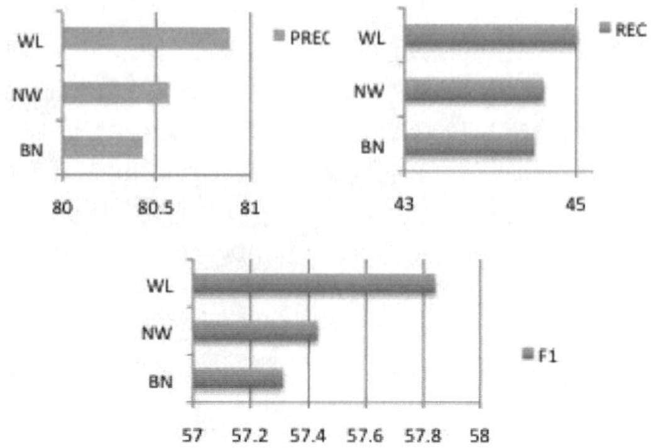

Figure 1: BC Data Genre and Performance correlation

DA-EGY Results: We apply the feature sets that yields the best result with and without the use of gazetteers in Table 3 to our second evaluation dataset DA-EGY. The reported result is the average of 5-fold cross validation. As proposed in (Zirikly and Diab, 2014), we omit ORG class because there is less than 0.05% instances of ORG in the annotated data, which does not represent a fair training data to the system. Our system outperforms the state-of-the-art results by $\approx$ 7% with the use of gazetteers, and $\approx$ 2% without the use of gazetteers. As shown in Table 4, we notice that FS15, which uses word2vec features and excludes BC features and gazetteers, generate very comparable results (72.61%) to the best gazetteers-free performance achieved 72.68%.

5 Conclusion & Future Work

In this paper we study the impact of word representations and embedding on Arabic NER system for social media data. We show that our proposed gazetteers-free features surpass other NER systems that use large gazetteers. This is a significant advantage since gazetteers are expensive to generate, especially in the area of social media due to the low coverage of dictionaries. We show that our proposed system improves NER performance and outperforms state-of-the-art results for Dialectal Arabic.

In future work, we would like to test the impact of cross-lingual word embedding and representation

[4] It should be noted that our use of the gazetteers is probably different from theirs thereby rendering our results with gazetteers incomparable to their results.

	LOC	ORG	PER	Overall		
	F1	F1	F1	PREC	REC	F1
BL	49.15	38.38	48.78	83.25	31.77	45.99
BL+WikiGaz (Darwish and Gao, 2014)	65.5	41.5	48.5	79.3	42.1	55
FS1=BL + EX-GAZ (LOC,ORG,PER)	52.37	41.72	57.09	83.07	37.44	51.62
FS2=BL+CAPS+POS[-1,0,1]	51.23	38.6	59.2	79.89	38.1	51.59
FS3=FS2 +PROC{3,2,1,0}+ENC0	51.73	39.55	60.78	79.01	39.53	52.7
FS4=FS3+isNum+isNoun	51.56	39.48	60.91	79.11	39.53	52.72
FS5=FS4+word2vec	53.18	38.37	62.74	79.54	40.57	53.74
FS6=FS4+BC	55.41	40.46	65.02	81.83	42.6	56.03
FS7=FS6+word2vec	56.78	39.74	65.58	82.01	43.12	56.52
FS8=FS7+EX-GAZ+PAR-GAZ	58.02	41.87	67.09	81.83	44.94	58.02
FS9=FS8+LVM-GAZ1	58.1	40.71	67.33	81.25	44.94	57.87
FS10=FS7+LVM-GAZ2	59.63	41.4	67.39	81.71	45.47	58.42
FS11=FS9+LVM-GAZ2	59.63	41.28	68.17	81.93	45.86	58.8
FS12=FS11+ASP+PERS	61.03	41.28	68.92	81.7	46.9	**59.59**
FS13=FS7+ASP+PERS	58.29	38.11	68.32	80.89	45.01	**57.84**

Table 3: Twitter NER Results

	LOC	PER	Overall		
	F1	F1	PREC	REC	F1
State-of-the-art	91.43	49.18	86.53	62.3	70.31
FS12	96.77	57.47	82.9	72.39	**77.12**
FS13	89.66	55.7	86.67	63.08	**72.68**
FS14	89.66	54.05	90	61.04	*71.86*
FS15	89.66	55.56	93.48	61.04	*72.61*

Table 4: DA-EGY NER Results

features on NER performance and test our system with numerous different domains.

6 Acknowledgment

This work was supported by the Defense Advanced Research Projects Agency (DARPA) Contract No. HR0011-12-C-0014, the BOLT program with subcontract from Raytheon BBN. We would like to thank three anonymous reviewers for their comprehensive feedback

References

Sherief Abdallah, Khaled Shaalan, and Muhammad Shoaib. 2012. Integrating rule-based system with classification for arabic named entity recognition. In *Computational Linguistics and Intelligent Text Processing*, pages 311–322. Springer.

Ahmed Abdul-Hamid and Kareem Darwish. 2010. Simplified feature set for arabic named entity recognition. In *Proceedings of the 2010 Named Entities Workshop*, NEWS '10, pages 110–115, Stroudsburg, PA, USA. Association for Computational Linguistics.

Alfred V. Aho and Margaret J. Corasick. 1975. Efficient string matching: An aid to bibliographic search. *Commun. ACM*, 18(6):333–340, June.

Yassine Benajiba and Paolo Rosso. 2008. Arabic named entity recognition using conditional random fields. In *Proc. of Workshop on HLT & NLP within the Arabic World, LREC*, volume 8, pages 143–153. Citeseer.

Yassine Benajiba, Paolo Rosso, and José-Miguel Benedí. 2007. Anersys: An arabic named entity recognition system based on maximum entropy. In *CICLing*, pages 143–153.

Yassine Benajiba, Mona Diab, and Paolo Rosso. 2008. Arabic named entity recognition using optimized feature sets. In *Proceedings of the Conference on Empirical Methods in Natural Language Processing*, pages 284–293. Association for Computational Linguistics.

Yassine Benajiba, Mona Diab, and Paolo Rosso. 2009. Arabic named entity recognition: A feature-driven study. *Audio, Speech, and Language Processing, IEEE Transactions on*, 17(5):926–934.

Yassine Benajiba, Imed Zitouni, Mona Diab, and Paolo Rosso. 2010. Arabic named entity recognition: Using features extracted from noisy data. In *Proceedings of the ACL 2010 Conference Short Papers*, ACLShort '10, pages 281–285, Stroudsburg, PA, USA. Association for Computational Linguistics.

Peter F Brown, Peter V Desouza, Robert L Mercer, Vincent J Della Pietra, and Jenifer C Lai. 1992. Class-based n-gram models of natural language. *Computational linguistics*, 18(4):467–479.

Kareem Darwish and Wei Gao. 2014. Simple effective microblog named entity recognition: Arabic as an example. In *Proceedings of the Ninth International Conference on Language Resources and Evaluation (LREC-2014), Reykjavik, Iceland, May 26-31, 2014.*, pages 2513–2517.

Kareem Darwish, Walid Magdy, and Ahmed Mourad. 2012. Language processing for arabic microblog retrieval. In *Proceedings of the 21st ACM International Conference on Information and Knowledge Management*, CIKM '12, pages 2427–2430, New York, NY, USA. ACM.

Kareem Darwish. 2013. Named entity recognition using cross-lingual resources: Arabic as an example. In *Proceedings of the 51st Annual Meeting of the Association for Computational Linguistics (Volume 1: Long Papers)*, pages 1558–1567, Sofia, Bulgaria, August. Association for Computational Linguistics.

Hal Daumé, III, Abhishek Kumar, and Avishek Saha. 2010. Frustratingly easy semi-supervised domain adaptation. In *Proceedings of the 2010 Workshop on Domain Adaptation for Natural Language Processing*, DANLP 2010, pages 53–59, Stroudsburg, PA, USA. Association for Computational Linguistics.

Ali Elsebai, Farid Meziane, and Fatma Zohra Belkredim. 2009. A rule based persons names arabic extraction system. *Communications of the IBIMA*, 11(6):53–59.

Sergio Ferrndez, Antonio Toral, scar Ferrndez, Antonio Ferrndez, and Rafael Muoz. 2007. Applying wikipedias multilingual knowledge to cross-lingual question answering. In *In Zoubida Kedad, Nadira Lammari, Elisabeth Mtais, Farid Meziane, and Yacine Rezgui, editors, NLDB, volume 4592 of Lecture Notes in Computer Science*. Springer.

Nizar Habash, Mona T Diab, and Owen Rambow. 2012. Conventional orthography for dialectal arabic. In *LREC*, pages 711–718.

Nizar Habash, Ryan Roth, Owen Rambow, Ramy Eskander, and Nadi Tomeh. 2013. Morphological analysis and disambiguation for dialectal arabic. In *Human Language Technologies: Conference of the North American Chapter of the Association of Computational Linguistics, Proceedings, June 9-14, 2013, Westin Peachtree Plaza Hotel, Atlanta, Georgia, USA*, pages 426–432.

Jun'ichi Kazama and Kentaro Torisawa. 2007. Exploiting wikipedia as external knowledge for named entity recognition. In *Joint Conference on Empirical Methods in Natural Language Processing and Computational Natural Language Learning*.

John Lafferty, Andrew McCallum, and Fernando CN Pereira. 2001. Conditional random fields: Probabilistic models for segmenting and labeling sequence data.

Vladimir I Levenshtein. 1966. Binary codes capable of correcting deletions, insertions and reversals. In *Soviet physics doklady*, volume 10, page 707.

Tomas Mikolov, Ilya Sutskever, Kai Chen, Greg S Corrado, and Jeff Dean. 2013. Distributed representations of words and phrases and their compositionality. In *Advances in Neural Information Processing Systems*, pages 3111–3119.

David Nadeau and Satoshi Sekine. 2007. A survey of named entity recognition and classification. *Lingvisticae Investigationes*, 30(1):3–26.

David Nadeau, Peter Turney, and Stan Matwin. 2006. Unsupervised named-entity recognition: Generating gazetteers and resolving ambiguity.

Naoaki Okazaki. 2007. Crfsuite: A fast implementation of conditional random fields (crfs).

Arfath Pasha, Mohamed Al-Badrashiny, Ahmed El Kholy, Ramy Eskander, Mona Diab, Nizar Habash, Manoj Pooleery, Owen Rambow, and Ryan Roth. 2014. Madamira: A fast, comprehensive tool for morphological analysis and disambiguation of arabic. In *In Proceedings of the 9th International Conference on Language Resources and Evaluation, Reykjavik, Iceland*.

Alan Ritter, Sam Clark, Mausam, and Oren Etzioni. 2011. Named entity recognition in tweets: An experimental study. In *Proceedings of the Conference on Empirical Methods in Natural Language Processing*, EMNLP '11, pages 1524–1534, Stroudsburg, PA, USA. Association for Computational Linguistics.

Khaled Shaalan and Mai Oudah. 2014. A hybrid approach to arabic named entity recognition. *Journal of Information Science*, 40(1):67–87.

Khaled Shaalan and Hafsa Raza. 2009. Nera: Named entity recognition for arabic. *Journal of the American Society for Information Science and Technology*, 60(8):1652–1663.

Khaled Shaalan. 2014. A survey of arabic named entity recognition and classification. *Comput. Linguist.*, 40(2):469–510, June.

Paul Thompson and Christopher C. Dozier. 1997. Name searching and information retrieval. In *In Proceedings of Second Conference on Empirical Methods in Natural Language Processing*, pages 134–140.

Joseph Turian, Lev Ratinov, and Yoshua Bengio. 2010. Word representations: A simple and general method for semi-supervised learning. In *Proceedings of the 48th Annual Meeting of the Association for Computational Linguistics*, pages 384–394. Association for Computational Linguistics.

Ayah Zirikly and Mona Diab. 2014. Named entity recognition system for dialectal arabic. In *Proceedings of the EMNLP 2014 Workshop on Arabic Natural Language Processing (ANLP)*, pages 78–86, Doha, Qatar, October. Association for Computational Linguistics.

Vector Space and Language Models for Scientific Document Summarization

John M. Conroy
IDA Center for Computing Sciences
17100 Science Drive
Bowie, MD 20708, USA
conroy@super.org

Sashka T. Davis
IDA Center for Computing Sciences
17100 Science Drive
Bowie, MD 20708, USA
stdavi3@super.org

Abstract

In this paper we compare the performance of three approaches for estimating the latent weights of terms for scientific document summarization, given the document and a set of citing documents. The first approach is a term-frequency (TF) vector space method utilizing a nonnegative matrix factorization (NNMF) for dimensionality reduction. The other two are language modeling approaches for predicting the term distributions of human-generated summaries. The language model we build exploits the key sections of the document and a set of citing sentences derived from auxiliary documents that cite the document of interest. The parameters of the model may be set via a minimization of the Jensen-Shannon (JS) divergence. We use the OCCAMS algorithm (Optimal Combinatorial Covering Algorithm for Multi-document Summarization) to select a set of sentences that maximizes the term-coverage score while minimizing redundancy. The results are evaluated with standard ROUGE metrics, and the performance of the resulting methods achieve ROUGE scores exceeding those of the average human summarizer.

1 Introduction

The volume of the scientific literature is vast and increasing. It is commonly impossible for researchers to read all the papers published even in their own specialty, thus it is natural to apply text summarization methods to scientific literature. The problem we consider is to summarize a scientific paper that has been cited multiple times, given the paper (*reference paper*) and a set of citing papers. Note that the citing papers give additional insights into the impact of the results presented in the original paper and also how the paper is perceived by colleagues. Following the approach of Qazvinian et al. (Qazvinian and Radev, 2008), we use the citing papers to help inform the summary, but also build a language model to cover the major sections of the paper such as the abstract and the results sections. Thus, we form a summary pooling information from the paper and how other authors citing the paper view the contributions of the paper.

The summarization system we consider for this task consists of the following components:

1. **Data Preprocessing and Segmentation**
   The reference document is processed, the individual sections of the paper (when present) are isolated and extracted, and the document is then sentence split.

2. **Term Selection**
   Terms are formed with stemmed word bigrams whose mutual information is significantly high.

3. **Latent Term Weight Estimation**
   We explore two distinct approaches:

   (a) **A Vector Space Model** based on a term-frequency (TF) matrix representation of the document and a nonnegative matrix factorization (NNMF) approximation for rank reduction.

   (b) **A Bigram Language Model** built on the selected bigrams for each document section. The global language model is a

Proceedings of NAACL-HLT 2015, pages 186–191,
Denver, Colorado, May 31 – June 5, 2015. ©2015 Association for Computational Linguistics

convex combination of the section models. Each term is given a weight, which is an estimate of the probability that a term would occur in a human-generated summary.

4. **Sentence Selection**
   We use the OCCAMS algorithm (Optimal Combinatorial Coverage Algorithm for Multi-Document Summarization) to select the sentences.

In this paper, we use the Biomedical Summarization data[1] recently released by the National Institute of Standards (NIST) to evaluate our approaches. The Biomedical data consists of 20 documents (*reference* papers), each with 10 documents that cite it (*citation* papers), a human-generated summary, and set of citation sentences extracted from the citation papers. (The citation sentences are the sentences of the citation papers that refer to the reference documents.)

In section 3 we describe in details how these data were preprocessed for the summarization task.

2 Related Work

In (Teufel and Moens, 2002) the authors use rhetorical status of statements in a scientific article to produce a summary. They use machine learning to identify rhetorical structure and produce extracted sentences from the source document by filling in a template to produce a summary. In (Qazvinian and Radev, 2008) the authors use the citation network to produce a summary of a scientific article and thereby put the focus on what other authors wrote about a paper as the prominent information to include in a summary of a paper in the scientific literature. They thus summarize a scientific document by what other authors have written about the document. In contrast with (Teufel and Moens, 2002) and (Qazvinian and Radev, 2008), in this paper, we use the sections of the document and machine learning to estimate the relative importance of the sections of the document as well as the citing sentences that reflect what other authors write about the referenced document. Jensen-Shannon (JS) divergence correlate as well or better with human judgments of a summary's quality than ROUGE scoring for multidocument summarization (Lin et al., 2006). In (Louis and Nenkova, 2009) the authors demonstrated that JS divergence between automatically generated summaries and the distribution of terms of the document yields a metric for evaluating summaries without the need for human-generated summaries. These results suggest that JS-divergence is correlated with the intrinsic quality of a summary. We therefore employ JS-divergence and use both the provided human summaries, and optionally the extracted text, to learn the distribution of terms as would be used in a human-generated summary.

3 Data Segmentation and Preprocessing

Each document from the NIST Biomedical collection contains one reference paper, a set of citation papers, and an annotation file containing citation sentences (*citances*). The vast majority of the biomedical papers (both reference and citation papers) had a common structure. All but two of the papers contained a well-defined *Abstract* or a *Summary* section; most papers contained a *Results* section; and all concluded with a *Reference Bibliography* section. We removed the Reference Bibliography because its content is inappropriate for summarization. The body of the reference paper was partitioned into three parts: abstract, results and other. The abstract and the result parts contained the body of the *Abstract* (or *Summary*) and the *Results* sections, respectively, if they were present. All remaining sections[2] of the paper were extracted and were used for forming the other part of the paper. We also extracted the citances from the annotation file into a separate part, called citations. We used the entire body of the reference paper except the *Reference Bibliography* and the citations part to build the vector space model, and we used the abstract, results, other, and citations parts for the language model approach for latent term weight estimation.

We trimmed the sentences of the abstract, results, other, and citations parts to remove quoted, parenthetical or citation text. Doing this trimming im-

[1]http://www.nist.gov/tac/2014/BiomedSumm.

[2]Some papers contained subject specific sections or *Methodology*, or *Discussion* sections but they were not common across the entire collection.

proves the fidelity of the summarization. Finally, all parts of the paper were segmented into individual sentences.

4 Term Selection

Term selection first begins by finding a good background model and then using it to select a set of stemmed word bigrams that occur *significantly more often than expected*, specifically, we calculate the frequency of each stemmed bigram in a document set as well as the frequency of the stemmed bigram in a background corpus of biomedical abstracts from PubMed (National Institute of Health, 2014). We employ the $G-$statistic, which is equivalent to a mutual information statistic. This statistic was first suggested by Ted Dunning (Dunning, 1993) to identify "surprise words" and in context of summarization, Lin and Hovy (Lin and Hovy, 2000) referred to them as "signature terms." The statistic computes likelihood ratio and the p-value is computed under the assumption null hypothesis that a given term occurs with the same probability in the background as the document set.

Here, instead of finding a small set of topic signature terms as proposed by (Lin and Hovy, 2000), we use Dunning's statistic to remove terms for which the p-value is 0.001 or larger. For this threshold about 40% of the bigrams will remain in lieu of a topic signature model where $10-50$ bigrams remain.

5 Sentence Selection

We use the OCCAMS algorithm (Davis et al., 2012) to select sentences for the final summary. OCCAMS uses techniques from combinatorial optimization (approximation schemes for budgeted maximal coverage and the knapsack problems) to select a set of minimally overlapping sentences, whose combined weight of terms covered is maximized. OCCAMS views the document as a set of sentences. Each sentence is viewed as a set of terms. The input to the algorithm is the sentences of the document; the lengths of the sentences, measured as the number of words; and the latent weights of the terms, computed in sections 6 and 7, for the two models we study. (Conroy et al., 2013) gives an improved version of the original OCCAMS algorithm (Davis et al., 2012) that computes four potential summaries and chooses the one of maximal combined term-weight coverage as the final summary. OCCAMS has a minimal sentence length parameter that one can use to discard sentences whose lengths (number of words) falls below the specified minimal-length threshold. The biomedical documents we summarized had a higher-than-average sentence length, and we used a threshold of 10 words per sentence, to generate our result summaries. Summaries containing longer sentences improve readability of the summaries generated (sentences containing nine words or less were discarded), while shorter sentences improve scores computed by automatic metrics.

6 Vector Space Model

The paper (Conroy et al., 2013) investigated the performance of a variety of vector space models together with a variety of algebraic dimensionality reduction techniques (LSA, LDA, and NNMF) to summarize multi-lingual documents. In this paper we consider a simple and well known vector space model for text, namely the term frequency model, and explore the use of NNMF to derive improved term weights for scientific document summarization. To build a term-by-sentence matrix we use the abstract, results, citances, and other parts of the reference paper, which is equivalent to taking the entire body of the paper excluding the *Reference Bibliogrpahy.* We use only bigram terms with high mutual information to form the terms of the document. The (i, j)th component of the matrix A is the frequency of the ith term in the jth sentence. We use the MATLAB^{TM} *nnmf()* function, with 100 random restarts and the alternating least squares option, to compute a rank k approximation of the column stochastic matrix derived from the term-sentence matrix A by scaling the columns to sum to 1. Let $\tilde{A}$ be this column stochastic matrix and the NNMF of this matrix gives $\tilde{A} \approx WH$, where W and H are nonnegative and W has k columns and H has k rows. The weights of the terms given to the OCCAMS algorithm are chosen to be the row sums of WH.

Table 1 shows ROUGE 1, 2, 3, and 4 scores of OCCAMS summaries given estimates of the latent weights of terms for values of the rank $k = 2, 4$, and 35. In our experiments we computed NNMF

System	R1	R2	R3	R4
TF	0.511	0.166	0.065	0.030
NNMF_2	0.509	0.172	0.073	**0.036**
NNMF_4	0.504	0.171	**0.074**	0.036
NNMF_35	**0.518**	**0.176**	0.070	0.033
Avg Human	**0.528**	**0.179**	**0.075**	**0.036**
Best Human	0.572	0.219	0.110	0.071

Table 1: Vector Space Model based on TF and NNMF

approximations for all values of $k \in [1, 50]$ but did not observe improvements of the score beyond the scores shown in Table 1. Our experiments show that the NNMF rank approximation of the matrix results in improved ROUGE scores compared to the baseline TF. It is also worth noting that the ROUGE scores of the best rank approximations are close to those of the averaged human ROUGE scores.

7 A Language Modeling Approach for Scientific Document Summarization

We consider a language modeling approach to estimate the importance of the terms in the referenced document to be summarized. This model is designed to estimate the probability that a term will occur in a human-generated summary of the referenced document. As described in section 3 a referenced document may be divided into abstract, results, and other parts and these in addition to the citances represent the "components" of the document, which are used to build the language model for the referenced document.

Specifically, we let $p_{i,j}^{(d)}$ be the estimate of the probability that term i occurs in document component j for the referenced document d. The estimate $\hat{p}_{i,j}^{(d)}$ is computed by the maximum likelihood estimate using the counts, and we then have

$$\sum_i \hat{p}_{i,j}^{(d)} = 1.$$

The probability that term i will occur in a human-generated summary of document d is given by $q_i^{(d)}$ and we estimated it for the purposes of training it in one of two ways. The first is simply the maximum likelihood model which sums the frequency observed in the human-generated summaries and then normalizes to form a probability distribution. We denote this estimate as $\hat{q}_i^{(d)}$.

The second estimate for $q_i^{(d)}$ uses a discount model and has a free parameter $\lambda^{(d)}$ with $0 \leq \lambda^{(d)} \leq 1$, which is used to compute a convex combination of the estimates $\hat{q}$ and the estimated probability distribution formed by human selected "referenced sentences." The referenced sentences are those sentences in the reference document that best support the information given in the citances and were selected by the humans as they were gathering information to create their summaries. We let $\hat{r}_i^{(d)}$ be the maximum likelihood estimate that term i occurs in a reference sentence. The discount model estimate of $q^{(d)}$ is then given by

$$\tilde{q}^{(d)} = \lambda \hat{r}^{(d)} + (1 - \lambda)\hat{q}^{(d)}.$$

While discount model provides an opportunity to smooth estimates, we defer its study to a later paper since 10 document sets proved insufficient to demonstrate a significant improvement.

7.1 Training the Language Model

We model the distribution of the terms in the human summaries as a simple mixture of the document components. As such, we expect that for a given document set d there exists a set of parameters α_i for $i = 1, 2, ..., k$ where k is the number of components in the document set, such that

$$\tau(\alpha, \lambda) = \sum_i \alpha_i p_{i,j}^{(d)} \approx \tilde{q}^{(d)}. \qquad (7.1.1)$$

Solving this equation in the least squares sense for both the parameters α and λ is the classical method of canonical correlation (Seber, 2004). Alternatively, we could seek to minimize a divergence function such as JS, i.e.,

$$[\alpha, \lambda] = \text{argmin JSD}(\sum_i \alpha_i p_{i,j}^{(d)}, \tilde{q}^{(d)}).$$

As first observed by (Lin et al., 2006) JS-divergence predicts as well as ROUGE, and it has continuous derivatives. The result of the training gives an optimal values of α and λ, and for each term t a term weight $\tau_t(\alpha, \lambda)$, which is an estimate of the probability that a term will occur in a human-generated summary given the component decomposition and the training data. The optional smoothing parameter, λ used for mixing human summaries with the set of human extracts can be forced to 1 and the optimal α can be computed from approximating the human abstract bigram distribution alone giving the term-weights for the unsmoothed probabilities. In addition to the term-weights, recall that a background model is used to discard bigrams with low mutual information as was described in section 4. The low mutual information terms are thus given a weight of 0.

7.2 Two Simple Language Models

Before discussing results of an optimized language model, we consider the special case of equal weighting of each document section. Recall that the sections of interest for summarization were limited to the abstract, results, other parts, and the citing sentences from the documents that reference the document to be summarized. We consider the following two simple language models on the set of significantly high mutual information bigrams. In the first model we build a language model by combining the four sections into one (LM_1), and in the second model we compute the maximum likelihood for each section of the document combine them with equal weighting (LM_4^{equal}). The ROUGE-1, 2, 3, and 4 scores of LM_1 and LM_4^{equal} as well as the best and average of the nine human summarizer scores are given in Table 7.2. The lengths of both the machine and human generated summaries were limited to 250 words. Each of the differences between the ROUGE scores of LM_1 and LM_4^{equal} are statistically significant at or above the 99% confidence level. We note that LM_1 performs comparably with TF baseline, whose term weights differ only by a scale factor. Furthermore, the equal weighting model scores higher than the average human and significantly better than even the NNMF methods given in section 6. Finally, we note that LM_4^{opt}, the language model that results via the JS optimization described in section 7.1, gives a slight improvement in each of the ROUGE scores, but there is no statistically significant difference between the ROUGE scores for LM_4^{opt} and LM_4^{equal}.

To measure the stability of the weighting coefficients learned by the optimization we performed 1000 trials of the optimization. In each trial a random subset of 10 of the reference papers and citances were chosen to perform the JS optimization. Figure 1 gives a notched box plot of the result of the experiment. The experiment demonstrates that the result section is given a significantly higher weight than the citations. Surprisingly the abstract is given the lowest weight. Note that the median abstract length of a doucment is about 145 words while human generated summaries are 250 words. Clearly, the human summarizers, having the freedom to write a summary longer than the median abstract length, chose to focused on the results section and the citances and did not draw mainly from the abstract.

System	R1	R2	R3	R4
LM_1	0.511	0.169	0.067	0.031
LM_4^{equal}	0.559	0.210	0.095	0.052
LM_4^{opt}	0.562	0.216	0.100	0.055
Avg Human	0.528	0.179	0.075	0.036
Best Human	0.572	0.219	0.110	0.071

Table 2: ROUGE Results for Three Language Models and a Comparison to Human Performance

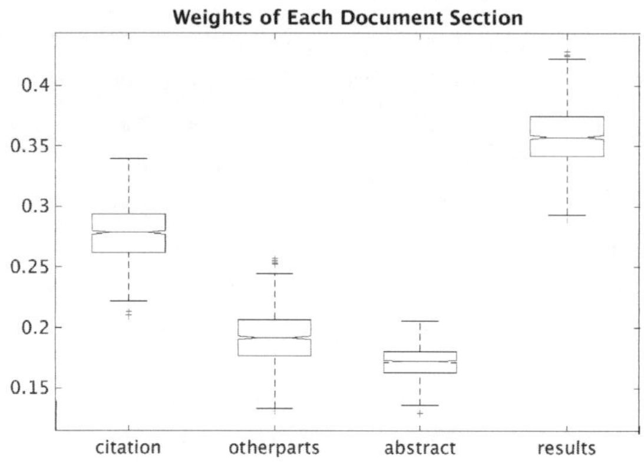

Figure 1: Language Model Coefficients for Document Sections

8 Conclusions

In this paper we compared the performance of a simple vector space model and two language modeling approaches for estimating the latent weights of the terms for scientific document summarization[3] that exploit the underlying structure of the document. Our vector space model uses the TF representation of the text and a low rank approximation of the term-sentence matrix using NNMF. The TF vector space model is a good basic model, but we showed that it benefits from low rank NNMF approximation. The ROUGE scores of the summaries computed with NNMF exceeded those of the basic TF and were close to the average human ROUGE score. However given the humanly generated segmentation of a scientific paper (the sections abstract, result, other, and citances of the document) gives rise to a stronger language model that we show achieves a performance exceeding that of the average human in four ROUGE measures.

Acknowledgments

The authors would like to thank Jeff Kubina for his selection of the background corpus, PubMed, which was used in this work. In addition, we like to thank Dianne P. O'Leary and Judith D. Schlesinger for fruitful discussion and feedback on the training summaries. Finally, we thank Julie M. Conroy for her editing of this paper and for the suggestions by Jeff Kubina and Libby Beer, all of which made for a clearer and stronger paper.

References

John M. Conroy, Sashka T. Davis, Jeff Kubina, Yi-Kai Liu, Dianne P. O'Leary, and Judith D. Schlesinger. 2013. Multilingual Summarization: Dimensionality Reduction and a Step Towards Optimal Term Coverage. In *MultiLing Workshop*, pages 55–63.

Sashka T. Davis, John M. Conroy, and Judith D. Schlesinger. 2012. OCCAMS - An Optimal Combinatorial Covering Algorithm for Multi-document Summarization. In Jilles Vreeken, Charles Ling, Mohammed Javeed Zaki, Arno Siebes, Jeffrey Xu Yu, Bart Goethals, Geoffrey I. Webb, and Xindong Wu, editors, *ICDM Workshops*, pages 454–463. IEEE Computer Society.

Ted Dunning. 1993. Accurate methods for the statistics of surprise and coincidence. *Computational Linguistics*, 19(1):61–74.

[3]The models were applied to the NIST Biomedical Summarization data.

Chin-Yew Lin and Eduard Hovy. 2000. The automated acquisition of topic signatures for text summarization. In *Proceedings of the 18th conference on Computational linguistics*, pages 495–501, Morristown, NJ, USA. Association for Computational Linguistics.

Chin-Yew Lin, Guihong Cao, Jianfeng Gao, and Jian-Yun Nie. 2006. An information-theoretic approach to automatic evaluation of summaries. In *Proceedings of the Main Conference on Human Language Technology Conference of the North American Chapter of the Association of Computational Linguistics*, HLT-NAACL '06, pages 463–470, Stroudsburg, PA, USA. Association for Computational Linguistics.

Annie Louis and Ani Nenkova. 2009. Automatically evaluating content selection in summarization without human models. In *Proceedings of the 2009 Conference on Empirical Methods in Natural Language Processing*, pages 306–314, Singapore, August. Association for Computational Linguistics.

The National Institute of Health. 2014. Pubmed. *http://www.ncbi.nlm.nih.gov/pubmed.*

Vahed Qazvinian and Dragomir R. Radev. 2008. Scientific paper summarization using citation summary networks. In *Proceedings of the 22Nd International Conference on Computational Linguistics - Volume 1*, COLING '08, pages 689–696, Stroudsburg, PA, USA. Association for Computational Linguistics.

G.A.F. Seber. 2004. *Multivariate observations*. Wiley series in probability and statistics. Wiley-Interscience.

Simone Teufel and Marc Moens. 2002. Summarizing scientific articles - experiments with relevance and rhetorical status. *Computational Linguistics*, 28:2002.

Unsupervised Topic Modeling for Short Texts Using Distributed Representations of Words

Vivek Kumar Rangarajan Sridhar*
AT&T Labs
1 AT&T Way, Bedminster, NJ 07920

Abstract

We present an unsupervised topic model for short texts that performs soft clustering over distributed representations of words. We model the low-dimensional semantic vector space represented by the dense distributed representations of words using Gaussian mixture models (GMMs) whose components capture the notion of *latent topics*. While conventional topic modeling schemes such as probabilistic latent semantic analysis (pLSA) and latent Dirichlet allocation (LDA) need aggregation of short messages to avoid data sparsity in short documents, our framework works on large amounts of raw short texts (billions of words). In contrast with other topic modeling frameworks that use word co-occurrence statistics, our framework uses a vector space model that overcomes the issue of sparse word co-occurrence patterns. We demonstrate that our framework outperforms LDA on short texts through both subjective and objective evaluation. We also show the utility of our framework in learning topics and classifying short texts on Twitter data for English, Spanish, French, Portuguese and Russian.

1 Introduction

A popular way to infer semantics in an unsupervised manner is to model a document as a mixture of latent *topics*. Several schemes such as latent semantic analysis (Deerwester et al., 1990), probabilistic latent semantic analysis (pLSA) (Hofmann, 1999) and latent Dirichlet allocation (LDA) (Blei et al., 2003) have been used to good success in inferring the high level meaning of documents through a set of representative words (*topics*). However, the notion of a document has changed immensely over the last decade. Users have embraced new communication and information medium such as short messaging service (SMS), chats, Twitter, Facebook posts, Instagram and user comments on news pages/blogs in place of emails and conventional news websites. Document sizes have been reduced from a few hundred words to few hundred characters[1] while the amount of data has increased exponentially.

Conventional topic models such as pLSA and LDA learn latent topics in a corpus by exploiting document-level word co-ocurrences. Hence, these models typically suffer from data sparsity (estimating reliable word co-occurrence statistics) when applied to short documents. A popular strategy to overcome this bottleneck is to aggregate short texts into longer documents based on user information, title category, etc. (Weng et al., 2010; Hong and Davison, 2010). However, these schemes are heuristic and highly dependent on the data. Furthermore, such metadata may not be available for short texts such as news titles, advertisements or image captions.

In this work, we present an unsupervised topic model that uses soft clustering over distributed representations of words. The distributed word representations are obtained by using a log-linear model and we model the low-dimensional semantic vector space represented by the dense word vectors using Gaussian mixture models (GMMs). The K components of the Gaussian mixture model can be considered as the latent topics that are captured by the model. Unlike long documents, these short messages do not have long distance syntactic or semantic dependencies and we find that the distributed representations learned over limited context windows is sufficient in capturing the distributional similarity of words within a message. In comparison with previous approaches to topic modeling, we completely ignore the distribution over documents and consider the entire corpus, thereby eliminating the need for aggregation over short messages. The framework presented here is

*The author is currently with Apple, Inc., and can be contacted at vrangarajansridh@apple.com.

[1]Twitter currently imposes a limit of 140 characters for each message

Proceedings of NAACL-HLT 2015, pages 192–200,
Denver, Colorado, May 31 – June 5, 2015.

unsupervised, language agnostic and scalable.

2 Related Work

In the *tf-idf* scheme (Salton and McGill, 1986), a collection of documents is represented as a $V \times D$ matrix where the rows denote the terms (words) and the columns contain *tf-idf* values for the chosen terms (words). However, the approach reveals little about the underlying semantic structure of the documents. Latent semantic analysis (LSA) (Deerwester et al., 1990) addressed the limitations of the *tf-idf* scheme by performing singular value decomposition (SVD) on the $V \times D$ matrix. The LSA features are linear combinations of the *tf-idf* features in a lower dimensional subspace and can capture linguistic notions such as polysemy and synonymy.

Probabilistic latent semantic analysis (pLSA) (Hofmann, 1999) improved on LSA by modeling each word as a sample from a mixture model, the components of which are multinomial random variables (*topics*). One of the main drawbacks of pLSA is that the topic distributions are learned for particular documents seen in training and consequently, the model is difficult to use on unseen documents. Moreover, the model size grows linearly with the size of the corpus and hence is prone to overfitting. Latent Dirichlet allocation (LDA) (Blei et al., 2003) is a generative model that overcomes some of the limitations of pLSI by using a Dirichlet prior on the topic distribution. The model can hence be used on unseen data and the parameters of the model do not grow with the size of training corpus.

LSA, pLSA and LDA have all been conventionally used on collection of documents that are typically at least a few hundred words. With the recent popularity of communication media such as SMS, Twitter, Facebook, Instagram, etc., many efforts (Weng et al., 2010; Hong and Davison, 2010) have addressed the application of topic models to short texts. (Weng et al., 2010) addressed the problem of identifying influential users on Twitter using a modified PageRank algorithm. They used LDA for inducing topics on user aggregated messages, i.e., a document is a collection of tweets from a single user. The work in (Hong and Davison, 2010) also experimented with different aggregation strategies to apply LDA for inducing topics. In (Ramage et al., 2010), a supervised version of LDA was used to model individual messages. However, such a scheme is not completely unsupervised and hence not desirable for large amounts of data than can span extremely large number of topics (billions of tweets, Facebook posts, image captions, etc.).

In contrast with previous approaches that have either modified LDA or the input to LDA (by aggregating short messages), our approach works on the entire corpus (e.g., billions of tweets or SMS messages) without any aggregation strategy and is completely unsupervised. We learn distributed representations of words over sufficiently long context windows and subsequently use Gaussian mixture models to parameterize the vector space represented by the distributed representations. Our framework is inspired by use of bottleneck features obtained from neural networks in hidden Markov model (HMM) based speech recognition (Grezl and Fousek, 2008). We can potentially use all the optimization and parallelization techniques used in HMM-based speech recognition to scale to large text data sets. The closest approach to that proposed in this work is the biterm topic model (BTM) (Yan et al., 2013) that learns topics over an entire corpus of short texts by directly modeling unordered word-pair co-occurrences (biterms) over the corpus. In our approach, the distributed representations capture longer word contexts, i.e., each word is projected into a vector that represents similarity between words within the contextual window. Hence, our approach can potentially capture context beyond unordered word-pair co-occurrences. Furthermore, since we use dense vectors to represent terms, our approach does not suffer from data sparsity issues typically encountered in co-occurrence statistics based topic models.

3 Distributed Word Representations

Distributed representation of words (also called word embeddings or continuous space representation of words) has become a popular way for capturing distributional similarity (lexical, semantic or even syntactic) between words. The basic idea is to represent each word in vocabulary V with a real-valued vector of some fixed dimension D, i.e., $w_i \in \mathbb{R}^D \;\; \forall \;\; i = 1, \cdots, V$. The idea of representing words in vector space was originally proposed in (Rumelhart et al., 1986; Elman, 1991). However, improved training techniques and tools

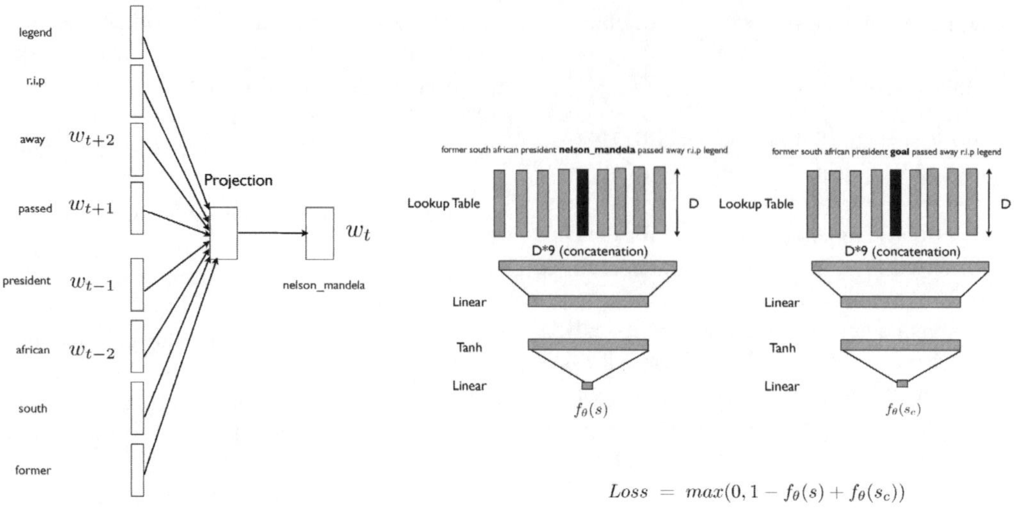

(a) Continuous Bag-of-Words Architecture

(b) Deep Neural Network Architecture

Figure 1: Illustration of obtaining distributed representations of words using two different approaches. An entire tweet can be captured with sufficient context. For Figure 1(b), θ denotes the parameters of the neural network while s and s_c denote the correct and corrupt windows, respectively.

in the recent past have made it possible to obtain such representations for large vocabularies.

Distributed representations can be induced for a given vocabulary V in several ways. While they are typically induced in the context of a deep neural network framework for a given task (Bengio et al., 2003; Collobert and Weston, 2008; Bengio et al., 2009; Turian et al., 2010; Mikolov et al., 2010), recent work in (Mikolov et al., 2013) has also shown that they can also be induced by using simple log-linear models.

Figure 1 shows two different architectures for inducing distributed representations. On the left side, the architecture for the "continuous bag-of-words" model (Mikolov et al., 2013) is shown while the deep learning architecture for inducing distributed representations in language models (Collobert and Weston, 2008) is shown on the right. Both these frameworks essentially perform a similar function in that the word representations are created based on contextual similarity. Since, the average sentence length for text media such as Twitter messages, SMS messages, Facebook posts, etc., is between 12-16 words, inducing distributed representations over similar length windows can capture the semantic similarity between the words in a message. In the next section, we demonstrate how this property can be exploited to perform topic modeling for short messages.

4 Gaussian Mixture Topic Model

We use a log-linear model for inducing the distributed representations using the continuous-bag-of-words architecture proposed in (Mikolov et al., 2013). The continuous-bag-of-words model is similar to the neural network language model (Bengio et al., 2003) with the non-linear layer replaced by a sum pooling layer, i.e., the model uses a bag of surrounding words to predict the center word. Since the implementation of this architecture was readily available through the word2vec tool[2], we used it for inducing the representations. We used hierarchical sampling for reducing the vocabulary during training and used a minimum count of 5 occurrences for each word. One can also use a deep neural network approach (Collobert and Weston, 2008) for inducing the representations. However, the training of these networks is extremely time consuming and we decided to use the simple log-linear model in this work. The framework presented here can work with distributed representations obtained with any methodology (latent semantic indexing, log-linear models, feedforward neural networks, convolutional neural networks, recurrent neural networks, etc.).

We use the continuous-bag-of-words

[2]https://code.google.com/p/word2vec/

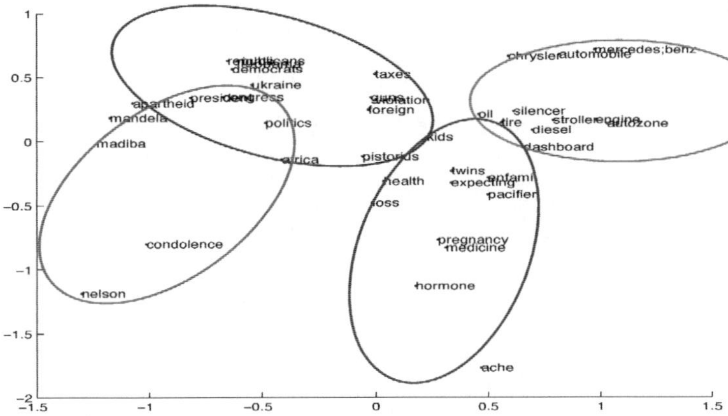

Figure 2: Illustration of fitting a Gaussian mixture model to distributed representations. The dimension of the distributed representations was reduced from 100 to 2 using principal component analysis and 4 GMM components were used.

model (Mikolov et al., 2013) to process all windows of length $wlen$ in a corpus and output a D-dimensional vector $\mathbf{d}_i$ for each word w_i in the vocabulary V. $wlen$ in our work is an odd number, i.e., $wlen = 11$ implies a left and right context of 5 words. Once we obtain the set of word embeddings $w_i \mapsto \mathbf{d}_i$, $\forall i \in V$, we use a Gaussian mixture model (GMM) to learn a parametric model for the distributed representations. Our idea is inspired from the use of bottleneck features obtained using neural networks for training HMM-based speech recognition systems (Grezl and Fousek, 2008). Our conjecture is that the Gaussian mixture model can learn the latent topics by clustering over the distributed representations that are already trained with a semantic similarity objective (positional and contextual similarity). The distributed representations for the vocabulary V can be represented as an $V \times D$ matrix where each row represents a word w_i in the vocabulary. If we choose to model this data with K Gaussian components, we need to estimate $\boldsymbol{\mu}_k, \boldsymbol{\Sigma}_k, p(k|w_i) \forall k \in K$, $w_i \in V$, namely the means, covariances and mixture weights. We denote the parameters for the kth component by θ_k. We can use the standard Expectation-Maximization (EM) algorithm for Gaussian mixture models to estimate the parameters[3] (Hastie et al., 2001). The EM algorithm was initialized with k-means clustering. We use diagonal covariance matrix approximation in this work, i.e., $\boldsymbol{\Sigma}_k, \forall k \in K$ are diagonal.

Given a new sentence $s' = \{w'_1, \cdots, w'_N\}$, we can perform decoding in the following way to assign the sentence to a particular topic k or a collection of topics since one can obtain the posterior distribution over the topics for each sentence.

$$k^* = \arg\max_{\theta_k} p(k|w'_1, \cdots, w'_N) \quad (1)$$

$$= \arg\max_{\theta_k} p(w'_1, \cdots, w'_N|k)p(k) \quad (2)$$

$$k^* = \arg\max_{\theta_k} p(k) \prod_{i=1}^{N} p(w'_i|k) \quad (3)$$

where $p(k)$ and $p(w'_i|k)$ are obtained from the Gaussian mixture model. The notion of latent topics in this model is represented by the K components of the GMM. Figure 2 shows an example of fitting a GMM to distributed representation of words.

The key difference between our approach and previous approaches to topic modeling is that we start with a dense vector representation for each word in place of a multinomial distribution that is typically learned as part of the topic modeling framework. Second, we do not use the notion of a document since the distributed representations are learned over windows over the entire corpus.

5 Data

We acquired a 10% random sample of Twitter firehose data for 2 weeks across all languages. As a first step, we filtered the tweets by language code. Since the language code is a property set in the

[3]The computation can be parallelized by chunking the $V \times D$ matrix, computing sufficient statistics over the chunks and finally accumulating the statistics.

	Language									
	en		**es**		**fr**		**pt**		**ru**	
Corpus	#voc	#sents	#voc	#sents	#voc	#sents	#voc	#sents	#voc	#sents
Twitter	8371078	178770137	5820863	74784082	1697619	14383118	1816744	22031792	2410668	16025128

Table 1: Statistics of the data used to induce distributed representation in each language. **en**: English, **es**: Spanish, **fr**: French, **pt**: Portuguese. #voc stands for the vocabulary and #sents denotes number of sentences.

user profile, the language code does not guarantee that all tweets are in the same language. We used a simple frequency threshold for language identification based on language specific word lists obtained from Wikitionary[4]. Subsequently, we performed some basic clean-up such as replacing usernames, hashtags, web addresses and numerals with generic symbols such as *_user_*, *_hashtags_*, *_url_* and *_number_*. Finally, we removed all punctuations from the strings and lowercased the text. In this work, we perform our experiments on English, Spanish, French, Portuguese and Russian.

We also formed a stop word list to eliminate extremely common as well as rare words from our topic models. For English, the stop word list comprised of words with frequency greater than 5 million or less than 5 in the training data. For Spanish, French, Portuguese and Russian, the stop list comprised of words with frequency greater than 25000 or less than 5 in the respective training data.

6 Experiments

First, we randomly replaced low frequency words (less than 4 occurrences) with an _UNK_ token to keep the vocabulary open and subsequently used the stop word list to filter the training data. Distributed representations using the continuous-bag-of-words log-linear model was used to obtain $w_i \mapsto \mathbf{d}_i, \forall i \in V$ in each language. We experimented with different dimensions of distributed representations as well as mixture components. Figure 3 shows some topics learned by the model and the terms that comprise the topics for a model learned with D=100 and K=200 on English Twitter data. The terms are ranked by probability.

Unsupervised topic modeling schemes are inherently difficult to evaluate quantitatively. Perplexity of trained models on a held-out set is typically used to objectively evaluate topic models (Blei et al., 2003). However, our scheme does not model the generation process of short text documents. Hence, we use a variety of subjective and objective topic coherence measures to evaluate our framework. We also present a comparison with a state-of-the-art technique for modeling short texts, namely, biterm topic model (BTM) (Yan et al., 2013).

We perform unsupervised topic modeling experiments on the phrasified English Twitter corpus using three schemes. We use LDA as a baseline and treat each tweet as an independent document without any aggregation. We also use the BTM topic model that has been proven to be a suitable fit for short texts. For LDA, we used the open-source implementation GibbsLDA++[5] and for BTM, we used the implementation associated with (Yan et al., 2013). [6]. All three schemes used identical data. We set the parameters $\alpha = 0.05$ and $\beta = 0.01$ for LDA and $\alpha = \frac{50}{K}$ and $\beta = 0.01$ for BTM. The parameters for LDA and BTM were optimized on held-out set with line search using topic coherence metric described in Eq 4. We performed training using our framework for varying window lengths ($wlen$), vector space dimension (D) and number of clusters (K). Specifically, we trained GMMs with the following parameters, $wlen = \{11, 13, 15, 17\}$, $D = \{50, 100\}$ and $K = \{50, 100, 200\}$.

First, we manually inspected the topics obtained by our unsupervised distributed representation framework. A sample of the topics is shown in Figure 3. Manual inspection of many of the topic clusters (top ranked words in each cluster) indicated promising results [7]. As a subsequent step, we asked three professional speech transcribers (also NLP annotators) to subjectively rate the utility of each topic (by displaying the top 50 words) on a 1-3 Likert scale. A rating of *1* indicates completely useless topic cluster while *3* indicates useful topic cluster. *Useful* was defined as a collection

[4]http://en.wiktionary.org/wiki/Wiktionary:Frequency_lists

[5]`http://gibbslda.sourceforge.net`

[6]`http://code.google.com/p/btm/`

[7]The topic clusters for all languages can be obtained from `https://github.com/annontopicmodel/unsupervised_topic_modeling/`. We are not able to share the sentence clusters due to Twitter's data policy.

c7	c113	c1	c3	c66
epictectus	dexter	❄	#nj	conservatives
confucius	portlandia	40°	#ottawa	politicians
sophocles	mulan	❄	#yyc	constitution
aristotle	jarhead	#fwinter	#melbourne	mandate
yiddish	starwars	#freezing	#toronto	alp
euripides	misfits	degrees	#indy	progressives
machiavelli	twilight	#ihatewinter	#vancouver	gop
#ultimatequotes	supernatural	blustery	#seattle	government
proverb	prometheus	#winterishere	#california	liberal
#bookbuzzr	avengers	brrrrr	#colorado	lnp
rumi	#thisistheend	#bundleup	#austin	tories
voltaire	jumpstreet	#socold	#philadelphia	bho
#proverb	simpsons	#hatewinter	#greenwich	propaganda
#wednesdaywisdom	sopranos	#toocold	#travelpics	repubs

Figure 3: Terms with the highest probability for sample latent topics over the entire English Twitter corpus. The topics were obtained by using $wlen$ = 15, D=100 and K=200.

Context	K	Fleiss' κ	Mean rating	Median rating
$wlen = 11$	50	0.89	2.2 ± 0.78	2
	100	0.81	2.11 ± 0.79	2
	200	0.82	2.15 ± 0.85	2
$wlen = 15$	50	0.70	2.24 ± 0.77	2
	100	0.80	2.17 ± 0.88	2.5
	200	0.78	2.11 ± 0.89	2.5
$wlen = 17$	50	0.79	2.18 ± 0.82	2
	100	0.68	2.3 ± 0.89	3
	200	0.54	2.18 ± 0.87	2
LDA	100	0.80	1.97 ± 1.01	2
BTM	100	0.78	1.84 ± 1.15	2

Table 2: Subjective evaluation of topic coherence across three annotators ($D = 50$)

of terms that indicated some meaningful semantic property (e.g., movie names, politics, headlines, superlatives, sad emoticons/words, etc.) that could be used for a categorization task. In cases of ambiguity, we asked the labelers to confer a rating of 2.

We computed the inter annotator agreement between the three labelers using Fleiss' kappa metric (Fleiss, 1971). The results are presented in Table 2. The inter-annotator agreement is quite high for the topic clusters induced with context windows $wlen$ of 11 and 15 words. The agreement is lower for model trained with longer context window perhaps indicating that a window of length 11 or 15 words is sufficient for tweets. The mean ratings are mostly higher than 2 and the median rating for $wlen = 15, K = \{50, 100\}$ are above 2. The subjective ratings are significantly better than LDA and BTM. Hence, subjective evaluation of topics learned using our framework are of consistently high quality.

In order to objectively measure the quality of topics, we also used *coherence score* (Mimno et al., 2011). Given a topic z and a set of top N words (ranked by likelihood) in z, $S^z = \{w_1^z, \cdots, w_N^z\}$, the coherence score is defined as:

$$C(z; S^z) = \sum_{n=2}^{N} \sum_{l=1}^{n-1} log \frac{D(w_n^z, w_l^z) + 1}{D(w_l^z)} \quad (4)$$

where $D(w)$ is the document frequency of word w and $D(w', w)$ is the co-document frequency of words w and w'. The coherence score was then averaged across all topics to obtain the mean coherence score for each scheme, i.e., we computed $\frac{1}{K}\sum_{k=1}^{K} C(z_k; S^{z_k})$. A high coherence score indicates a good topic cluster. Figure 4 shows the average topic coherence score over top N words across varying $wlen$ by fixing $D = 50$ and $K = 50$. The topic clusters are more coherent for $wlen = 11$ at lower values of N but for higher values of N, the model with $wlen = 13$ performs better. Since our vector space GMM model learns topic distributions across the entire corpus, many clusters have a large number of terms with high likelihoods. As a result, it is more appropriate to choose a model with high topic coherence for large values of N.

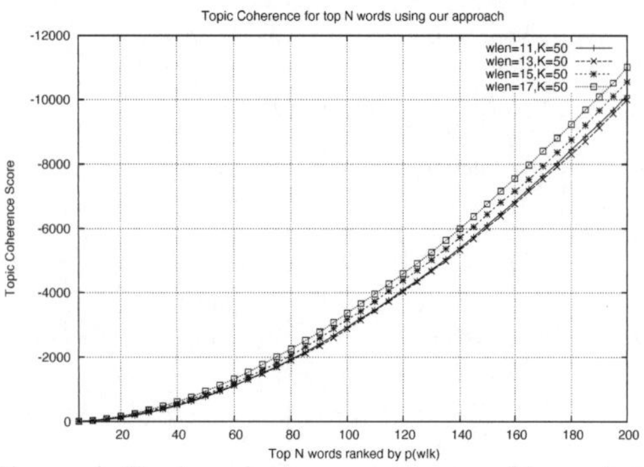

Figure 4: Topic coherence versus top N words in each topic for different values of $wlen$

Next, we analyze the effect of dimension of the vector space model on the topic modeling framework. Figure 5 plots the average topic coherence for varying D. We find that for $D = 100$, the model with lower K achieves better topic coherence. In contrast, for $D = 50$, the model with $K = 200$ is objectively better than the models with $K = \{50, 100\}$. In the former case, the number of topics is smaller and hence a higher dimension is separating the vectors in a better fashion while in the latter case, the increased number of topics achieves better separation even with smaller dimension vectors. One can balance the choice of K and D based on the size of data and desired clusters to be learned.

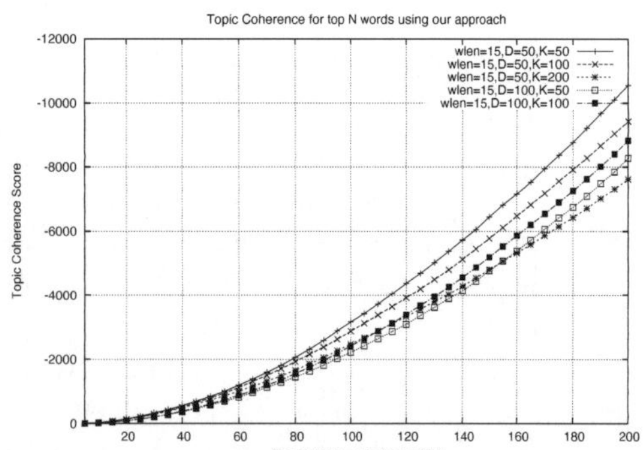

Figure 5: Topic coherence versus top N words in each topic for different values of D

In Figure 6, we plot the topic coherence score for different cluster sizes. The plot shows that for a given N, the best coherence score is obtained for

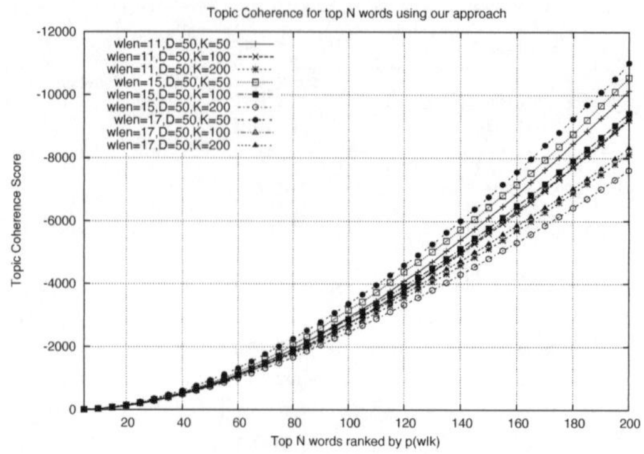

Figure 6: Topic coherence versus top N words in each topic for different values of K

$wlen = 15, D = 50, K = 200$. In general for a large dataset with millions of tweets, $K = 200$ results in better clustering since there are many topics in the data. The model with $wlen = 15$ is interesting since the context window is about the same as the average length of a tweet. The topic coherence scores for $D = 100, K = 200$ were consistently lower than that of the above presented results. It may again be due to the balance needed in the separation of topics due to vector space dimension versus the total number of GMM components. Finally, Figure 7 plots the topic coherence score for our approach, BTM and LDA. The results clearly indicate that our framework performs extremely well on short texts. While previous results using the BTM approach was only performed on a few million tweets, our experiments are performed on 178M tweets for English. The performance of LDA and BTM are very similar while our approach achieves significantly higher topic coherence scores. Finally, Figure 8 shows the topic coherence for Spanish, French, Portuguese and Russian. Our proposed scheme clearly outperforms LDA on large collections of short texts across languages.

7 Discussion

Conventional topic modeling schemes such as pLSA and LDA need to make modifications when applied on short texts and messages through aggregation strategies. We are not confounded with such a problem since our framework works on large amounts of raw short texts without the need for any aggregation strategy. For media such as Twitter, Facebook or SMS, aggregation over users

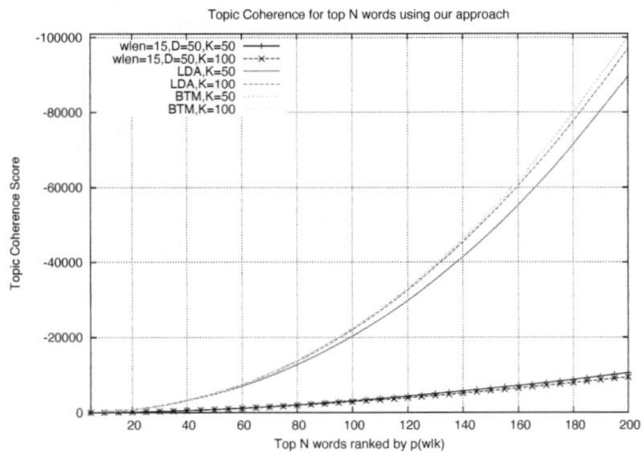

Figure 7: Topic coherence versus top N words in each topic for our scheme, LDA and BTM for English tweet data

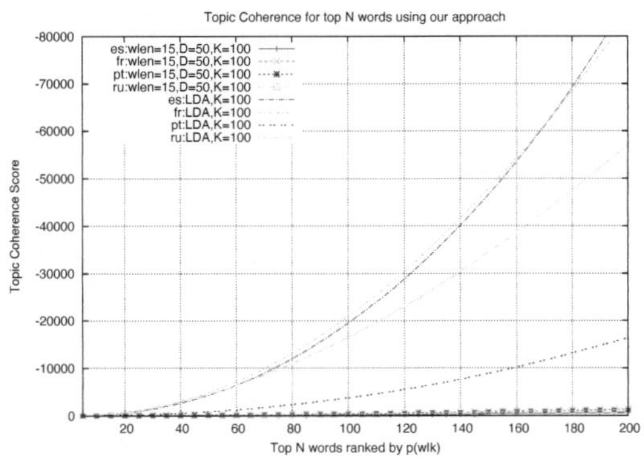

Figure 8: Topic coherence versus top N words in each topic for our scheme and LDA across languages

or location is not a good strategy since the interests of users is diverse and can change quickly. Besides such information is not available for news titles, image captions, etc. Our conjecture is that even for longer documents (emails, news pages, etc.), applying our scheme at the sentence level can be used to accrue topics over the document. The bottleneck is mainly due to the span of windows that one can use to learn reliable distributed representations of words.

We used a log-linear model for learning distributed representations of words in this work. However, our scheme can work with distributed representations obtained by neural networks or latent semantic indexing. The key requirement for distributed representations to work with our GMM framework is that they need to represent good partitioning of semantic concepts in the vector space $\mathbb{R}^D$, where D is the dimensionality of the vector space.

The GMM estimation in this work was simplified due to the assumption of diagonal covariance matrices for the components. We conjecture that the performance can be further improved with full covariance matrices at the cost of computational overhead involved in the Cholesky decomposition. However, the diagonal covariance assumption improves training time as the GMM parameter estimation can be parallelized.

For short texts, the likelihood of a message containing more than 2 or 3 topics is quite low. The decoding scheme presented in this work can obtain a complete posterior distribution over all topics (GMM components) for each message. However, we found that the a large proportion of messages (over 80%) contained only one topic, i.e., the posterior distribution peaks for a particular GMM component. Our scheme can potentially be used for a variety of monitoring tasks such as detection of offensive posts, removal of adult content, advertisement detection, targeted advertising (retail, entertainment, sports), sentiment classification, etc., since such posts are all clustered together.

8 Conclusion

We presented a novel unsupervised topic modeling framework for short texts that uses distributed representations of words and phrases. Our framework models the low-dimensional semantic vector space represented by the dense word vectors using Gaussian mixture models. By learning representations over sufficiently long context windows, we find that one can learn robust word embeddings that can be exploited to learn the semantics of entire short messages. The work presented here was inspired by the use of bottleneck features in HMM-based speech recognition and one can potentially use all the optimization techniques used to estimate GMMs over large datasets (thousands of hours of speech) for modeling large amounts of text. Our experimental results indicate that our scheme can reliably learn latent topics and can be used to categorize short messages with high fidelity in comparison with LDA and biterm topic model. Our scheme is language agnostic and we demonstrated the utility of our scheme in English, Spanish, French, Portuguese and Russian tweets.

References

Y. Bengio, R. Ducharme, P. Vincent, and C. Jauvin. 2003. A neural probabilistic language model. *Journal of Machine Learning Research*, 3:1137–1155.

Y. Bengio, J. Louradour, R. Collobert, and J. Weston. 2009. Curriculum learning. In *Proceedings of ICML*.

David M. Blei, Andrew Y. Ng, and Michael I. Jordan. 2003. Latent dirichlet allocation. *Journal of Machine Learning Research*, 3.

R. Collobert and J. Weston. 2008. A unified architecture for natural language processing: deep neural networks with multitask learning. In *Proceedings of ICML*.

C. De Marcken. 1996. *Unsupervised Language Acquisitiong*. Ph.D. thesis, Massachusetts Institute of Technology.

S. Deerwester, S. T. Dumais, G. W. Furnas, T. K. Landauer, and R. Harshman. 1990. Indexing by latent semantic analysis. *Journal of the American Society for Information Science*, 41.

J. L. Elman. 1991. Distributed representations, simple recurrent networks, and grammatical structure. *Machine Learning*, 7(2-3):195–225.

J. L. Fleiss. 1971. Measuring nominal scale agreement among many raters. *Psychological Bulletin*, 76(5):378382.

F. Grezl and P. Fousek. 2008. Optimizing bottle-neck features for LVCSR. In *Proceedings of ICASSP*, pages 4729–4732.

T. Hastie, R. Tibshirani, and J. Friedman. 2001. *The Elements of Statistical Learning*. Springer Series in Statistics. Springer New York Inc.

Thomas Hofmann. 1999. Probabilistic latent semantic indexing. In *Proceedings of the 22Nd Annual International ACM SIGIR Conference on Research and Development in Information Retrieval*.

Liangjie Hong and Brian D. Davison. 2010. Empirical study of topic modeling in twitter. In *Proceedings of the First Workshop on Social Media Analytics*.

C. Kit and Y. Wilks. 1999. Unsupervised Learning of Word Boundary with Description Length Gain. In *Proceedings of Workshop on Computational Natural Language Learning CoNLL*.

T. Mikolov, S. Kopecký, L. Burget, J. Černocký, and S. Khudanpur. 2010. Recurrent neural network based language model. In *Proceedings of Interspeech*.

T. Mikolov, K. Chen, G. Corrado, and J. Dean. 2013. Efficient estimation of word representations in vector space. In *Proceedings of Workshop at ICLR*.

David Mimno, Hanna M. Wallach, Edmund Talley, Miriam Leenders, and Andrew McCallum. 2011. Optimizing semantic coherence in topic models. In *Proceedings of the Conference on Empirical Methods in Natural Language Processing*, EMNLP '11.

D. Ramage, S. Dumais, and D. Liebling. 2010. Characterizing microblogs with topic models. In *International AAAI Conference on Weblogs and Social Media*.

J. Rissanen. 1978. Modeling by shortest data description. *Automatica*, 14:465471.

D. E. Rumelhart, G. E. Hinton, and R. J. Williams. 1986. Parallel distributed processing: Explorations in the microstructure of cognition, vol. 1. chapter Learning Internal Representations by Error Propagation, pages 318–362.

G. Salton and M. J. McGill. 1986. *Introduction to Modern Information Retrieval*. McGraw-Hill, Inc., New York, NY, USA.

C. E. Shannon. 1948. A Mathematical Theory of Communication. *Bell System Technical Journal*, 27:379423.

S. Sista, R. Schwartz, T. R. Leek, and J. Makhoul. 2002. An algorithm for unsupervised topic discovery from broadcast news stories. In *Proceedings of HLT*, pages 110–114.

J. Turian, L. Ratinov, and Y. Bengio. 2010. Word representations: a simple and general method for semi-supervised learning. In *Proceedings of ACL*.

Jianshu Weng, Ee-Peng Lim, Jing Jiang, and Qi He. 2010. Twitterrank: Finding topic-sensitive influential twitterers. In *Proceedings of the Third ACM International Conference on Web Search and Data Mining*.

Xiaohui Yan, Jiafeng Guo, Yanyan Lan, and Xueqi Cheng. 2013. A biterm topic model for short texts. In *Proceedings of the 22Nd International Conference on World Wide Web*, WWW '13.

Estimating User Location in Social Media with Stacked Denoising Auto-encoders

Ji Liu and Diana Inkpen
School of Electrical Engineering and Computer Science
University of Ottawa, Ottawa, Ontario, Canada
rexliu01@gmail.com, Diana.Inkpen@uOttawa.ca

Abstract

Only very few users disclose their physical locations, which may be valuable and useful in applications such as marketing and security monitoring; in order to automatically detect their locations, many approaches have been proposed using various types of information, including the tweets posted by the users. It is not easy to infer the original locations from textual data, because text tends to be noisy, particularly in social media. Recently, deep learning techniques have been shown to reduce the error rate of many machine learning tasks, due to their ability to learn meaningful representations of input data. We investigate the potential of building a deep-learning architecture to infer the location of Twitter users based merely on their tweets. We find that stacked denoising auto-encoders are well suited for this task, with results comparable to state-of-the-art models.

1 Introduction

Many real-world applications require the knowledge of the actual locations of users. For example, online advertisers would like to target potential buyers in particular regions. There are easy ways to obtain user locations, for example, social media service providers allow users to provide their locations, mostly through GPS locating or by manual specification. However, only a small proportion of users actually provide location information. The proportion of users who specify their locations in their profiles is reported to be 14.3% by Abrol et al. (2012); self-reported locations also tend to be unreliable because users can practically type anything they want, such as *In your backyard* or *Wonderland*. When it comes to per-tweet GPS tagging, only 1.2% of all users use this functionality (Dredze et al., 2013). In view of such extreme sparsity, researchers have developed various ways of inferring users' locations using information such as interactions between users, locations declared by users in their social media profiles, users' time zones, the text they generate, etc. The relation between geographical location and language has been studied since the 19th century as a sub-field of sociolinguistics known as dialectology (Petyt, 1980; Chambers, 1998).

In this work, our concern is how to estimate users' locations from the textual data that they generate on social media, and in particular to infer Twitter users' location using the messages they post on their Twitter accounts. For each user, we put together all the tweets written by that user, in order to predict his/her physical location. We focus on predicting users' locations with a deep learning architecture built with denoising auto-encoders proposed first by Vincent et al. (2008), since this approach was not yet applied to this task. The contribution of our work consists in designing models for solving the task and in finding the right parameter values to make the proposed models achieve good results. The first model predicts the U.S. region where the user is located and his/her U.S. state, while the second model predicts the longitude and latitude of the user's location.

Proceedings of NAACL-HLT 2015, pages 201–210,
Denver, Colorado, May 31 – June 5, 2015.

2 Related Work

2.1 Location Prediction Using Twitter Data

Many methods have been proposed to predict users' locations based on social network structure (Backstrom et al., 2010), (Jurgens, 2013), (Rout et al., 2013). Here we focus on the methods that predict users' locations based on the social media texts they generate. One of the very first is by Cheng et al. (2010), who first learned the location distribution for each word, then inferred the location of users at U.S. city level according to the words in their tweets. Specifically, they estimated the posterior probability of a user being from a city c given his/her tweets t by computing:

$$P(c|t) = \prod_{w \in t} P(c|w) \times P(w) \qquad (1)$$

where w is a word contained in this user's tweets. To improve the initial results, they also used several smoothing techniques such as Laplace smoothing and so-called *data-driven geographic smoothing* and *model-based smoothing*. Their best model managed to make accurate predictions (less than 100 miles away from the actual location) 51% of the time, and the average error distance is 535.564 miles. It is worth noting that the size of the dataset in their work is large, containing 4,124,960 tweets from 130,689 users.

Eisenstein et al. (2010) adopted a topic model approach. They treated tweets as documents generated by two latent variables, i.e., topic and region, and train a system they call *geographic topic model*, which could predict authors' locations based on text alone. Like Cheng et al. (2010), their model also relied on learning regional word distributions. The average distance from the model's prediction to the actual location is 900 kilometres. By comparison, their dataset is much smaller, containing 380,000 tweets from 9,500 users. This dataset is made available and has been used by a number of works.

Roller et al. (2012) used a variant of K-Nearest Neighbours (kNN); they divided the geographic surface of the Earth into *grids* and then constructed a pseudo-document for each grid; a location for a test document was chosen based on the most similar pseudo-document. Another type of model is a variant of Gaussian mixture models (GMMs) proposed by Priedhorsky et al. (2014). Their approach resembles that of Cheng et al. (2010) in constructing location-sensitive n-grams; besides tweets, they also used information such as users' self-reported locations and time zones for prediction.

2.2 Deep Neural Networks

In this section, we present the artificial neural network architectures that will appear in the subsequent sections.

2.2.1 Feedforward Artificial Neural Networks

A feedforward neural network usually has an input layer and an output layer. If the input layer is directly connected to the output layer, such a model is called a *single-layer perceptron*. A more powerful model has several layers between the input layer and the output layer; these intermediate layers are called *hidden layers*; this type of model is known as a *multi-layer perceptron* (MLP). In a perceptron, neurons are interconnected, i.e., each neuron is connected to all neurons in the subsequent layer. Neurons are also associated with activation functions, which transform the output of each neuron; the transformed outputs are the inputs of the subsequent layer. Typical choices of activation functions include the identity function, defined as $y = x$; the hyperbolic tangent, defined as $y = \frac{e^x - e^{-x}}{e^x + e^{-x}}$ and the logistic sigmoid, defined as $y = \frac{1}{1+e^{-x}}$. To train a MLP, the most commonly used technique is *back-propagation* (Rumelhart et al., 1985). Specifically, the errors in the output layer are back-propagated to preceding layers and are used to update the weights of each layer.

2.2.2 Deep Neural Network Architecture

An artificial neural network (ANN) with multiple hidden layers, also called a Deep Neural Network (DNN), try to mimic the deep architecture of the brain and it is believed to perform better than shallow architectures such as logistic regression models and ANNs without hidden units. The effective training of DNNs is, however, not achieved until the work of Hinton et al. (2006) and Bengio and Lamblin (2007). In both cases, a procedure called *unsupervised pre-training* is carried out before the final supervised fine-tuning. The pre-training significantly decreases error rates of Deep Neural Networks on a number of ML tasks such as object recognition and speech recognition.

The details of DNN's are beyond the scope of this paper; interested readers can refer to the work of Hinton et al. (2006), Bengio and Lamblin (2007), Vincent et al. (2008) and the introduction by Bengio et al. (2013).

2.3 Deep Neural Networks Applied to NLP

Data representation is important for machine learning (Domingos, 2012). Many statistical NLP tasks use hand-crafted features to represent language units such as words and documents; these features are fed as the input to machine learning models. One such example is emotion or sentiment classification which uses external lexicons that contain words with emotion or sentiment prior polarities (Ghazi et al., 2014; Aman and Szpakowicz, 2008; Melville et al., 2009; Li et al., 2009). Despite the usefulness of these hand-crafted features, designing them is time-consuming and requires expertise.

A number of researchers have implemented DNNs in the NLP domain, achieving state-of-the-art performance without having to manually design any features. The most relevant to ours is the work of Glorot et al. (2011), who developed a deep learning architecture that consists of stacked denoising auto-encoders (SDA) and apply it to sentiment classification of Amazon reviews. Their stacked denoising auto-encoders can capture meaningful representations from reviews and outperform state-of-the-art methods; due to the unsupervised nature of the pre-training step, this method also performs domain adaptation well.

In the social media domain, Tang et al. (2013) extracted representations from Microblog text data with Deep Belief Networks (DBNs) and used the learned representations for emotion classification, outperforming representations based on Principal Component Analysis and on Latent Dirichlet Allocation.

Huang and Yates (2010) showed that representation learning also helps domain adaptation of part-of-speech tagging, which is challenging because POS taggers trained on one domain have a hard time dealing with unseen words in another domain. They first learned a representation for each word, then fed the learned word-level representations to the POS tagger; when applied to out-of-domain text, it can reduce the error by 29%.

3 Methods

3.1 Datasets

In order to compare the performance of our system with that of other systems, we choose a publicly available dataset from Eisenstein et al. (2010) [1], which has been used by several other researchers. It includes about 380,000 tweets from 9,500 users from the contiguous United States (i.e., the U.S. excluding Hawaii, Alaska and all off-shore territories). The dataset also provides geographical coordinates of each user. A similar but much larger dataset that we use is from Roller et al. (2012) [2]; it contains 38 million tweets from 449,694 users, all from North America. We regard each user's set of tweets as a training example (labelled with location), i.e., $(x^{(i)}, y^{(i)})$ where $x^{(i)}$ represent all the tweets from the i-th user and $y^{(i)}$ is the location of the i-th user. Meta-data like user's profile and time zone will not be used in our work.

3.2 Our Models

We define our work as follows: first, a classification task puts each user into one geographical region (see Section 4 for details); next, a regression task predicts the most likely location of each user in terms of geographical coordinates, i.e., a pair of real numbers for latitude and longitude. We present one model for each task.

3.2.1 Model 1

The first model consists of three layers of denoising auto-encoders. Each code layer of denoising auto-encoders also serves as a hidden layer of a multiple-layer feedforward neural network. In addition, the top code layer works as the input layer of a logistic regression model whose output layer is a softmax layer.

Softmax Function The softmax function is defined as:

$$softmax_i(\mathbf{z}) = \frac{e^{\mathbf{z}_i}}{\sum_{j=1}^{J} e^{\mathbf{z}_j}} \tag{2}$$

[1] http://www.ark.cs.cmu.edu/GeoTwitter

[2] https://github.com/utcompling/textgrounder/wiki/RollerEtAl_EMNLP2012

where the numerator z_i is the ith possible input to the softmax function and the denominator is the summation over all possible inputs. The softmax function produces a normalized probability distribution over all possible output labels. This property makes it suitable for multiclass classification tasks. Consequently, a softmax layer has the same number of neurons as the number of possible output labels; the value of each neuron can be interpreted as the probability the corresponding label given the input. Usually, the label with the highest probability is returned as the prediction made by the model.

In our model, mathematically, the probability of a label i given the input and the weights is:

$$\begin{aligned} &P(Y=i|x^N,W^{(N+1)},b^{(N+1)}) \\ &= softmax_i(W^{(N+1)}x^N+b^{(N+1)}) \\ &= \frac{e^{W_i^{(N+1)}x^N+b_i^{(N+1)}}}{\sum_j e^{W_j^{(N+1)}x^N+b_j^{(N+1)}}} \end{aligned} \quad (3)$$

where $W^{(N+1)}$ is the weight matrix of the logistic regression layer and $b^{(N+1)}$ are its biases. N is the number of hidden layers, in our case $N=3$. x^N is the output of the code layer of the denoising auto-encoder on top. To calculate the output of i-th hidden layer (i = 1 ... N), we have:

$$x^i = s(W^{(i)}x^{i-1}+b^{(i)}) \quad (4)$$

where s is the activation function, $W^{(i)}$ and $b^{(i)}$ correspond to the weight matrix and biases of the i-th hidden layer. x^0 is the raw input generated from text[3], as specified in section 4. We return the label that maximizes Equation (3) as the prediction, i.e.:

$$i_{predict} = \arg\max_i P(Y=i|x^N,W^{(N+1)},b^{(N+1)}) \quad (5)$$

We denote this model as SDA-1.

3.2.2 Model 2

In the second model, a multivariate linear regression layer replaces a logistic regression layer on top. This produces two real numbers as output, which can be interpreted as geographical coordinates. Therefore the output corresponds to locations

[3]Explained in Section 3.3

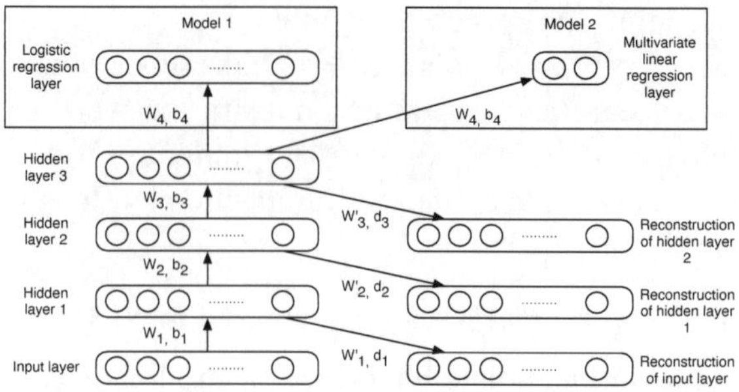

Figure 1: Illustration of the two proposed models SDA-1 and SDA-2.

on the surface of Earth. Specifically, the output of model 2 is:

$$y_i = W_i^{(N+1)}x^N + b_i^{(N+1)} \quad (6)$$

where $i \in \{1,2\}$, $W^{(N+1)}$ is the weight matrix of the linear regression layer and $b^{(N+1)}$ are its biases, x^N is the output of the code layer of the denoising auto-encoder on top. The output of i-th hidden layer (i = 1 ... N) is computed using Equation (4), which is the same as Model 1. The tuple (y_1, y_2) is then the pair of geographical coordinates produced by the model. We denote this model as SDA-2. Figure 1 shows the architecture of both models. They have with three hidden layers. The models differ only in the output layers. The neurons are fully interconnected. A layer and its reconstruction and the next layer together correspond to a denoising auto-encoder. For simplicity, we do not include the corrupted layers in the diagram. Note that models SDA-1 and SDA-2 are not trained simultaneously, nor do they share parameters.

3.3 Input Features

To learn better representations, a basic representation is required to start with. For text data, a reasonable starting representation is achieved with the *Bag-of-N-grams* features (Glorot et al., 2011; Bengio et al., 2013).

The input text of Twitter messages is preprocessed and transformed into a set of Bag-of-N-grams **frequency** feature vectors. We did not use binary feature vectors because we believe the frequency of n-grams is relevant to the task at hand. For example, a user who tweets *Senators* 10 times is more likely to be from Ottawa than another user who tweets it just once. (The latter is more likely to be someone from Montreal who tweets *Senators* simply because the Canadiens happen to be defeated by the Senators that time.) Due to computational limitations, we consider only the 5000 most frequent unigrams, bigrams and trigrams[4]. We tokenized the tweets using the *Twokenizer* tool from Owoputi et al. (2013).

3.4 Statistical Noises for Denoising Auto-encoders

An essential component of a DA is its statistical noise. Following Glorot et al. (2011), the statistical noise we incorporate for the first layer of DA is the masking noise, i.e., each active element has a probability to become inactive. For the remaining layers, we apply Gaussian noise to each of them, i.e., a number independently sampled from the Gaussian distribution $\mathcal{N}(0, \sigma^2)$ is added to each element of the input vector to get the corrupted input vector. Note that the Gaussian distribution has a 0 mean. The standard deviation of the Gaussian distribution σ decides the degree of corruption; we also use the term *corruption level* to refer to σ.

3.5 Loss Functions

3.5.1 Pre-training

In terms of training criteria for unsupervised pre-training, we use the squared error loss function:

$$\ell(x,r) = ||x-r||^2 \tag{7}$$

where x is the original input, r is the reconstruction. The squared error loss function is a convex function, so we are guaranteed to find the global optimum once we find the local optimum.

The pre-training is done by layers, i.e., we first minimize the loss function for the first layer of denoising auto-encoder, then the second, then the third. We define the decoder weight matrix as the transposition of the encoder weight matrix.

3.5.2 Fine-tuning

In the fine-tuning phase, the training criteria differ for model 1 and model 2. It is a common practice to use the *negative log-likelihood* as the loss function of models that produce a probability distribution, which is the case for model 1. The equation for the negative log-likelihood function is:

$$\begin{aligned}&\ell(\theta = \{W,b\},(x,y))\\ &= -\log(P(Y=y|x,W,b))\end{aligned} \tag{8}$$

where $\theta = \{W,b\}$ are the parameters of the model, x is the input and y is the ground truth label. To minimize the loss in Equation (8), the conditional probability $P(Y=y|x,W,b)$ must be maximized, which means the model must learn to make the correct prediction with the highest confidence possible. Training a supervised classifier using the negative log-likelihood loss function can be therefore interpreted as maximizing the likelihood of the probability distribution of labels in the training set.

On the other hand, model 2 produces for every input a location $\hat{y}(l\hat{a}t, l\hat{o}n)$, which is associated with the actual location of this user, denoted by $y(lat, lon)$. Given latitudes and longitudes of two locations, their great-circle distance can be computed by first calculating an intermediate value $\Delta\sigma$ with the Haversine formula (Sinnott, 1984):

$$\Delta\sigma = \arctan\left(\frac{\sqrt{(\cos\phi_2\sin\Delta\lambda)^2 + (\cos\phi_1\sin\phi_2 - \sin\phi_1\cos\phi_2\cos\Delta\lambda)^2}}{\sin\phi_1\sin\phi_2 + \cos\phi_1\cos\phi_2\cos\Delta\lambda}\right) \tag{9}$$

Next, calculate the actual distance:

$$d((\phi_1,\lambda_1),(\phi_2,\lambda_2)) = r\Delta\sigma \tag{10}$$

where ϕ_1, λ_1 and ϕ_2, λ_2 are latitudes and longitudes of two locations, $\Delta\lambda = \lambda_1 - \lambda_2$, r is the radius of the Earth. Because d is a continuously differentiable function with respect to ϕ_1 and λ_1 (if we consider (ϕ_1, λ_1) as the predicted location, then (ϕ_2, λ_2) is the actual location), and minimizing d is exactly what model 2 is designed to do, we define the loss function of model 2 as the great-circle distance between the estimated location and the actual location:

$$\begin{aligned}&\ell(\theta = \{W,b\},(x,y))\\ &= d(Wx+b,y)\end{aligned} \tag{11}$$

where $\theta = \{W,b\}$ are the parameters of the model, x is the input and y is the actual location. [5]

[4]Not all of these 5000 n-grams are necessarily good location indicators, we don't manually distinguish them; a machine learning model after training should be able to do so.

[5]Alternatively, we also tried the loss function defined as the

Now that we have defined the loss functions for both models, we can train them with back-propagation (Rumelhart et al., 1985) and Stochastic Gradient Descent (SGD).

4 Experiment

4.1 Metrics

We train the stacked denoising auto-encoders to predict the locations of users based on the tweets they post. To evaluate SDA-1, we follow Eisenstein et al. (2010) and define a classification task where each user is classified as from one of the 48 contiguous U.S. states or Washington D.C. The process of retrieving a human-readable address including street, city, state and country from a pair of latitude and longitude is known as *reverse geocoding*. We use MapQuest API [6] to reverse geocode coordinates for each user. We also define a task with only four classes, the West, Midwest, Northeast and South regions, as per the U.S. Census Bureau.[7] The metric for comparison is the classification accuracy defined as the proportion of test examples that are correctly classified. We also implement two baseline models, namely a Naive Bayes classifier and an SVM classifier (with the RBF kernel); both of them take exactly the same input as the stacked denoising auto-encoders.

To evaluate SDA-2, the metric is simply the mean error distance in kilometres from the actual location to the predicted location. Note that this is the distance on the surface of the Earth, also known as the great-circle distance. See Equations (9)-(10) for its computation. In Section 5.2, we applied two additional metrics, which are the median error distance and the percentage of predictions less than 100 miles away from the true locations, to comply with previous work. Similarly, we implement a baseline model which is simply a multivariate linear regression layer on top of the input layer. This baseline model is equivalent to SDA-2 without hidden layers. We denote this model as baseline-MLR. After we have obtained the performance of our models, they will be compared against several existing models from previous work.

4.2 Early Stopping

We define our loss functions without regularizing the weights; to prevent overfitting, we adopt the early-stopping technique (Yao et al., 2007); i.e., training stops when the model's performance on the validation set no longer improves. Specifically, we adopt the *patience* approach (Bengio, 2012), which is illustrated in pseudocode:

```
initialization
patience=20, iteration=1;
while iteration <patience do
    update parameters;
    if the performance improves then
        patience := max(patience, iteration*2);
    end
    iteration +=1
end
```

Algorithm 1: Early stopping.

4.3 Splitting the Data

To make the comparisons fair, we split the Eisenstein dataset in the same way as Eisenstein et al. (2010) did, i.e., 60% for training, 20% for validation and 20% for testing. The Roller dataset was provided split, i.e., 429,694 users for training, 10,000 users for validation and the rest 10,000 users for testing; this is the split we adopted.

4.4 Tuning Hyper-parameters

One of the drawbacks of DNNs is a large number of hyper-parameters to specify (Bengio, 2012). The activation function we adopt is the sigmoid function $y = \frac{1}{1+e^{-x}}$, which is a typical choice as the non-linear activation function. For the size (the number of neurons) of each hidden layer, usually a larger size indicates better performance but higher computational cost. Since we do not have access to extensive computational power, we set this hyper-parameter to 5000, which is equal to the size of the input layer. As for the corruption level, the masking noise probability for the first layer is 0.3; the

average squared error of output numbers, which is equivalent to the average Euclidean distance between the estimated location and the true location; this alternative model did not perform well.

[6] http://www.mapquest.com

[7] http://www.census.gov/geo/maps-data/maps/pdfs/reference/us_regdiv.pdf

Gaussian noise standard deviation for other layers is 0.25. These two values are chosen because they appear to work well in our experiments based on the validation dataset. The Mini-batch size chosen for stochastic gradient descent is 32, which is a reasonable default suggested by Bengio (2012). For the learning rates, we explore different configurations in the set $\{0.00001, 0.0001, 0.001, 0.01, 0.1\}$ for both pre-learning learning rate and fine-tuning learning rate. Lastly, the pre-training stops after 25 epochs, which usually guarantees the convergence. Fine-tuning stops after 1000 epochs; because of the early stopping technique described in Section 4.2, this number is rarely reached.

4.5 Implementation

Theano (Bergstra et al., 2010) is a scientific computing library written in Python. It is mainly designed for numerical computation. A main feature of Theano is its symbolic representation of mathematical formulas, which allows it to automatically differentiate functions. We train our model with stochastic gradient descent which requires the computation of gradients, either manually or automatically. Since Theano does automatic differentiation, we no longer have to manually differentiate complex functions like Equation (9). We implemented SDA-1, SDA-2[8] and the baseline multivariate linear regression model with Theano.

Scikit-learn (Pedregosa et al., 2011) is a machine learning package written in Python. It includes most standard machine learning algorithms. The two baseline models compared against SDA-1 (Naive Bayes and SVM) are implemented using the Scikit-learn package.

5 Results

5.1 Evaluation on the Eisenstein Dataset

The SDA-1 model yields an accuracy of 61.1% and 34.8%, for region classification and state classification, respectively. The results of all models are shown in Table 1. Among all previous works that use the same dataset, only Eisenstein et al. (2010) report the classification accuracy of their models; to present a comprehensive comparison, all models from their work, not just the best one, are listed. Student's t-tests suggest that the differences between SDA-1 and the baseline models are statistically significant at a 99% level of confidence[9].

It can be seen that our SDA-1 model performs best in both classification tasks. It is surprising to find that the shallow architectures that we implemented, namely SVM and Naive Bayes, perform reasonably well. They both outperform all models in (Eisenstein et al., 2010) in terms of state-wise classification. A possible explanation is that the features we use (frequencies of n-grams with n = 1, 2, 3) are more indicative than theirs (unigram term frequencies).

	Model	Classif. Acc. (%) Region (4-way)	State (49-way)
Eisenstein et al. (2010)	Geo topic model	58	24
	Mixture of unigrams	53	19
	Supervised LDA	39	4
	Text regression	41	4
	kNN	37	2
Our models	**SDA-1**	**61.1**	**34.8**
	Baseline-Naive Bayes	54.8	30.1
	Baseline-SVM	56.4	27.5

Table 1: Classification accuracy for SDA-1 and other models

Table 2 shows the mean error distance for various models trained on the same dataset. The difference between SDA-2 and the baseline model is statistically significant at a level of confidence of 99.9% [10]. Our model has the second best results and performs better than four models from previous work. In addition, the fact that SDA-2 outperforms the baseline model by a large margin shows the advantages of a deep architecture and its ability to capture meaningful and useful abstractions from input data.

5.2 Evaluation on the Roller Dataset

Table 3 compares the results from various models on the Roller dataset. The model by Han et al. (2014), which included extensive feature engineering, outperformed other models. In addition it achieves the

[8]Our code is available at https://github.com/rex911/usrloc

[9]We are unable to conduct t-tests on the Eisenstein models, because of the unavailability of the details of the results produced by these models.

[10]We are unable to conduct t-tests on the other models, because of the unavailability of the details of the results produced by these models.

Model	Mean Error Distance(km)
Eisenstein et al. (2011)	845
SDA-2	**855.9**
Priedhorsky et al. (2014)	870
Roller et al. (2012)	897
Eisenstein et al. (2010)	900
Wing and Baldridge (2011)	967
Baseline-MLR	1268

Table 2: Mean error distance of predictions for SDA-2 and models from previous work.

best results by utilizing about 90% of all 214,000 features; when using the top 3% (6420) features, the Accuracy was 10% [11]. The SDA-2 model, despite the computational limitation, achieved better results than that of Roller et al. (2012) using just 5,000 features.

Model	Mean error (km)	Median error (km)	Acc. %
Roller et al. (2012)	860	463	34.6
Han et al. (2014)	NA	260	45
Han et al. (2014) using top 3% features (6420)	NA	NA	10
SDA-2	733	377	24.2

Table 3: Results from SDA-2 and the best models of previous work; *NA* indicates *Not Available*

6 Conclusion and Future Work

The experimental results show that our SDA-1 model outperformed other empirical models; our SDA-2 model's performance is reasonable. We demonstrate that a DNN is capable of learning representations from raw input data that helps the inference of location of users without having to design any hand-engineered features. The results also show that deep learning models have the potential of being applied to solve real business problems that require location detection, in addition to their recent success in natural language processing tasks and to their well-established success in computer vision and speech recognition.

We should point out the comparisons in Section 5 are approximate because our models use unigram, bigram and trigrams, while some of the models with compared with use only unigram; instead, our models use a smaller number of features, especially compared to the model of Han et al. (2014).

We believe a better model can yet be built. For example, our exploration for hyper-parameters is by no means exhaustive, especially for the mini-batch size and the corruption levels, due to the very high running time required. It would be interesting to find out the optimal set of hyper-parameters. More computational capacity also allows the construction of a more powerful DNN. For example, in our models, the hidden layers have a size of 5000, which is equal to the size of input layer; however, a hidden layer larger than the input layer learns better representations (Bengio et al., 2013).

The datasets we use does not have a balanced distribution. Users are densely distributed in the West Coast and most part of the East, whereas very few are located in the middle. Such label imbalance has a negative effect on statistical classifiers, and adversely affects regression models because many target values will never be sampled.

In future work, we plan to collect a dataset uniformly distributed geographically, and the locations do not have to be limited to the contiguous United States. Alternatively, one may notice that the distribution of users is similar to that of the U.S. population, therefore it is possible to use the U.S. census data to offset such a skewed distribution of users. It could also benefit to choose the 5000 features more carefully, instead of simply selecting the most frequent ones. In addition, the input of our system consists only of tweets, because we are mostly interested in recovering users' location from the language they produce; however, real applications require a higher accuracy. To achieve this, we could also incorporate information such as users' profiles, self-declared locations, time zones and interactions with other users. Another type of stacked denoising auto-encoder is one that only does unsupervised pre-training, then the output of the code layer is regarded as input into other classifiers such as SVM (Glorot et al., 2011). It would be interesting to compare the performance of this architecture and that of an SDA with supervised fine-tuning, with respect to our task.

[11] Only this metric was reported by the author in the top 3% features configuration

References

S Abrol, L Khan, and B Thuraisingham. 2012. Tweecalization: Efficient and intelligent location mining in twitter using semi-supervised learning. In *Proceedings of the 8th International Conference on Collaborative Computing: Networking, Applications and Worksharing (CollaborateCom 2012)*, pages 514–523.

Saima Aman and Stan Szpakowicz. 2008. Using roget's thesaurus for fine-grained emotion recognition. In *Proceedings of IJCNLP*, pages 312–318.

Lars Backstrom, Eric Sun, and Cameron Marlow. 2010. Find me if you can: Improving geographical prediction with social and spatial proximity. In *Proceedings of the 19th International Conference on World Wide Web*, WWW '10, pages 61–70, New York, NY, USA. ACM.

Yoshua Bengio and Pascal Lamblin. 2007. Greedy layer-wise training of deep networks. *Advances in Neural Information Processing Systems*, 19(153).

Yoshua Bengio, Aaron Courville, and Pascal Vincent. 2013. Representation learning: A review and new perspectives. *Pattern Analysis and Machine Intelligence*, 35(8):1798 – 1828.

Yoshua Bengio. 2012. Practical recommendations for gradient-based training of deep architectures. *Neural Networks: Tricks of the Trade*, 7700:437–478.

James Bergstra, Olivier Breuleux, Frédéric Bastien, Pascal Lamblin, Razvan Pascanu, Guillaume Desjardins, Joseph Turian, David Warde-Farley, and Yoshua Bengio. 2010. Theano: a CPU and GPU math expression compiler. In *Proceedings of the Python for Scientific Computing Conference (SciPy)*, volume 4, page 3.

John Kenneth Chambers. 1998. *Dialectology*. Cambridge University Press.

Zhiyuan Cheng, James Caverlee, and Kyumin Lee. 2010. You are where you tweet: a content-based approach to geo-locating Twitter users. In *Proceedings of the 19th ACM International Conference on Information and Knowledge Management (CIKM '10)*, volume October 26, pages 759–768, Toronto.

Pedro Domingos. 2012. A few useful things to know about machine learning. *Communications of the ACM*, 55(10):78–87.

Mark Dredze, Michael J Paul, Shane Bergsma, and Hieu Tran. 2013. Carmen: A twitter geolocation system with applications to public health. In *Proceedings of the AAAI Workshop on Expanding the Boundaries of Health Informatics Using AI (HIAI)*.

Jacob Eisenstein, Brendan O'Connor, Noah A Smith, and Eric P Xing. 2010. A latent variable model for geographic lexical variation. In *Proceedings of the 2010 Conference on Empirical Methods in Natural Language Processing*, EMNLP '10, pages 1277–1287, Stroudsburg, PA, USA. Association for Computational Linguistics.

Jacob Eisenstein, Amr Ahmed, and Eric P Xing. 2011. Sparse additive generative models of text. In *Proceedings of the 28th International Conference on Machine Learning (ICML'11)*, pages 1041–1048.

Diman Ghazi, Diana Inkpen, and Stan Szpakowicz. 2014. Prior and contextual emotion of words in sentential context. *Computer Speech & Language*, 28(1):76–92, January.

Xavier Glorot, Antoine Bordes, and Yoshua Bengio. 2011. Domain Adaptation for Large-Scale Sentiment Classification: A Deep Learning Approach. In *Proceedings of the 28th International Conference on Machine Learning (ICML'11)*, pages 513–520.

Bo Han, Paul Cook, and Timothy Baldwin. 2014. Text-based twitter user geolocation prediction. *Journal of Artificial Intelligence Research (JAIR)*, 49:451–500.

Geoffrey E Hinton, Simon Osindero, and Yee-Whye Teh. 2006. A fast learning algorithm for deep belief nets. *Neural Computation*, 18(7):1527–54, July.

Fei Huang and Alexander Yates. 2010. Exploring representation-learning approaches to domain adaptation. In *Proceedings of the 2010 Workshop on Domain Adaptation for Natural Language Processing*, pages 23–30.

David Jurgens. 2013. That's what friends are for: Inferring location in online social media platforms based on social relationships. In *Proceedings of the Seventh International Conference on Weblogs and Social Media, ICWSM 2013, Cambridge, Massachusetts, USA, July 8-11, 2013*.

Tao Li, Yi Zhang, and Vikas Sindhwani. 2009. A non-negative matrix tri-factorization approach to sentiment classification with lexical prior knowledge. In *Proceedings of the Joint Conference of the 47th Annual Meeting of the ACL and the 4th International Joint Conference on Natural Language Processing of the AFNLP*, pages 244–252. Association for Computational Linguistics, August.

Prem Melville, Wojciech Gryc, and Richard D. Lawrence. 2009. Sentiment analysis of blogs by combining lexical knowledge with text classification. In *Proceedings of the 15th ACM SIGKDD International Conference on Knowledge Discovery and Data Mining (KDD'09)*, page 1275, New York, New York, USA, June. ACM Press.

Olutobi Owoputi, Brendan OConnor, Chris Dyer, Kevin Gimpel, Nathan Schneider, and Noah A Smith. 2013. Improved part-of-speech tagging for online conversational text with word clusters. In *Proceedings of NAACL-HLT*, pages 380–390.

F. Pedregosa, G. Varoquaux, A. Gramfort, V. Michel, B. Thirion, O. Grisel, M. Blondel, P. Prettenhofer,

R. Weiss, V. Dubourg, J. Vanderplas, A. Passos, D. Cournapeau, M. Brucher, M. Perrot, and E. Duchesnay. 2011. Scikit-learn: Machine learning in Python. *Journal of Machine Learning Research*, 12:2825–2830.

K Malcolm Petyt. 1980. *The study of dialect: An introduction to dialectology*. Andre Deutsch.

Reid Priedhorsky, Aron Culotta, and Sara Y. Del Valle. 2014. Inferring the origin locations of tweets with quantitative confidence. In *Proceedings of the 17th ACM Conference on Computer Supported Cooperative Work & Social Computing (CSCW '14)*, pages 1523–1536, New York, USA, February. ACM Press.

Stephen Roller, Michael Speriosu, Sarat Rallapalli, Benjamin Wing, and Jason Baldridge. 2012. Supervised text-based geolocation using language models on an adaptive grid. In *Proceedings of the 2012 Joint Conference on Empirical Methods in Natural Language Processing and Computational Natural Language Learning*, pages 1500–1510. Association for Computational Linguistics, July.

Dominic Paul Rout, Kalina Bontcheva, Daniel Preotiuc-Pietro, and Trevor Cohn. 2013. Where's @wally?: a classification approach to geolocating users based on their social ties. In *24th ACM Conference on Hypertext and Social Media (part of ECRC), HT '13, Paris, France - May 02 - 04, 2013*, pages 11–20.

David E Rumelhart, Geoffrey E Hinton, and Ronald J Williams. 1985. Learning internal representations by error propagation. Technical report, DTIC Document.

Roger W Sinnott. 1984. Virtues of the haversine. *Sky and Telescope*, 68:158.

Duyu Tang, Bing Qin, Ting Liu, and Zhenghua Li. 2013. Learning Sentence Representation for Emotion Classification on Microblogs. *Natural Language Processing and Chinese Computing*, 400:212–223.

Pascal Vincent, Hugo Larochelle, Yoshua Bengio, and Pierre-Antoine Manzagol. 2008. Extracting and composing robust features with denoising autoencoders. *Proceedings of the 25th International Conference on Machine Learning (ICML'08)*, pages 1096–1103.

Benjamin P. Wing and Jason Baldridge. 2011. Simple supervised document geolocation with geodesic grids. In *Proceedings of the 49th Annual Meeting of the Association for Computational Linguistics: Human Language Technologies (ACL HLT '11)*, pages 955–964. Association for Computational Linguistics, June.

Yuan Yao, Lorenzo Rosasco, and Andrea Caponnetto. 2007. On early stopping in gradient descent learning. *Constructive Approximation*, 26(2):289–315.

Author Index

Association for Computational Linguistics
209 N. Eighth Street
Stroudsburg, Pennsylvania 18360

CURRAN ASSOCIATES INC
proceedings
.com